IMAGINING EARLY MODERN LONDON

*Perceptions and Portrayals of the City from Stow to Strype,
1598–1720*

The 120 years that separate the first publication of John Stow's famous *Survey of London* in 1598 from John Strype's enormous new edition of the same work in 1720 witnessed London's transformation into a sprawling Augustan metropolis, very different from the compact medieval city so lovingly charted in the pages of Stow.

Imagining Early Modern London takes Stow's classic account of the Elizabethan city as a starting point for an examination of how generations of very different Londoners – men and women, antiquaries, merchants, skilled craftsmen, labourers, and beggars – experienced and understood the dramatically changing city. A series of interdisciplinary essays explores the ways in which Londoners interpreted and memorialized their past, how individuals located themselves mentally, socially, and geographically within the city, and how far the capital's growth was believed to have a moral influence upon its inhabitants. Using a wide range of sources, the contributors recapture vividly the varying impact of the changing urban environment on the lives and minds of early modern Londoners.

J. F. MERRITT is Research Fellow in History, University of Sheffield. She has written extensively on London history and is the author of *The Social World of Early Modern Westminster: Abbey, Court and Community, 1525–1640* (Manchester, forthcoming).

IMAGINING EARLY MODERN LONDON

Perceptions and Portrayals of the City from Stow to Strype,
1598–1720

EDITED BY

J. F. MERRITT

CAMBRIDGE
UNIVERSITY PRESS

CAMBRIDGE UNIVERSITY PRESS
Cambridge, New York, Melbourne, Madrid, Cape Town, Singapore, São Paulo

Cambridge University Press
The Edinburgh Building, Cambridge CB2 8RU, UK

Published in the United States of America by Cambridge University Press, New York

www.cambridge.org
Information on this title: www.cambridge.org/9780521773461

First published 2001
This digitally printed version 2007

A catalogue record for this publication is available from the British Library

Library of Congress Cataloguing in Publication data
Imagining early modern London: perceptions and portrayals of the city from
Stow to Strype, 1598–1720 / edited by J. F. Merritt.
p.   cm.
Largely revised papers of a conference held at the
Institute of Historical Research in July 1998.
Includes bibliographical references and index.
ISBN 0 521 77346 6
1. London (England) – History – 17th century – Congresses.
2. Stow, John, 1525?–1605. Survey of London – Congresses.
3. London (England) – History – 18th century – Congresses.
4. London (England) – Historiography – Congresses.
5. Strype, John, 1643–1737 – Congresses.
I. Merritt, J. F.
DA681.143 2001
942.1′06–dc21   2001025392

ISBN 978-0-521-77346-1 hardback
ISBN 978-0-521-03758-7 paperback

Contents

List of illustrations   *page* vii

Notes on the contributors   viii

Acknowledgements   xi

List of abbreviations   xii

Introduction. Perceptions and portrayals of London 1598–1720   1
J. F. Merritt

MEMORIALIZING THE CITY

1   John Stow and nostalgic antiquarianism   27
Patrick Collinson

2   The reshaping of Stow's *Survey*: Munday, Strype, and the Protestant City   52
J. F. Merritt

3   The arts and acts of memorialization in early modern London   89
Ian W. Archer

SPACE, SOCIETY, AND URBAN EXPERIENCE

4   City, capital, and metropolis: the changing shape of seventeenth-century London   117
Vanessa Harding

5   Gendered spaces: patterns of mobility and perceptions of London's geography, 1660–1750   144
Robert B. Shoemaker

Contents

6 The publicity of poverty in early eighteenth-century 166
London
Tim Hitchcock

7 'To recreate and refresh their dulled spirites in the sweet 185
and wholesome ayre': green space and the growth of the
city
Laura Williams

INVERSION, INSTABILITY, AND THE CITY

8 From Troynouvant to Heliogabulus's Rome and back: 217
'order' and its others in the London of John Stow
Peter Lake

9 Perceptions of the crowd in later Stuart London 250
Tim Harris

10 'Making fire': conflagration and religious controversy in 273
seventeenth-century London
Nigel Smith

Index 294

Illustrations

1. London in *c.* 1560, from Braun and Hogenberg's   *page* 119
   Civitates Orbis Terrarum (1572)
2. John Oliver's 'A Mapp of the Cityes of London and   120
   Westminster and Burrough of Southwark with their
   Suburbs as it is now Rebuilt since the late dreadfull
   Fire' (*c.* 1680)
3. John Ogilby and William Morgan's 'Large and Accurate   126
   Map of the City of London' (*c.* 1676)
4. Wenceslaus Hollar's 'Westminster and London' (*c.* 1658)   129
5. John Ogilby and William Morgan's 'Large and Accurate   136
   Map of the City of London' (*c.* 1676)
6. William Faithorne's 'An Exact Delineation of the Cities   142
   of London and Westminster and the Suburbs' (1658)

All illustrations reproduced by the kind permission of the Guildhall Library, London.

Notes on the contributors

IAN W. ARCHER is Fellow, Tutor, and University Lecturer at Keble College, Oxford. He is the author of *The Pursuit of Stability: Social Relations in Elizabethan London* (1991) and the *History of the Haberdashers' Company* (1991), as well as a number of articles on the social and cultural history of early modern London. He is General Editor of the Royal Historical Society Bibliography on British History, and his current research is on charity.

PATRICK COLLINSON is Regius Professor of Modern History, Emeritus, in the University of Cambridge, and a Fellow of Trinity College. He is a Fellow of the British Academy. Professor Collinson is the author of *The Elizabethan Puritan Movement* (1967), *The Religion of Protestants: The Church in English Society, 1559–1625* (1982), and other studies of religion, politics, and society in sixteenth- and seventeenth-century England, and has co-authored histories of Canterbury Cathedral and Emmanuel College, Cambridge.

VANESSA HARDING is Senior Lecturer in London History at Birkbeck College, University of London. Much of her work focuses on aspects of the relationship between Londoners and their physical environment in the medieval and early modern period, including population growth, the property market, the history of open space, and the problems associated with the burial of the dead. Her study of the living and the dead in early modern London and Paris will appear soon.

TIM HARRIS, formerly a Fellow of Emmanuel College, Cambridge, is now Professor of History at Brown University, Providence, R.I. His publications include *London Crowds in the Reign of Charles II* (Cambridge, 1987), *Politics under the Later Stuarts* (London, 1993), *Popular Culture in England, c. 1500–1850* (London, 1995), and (co-edited with

Paul Seaward and Mark Goldie) *The Politics of Religion in Restoration England* (Oxford, 1990). He is currently editing a collection of essays on *The Politics of the Excluded* in early modern England (to be published by Macmillan) and writing a book entitled *British Revolutions: The Making of the Modern Nation, 1660–1707* (under contract with Penguin). He is also involved in a team project to edit the Roger Morrice 'Ent'ring Books' for publication by the Parliamentary History Records Society.

TIM HITCHCOCK is Reader in Eighteenth-Century History at the University of Hertfordshire. He has published widely on eighteenth-century poverty, sexuality, and masculinity. His recent books include *English Sexualities, 1700–1800* (1997) and, with Michele Cohen, *English Masculinities, 1660–1800* (1999).

PETER LAKE teaches early modern English history at Princeton University. He has written on the religion, politics, and culture of Elizabethan and early Stuart England. His most recent book is *The Boxmaker's Revenge*, published by Manchester and Stanford University Presses. He is currently completing an even longer book, in collaboration with Michael Questier, *Anti-Christ's Lewd Hat: Puritans, Papists and Players in Post-Reformation England*.

J. F. MERRITT is Research Fellow in the History Department of the University of Sheffield and Director of the Stuart London Project there. Her interests focus on the social, cultural, and religious history of early modern London. She has published (ed.), *The Political World of Thomas Wentworth, Earl of Strafford, 1621–1641* (Cambridge, 1996), *The Social World of Early Modern Westminster: Abbey, Court and Community, 1525–1640* (Manchester, forthcoming), and a number of articles on early modern London. Her next project is a book on religion and society in early modern London.

ROBERT B. SHOEMAKER is Senior Lecturer in History at the University of Sheffield. He is the author of *Prosecution and Punishment: Petty Crime and the Law in London and Rural Middlesex, 1660–1725* (1991) and *Gender in English Society 1650–1850: The Emergence of Separate Spheres?* (1998). He is currently writing a book on the decline of public conflict in eighteenth-century London, focusing on changing patterns of public insult, violence, and popular protest.

NIGEL SMITH has been Professor of English at Princeton University since September 1999, having previously been Fellow and Tutor in English at Keble College, and Reader in English, University of Oxford. He is the author of *Perfection Proclaimed: Language and Literature in English Radical Religion, 1640–1660* (1989) and *Literature and Revolution in England, 1640–1660* (1994). He is currently completing the Longman Annotated English Poets edition of Andrew Marvell.

LAURA WILLIAMS was formerly a Museum Officer for the London Borough of Redbridge, where she helped to set up a new social history museum. She is now a Policy and Research Officer at the Heritage Lottery Fund. She wrote her PhD thesis on 'The greening of English towns, 1660–1760', under the supervision of Peter Borsay at the University of Wales, and is currently preparing the thesis for publication.

Acknowledgements

Many of the papers in this volume are derived from a conference, 'Imagining the City: Perceptions and Portrayals of Early Modern London from Stow to Strype', held at the Institute of Historical Research in July 1998. This conference formed one aspect of the Leverhulme-funded Stuart London Project, and I would like to thank the Leverhulme Trust and the British Academy for their financial support, as well as all those whose participation made this such a lively and stimulating occasion. Dr Vanessa Harding should especially be thanked for her help and hospitality at the time of the conference.

The contributors to this volume deserve special thanks for their speed and efficiency in completing their chapters, and in some cases for their good-natured tolerance of minor editorial intervention. I would also like to thank William Davies of Cambridge University Press for his encouragement and support in bringing the volume to fruition.

The final stages of editorial work were carried out in the congenial surroundings of the Department of History at Sheffield, and with the able computer support of Allen Foster. I would also like to thank my husband, Anthony Milton, for cheering the project along and acting as a sympathetic sounding-board for my ideas. Finally, I must thank Professor Caroline Barron, who first suggested that I carry out a more detailed study of John Strype's edition of the *Survey of London*, and whose multi-faceted interest in London's history continues to act as an inspiration.

Abbreviations

BL	British Library
Bodl.	Bodleian Library
CLRO	Corporation of London Record Office
CSPD	*Calendar of State Papers, Domestic*
CSPVen	*Calendar of State Papers, Venetian*
CUL	Cambridge University Library
CWA	Churchwardens' Accounts
GL	Guildhall Library
HMC	Historical Manuscripts Commission
LMA	London Metropolitan Archives
LPL	Lambeth Palace Library
PRO	Public Record Office
Stow, *Survey*	John Stow, *A Survey of London* (1598; 1603), ed. C. L. Kingsford (2 vols., Oxford, 1908, repr., 1971)
Strype, *Survey*	John Strype, *A Survey of the Cities of London and Westminster* (2 vols., 1720)
VM	Vestry Minutes
WCA	Westminster City Archives

Note: The place of publication for works cited in footnotes is London, unless otherwise specified.

Perceptions and portrayals of London 1598–1720

J. F. Merritt

The year 1598 saw the first publication of what has become the most famous single work about England's capital – John Stow's *Survey of London*. Stow's survey was in part a description of a city that had already disappeared: as he explained to his readers, 'what London hath beene of ancient time, men may here see, as what it is now every man doth beholde'.[1] Some 120 years later, a long-awaited work with the same title finally emerged. This was an enlarged and updated version of Stow's *Survey*, compiled by the famous ecclesiastical historian John Strype. This was in its own way as monumental as Stow's original work, filling two substantial folio volumes with its vastly expanded text. In the period between the two works, London had been dramatically transformed. When Stow wrote, the city had already undergone the cultural trauma of the Reformation, but it was also in the throes of major demographic change. Its population had expanded significantly over the previous fifty years, and London *c*. 1600 was home to roughly 200,000 people. By 1720, when John Strype produced a new edition of Stow's work, the city had assumed the character of an enormous metropolis, its population had soared to more than half a million people, and it was comfortably the biggest city in Europe.[2] Most of this massive demographic expansion took place in suburban areas, formally outside the City's jurisdiction, leaving less than half of London's population within the City of London proper by the

[1] Stow, *Survey*, I.xcviii.
[2] For an excellent up-to-date overview of scholarship on London's development in this period, see J. Boulton, 'London 1540–1700', in P. Clark (ed.), *The Cambridge Urban History of Britain 1540–1700* vol. II (Cambridge, 2000). On London's population in a comparative context see *ibid.*, pp. 316–17; V. Harding, 'The population of London 1550–1700: a review of the published evidence', *London Journal* 15 (1990), 112; J. de Vries, *European Urbanization 1500–1800* (1984), pp. 170–8.

Restoration.[3] This burgeoning metropolis encompassed great contrasts, including not only areas of great poverty but also what contemporaries increasingly identified as a socially distinctive 'West End'.[4] The resulting urban sprawl was daunting. Indeed, in 1722 one William Stow estimated that a perambulation of the city streets like that conducted earlier by John Stow would have to cover some 250 miles, and include 2,175 streets.[5] In tandem with the relentless extension of the capital's built-up area were new patterns of consumption which in themselves altered the urban environment, with its more negative manifestations seen in new problems of traffic and air pollution.[6] The face of the old City had itself been ravaged by the destruction of the Great Fire, while the Civil War had decisively fractured its religious unity.

The span between these two editions of the *Survey of London* seems an appropriate one to adopt, given the rapid changes that overtook the capital during that period. The demographic and economic changes of this timescale are relatively well known, but an approach which asks how Londoners experienced and understood their city over the same period takes us into less familiar territory. By beginning with Stow, we can start not just with the late sixteenth century, but with one man's memories of the pre-Reformation city, a city which still cast its shadow, even if indirectly, over the seventeenth-century capital. Taking Strype's edition as our closing point brings us forward to the Georgian city and also allows us to cross the traditional historiographical divide represented by the Civil War.

The manner in which texts such as the *Survey of London* formally provided a structure for London's history is our necessary starting

---

[3] Recent estimates suggest that the population of metropolitan Westminster, Middlesex, and Surrey increased eightfold between 1580 and 1695, compared with little or no overall increase in the City and its liberties: Boulton, 'London 1540–1700', p. 317, citing R. Finlay, *Population and Metropolis: The Demography of London 1580–1650* (Cambridge, 1981), pp. 51–66 and R. Finlay and B. Shearer, 'Population growth and suburban expansion', in A. L. Beier and R. Finlay (eds.), *London 1500–1700: The Making of the Metropolis* (1986), pp. 37–59.

[4] M. J. Power, 'The east and west in early-modern London' in E. W. Ives, R. J. Knecht, and J. J. Scarisbrick (eds.), *Wealth and Power in Tudor England* (1978), pp. 167–85; M. J. Power, 'The social topography of Restoration London', in Beier and Finlay, *London 1500–1700*, pp. 199–223. The actual term 'West End', however, was only beginning to come into use during our period, with contemporaries more often referring to 'the fashionable end of the town': E. Jones, 'The first West End comedy', *Proceedings of the British Academy* 68 (1983), 225–7.

[5] William Stow, *Remarks on London. Being an Exact Survey of the Cities of London and Westminster* (1722), preface.

[6] Boulton, 'London 1540–1700', pp. 324–6.

point. The authors of such works offer obvious and rich subjects for the analysis of the shifting perceptions of individual inhabitants. But to recapture something of the mental world of a broader swathe of early modern Londoners, the contributors to this volume have also moved forward from the works of historical commentary and scholarship provided by Stow and Strype. Their sources extend from livery company, church court, and parochial records to murder pamphlets, diaries, letters, and architectural treatises. The use of such a variety of materials also acknowledges the difficulty of reconstructing contemporary experience. Men and women, recent migrants, merchants, skilled craftsmen, labourers, and beggars may not only have conceptualized the capital in different ways, but they also left us quite different materials for the study of their behaviour and impressions.

The questions about the early modern metropolis addressed in this volume fall into three broad categories. The first set of questions focuses on issues of continuity. Historians are keen to identify the undoubted changes that occurred during the early modern period, but to what extent did contemporaries perceive a disjunction between the physical size, culture, and social relationships of London past and present? A second set of questions leads us to consider the nature of metropolitan experience. Did understandings of the metropolis alter to fit the changing shape of the city? How did individuals locate themselves – mentally and geographically – within the city? And did changes in the capital's population, physical extent, and economic complexity affect social interaction? These topics bring us to a third related series of issues: evaluations of London's urbanization. Embedded in many contemporary representations of London was the assumption that the capital's growth had a moral impact upon its citizens. But how negative was the assumed impact of the developing city, and in what ways did people believe that the deleterious effects of urbanization could be controlled and countered? And what implications did such ideas have for the manifold ways in which London was not only perceived, but portrayed? From the just-remembered, pre-Reformation London of John Stow to the thrusting, Augustan metropolis which emerges from the pages of Strype, the following chapters turn their attention to these questions.

I

To understand how Londoners interpreted the changes which overtook the early modern city, we must also ask how they understood
and related to London's past. We begin with John Stow himself,
perhaps the most famous encomiast of the pre-Reformation city. For
Stow was writing at a time when London had already undergone a
major cultural transformation over the course of a single lifetime.
Not only had the capital greatly increased in size and population,
but it had also undergone the trauma of the Protestant Reformation.
Stow's *Survey* is thus famously a paean of praise for his own city, but
also a heavily nostalgic one which lingers lovingly over the past but
(more often than not) deplores more recent events. Patrick Collinson
(ch. 1) reminds us of just how far Stow was guilty of a 'selective
nostalgia'. Stow's is a vision which presupposes a changeless London
for the 400 years from the writings of Fitzstephen until the 1530s,
when the old London had changed suddenly and decisively. But
there was more than an old man's regretful nostalgia for what has
passed – there was a strong confessional element, too. In Stow's text
there is an implicit conflation of desecration, the triumph of selfish
individualism over communal endeavour, and the emergence of
Protestantism. Nor is this conflation accidental. As Professor Collinson emphasizes, Stow was not simply a man vaguely hankering
after old ways. In the 1560s he was clearly a man with links to a
more assertive and combative confessional Catholicism, although
the official and damaging enquiry into his reading at the end of this
decade seems to have forced him to adopt more circumspect ways
and to avoid direct contact with the forces of political Catholicism.

Stow's *Survey* is in part a work of memory, and Ian Archer (ch. 3)
traces the many other ways in which memory and the past lived on
in the London of the early seventeenth century. He provides a vivid
account of how livery company halls and parish churches might act
as 'theatres of memory'. Here the new acts of charity of those dying
in the post-Reformation city were memorialized by means of a
variety of monuments and rituals which echoed and imitated the
forms of memorialization used in the pre-Reformation church.
Continuity was thus achieved in a way which not only smoothed
over the awkward disjunctions between the immediate and the more
distant past, but which also helped to reinforce the power and
authority of the present governors. Dr Archer reminds us too of the

degree to which these rituals could serve to legitimate a set of unequal power relations, the desire for memorialization also being tied to urgent present-day concerns.

The understanding of links between London's past and present is a major theme in my own chapter (ch. 2). This chapter focuses more directly on the fortunes of Stow's famous text as it was adapted and dramatically expanded during the course of the seventeenth and early eighteenth centuries. Stow's religious nostalgia for an earlier and more compact city might seem to present problems for those trying to celebrate the growing capital within an updated *Survey*. Nevertheless, as this chapter shows, Stow's later editors and 'continuators' found their own ways of adjusting Stow's message to suit the changing Protestant city. Stow's first editor, Anthony Munday, for example, found it possible to engage with the medieval past while placing it in a triumphalist celebration of continuity with the present. In the aftermath of political upheavals, such as the Civil War and the Glorious Revolution, different writers raided Stow to create their own variously nostalgic or triumphalist readings of the recent past. By the time that we come to Strype's monumental volumes of 1720, we find Stow's original text carefully presented *within* that of Strype. This manner of presentation acted to preserve in readers' minds a medieval city that had long since disappeared in the face of new urban development and the ravages of the Great Fire. The blending of new and old accounts permitted the post-Fire city to retain its bearings, sense of identity, and continuity with the older city. At the same time, this blend ensured that Stow's nostalgia was partly neutralized by the provision of new information which lauded Protestant achievements, celebrated new developments in the city, and avoided the older historian's conflation of vice and individualism with the expanding city and its new religion.

This strange mélange of new and old, and insistence on continuity in the face of destructive change, is also evident in the reaction to the most traumatic upheaval of all, that of the Great Fire. The destruction of the city did not simply represent the loss of physical buildings. London was also a place permeated with meanings, a theatre of memory.[7] It is all the more striking, then, to note that the post-Fire city was generally rebuilt along the old lines. Despite all the

---

[7] C. Wall, *The Literary and Cultural Spaces of Restoration London* (Cambridge, 1998), p. 53 (and generally ch. 2).

grandiose schemes for a dramatically different, refashioned city, the old city was in effect restored, in a piecemeal and idiosyncratic fashion. It is true that the skyline was transformed, the appearance of streets changed dramatically, and the classical style made major inroads; but property boundaries were scarcely altered, the street plan remained the same (apart from where streets were widened), and the old alleys as well as the medieval courtyard houses were rebuilt.[8] There were compelling economic and legal reasons for this restoration of the old city;[9] but Cynthia Wall has recently argued for the presence of cultural factors as well. If the city contained a 'whole abstract network of associative meaning', then it was necessary to restore it in order to preserve such meaning. There would have been an understandable desire to reconstruct the patterns and memory of the old city, a 'cultural preference for recovering the London known and lost, rather than creating a London new and unknown', a desire 'to reinscribe London with familiar spatial meaning'.[10] The very act of recording and surveying the city, carried out so systematically by the post-Fire authorities, was itself a form of memorialization.[11] And like any act of memorialization – indeed, like Stow's own printed *Survey* – it froze and formalized in a more regulated fashion the more randomly evolving past.

Both the Reformation and the Great Fire, then, represented traumatic interruptions in the city's history, and contemporaries dealt with them in a parallel fashion. Partly, they emphasized the positive side of the new – the advent of the true religion and its good works, or the glorious new post-Fire buildings. But in both cases, too, change was neutralized and re-interpreted by a stress on continuity, in cultural and spatial terms, with the preservation of the street plan of the old city, and of Stow's celebration of it.

II

As the city continued to sprawl beyond its traditional boundaries, it posed serious problems for its inhabitants. Memorialization had an

---

8 S. Porter, *The Great Fire of London* (Stroud, 1996), ch. 6. For a similar stress on elements of continuity with traditional patterns of building, even in the western suburbs unaffected by the Fire, see E. McKellar, *The Birth of Modern London* (Manchester, 1999).

9 T. F. Reddaway, *The Rebuilding of London After the Great Fire* (1951), chs. 1–4, 6.

10 Wall, *Literary and Cultural Spaces*, pp. 39–41.

11 Reddaway, *Rebuilding*, chs. 4 and 6; Wall, *Literary and Cultural Spaces*, ch. 3.

obvious value in investing places and buildings with a sense of identity and meaning. But how were Londoners to locate themselves mentally within the city, and how were they to gain sufficient information to find their way around? Would they develop a new metropolitical self-identity to match the ever-expanding city? Or would they retreat into the smaller districts of the increasingly fragmented metropolis?

Part of the problem of retaining a sense of the enlarged city was that of knowledge acquisition. As Vanessa Harding remarks (ch. 4), John Stow was writing at perhaps the latest time when it was possible for one man to have a personal knowledge of the whole extent of the city (indeed, some would suggest, at a point at which 'the capital ceased to be seen as one entity to those inhabiting it').[12] Stow's *Survey* was in itself a substitute for first-hand knowledge, as were the later guidebooks. There is evidence that Stow's work was used as a guidebook as well as a work of reference kept in parochial libraries. While the later folio continuations of the *Survey of London* by Munday and Strype may not have been easily portable, there is evidence that their owners came to value them as more personal documents, carefully updating material in them by hand and correcting points of detail.[13]

Paul Slack has also suggested that the availability of new and improved city maps, prospects, street plans, and directories may have provided the visual aids which could ensure that people's 'mental maps' preserved a broader sense of the metropolis.[14] There was certainly an explosion in the maps produced in the 1670s and early 1680s, but this partly resulted from the need to survey the new city, and the destruction of stocks of previous maps in the Great Fire. Ogilby and Morgan's map of the rebuilt city in 1676 was truly

[12] J. Boulton, *Neighbourhood and Society* (Cambridge, 1987), p. 293, citing P. Burke, 'Some reflections on the pre-industrial city', *Urban History Yearbook* (1975), 19; P. Burke, 'Urban history and urban anthropology of early modern Europe', in D. Fraser and A. Sutcliffe (eds.), *The Pursuit of Urban History* (1983), p. 81; Finlay, *Population and Metropolis*, p. 155.

[13] X. Baron (ed.), *London 1066–1914* (3 vols., Mountfield, 1997), I, p. 335. See for example Bodl., L.3.7 (Art.) – a copy of the 1633 edition of the *Survey* with MS additions after p. 598 noting lord mayors and epitaphs in churches. Even substantial folio volumes could be used directly as travel guides: the young Bulstrode Whitelocke took Camden's *Britannia* with him as a guide on his travels: R. Spalding, *The Improbable Puritan* (1975), p. 36.

[14] P. Slack, 'Perceptions of the metropolis in seventeenth-century England', in P. Burke, B. Harrison, and P. Slack (eds.), *Civil Histories* (Oxford, 2000), pp. 170–2; for discussion of individual maps and their extent see J. Howgego, *Printed Maps of London c.1533–1850* (2nd edn, 1978).

impressive, but nothing on so large a scale covering the entire city would be produced again until the mid-nineteenth century.[15] By 1722 William Stow was very dismissive. 'Our Maps, or Prospects of London, Westminster and Southwark', he commented, were 'made more for Ornament than Use, [and] do not describe a fourth part of the Places contain'd in 'em'. Even if a map were to be 30 feet long and 20 feet deep, Stow claims, it would not comprehend the town in an exact scale of feet and one would undoubtedly need a magnifying glass to find relevant details. In addition, 'as it is many Years since these Maps of London were made, they must be now most imperfect'.[16]

William Stow was, of course, anxious to emphasize the deficiencies of maps in order to boost the case for his own street directory, and he certainly ignored the value of the smaller ward maps being produced at this time.[17] His own directory might be seen as evidence of a golden age of user-friendly guides, yet his preface gives equal evidence of the confusion created by the expanding capital.[18] He intended his 'Pocket-Companion' partly as a guide for coachmen and porters, since none of them knew all the streets of London now: 'So large is the Extent of London, Westminster and Southwark, with their Suburbs and Liberties, that no Coachman nor Porter knows every Place in them.' William Stow's book would guide them, and prevent 'their losing any more Portmanteaus, Trunks, Boxes, or Parcels'. He also hoped to standardize the increasingly chaotic use of postal addresses. It was intended 'to show People how to spell and write proper their Superscriptions on Letters; for a bad Hand and wrong Orthography, or false spelling . . . have caus'd the Miscarriage of many Letters'. He also noted that letters sometimes miscarried because people did not know in which part of London a road was situated – there were, for example, fifteen different King Streets![19] For all that the later seventeenth and early eighteenth centuries may have given rise to a plethora of maps, street directories, and other

[15] Porter, *Great Fire*, pp. 165–6; P. Glanville, *London in Maps* (1972), pp. 26–8; R. Hyde, 'Ogilby and Morgan's City of London Map, 1676', introduction to *The A to Z of Restoration London* (London Topographical Society, no. 145, 1992).

[16] Stow, *Remarks*, preface.

[17] On ward maps see R. Hyde, *Ward Maps of the City of London* (London Topographical Society, no. 154, 1999).

[18] On street directories, see C. W. F. Goss, *The London Directories 1677–1855* (1932); Slack, 'Perceptions', pp. 172–3; M. Harris, 'London Guidebooks before 1800', in R. Myers and M. Harris (eds.), *Maps and Prints: Aspects of the English Booktrade* (Oxford, 1984), pp. 42–4.

[19] Stow, *Remarks*, preface.

guides to the metropolis, it remains debatable how far these guides really overcame the problems of comprehending the extent of the expanding city. On the level of the individual, there seems little reason to doubt the comment of the Scottish visitor Robert Kirk in 1690 that 'the city is a great vast wilderness. Few in it know the fourth part of its streets. The most attend their business, and an inquisitive stranger will know more of the varieties of the city than an hundred inhabitants.'[20]

If people experienced difficulty in navigating through the streets of London, they had even greater difficulty in gaining first-hand news of what was happening in those streets. The emergence of newspapers might help to bridge this knowledge gap, but not everyone could read them. As Kirk remarked: 'Few in it know the fourth part of its streets, far less can they get intelligence of the hundredth part of its streets, far less can they get one hundredth part of the special affairs and remarkable passages in it, unless by printed public papers, which come not to every man's notice.'[21] Information gleaned from newspapers was, of course, qualitatively different from that gained by verbal reports. For many people, parts of the city may have been becoming places that they read about, rather than places with which they had some tenuous personal link. It is also important to remember that both guidebooks and more scholarly surveys were highly selective in which features and aspects of the capital they portrayed and even which portions of the city received most attention. Stow, Munday, Strype, and others all created their own different 'Londons', based on a distinctive range of priorities and experience. As the Jacobean preacher Thomas Adams commented, London could 'not unfitly be compared to certain pictures that represent to divers beholders, at divers stations, divers forms'.[22] In this way, individuals may have fashioned their own sense of the metropolis.[23]

Printed guides, newspapers, songs and plays, gossip, rumour, oral

20 D. MacLean and N. Brett-James (eds.), 'London in 1689–90. By Rev. Robert Kirk, MA (Part I)', *Transactions of the London and Middlesex Archaeological Society*, new series, 6 (1933), 333.

21 *Ibid.* On the growth of newspapers see e.g. M. Harris, *London Newspapers in the Age of Walpole* (1987); R. B. Walker, 'Advertising in London newspapers, 1650–1750', *Business History* 15 (1973), 112–30.

22 'The City of Peace' (1612) in *Works*, ed. J. Angus (3 vols., Edinburgh, 1861–2), III, p. 331; L. Manley, *Literature and Culture in Early Modern London* (Cambridge, 1995), p. 2.

23 This is the world of mental maps, 'the highly subjective ways in which people may experience in their own minds the shapes of the public spaces they inhabit': Jones, 'The first West End comedy', 227; P. Gould and R. White, *Mental Maps* (2nd edn, 1986).

tradition, and other second-hand information would all have played a part in the creation of each individual's mental map of the city. But the extent of the city that was experienced first-hand also helped to determine such mental maps. London's expansion inevitably meant that it was virtually impossible for people to gain experience of the entire metropolis. But how far did they range within the city? Here Robert Shoemaker (ch. 5) notes the importance of gender, occupation, social status, wealth, and cultural attitudes. The immediate neighbourhood may have been very important to Londoners, but at the same time people of both sexes frequently moved outside their parish and neighbourhood (even if in the case of most people they did not move very far), for reasons of business, leisure, and accommodation, or just to make social calls. His research suggests a relative lack of metropolis-wide movement, with the greatest mobility to be found among the highest and lowest social classes, and with women's mobility, in particular, being seriously underestimated in contemporary writing about the capital. Dr Harding, too, notes that while individuals might move within tight networks of neighbours and other local acquaintants, they also pursued idiosyncratic social circuits that could make them familiar with many other parts of the city, propelled there by business, shopping, religious contacts, or pleasure. New foci of urban social activity emerging in the later seventeenth century can only have made such individual social circuits still more varied.

Similarly, the changing use of language reflected the city's shifting cultural topography. This is most clearly seen in the language of urban description, where reference to purely jurisdictional boundaries might be found wanting. William Stow, for example, admitted to bowing to custom in his street directory, by designating certain Westminster parishes as part of London. As he explained, he only labelled St Margaret's parish as Westminster (omitting populous parishes such as St Clement Danes, St Martin in the Fields and the rest, which should technically have been included) 'because Use and Custom having gain'd so far as to ascribe them to London, and the Directions herein being so plain . . . I would not altogether deviate from what has been habitual to the Generality of the common People by long Practice.'[24] These western parts of the metropolis

[24] Stow, *Remarks*, preface. This was not merely a matter of linguistic slippage, but also reflected important political and cultural developments in the area, and the frustration of efforts towards the town's incorporation. For attempts to develop a distinctive identity for

also gave rise to other distinctions. Emrys Jones, for example, has charted the use of the terms 'Town' and 'West End' as emerging conceptual identities, which did not, however, always match social reality.[25] Robert Shoemaker similarly notes how by the eighteenth century the term 'Westminster' was often used to denote a smaller area than the city, and one which drew more on the legal and political connotations of Westminster as a place name.[26] Finally, Jeremy Boulton's work should remind us that usage was unlikely to have been uniform throughout the capital. The Boroughside residents of early seventeenth-century Southwark, for example, employed very vague general terminology to describe neighbourhoods other than their own, while being most conscious of their immediate surroundings.[27]

From looking at how Londoners located themselves and others within the metropolis, one might ask what effect the city had on individuals and their social relationships. The city is often spoken of in terms of the opportunities that it offered for anonymity, for people to be free-floating private individuals, creating their own identities free from the restrictions of birth and background. Yet the researches of Boulton, Shoemaker, Gowing, and Harding present us with other images, of tightly focused, even claustrophobic local communities.[28] Dr Boulton has charted the workings of a 'local social system' in early seventeenth-century Southwark, noting that most social and economic activity was locally based.[29] London was, after all, becoming increasingly fragmented culturally, socially, and economically in this period, with its different areas characterized by distinctive living patterns, health, social structure, household size, and social

Westminster as a whole in the period before the Civil War, see J. F. Merritt, 'Introduction', *The Social World of Early Modern Westminster: Abbey, Court and Community, 1525–1640* (Manchester, forthcoming).

[25] Jones, 'The first West End comedy'. The development of the notion of the 'Town' is obviously also echoed by the later emerging 'west end–city–east end' terminology to describe differences within the metropolis. On the role of bills of mortality in shaping assumptions about the character of different districts, particularly in relation to the suburbs, see J. Robertson, 'Reckoning with London: interpreting the Bills of Mortality before John Graunt', *Urban History* 23 (1996), 325–50.

[26] Ironically, this more circumscribed usage had its roots in the original medieval vill of Westminster: see G. Rosser, *Medieval Westminster* (Oxford, 1989), pp. 251–3.

[27] Boulton, *Neighbourhood*, p. 293. Cf. also Gould and White, *Mental Maps*, pp. 12–17; Burke, 'Urban history', p. 76.

[28] Boulton, *Neighbourhood*, ch. 9; L. Gowing, *Domestic Dangers* (Oxford, 1996), pp. 21–4. See also the thoughtful discussion in I. Archer, *The Pursuit of Stability: Social Relations in Elizabethan London* (Cambridge, 1991), pp. 74–82.

[29] Boulton, *Neighbourhood*, pp. 228–88; Burke, 'Urban history', p. 76.

dynamics. James Boswell would later comment that 'one end of London was like a different country from the other in look and manners'.[30] The sense of belonging generated by a locality and its institutions may well have shifted during the later part of our period. As Vanessa Harding observes, the parishes and wards into which John Stow's perambulation divided London (and which John Strype's *Survey* doggedly followed) would not have had the same resonance as personal signifiers by Strype's time. The wards were certainly becoming less meaningful, although the position of the parish was more complex. Parochial worship no longer embraced the entire community, and the growth of suburban parishes, along with the amalgamation or subdivision of others, may have made them less 'self-evidently a neighbourhood'. Nevertheless, the fact that parishes increasingly took on more administrative duties, especially control of taxation and poor relief, along with the provisions of the 1662 Act of Settlement, may have served to increase the immediate significance of parochial identity for the individual Londoner. A stronger feeling of loyalty and identity may have attached to a smaller immediate neighbourhood, or even a street or alleyway. Yet even the latter was subject to change. Harding reminds us that in some areas new housing patterns may have militated against a sense of neighbourhood. As the built environment became more dense and congested, the spatial obscurity of new dwellings may actually have obscured the identity of the men and women who lived there.

But the dichotomy between anonymity and tight neighbourhood identities seems in part to be a false one. Residents of early seventeenth-century Boroughside clearly enjoyed contacts beyond the neighbourhood that was so important to them, and Dr Boulton has emphasized that it was *not* 'a *self enclosed* neighbourhood, an inward looking urban community'. The American urban sociologist Robert Park's remark about the city being 'a mosaic of little worlds' has often been paraphrased by historians, but in the same sentence Park emphasized that the existence of these 'little worlds' makes it possible for individuals 'to pass quickly and easily from one moral

---

[30] Quoted in Manley, *Literature and Culture*, pp. 134–5. Similarly, by the late eighteenth and early nineteenth century, the trend in London historical writing was more towards individual histories of the parishes, villages, and towns that had been absorbed by the metropolis: R. Sweet, *The Writing of Urban Histories in Eighteenth-Century England* (Oxford, 1997), p. 253.

milieu to another, and encourages the fascinating but dangerous experiment of living at the same time in several different contiguous but otherwise widely separated, worlds'.[31] The early modern city was not fragmented into a mosaic of individually self-sufficient communities, but seems instead more like a complex web of interwoven communities, where, over the course of a lifetime, individuals might vary their involvement. But everyone also had potential access to the 'anonymity' of city life, in the shape of other 'foreign' parts of the capital, and most of all in the public streets, squares, and gardens. It was the street, most of all, which provided the forum for the free-floating, depersonalized existence which is sometimes taken to typify city life, and which explains both the attraction of the street and also its sense of danger.[32]

These points are vividly captured in Tim Hitchcock's study of the 'public poor'. As Hitchcock notes (ch. 6), beggars were virtually the living embodiment of urban anonymity. Their obvious strategy was to seek out the most public streets and spaces. And it was here, of course, where everyone was in a sense 'anonymous'. As Dr Hitchcock observes, the relative lack of private prosecutions of beggars may have reflected the fact that 'because the street was everyone's business, it was no-one's business'. But beggars were not quite the mobile 'modern' individuals, surviving on impersonal financial transactions, cut off from local connections, that they might seem. The legal settlement of men and women prosecuted for begging shows that they were much more strongly connected to the local community than might be imagined, while the increase in short-distance migration within the city may well have meant that they had relatives and connections within a reasonable distance of their activities. Yet how might such individuals respond to a more general assumption of their anonymity? This is a difficult question and perhaps few of the 'beggarly self-employed' would have responded as robustly as Silas Wegg, the nineteenth-century character Charles Dickens created in *Our Mutual Friend*. Wegg presides over his own particular pitch, his stall placed 'over against' a large corner house

[31] Burke, 'Urban history', p. 77; Boulton, *Neighbourhood*, p. 293.
[32] On city streets see P. Corfield, 'Walking the city streets. The urban odyssey in eighteenth-century England', *Journal of Urban History* 16 (1990), 132–74; Wall, *Literary and Cultural Spaces*, ch. 4; P. Griffiths, 'Meanings of nightwalking in early modern England', *The Seventeenth Century* 13 (1998), 212–38; M. Ogborn, *Spaces of Modernity. London's Geographies 1680–1780* (New York, 1998), ch. 3.

not far from Cavendish Square. He likes to cultivate a sense of knowing this house and its occupants. He always speaks of it authoritatively as 'Our House' and even dubs its inhabitants with his own invented names, 'Uncle Parker' and 'Master George', though, as the narrator tells us, 'his knowledge of its affairs was mostly speculative and all wrong'. On the basis of a few odd jobs undertaken for servants of the house, he has also 'settled it with himself . . . that he was one of the house's retainers and owed vassalage to it and was bound to leal and loyal interest in it'. Wegg invents a false set of social relationships with these prosperous residents, partly, it would seem, to compensate for his very anonymity in their eyes.[33]

Tim Hitchcock's suggestion is that the increase in 'public' spaces in eighteenth-century London may have provided the impetus for more 'stationary' begging. As begging became more public, so the poor came to seem more anonymous, and the responsibility of communities towards them less clear. Eighteenth-century policy towards the poor similarly came to treat them more and more as individuals with no home or connections. The anonymizing of the poor may thus reflect in part an interaction of elite perception with a response to some of the practical consequences of the changing architecture of the capital.

III

The expanding city may have created both opportunities and confusion for its inhabitants, but how did contemporaries represent and evaluate such growing urbanization? How far did people see such development as bringing physical and moral problems? Did this create an ambivalent attitude towards urban development, and if so, how did contemporaries seek to rectify the problems that were generated by urbanization?

There had always been a tradition of perceiving the city and its growth in a positive way. Classical and Renaissance humanist authors had praised cities as the ideal form of social organization, and chorographers and pageant-writers followed their lead in praising London as a centre of civilization, in its government, religion, arts, and learning.[34] Trade and commerce could also win

---

[33] Charles Dickens, *Our Mutual Friend*, ed. S. Gill (Harmondsworth, 1971), pp. 87–9.
[34] G. K. Paster, *The Idea of the City in the Age of Shakespeare* (Athens, Ga., 1989), ch. 1; Slack, 'Perceptions', pp. 163, 164–5.

applause, with Tudor social analysts praising the projector as a hero, and lord mayors' pageants extolling the glories of trade and its benefits for all, depicting urban growth as a source of wealth and energy for the whole country.[35] Equally established, however, was a more doubtful and ambivalent view, which feared the impact of an urban development spinning out of control. The *Survey of London* tradition was essentially encomiastic, but Stow's own account was carefully nuanced, with an underlying critical edge. Nor were doubts about the wisdom of urban growth in short supply in the early modern period. In part, this was prompted by a sharp awareness of the practical difficulties linked to urban expansion, particularly in the development of suburban areas outside the City of London proper. Not entirely without reason, suburban growth was associated with poverty, disease, and potential social unrest. There were also fears that London's commercial predominance was distorting the national economy – the capital's distended shape and distorting economy invited images of an overgrown monster that disrupted all around it.[36]

At the same time, more traditional doubts about the moral impact of the city on its inhabitants found full expression. Distrust of urban living dated back to classical times, but was no less potent for that.[37] Some fears related to commerce – there were worries that money subverted all other values, and that the marketplace undermined more fixed social relationships and hierarchies.[38] Traditional juxtapositions of the simple honour of the country and the sophisticated immorality of the city had often focused on the image of the humble and awestruck countryman being tricked or corrupted when visiting the city.[39] The high rates of immigration into the early modern city, and the relatively high percentage of the overall population with direct experience of the capital, must have made such cony-catching pamphlets seem all the more relevant and more generally served to intensify the city/country dialectic in the eyes of contemporaries.[40]

[35] Manley, *Literature and Culture*, pp. 106–10, 288.
[36] Archer, *Pursuit*, pp. 12–13, 38–9, 225–30, 235. On London's economic dominance, see Slack, 'Perceptions', p. 166; Manley, *Literature and Culture*, pp. 133–4, 198.
[37] Paster, *Idea of the City*, ch. 1; Manley, *Literature and Culture*, p. 73.
[38] Manley, *Literature and Culture*, pp. 90–8.
[39] *Ibid.*, pp. 110–13.
[40] It has been estimated that one in eight of the survivors of all those born in England came to reside in London at some point in their lives in the period between 1550 and 1650. A similar figure of one in six has been assigned to the period 1650 to 1750: E. A. Wrigley, 'A simple model of London's importance in changing English society and economy 1650–1750', *Past*

Peter Lake's chapter provides us with a detailed analysis of the process by which certain writings demonized contemporary urban life. In a range of literature – sermons and plague pamphlets which deplored the sins of the city, plays which denounced or satirized the evils of the city, and popular murder pamphlets which gave graphic and morally charged accounts of the evils committed in the capital – Lake shows how authors produced an inverted image of London's glories as painted in familiar celebratory accounts. In this literature, the crimes and sins committed in London were enumerated, and in the process the city itself identified as the initiator of moral decay. Under its corrupt sway, inhabitants plunged into lives of debauchery and even murder. These were not, moreover, simply accounts of the fortunes of an underclass. As Lake shows, the principal actors whose doom was portrayed in these pamphlets and plays were sometimes members of the elite, brought down by the perilous attractions of London's depravity.[41]

Professor Lake also argues, however, that this literature did not work simply by inverting the positive celebrations of the city. Good and bad were almost necessarily seen as different sides of the same coin – virtue could easily slide into vice, as they only differed from each other in degree. Those vices which brought down God's angry punishment were arguably the activities that helped to generate the city's oft-praised wealth. In one sense, therefore, the reform of the sins enumerated in the pamphlets was ultimately impossible, since many of these sins were inherent in the very nature of successful urban living and economic relations. Thomas Dekker captured precisely this ambivalence when he addressed the city in his *The Seven Deadly Sinnes of London* (1606):

Thou art the goodliest of thy neighbours, but the prowdest; the wealthiest, but the most wanton. Thou hast all things in thee to make thee fairest, and all things in thee to make thee foulest; for thou art attir'de like a Bride, drawing all that looke upon thee, to be in love with thee, but there is much harlot in thine eyes.[42]

Dekker himself, as well as his contemporaries Jonson and Middleton,

---

& *Present* 37 (1967), 48–50; Finlay, *Population and Metropolis*, p. 9; Boulton, *Neighbourhood*, pp. 3–5; M. J. Kitch, 'Capital and kingdom: migration to later Stuart London', in Beier and Finlay, *London 1500–1700*, pp. 224–51.

41 On much of this literature see also Manley, *Literature and Culture*, chs. 6 and 8; Archer, *Pursuit*, pp. 204–11.

42 Quoted in Paster, *Idea of the City*, p. 3; Manley, *Literature and Culture*, p. 142.

was, of course, capable of apotheosizing the city and its merchants in pageants as well as satirizing them in city comedies.

Ambivalence, then, seems a dominant characteristic of writings about the capital. Far less detailed work has been done on writings about London in the period after 1660, but some interesting suggestions have emerged in more recent work. Paul Slack has suggested that 'the balance of opinion became perceptibly more favourable' later in the century towards the notion of urban expansion. While the nature of the balance requires more research, it is undoubtedly the case that Slack has identified the development of a form of elite discourse which was more comfortable with notions of urban culture and urban growth. The traditional themes of pro-urban literature were now boosted by the newly fashionable language of improvement and quantification, which, bristling with figures and tables, saw the continuing expansion of the city and its economy as a vital sign of the health of the country at large.[43] The economic argument may have been won, but, despite these positive messages, older negative discourses persisted in parallel with these new developments, and in forms that would have been recognizable to a much earlier audience. There is ample evidence that the morally ambiguous low-life pamphlets were alive and well in the later period. The sins of the city continued to be condemned. The familiar scenario of the country yokel visiting the corrupt city was still replayed.[44] The image of the city as a whore, propounded by classical authors and repeated by Thomas Dekker, can still be found in the eighteenth century.[45] Guidebooks and pamphlets continued to denounce London as wicked, brutal, unmanageable, and overgrown, depicting crime and commerce as intertwined in a sink of corruption. Even beyond the familiar pamphlet exposés of low life in the city, one commentator has noted 'a more general trend of London malediction prominent in the literature of the mid-[eighteenth] century'.[46]

---

[43] Slack, 'Perceptions', pp. 162, 173–8.

[44] Corfield, 'Walking the streets', 138–9; M. Byrd, *London Transformed* (New Haven, 1978), pp. 20–4.

[45] Paster, *Idea of the City*, pp. 3, 4–5, 20–1, 26–7, 220; Manley, *Literature and Culture*, p. 142; Byrd, *London Transformed*, pp. 56–7, 77–8, 114, 133–4, 159–60.

[46] Byrd, *London Transformed*, pp. 21–3, 85–6. The early eighteenth century also witnessed one of the most striking examples of the intrusion of the 'monstrous' language of the satire and city comedies into the normally encomiastic arena of civic appraisal with the publication of Daniel Defoe's *View*, although whether this represented an astute subversion of a genre rather than a more long-term expansion of the domain of the cony-catching pamphlets is open to question: Manley, *Literature and Culture*, p. 167.

The sense of moral ambivalence about the expanding city thus seems to have remained, even as the range of literary genres offering either positive or negative images of the city proliferated.

The intimate and sometimes paradoxical link between London's vices and its virtues is articulated most strikingly in Bernard Mandeville's remarkable claim that the City's filthy streets were a crucial manifestation of the metropolis's health. Filth was the creation of a thriving city. If people 'have any Concern in its Welfare, they will hardly ever wish to see the Streets of it less dirty . . . Now would I ask if a good Citizen . . . might not assert that dirty streets are a necessary Evil inseparable from the Felicity of London.'[47] Not all shared Mandeville's view, and Laura Williams's chapter traces the ways in which London's parks were partly seen as a means of reforming the city's environmental 'evils'. Green spaces were more formally and self-consciously integrated into the urban landscape than ever before. Nor were they considered merely escapist oases from the foul air of the city. Commentators such as Evelyn believed that natural elements could *actively* purify the air. Physical exercise in the park was a cleansing ritual for the individual, but also comfortably dovetailed with medical notions of the importance of circulation in nature, which could themselves be imprinted on wider conceptions of the city as an organism. The importance of London's green spaces was also more than a matter of overcoming the physical unhealthiness of the capital. The equation of urban pollution with moral decay found within contemporary discourse also meant that green spaces, and the vigorous exercise conducted within them, were considered integral to the *moral* cleansing of the capital. Recourse to nature, therefore, held the potential to correct the moral imbalances of city life in all its forms.

But this also meant that green spaces acquired connotations of social exclusivity as the seventeenth century progressed. Of course they had partly held such associations even earlier, with areas such as Hyde Park being specifically dedicated to the socially exclusive sport of hunting once King Henry VIII had decided to build Whitehall Palace nearby.[48] But increasingly in the seventeenth century, clean air and pleasant views became the trappings of social

---

[47] Bernard Mandeville, *The Fable of the Bees* (1714), preface, quoted in Ogborn, *Spaces of Modernity*, pp. 86–7.
[48] For a discussion of the profound long-term impact of the siting of Whitehall Palace on the use of space in the western suburbs, see Merritt, *Social World*, ch. 6.

respectability. This inevitably brought with it an increasing concern that access should be regulated, as seen both in the restrictions on access to St James's Park, and in the development of the planned square, partly railed in – 'a "public" space reserved for private consumption'. This retreat from urban contamination also preserved the fortunate individual from the 'moral miasma' and 'social contagion' of lesser citizens. The orderly containment of nature, rather than nature in its wild and untrammelled state, was most admired. But the value placed upon parks and green spaces should not, Williams argues, be perceived as expressive of 'anti-urban' sentiment. Green spaces might evoke some rural associations, but just as importantly, they provide the perfect setting for urbane sociability. Here were rustic virtues but urban amenities, and a 'country' which was controlled and packaged for use when required. Nature and the country might be seen as corrective and redemptive, but the aim was to restore a balance which would harmonize the best aspects of the city, rather than to flee from the city itself.

Nevertheless, as Dr Williams notes, even the parks and open spaces were not entirely immune to the Janus-faced depictions which typified London's other amenities. Different literary genres depicted the city's parks as well-springs of vice just as much as havens of moral regeneration. The preacher Robert Elborough, for example, attributed the Fire of London partly to God's vengeance for the breaking of the sabbath 'by our Moore-fields walkes and Hide-park Recreations'.[49] In a different vein, John Evelyn's *A Character of England* pursued equally negative images. The assembly of coaches in Hyde Park, for example, was a disorganized rabble that he compared to 'a Regiment of Carre-men'; people had to pay for access to the park when it should be free; in the Spring Garden people walked far too fast, 'at such a rate, as you would think all the ladies were so many Atlantas contending with their Wooers'; and above all the parks themselves were centres of vice.[50] The depiction of parks as sites of immorality was partly, of course, simply a statement of fact, but it also undoubtedly drew on the more traditional negative images of

---

[49] Robert Elborough, *Londons Calamity by fire Bewailed and Improved* (1666), p. 14; Wall, *Literary and Cultural Spaces*, pp. 9–10.

[50] John Evelyn, *A Character of England* (1659), pp. 60–2. Evelyn associates republicanism with the chaotic landscape: see Manley, *Literature and Culture*, p. 164; M. Jenner, 'The politics of London air: John Evelyn's *Fumifugium* and the Restoration', *Historical Journal* 38 (1995), 535–51.

unenclosed lands as places of disorder and corrupt assignation, which Peter Lake has noted.[51] In the later eighteenth century, as Miles Ogborn has shown, contemporaries expressed concern that a venue such as Vauxhall Gardens allowed the social identities of visitors to blur dangerously, a concern shared by earlier park-builders, but one now increased with what were taken to be the parallel urban trends of growing commercialization and commodification.[52]

This schizophrenic treatment of the city can also be seen, as Tim Harris's chapter demonstrates, in contemporaries' different views of that most worrying symptom of urban disorder, the London crowd. Since classical times, of course, the crowd had supported a positive as well as a negative image, standing as the emblem of the city, and classical notions of civic republicanism were everywhere in the pageants and plays of the early modern city.[53] 'What is the city but the people?' demands the tribune Sicinius in Shakespeare's *Coriolanus*, 'as if uttering an accepted commonplace', to which the crowd of citizens echoes 'True, the people are the city.'[54] But here, as several commentators have noted, there is an ambiguity. Sicinius in one sense is asserting that the city is its inhabitants rather than its buildings, but he is also perversely twisting a legal maxim in order to imply that only the 'rabble of Plebeians' who accompany him are the people and the city. In the play, Sicinius gives the statement a deliberately inflammatory, populist emphasis.[55] 'Vox populi' could be a powerful form of legitimation, but the question was *which* crowds represented the 'real' voice of London. This was a question raised with particular urgency in the later seventeenth and early eighteenth century, the 'golden age' of the London crowd. John Strype had done his best to avoid the topic, but when he touched on these crowds he was anxious to insist that these notorious mobs did not include proper apprentices.[56] As Tim Harris demonstrates,

---

[51] But the landscape was ever the subject of strong feeling, and in 1549 petitioners objecting to the enclosure of fields in the parish of St Martin in the Fields had argued conversely, that the hedges associated with enclosure not only undermined the livelihood of locals, but also positively encouraged immorality by providing cover for prostitutes and their clients: J. Kitto, *St Martin in the Fields. The Accounts of the Churchwardens 1525–1603* (1901), pp. 579–80.

[52] Ogborn, *Spaces of Modernity*, ch. 4.

[53] Manley, *Literature and Culture*, pp. 276–7; Paster, *Idea of the City*, pp. 127–8, 142–4, 147.

[54] *Coriolanus* 3.1.198–9, ed. L. Bliss (New Cambridge Shakespeare, Cambridge, 2000); Paster, *Idea of the City*, p. 65.

[55] *Coriolanus*, (Bliss edition), p. 190; *Coriolanus*, ed. Philip Brookbank (Arden Shakespeare, London, 1976), p. 207n.

[56] Strype, *Survey*, II.v.332–3.

however, other commentators were not averse to celebrating the political activities of the London crowd when they took it to be in defence of their own values. Depictions of 'good' and 'bad' crowd agitation often drew on precisely the same features that we have encountered in Professor Lake's discussion – here was the rhetorical form of *paradiastole* with a vengeance. As Harris suggests, in the politically polarized world of late seventeenth- and early eighteenth-century London, the question was less one of what the crowd had done, but whether the crowd support 'was of the right kind and for the right reasons'.

Arguably, at the heart of these ambiguous treatments of popular activism in London was the broader question of the precise nature of the city's political loyalty, and how civic political activity should be portrayed. Even Stow in an appendix to the *Survey* had published a short tract (probably by James Dalton) which, in mounting an enthusiastic defence of the city, had praised its role in acting as a bridle against tyranny.[57] Strype would later encounter serious difficulties in trying to create a narrative which would celebrate the city's defence of its liberties and of true religion while also emphasizing its loyalty to the Crown. He ultimately found his solution in creating two entirely separate chapters, rather than resolving the conundrum within a single discourse.[58]

Nigel Smith's chapter reminds us that radical religious groups possessed their own highly potent images of the city, which intersected with a more traditional literature of complaint. Radical religious writers (as well as hack-writers such as Dekker and Goodcole) painted a lurid picture of London's scarlet sins and the likelihood of God's judgement upon a vice-ridden city. By the mid-seventeenth century, however, radical discourse took on an increasingly apocalyptic tone, and its millenarian thrust generated a whole series of urban-specific images. The prominence of cities in millenarian texts positively invited radicals to visualize London in apocalyptic terms. Radical visionaries such as Anna Trapnel quite naturally located their own millennial narratives within London itself: her divine visions were not just urban in character, they also contained specific topographical allusions to parts of the capital. The fact that the city was familiarly viewed as a site for apocalyptic

---

[57] Stow, *Survey*, II, 196–217.
[58] See below, pp. 81–3.

destruction also prompted the ready use of the image of fire within such texts.

Fire, of course, is an element which held particularly strong resonances for densely populated urban communities. Like plague epidemics, outbreaks of fire regularly prompted contemporaries to examine urban life for sources of divine displeasure.[59] God's providential judgement on a sinful city and prophetic utterances were the staple of this form of literature.[60] But this negative focus on fire as a manifestation of God's dreadful judgement was not the only aspect of fire that aroused interest. Fire might also be seen as purgative, even inspirational. For those men and women with a more radical religious agenda, for whom prophecy derived most readily from personal inspiration and the Book of Revelation, fire could have a vital positive significance. Fire was certainly destructive, but it was also purifying. Smith suggests that this association was so powerful for the radical Finch, that he may have even assisted the fulfilment of this much-desired prophecy through his own efforts. The multiple significances of London's fires, beyond the purely destructive, can also be observed in the writings of less radical authors, such as the astrologer Francis Bernard. Bernard's treatment of the city as a single body or organism convinced him that he could cast London's horoscope. In this calculation, each past fire was equated with a fever ravaging a human body and on this basis Bernard believed that he could predict the exact week in which future fires would occur.[61] It was commonplace for writers after the Great Fire to suggest that the cataclysm had been a useful purgative in ridding the city of some of its older buildings. One contemporary commentator remarked of

---

[59] For the many meanings that fire held for one early modern Londoner, see the interesting discussion in P. Seaver, *Wallington's World: A Puritan Artisan in Seventeenth-Century London* (Stanford, 1985), pp. 54–6.

[60] E.g. A. Walsham, *Providence in Early Modern England* (Oxford, 1999), pp. 117–24, 126, 137–8, 155–6. Such providential interpretations of fire in the capital continued even into the nineteenth century. In 1854, one pamphleteer warned that the recent burnings of the Houses of Parliament, the Royal Exchange, and the Armoury in the Tower were not accidents, but were partly judgements on the City for its sins. As the richest, largest, and most luxurious city in the world, London was prophesied in the Book of Revelation as the idolatrous Babylon. The Catholic powers, the writer declared, 'shall ravage and utterly destroy London': anon., *London, the Subject of Fearful Predictions, contained in the Revelation of St John* (1854), pp. 12, 13–23, 24, 29, 31. The writer also managed to feed London's earlier history into his prophetic interpretation, including Laud and Cromwell (*ibid.*, pp. 17–19).

[61] K. Thomas, *Religion and the Decline of Magic* (1971), p. 388. Bernard makes his claims writing to Lilly in 1664: Thomas does not record whether this infallible system managed to predict the Great Fire. Lilly would later himself be accused of suspicious advance knowledge of the Great Fire in prophecies that he had published in 1651 (*ibid.*, p. 488).

urban fires in general: 'it is observed that every town is bettered exceedingly by being purified by fire'.[62] But the purifying role of fire could also be emphasized in a more directly medical way. In his 1720 edition of the *Survey of London*, Strype ends his account of the Fire by quoting the observations of the medical doctor, John Woodward. Woodward suggested that levels of infectious disease within the capital had dropped since the Fire due to improvements in sewers and housing and claimed that London was now 'the most Healthy City in the World'. Therefore, in the celebratory pages of the *Survey*, the fire may have resulted in lamentable losses, but its ultimate impact has been cleansing, indeed quite literally, purifying.[63]

The authors of this volume have consistently sought to look behind the larger processes of change at work in the early modern capital in order to consider the human, the particular, and the personal. Max Byrd has observed of the eighteenth century that as London grew 'larger and larger, more and more unmanageable', so there was 'an increasing effort to humanize the city, to bring it to terms with the human scale of imagination, to force what is beyond comprehension back into traditional forms of comprehension'.[64] Byrd suggests that such efforts are 'paradoxical', but they seem all of a parcel with the efforts from Stow onwards to make the expanding city more knowable, to provide it with a past and a fully mapped present, partly as a means of accommodating change. In the same way, the city's formalized green spaces helped to provide a reassuring counter to rapid urban development. It is these efforts to explain and master the changing city, whether in texts or in the daily lives of individuals, which we have been seeking to study.

In part, the result has been to reinstate citizens as active participants in the changing city – not simply as passive observers of a developing cityscape, but as individuals making creative, pragmatic responses to a changing urban environment. These responses were enormously varied, but partly seem to have reflected the more general dialectics of fragmentation and integration, local and metropolitical identity, positive and negative evaluation, continuity and

[62] Porter, *Great Fire*, p. 157; Wall, *Literary and Cultural Spaces*, p. 42; Thomas De Laune, *Angliae Metropolis* (1690), pp. 10, 20–1, 45; Stow, *Remarks*, dedicatory epistle.
[63] Strype, *Survey*, 1.i.240. Such assessments were, of course, overly sanguine, see Boulton, 'London 1540–1700', p. 319.
[64] Byrd, *London Transformed*, p. 4.

change, that typified the early modern metropolis. Here were new inflections and new features, but a world of change that was still partly rooted in the past – a past that was redefined, bowdlerized, and reconstructed, but yet remained an important part of the imagination of early modern Londoners.

Memorializing the city

CHAPTER I

John Stow and nostalgic antiquarianism

Patrick Collinson

John Stow might have anticipated Peter Laslett by 350 years, calling his *Survey of London The World We Have Lost*. While Stow never employed the expression 'Merry England', his preoccupation with 'that declining time of charity'[1] makes his book the most extended treatment of the Merry England refrain in all English literature: a mythical story about a world enjoying plenty, but attentive to want, a socially harmonious world consolidated and sweetened by charity, a festive world, in which generosity spilled over freely from the full cup of seasonal pastimes, an open world, and, above all, a religious world. Stow's *Survey* poses on almost every page the questions which all Merry England studies are bound to address.[2] Did Merry England ever exist? And if it did, are selective memories of its fall, or demise, to be trusted? For the myth of the life of Merry England depends upon the companion myth of its death. Later ages placed Merry England in the very years in which Stow lived and constructed his partly mythical London, while still later generations located it in epochs which Stow never lived to see. As Sir Keith Thomas has explained, Merry England was always the day before yesterday.[3] In Victorian fiction, it was associated with the stage coach in its last days, before steam put an end to it, as, for example, in Thackeray's *The Newcomes*: 'The island rang, as yet, with the tooting horns and rattling teams of mail-coaches; a gay sight was the road in merry England in those days.'[4]

Ian Archer has written on the Elizabethan London which Stow somehow failed to notice in his chapter, 'The nostalgia of John

---

[1] Stow, *Survey*, II.89.
[2] Ronald Hutton, *The Rise and Fall of Merry England: The Ritual Year 1400–1700* (Oxford, 1994).
[3] Keith Thomas, *The Perception of the Past in Early Modern England*, The Creighton Trust Lecture 1983 (1983).
[4] W. M. Thackeray, *The Newcomes*, ed. D. Pascoe (Oxford, 1996), p. 108.

Stow'.[5] But it is not my intention to compare Stow's nostalgic perceptions with reality. This essay has the more limited aim of scrutinizing and nuancing what might be called Stow's selective nostalgia, relating it to a religious position and religious attitudes which were evidently in a process of evolution throughout the forty years of his antiquarian activity. To this I shall add two contrasted points of contemporary reference: Richard Carew's *Survey of Cornwall*, where present-tenseness contrasts with the past-tenseness of Stow's constantly reiterated 'of old time'; and William Lambarde's *Perambulation of Kent*, where the crudest Anti-Romanism stands in stark contrast to Stow's religious conservatism. And yet, not only did Lambarde's *Perambulation* provide Stow with the model for his *Survey*. Stow referred to Lambarde as 'my loving friend': a touching tribute to the latitude of shared antiquarian enthusiasm.[6]

I

Although Stow's nostalgia is suffused throughout his text, including the ward-by-ward itinerary of the city which accounts for its bulk, its most explicit and intense expression comes in his descriptions of 'Orders and Customes', 'Sports and Pastimes', the military musters held at midsummer (the Standing and Marching Watches), and the section headed 'Honor of Citizens, and worthinesse of men in the same'. These self-contained cultural-historical essays depended on the *Descriptio Nobilissimae Civitatis Londoniae* which prefaced William Fitzstephen's life of Thomas Becket, which Stow also prints in full as an appendix, 'the said Author being rare'.

Stow's Fitzstephen was not only 'rare'. He wrote in the late twelfth century, so that while we are distanced from the first edition of Stow's *Survey* by four centuries, rather more than four hundred years separated Stow from Fitzstephen. Yet Stow compresses the centuries. Having quoted Fitzstephen at length on orders and customs, 'the estate of things in his time', Stow writes: 'whereunto may be added the present, by conference whereof, the alteration will easily appeare'. The implication is of a world which had remained more or less static until a vaguely defined moment which seems to

[5] Ian Archer, 'The nostalgia of John Stow', in David L. Smith, Richard Strier, and David Bevington (eds.), *The Theatrical City: Culture, Theatre and Politics in London, 1576–1649* (Cambridge, 1995), pp. 17–34.
[6] Stow, *Survey*, I.1; II.253.

correspond to the years of Stow's own childhood, the 1530s. The great changes which he alleges, and regrets, had all or mostly happened in his own lifetime, not in the four centuries which distanced him from his rare author. Now, no more than Stow was Fitzstephen a kind of historical camera, recording a series of accurate images of the real London of his day. His *Descriptio* was an early rhetorical exercise in praise of famous cities, a long tradition culminating in the many cartographical and literary descriptions of Renaissance cities, of which Stow appears to have had no knowledge, or none which he discloses.[7] So Stow's principal source is itself an unrealistic, rose-tinted picture of the London he thought he had lost.

Fitzstephen's London is made the occasion for some of Stow's sharpest complaints about the new London. According to Fitzstephen, the only plagues to afflict the city, 'solae pestes', were immoderate drinking and frequent house fires. Stow thought that in these respects there had been some improvement, since the poor could no longer afford strong beers and wines and most new building was in stone and tile. But now there were new 'enormities', especially encroachments on highways, lanes, and common ground, and the problem of heavy, uncontrolled traffic: 'for the world runs on wheeles with many, whose parents were glad to goe on foote'.[8] What Fitzstephen recorded, or alleged, about the great men of his time keeping house in the city, 'as if they were Citizens and free men of London', provoked Stow's lament for the decline of that charity 'of olde time given', recalling what he himself had seen as a child, over the garden wall: Thomas Cromwell's servants doling out bread, meat, and drink to as many as two hundred persons every day, 'for he observed that auncient and charitable custome as all prelates, noble men, or men of honour and worship his predecessors had done before him'.[9]

Above all, it was Fitzstephen who inspired Stow's fervently nostalgic calendrical rehearsal of traditional customs and pastimes, all supplied in the past tense. This festive calendar was more civic,

[7] Xavier Baron, 'Medieval traditions in the English Renaissance: John Stow's portrayal of London in 1603', in Rhoda Schnur (ed.), *Acta Conventus Neo-Latini Hafniensis: Proceedings of the Eighth International Congress of Neo-Latin Studies*, Medieval & Renaissance Texts & Studies 120 (Binghamton, N.Y., 1994), pp. 133–41.

[8] Stow, *Survey*, 1.83–4.

[9] *Ibid.*, 1.84–9.

less religious and liturgical, than the structure of the festive half of the year described by Hutton in his *Rise and Fall of Merry England*, or by Eamon Duffy in *The Stripping of the Altars*.[10] But it began with Christmas, lords of misrule in every great house, presiding over 'fine and subtle disguisinges, Maskes and Mummeries', everyone's house and the parish churches decked with holly, ivy, bays, and 'whatsoever the season of the yeare aforded to be greene'. This sort of thing went on until Candlemas. The only springtime custom which Stow described was the practice of fetching twisted trees or withies out of the woods into people's houses, which must have been what in other parts of the country was called 'palming'. Then to Mayday and Maytime, a wholly secular celebration.

I find also that in the moneth of May, the Citizens of London of all estates, lightly in every Parish, or sometimes two or three parishes ioyning togither, had their severall mayings, and did fetch in Maypoles, with diuerse warlike shewes, with good Archers, Morice dauncers, and other deuices for pastime all the day long, and towards the Euening they had stage playes, and Bonefiers in the streets.[11]

Midsummer was marked by standing and marching watches, as many as two thousand men and more processing through the streets 'all in bright harnes', with drums and fifes, trumpeters on horseback, together with pageants and morris dancers. Here Stow's chronology is more exact. The Midsummer Watch came to its historical climax on 8 May 1539, when as many as fifteen thousand citizens dressed up and marched from London to Westminster 'in three great battailes'. But boom was followed by bust. Henry VIII – ostensibly considering the heavy cost to the citizens, but also security – suppressed the watch, which was briefly but abortively revived in 1548. This was a matter close to Stow's heart. In his *Summarie of Englyshe Chronicles* he had recorded that in 1564, 'through the earnest suite of the armourers', a standing watch was held at midsummer (no marching), which he implied was a poor show, but as chargeable as the marching watches of the past. This was repeated in 1565 and 1567, but Stow has no reference to the watches after that; nor, as Ian Archer has pointed out, to the lord mayor's inaugural show which filled the vacuum left by the midsummer watches, leaving the quite

---

[10] Eamon Duffy, *The Stripping of the Altars: Traditional Religion in England, c.1400–c.1580* (New Haven and London, 1992).
[11] Stow, *Survey*, I.91–9.

misleading impression that now there were no more costly and spectacular shows to liven up London's streets.[12]

One thing conspicuously missing from Stow's mostly secular London calendar is the feast of Corpus Christi. Corpus Christi celebrations in provincial towns and cities such as Coventry, Beverley, and York, and the great play cycles performed in the context of the feast, were a cultural manifestation of a manufacturing and trading society composed of crafts, which were in competition, the plays serving, in Mervyn James's words, to defuse the 'tension between social wholeness and social differentiation', while sometimes occasioning the very conflict they were intended to prevent.[13] Stow's silence on the subject is a reminder that while the economic fabric of London, no less than that of provincial towns, was one of crafts and guilds, its political structure was composed of wards; and that the great London play cycles (now sadly lost) had no basis in the city guilds and no connection with Corpus Christi, but were organized and controlled by the city fathers, and performed by professional actors, often for the entertainment of royalty.[14] Stow reproduces Fitzstephen's account of summer and winter sports and pastimes, including skating, and merely adds 'these or the like exercises haue beene continued till our time', specifying stage plays, with a few meagre details. 'Of late time in place of those Stage playes, hath beene vsed Comedies, Tragedies, Enterludes, and Histories, both true and fayned: For the acting whereof certaine publike places haue beene erected': which, notoriously, is all that Stow tells us about the theatre of Shakespeare's early and triumphant years. In 1598 he had mentioned two of those 'public places': the Theatre and the Curtain. But in 1603 even those names were deleted.[15]

---

[12] *Ibid.*, 1.99–104; John Stow, *A Summarie of Englyshe Chronicles* (1570 edn), fos. 402r, 405v; (1587 edn), pp. 327, 330, 334; Archer, 'The nostalgia of John Stow', pp. 24–5. But see Lawrence Manley's essay on Stow accompanying Ian Archer's 'Of sites and rites' in *The Theatrical City*, pp. 47–8. There is a lavish description of an early seventeenth-century lord mayor's show in Thomas Middleton, *The Triumphs of Truth: A Solemnity Vnparalleld for Cost, Art, and Magnificence, at the Confirmation and Establishment of that Worthy and true Nobly-minded Gentleman, Sir Thomas Middleton, Knight; in the Honorable Office of his Maiesties Lieuetenant, the Lord Maior of the thrice Famous Citty of London* (London, 1613).

[13] Mervyn James, 'Ritual, drama and social body in the late medieval English town', in M. James, *Society, Politics and Culture: Studies in Early Modern England* (Cambridge, 1986), pp. 16–47; Charles Phythian-Adams, 'Ceremony and the citizen: the communal year at Coventry, 1450–1550' in Peter Clark and Paul Slack (eds.), *Crisis and Order in English Towns 1500–1700: Essays in Urban History* (Cambridge, 1972), pp. 57–85.

[14] This point was clarified for me by Professor Caroline Barron.

[15] Stow, *Survey*, 1.93; 11.236.

Stow's nostalgia reached its apogee in his account of the festivities associated with two other religious feasts of the dog days of high summer, St John the Baptist's Day and Saint Peter's Day, together with their preceding vigils, when

in the Euenings after the Sunne setting, there were vsually made Bonefiers in the streetes, euery man bestowing wood or labour towards them: the wealthier sort also before their doores neare to the said Bonefiers, would set out Tables on the Vigiles, furnished with sweete breade, and good drinke, and on the Festiuall dayes with meates and drinks plentifully, whereunto they would inuite their neighbours and passengers also to sit, and bee merrie with them in great familiaritie, praysing God for his benefites bestowed on them. These were called Bonefiers aswell of good amitie amongest neighbours that, being before at controuersie, were there by the labour of others, reconciled, and made of bitter enemies, louing friendes, as also for the vertue that a great fire hath to purge the infectyon of the ayre.[16]

The doorways of houses were festooned with green branches and flowers, while glass lamps with oil in them burning all night hung on branches of iron curiously wrought, each carrying hundreds of lights. Here was the ever seductive myth of community.

We may notice some other striking examples of nostalgic memory in the walkabout chapters of the *Survey*. There is a memorable description of Houndsditch, a row of almshouses for poor bedridden folk, each with a little garden plot behind, the sick old pensioners as visible through their windows as a rather different class of person in modern Amsterdam, 'a clean linnen cloth lying in their window, and a payre of Beades to shew that there lay a bedred body, vnable but to pray onely'. And there devout men and women would go on Fridays, to bestow their charitable alms. But more recently the whole area had been taken over by brokers and dealers in second-hand clothes, which, remarked C. L. Kingsford, was what the district was still known for in 1908.[17]

There is a horror story of what happened to the Priory of Christ Church, called Holy Trinity, in Aldgate, which had come into the possession of Sir Thomas Audley. The great church was demolished, and there was such a glut of stone that any man in the city could have a cartload brought to his door for sixpence or sevenpence, carriage included. The church of the Crutched Friars had become a carpenter's yard, a tennis court, and a glass factory. St Mary Spittle

16 *Ibid.*, I.101.   17 *Ibid.*, I.128; II.289.

in Bishopsgate Ward had been 'an Hospitall of great reliefe'. But now, in its place, were 'many faire houses builded, for receipt and lodging of worshipfull persons'. Much of the great complex of buildings which made up the Austin Friars had been demolished, and the marquess of Winchester had sold the monuments of noblemen and the paving, which had cost thousands of pounds, for a hundred, 'and in place thereof made fayre stabling for horses'.[18] It looks as if Margaret Aston's essay on 'The Dissolution and the sense of the past' could well have been written without reference to any text other than Stow's *Survey*.[19]

A strong moral is drawn from the strange story of Moorfields in the sixteenth century, first drained and enclosed, then opened up again for archery practice and other forms of recreation, but then re-enclosed, with gardens and summer houses, 'in worse case than euer . . . not so much for vse or profite, as for shewe and pleasure, bewraying the vanity of mens mindes, much vnlike to the disposition of the ancient Cittizens, who delighted in the building of Hospitals, and Almes houses for the poore, and therein both imployed their wits, and spent their wealthes in preferment of the common commoditie of this our Citie'.[20]

But as Stow walked from ward to ward, parish to parish, it was the wanton destruction of tomb monuments which made a constant, distressing refrain. At St Michael's Cornhill, where Stow's father and grandfather were buried, the tombs of two notable citizens having been pulled down, 'no monument remayneth of them', 'notwithstanding their liberality to that Church and Parrish'. St Botolph's in Billingsgate once had 'many fayre monuments', now 'al destroyed by bad and greedy men of spoyle'. The tombs in St Magnus the Martyr at the foot of London Bridge were 'for the most part utterly defaced'. The Franciscan church of the Grey Friars, rechristened Christ Church by Henry VIII, was stuffed with notable burials, of which Stow lists no less than 138, including the foundress, Edward I's queen, Queen Isabel, the consort of Edward II, a daughter of Edward III, the wife of Robert the Bruce, and Sir Thomas Mallory. 'All these and fiue times so many more haue bin

---

[18] *Ibid.*, I.143–4, 148, 166–7, 176–7.
[19] Margaret Aston, 'English ruins and English history: the Dissolution and the sense of the past', in M. Aston, *Lollards and Reformers: Images and Literacy in Late Medieval Religion* (1984), pp. 313–37.
[20] Stow, *Survey*, II.76–8.

buried there, whose Monuments are wholly defaced.' In Shoreditch church the vicar had stripped all the memorial brasses from the graves, the action either of 'a preposterous zeale, or of a greedy mind'.[21] Stow told John Manningham that he had omitted many new monuments from his *Survey*, 'because those men have bin the defacers of the monumentes of others, and soe thinkes them worthy to be deprived of that memory whereof they have injuriously robbed others'.[22]

II

If we attempt to dissect Stow's nostalgic antiquarianism, what do we find? First, and most simply, the values of an old man, seventy-three years of age when the *Survey* was first published, someone who lived in the past, had no enthusiasm for the present, and no words for the future. Stow had spoken with 'some ancient men' who had seen King Richard the Third and who could describe his physical appearance, 'comely enough, onely of low stature', and he passed this on to Sir George Buck in the seventeenth century, just as in the next millennium I may tell my grandchildren about the tiny and nearly globular Queen Victoria whom my father saw with his own eyes, riding in a coach in Hyde Park in the late nineteenth century.[23] As a child, Stow had walked every day to the fields beside the Tower to buy a halfpenny-worth of milk, which was three pints in summer, a quart in winter, 'always hot from the Kine, as the same was milked and strained'.[24] By the time he wrote, the countryside had retreated far down the Mile End Road, beyond Whitechapel. I myself grew up on a Suffolk farm where I rode on the backs of gentle carthorses, fed the pigs, and took part in the harvest with everyone else in the village. That farm no longer exists. The ponds in which I used to fish and catch newts have long since dried up. Old men hate change.

Stow was an historical ecologist before his time. All the old open spaces were filling up, the fields where the Stow family's milk had come from 'let out for Garden plots, Carpenters yardes, Bowling Allies, and diuerse houses thereon builded'. No more than forty

[21] *Ibid.*, I.197, 207–8, 212, 319–22; II.75.
[22] R. P. Sorlien (ed.), *The Diary of John Manningham* (Hanover, N.H., 1976), p. 154.
[23] George Buck, *The History of the Life and Reigne of Richard the Third* (1647), p. 79.
[24] Stow, *Survey*, I.126.

years before he wrote, Hog Lane which ran to the north towards Bethlehem Hospital (and nowadays Liverpool Street Station) had been lined with elm trees, 'with Bridges and easie stiles to passe ouer into the pleasant fieldes, very commodious for Citizens therein to walke, shoote, and otherwise to recreate and refresh their dulled spirites in the sweete and wholesome ayre', which was now 'made a continuall building throughout'.[25]

Such nostalgia for the raped and now distant countryside is a potent urban myth, symbolized by all that greenery allegedly brought in at Christmas and in the month of May, and it is impossible to say how many sixteenth-century Londoners were consciously moved by it. As for Stow's account of May morning, partly suggested by Fitzstephen's lyrical description of twelfth-century London's rural setting, and perhaps by the poets whom Stow knew so well, from Chaucer to Lydgate, this certainly reads like a pleasant fiction: 'Euery man, except impediment, would walke into the sweete meadowes and greene woods, there to reioyce their spirites with the beauty and sauour of sweete flowers, and with the harmony of birds.'[26]

Stow took particular exception to the creation of the East End. He objected to the encroachment of 'filthy cottages' and other 'purprestures' on what had once been open and common fields, making an 'unsauery and unseemly' passage into the city from that direction.[27] And he was equally disturbed by the abandonment of the great houses within the walls on the east side of the city, creating more slums and equally destructive of old-style community. For example, Northumberland House, two minutes' walk from Stow's own house by Aldgate pump, and once the town house of the Percies, had first been converted into a complex of bowling alleys and dicing houses, but then, when the competition of other unlawful gaming houses proved too severe, it was opportunistically developed as small cottages, 'for strangers and others'.[28] But it was none of Stow's business to tell us how the underlying problem of immigration and overcrowding was being created, addressed, and managed, which is the contested preoccupation of our modern historians of early modern London: Pearl, Foster, Rappaport, Archer, Boulton.[29]

[25] *Ibid.*, I.126–7.   [26] *Ibid.*, I.98.
[27] *Ibid.*, II.72.   [28] *Ibid.*, I.149.
[29] Valerie Pearl, 'Social policy in early modern London', in H. Lloyd-Jones, B. Worden, and V. Pearl (eds.), *History and Imagination: Essays in Honour of H. R. Trevor-Roper* (1981), pp. 115–31;

Stow was less exercised by ribbon development along the roads
leading towards Hoxton and Hackney, and thoroughly complacent
about the growth of the newly fashionable London to the west,
beyond Temple Bar and along the Strand into Westminster. The
expressions used in those passages are 'faire buildings', 'diuers fayre
houses', 'diuers fayre Tenements lately builded'.[30] But as we gather
from some of the most spine-chilling passages in Defoe's *Journal of the
Plague Year*, inhabitants of Aldgate were not necessarily well informed
about what went on in St Martin's Lane.

The ecological strand in Stow's *Survey* weaves its way in and out of
three related themes and preoccupations: open and enclosed, public
and private, innocence and sophisticated corruption. 'Of olde time',
on holy days, and after evening prayer, the youths of the city had
exercised themselves at their masters' doors with cudgel play, while
their sisters danced for garlands 'hanged thwart the streetes': 'which
open pastimes in my youth, being now suppressed, worser practises
within doores are to be feared'. What, asked Stow, am I to say about
the daily exercises in the long bow, 'now almost cleane left off and
forsaken? I ouerpass it: for by the meane of closing in the common
grounds, our Archers for want of roome to shoote abroad, creepe
into bowling Allies, and ordinarie dicing houses, nearer home,
where they have roome enough to hazard their money at vnlawfull
games: and there I leaue them to take their pleasures.'[31]

The development of part of the churchyard of St Botulph's
Bishopsgate to create Petty France, a collection of houses let out to
French immigrants, was, reported Stow, the work of some citizens
'that more regarded their owne priuate gaine, then the common
good of the Cittie'. And then, much closer to home, there was the
shocking story of how Thomas Cromwell, without a by-your-leave,
had encroached twenty-two feet into Stow's father's garden, in the
course of the operation moving a garden house out of the way on
rollers 'ere my father heard thereof, no warning was given him'. A
symbol of the new age was the ambitious house built in Bishopsgate

F. F. Foster, *The Politics of Stability. A Portrait of the Rulers in Elizabethan London* (1977); Steve
Rappaport, *Worlds Within Worlds: Structures of Life in Sixteenth-Century London* (Cambridge,
1989); Ian W. Archer, *The Pursuit of Stability: Social Relations in Elizabethan London* (Cambridge,
1991); Jeremy Boulton, *Neighbourhood and Society: A London Suburb in the Seventeenth Century*
(Cambridge, 1987).
[30] Stow, *Survey*, II.74, 98, 101–2.
[31] *Ibid.*, I.95, 104.

and known for generations as 'Fishers Folly', about which 'men haue not letted to speake their pleasure'.[32]

What all this added up to was a catastrophic collapse of age-old and traditional charity, which in Stow's perception seems to have been equivalent to the end of citizenship and community as he had known it. Ian Archer has dealt thoroughly with this matter. Hospitality, together with face-to-face, informal, charity may have been in decline in Stow's lifetime. It is impossible to say. But 'there can be no doubting the huge surge in philanthropic giving in the sixteenth century', a 'massively increased participation in giving to the poor', and this is a finding which could never be inferred from Stow.[33]

III

Was the taproot of Stow's nostalgic antiquarianism religious, the attitude of an essentially unreconstructed English Catholic, as it were a denizen of the pages of Duffy's *Stripping of the Altars*? A good case can be made for a strong link between antipathy to the Reformation and all that flowed from it and what might be called the antiquarian bug, and it is made by Richard Cust for certain Midland antiquarians, such as the Leicestershire gentleman Sir Thomas Shirley, and the Staffordshire chorographer Sampson Erdeswicke, Stow's exact contemporary. Catholic antiquarians compensated for their exclusion from many areas of public life by celebrating their ancient lineage with elaborate armorial displays, in their houses and parish churches, where they erected tombs which were assertive genealogical and heraldic statements. Here was the summoning up of the ghost of a past world to redress the unequal balance of the new. Lord Lumley up in County Durham is another good example of the same phenomenon.[34]

Stow, as a London citizen, whose trade was tailoring, and whose greatest adventure into public life was as a conner of ale, was not, to be sure, moved by the same grandiose motives as an Erdeswicke or a Lumley. His friend William Camden makes a more relevant point of

---

[32] *Ibid.*, I.164, 179, 165–6.
[33] Archer, 'The nostalgia of John Stow', p. 27.
[34] Richard Cust, 'Catholicism, antiquarianism and gentry honour: the writings of Sir Thomas Shirley', *Midland History* 23 (1998), 40–70; Mervyn James, *Family, Lineage and Civil Society: A Study of Society, Politics and Mentality in the Durham Region, 1500–1640* (Oxford, 1974), pp. 108–10.

reference. Camden's dislike of what he once called 'protestantes
effervescentes' runs through his *Annales* of Elizabeth like bindweed.[35]
And the Preface to his *Britain* contains this affirmation:

There are certaine, as I heare who take it impatiently that I have
mentioned some of the most famous Monasteries and their founders. I am
sory to heare it, and with their good favour will say thus much, They may
take it as impatiently, and peradventure would have us forget that our
ancestoures were, and we are of the Christian profession when as there are
not extant any other more conspicuous, and certaine Monuments, of their
piety, and zealous devotion toward God. Neither were there any other
seed-gardens from whence Christian Religion, and good learning were
propagated over this isle, howbeit in corrupt ages some weeds grew out
over-ranckly.[36]

The 'weeds' were not some polite deference to Protestant prejudice.
Camden was some kind of Protestant, who had suffered for his
convictions in Catholic Oxford, not to be sure at the stake but
perhaps by what some would regard as a worse fate, failure to gain a
fellowship at All Souls, which, in a letter to Archbishop Ussher, he
attributed to 'defending the religion established'.[37] This takes us into
the problematical, and perhaps unprofitable, business of determining
what religious labels it may or may not be appropriate to pin on
representatives of the generation whose lives were intercepted and
diverted by the Protestant Reformation.

An exception to prove the rule of the linkage between antiquarianism and a conservative religious outlook is the very unproblema-
tical William Lambarde. But if Sir Thomas Shirley was
compensating for a present which had deprived him of his past,
Lambarde as a newcomer to Kent was creating for himself his own
instant heritage. In what has been written about his *Perambulation of
Kent*,[38] not enough has been made of Lambarde's virulent and even,
in Camden's phrase, effervescent, Protestantism, no doubt because

35 Patrick Collinson, 'One of us? William Camden and the making of history', *Transactions of
    the Royal Historical Society*, 6th series, 8 (1998), 139–63, and esp. 156.
36 William Camden, tr. Philemon Holland, *Britain* (1610), 'The Author To The Reader'. This
    preface, including this statement, addressed to an English rather than a continental
    readership, appeared for the first time in 1610.
37 Thomas Smith (ed.), *V. Cl. Gulielmi Camdeni et Illustrium Virorum ad G. Camdenum Epistolae*
    (1691), pp. 246–8.
38 I cite the 1596 edition of *A Perambulation of Kent: Conteining the Description, Hystorie and Customes
    of that Shyre*, first published in a limited edition of 600 copies (intended for the Kentish
    gentry?) in 1576. Lambarde was republished in 1826, an edition reprinted in facsimile and
    edited by Richard Church (Bath, 1970).

attention has been concentrated on his Anglo-Saxon interests and learning, evidenced, for example, in Lambarde's extensive discussion of the Kentish law of gavelkind, and in the extent of his indebtedness to other Anglo-Saxon scholars, and especially to the mysterious Laurence Nowell.[39] But anti-popery is a very conspicuous feature of the *Perambulation*, apparent in such small details as a comment on the foundation of the nunnery of Minster in Thanet, with the foundress 'instructed belike by some Monkish counsellor'.[40]

Lambarde's longest continuous narratives were accounts of gross popish superstition. Such was the sensational story of the Maid (or Nun) of Kent, whose exploits had been engineered by 'the enimie of mankinde and Prince of darknesse', the bishops, priests, and monks with closed eyes winking, the Devil and his agents 'with open mouth laughing at it' (more than a thousand words); the conjuring Rood of Boxley (1,500 words): 'if I should thus leave Boxley, the favourers of false and feyned Religion would laugh in their sleeves, and the followers of Gods trueth might iustly cry out and blame me'.[41] John Bale, who also combined a genuine and learned passion for antiquity with an Ian Paisley-like hatred of all forms of monkery and popish superstition, could hardly have done better.

Lambarde pulled all the stops out when his chorographical itinerary brought him to Canterbury and to the great monasteries of Christ Church and St Augustine, 'two irreligious Synagogues' 'harborowes of the Devil and the Pope'. It was no wonder that Canterbury, like Walsingham, was now 'in a maner waste', since that was where God in times past had been blasphemed most. Lambarde's attitude to ruined abbeys differs from Camden's:

In which part, as I cannot on the one side, but in respecte of the places themselves pitie and lament this generall decay, not onely in this Shyre, but in all other places of the Realme also: So on the other side, considering the maine Seas of sinne and iniquitie, wherein the worlde (at those daies) was almost wholy drenched, I must needes take cause, highly to praise God that hath thus mercifully in our age delivered us, disclosed Satan, unmasked

---

[39] Robin Flower, 'Laurence Nowell and the discovery of England in Tudor times', *Proceedings of the British Academy* 21 (1935), 47–74. Flower's misidentification of Nowell is corrected in Retha Warnicke, 'Notes on a Court of Requests case of 1571', *English Language Notes* (Boulder, Colo., 1973), and in her *William Lambarde; Elizabethan Antiquary 1536–1601* (1973). See ch. 4, 'The antiquary'.

[40] *A Perambulation*, p. 99.

[41] *Ibid.*, pp. 187–94, 227.

these Idoles, dissolved their Synagogs, and raced to the grounde all monuments of building erected to superstition, and ungodlynesse.[42]

Lambarde's 'pitie and lament' were not crocodile tears. Paradoxically, he, and that hot Protestant Bale, bitterly regretted the dispersal of the monastic libraries and the loss of their manuscripts, an aspect of the religious alteration which the conservative Stow never mentions.[43] But it appears that Lambarde would have been the last to complain if Canterbury Cathedral had been turned into a quarry: which is what happened to St Augustine's. The flip-side, as it were, of Lambarde's fierce anti-popery was the account, in his second edition, of the fleet riding at anchor at Chatham, 'these most stately and valiant vessels', 'such excellent ornaments of peace, and trustie aides in warre', 'this triumphant spectacle'.[44]

Lambarde regarded the murder of Thomas Becket as an unlawful crime, but asked 'whether such a life deserved not such a death'?[45] In stark contrast, John Stow's interest in Becket was as a person of honour, wisdom, and virtue, a local boy made good, following Fitzstephen with the marginal comment: 'A Shiriffes clarke of London became Chancellor of England, and Archbishop of Canterburie.'[46]

This brings us back to Stow's religion. There is not any doubt that he regretted the 'preposterous' zeal which had made a holocaust of so much of London's past, and that he deplored all acts of iconoclasm, especially when they were as senseless as the decapitation of the images of Lud and other ancient kings which had 'beautified' Ludgate, the act of those who 'iudged every Image to be an Idoll'.[47] Stow's detailed account of the regularly repeated acts of unlawful violence perpetrated against the images on the cross in Cheapside leave us in no doubt where he stood on that matter. In 1581 the target was 'the image of the blessed virgin, at that time robbed of her son, and her armes broken, by which she staid him on her knees: her whole body also was haled with ropes and left likely to fall'. In 1595 repairs were carried out, and in the year following 'a new misshapen son, as borne out of time, all naked was laid in her armes, the other images broke as afore'. But then, in 1600, between

---

[42] *Ibid.*, pp. 296–8.
[43] I owe this point to Dr Thomas Freeman.
[44] *A Perambulation*, pp. 346–50. Lambarde provides a list of all ships present in December 1596, the 'Estate of the Navie Royall', forty vessels.
[45] *A Perambulation*, p. 305.
[46] Stow, *Survey*, I.105.   [47] *Ibid.*, I.38.

the two editions of the *Survey*, the image of Our Lady was yet again defaced 'by plucking off her Crowne, and almost her head, taking from her her naked child, and stabbing her in the breast etc.'. 'Thus much for the crosse in west Cheape.'[48]

What mordant pleasure Stow derived from the story of St Andrew Undershaft, the church round the corner from his home! The shaft after which the church was named was the principal maypole of the city which had not been set up since the racial riots of the 'evil' May Day of 1517, and it hung on iron hooks under the eaves of neighbouring houses. In 1549, the curate of the parish of St Katherine Christ Church, a certain 'Sir Stephen', preaching at Paul's Cross, denounced the shaft as an idol and demanded that the quaint and in his perception superstitious names of such churches be altered. According to Stow's account, this man was a fanatical extremist who had once preached out of an elm tree in his chuchyard. The effect of the sermon was that the neighbours over whose doors the shaft had hung for thirty-two years, after a good dinner, hauled the thing down and sawed it up for firewood. 'Thus was this Idoll (as he tearmed it) mangled, and after burned.' Soon afterwards there happened the 'commotions' of the summer of 1549, in the midst of which, with martial law in force, a man from Romford, the local bailiff, was hanged for incautious words spoken to the same curate. The summary execution happened on Stow's very doorstep. This was a gross miscarriage of justice and the victim was a popular figure. Stow tells us that the villain of the piece immediately left London and was never heard of again.[49]

All this was consistent with the views of a non-effervescent Protestant, which is what Hugh Trevor-Roper supposed Stow to have been. But had that always been the case? C. L. Kingsford knew that there was more to it than that, but was swayed by a somewhat anachronistic view of Elizabethan religion typical of the time in which he wrote: 'Whatever lurking sympathy he might have felt for the old faith was lost in the deep loyalty of a true Elizabethan.'[50] That sounds more like Lambarde.

We must deal with another, and still more questionable reading of Stow. Barrett Beer, in an article based on a reading of successive

---

[48] *Ibid.*, 1.266–7. [49] *Ibid.*, 1.143–5.
[50] H. R. Trevor-Roper, 'John Stow' in *Renaissance Essays* (1985), pp. 94–102; Kingsford's Introduction to the *Survey*, 1.xxx.

editions of Stow's *Chronicles*, regarded Stow as a representative and
detached layman, the man in the street, who viewed the Reformation 'from the outside'. Beer even suggested that Stow 'never really
grasped the significance of the religious revolution through which he
lived'.[51]

There is no need to make things up. There is some evidence. In
February 1569, Stow came under suspicion as a closet Catholic. The
circumstances are obscure but had to do with Stow's possession of a
manifesto circulated by the Spanish ambassador on behalf of the
duke of Alva. Although Stow was called to answer before the lord
mayor, this would probably not have happened if he had not been
shopped by his younger brother Thomas, with whom Stow was on
the worst possible terms. Thomas knew about his brother's books
and papers and suspected him of dabbling in witchcraft. 'I will make
all the world know what artes he practysythe.'[52] A few days after
Stow's court appearance, he was visited by what might be called the
bishop of London's thought police, and his library and papers were
searched. After his chaplain had reported on what was found,
Bishop Grindal sent a report to the Privy Council and wrote to
William Cecil in his own hand, which suggests that the matter was
taken seriously.[53]

Historians have not made very much of this episode. There has
been a tendency to focus on Stow's collections of chronicles and
other papers, and what Grindal's chaplain chose to call 'phantasti-
call popishe bokes prynted in the old tyme', pretty harmless stuff.
But the chaplain paid little or no attention to this material, whereas
he prepared a catalogue of 'such bokes as have been lately sett furth
in this realme or beyonde the seas for defense of papistrye'. These,
he claimed, declared Stow to be 'a great fautor of papistrye'. The
chaplain was quite right. The books in question were not old and
fantastical but a fairly complete library of the up-to-date Catholic
literature of the English Counter-Reformation. There were over
thirty titles, including Bishop Bonner's Catechism and *Homilies*,

[51] Barrett L. Beer, 'John Stow and the English Reformation, 1547–1559', *The Sixteenth-Century
Journal* 16 (1985), 257–71.
[52] Stow, *Survey*, I.xvi–xviii, lvi.
[53] Bishop Edmund Grindal to Sir William Cecil, 24 February 1568(9), enclosing a letter from
Thomas Wattes to Grindal, 21 February 1568(9), together with 'A Catalog of such unnlawfull
bookes as were founde in the studye of John Stowe of London'; BL, MS Lansdowne 11, fos.
4–8. The catalogue was printed by John Strype in his *Life of Edmund Grindal* (Oxford, 1821),
pp. 516–19.

Richard Smith's *A Bouclier of the Catholike Fayth* (1554) and his *Defence of the Blessed Mass* and *Assertion and Defence of the Sacramente of the Alter* (both 1546), Bishop Stephen Gardiner's *Explication and Assertion of the True Catholique Fayth Touchyng the Sacrament of the Aulter* (Rouen, 1551), Bishop Thomas White's sermon on the real presence (1554), Miles Hogarde's *Displaying of the Protestants* (1556), and two much more recent imports from Catholic presses overseas, Thomas Stapleton's translation of Bede (1565), in effect a retort to Foxe's *Book of Martyrs*, and Thomas Dorman's book against Bishop Jewel, *A Proufe of Certeyne Articles in Religion* (1564). This does not sound like the bedside reading of a man who never really grasped the significance of what was going on in the Reformation. These were apologetical and polemical works, not books of devotion. What made Stow such a dedicated student of the doctrine of the real presence?

If Bishop Grindal's chaplain had paid closer attention to Stow's own papers and manuscripts, he might have been alerted to a kind of diary which finished up in a Lambeth Palace Library MS, a document of considerable interest if we are trying to pin Stow down, religiously, and a source of the utmost importance for the religious history of London in the 1560s.[54]

This piece of contemporary history suggests a fascination with religious weirdos, of whom early Elizabethan London afforded several examples, including two inmates of Bedlam, John More, who claimed to be Christ; and William Jefferey, who had appointed himself More's apostle, Saint Peter; and the self-confessed usurer, Richard Allington, who recounted on his deathbed many strange visions, with devils 'lyke puppets, they came up and downe my chamber'. 'And maisters, I can not tell of what religion you be that heare, nor I care not': 1,600 words of this.[55] For the year 1562, Stow records the summary arrest of a priest for preparing to say mass in Lady Cary's house in Fetter Lane, the hauling of the priest to prison with the crowd baying for his blood, 'mokynge, derydynge, cursynge, and wyshynge evyll to hym', 'well was he or she that cowld get a plucke at hym or gyve hym a thumpe with theyr fyst or spyt in his face' – and note, says Stow, the priest had not actually said mass but was only dressed and ready for it; the ladies of quality who had been

---

[54] James Gairdner (ed.), *Three Fifteenth-Century Chronicles With Historical Memoranda by John Stow the Antiquary, And Contemporary Notes of Occurrences Written by Him in the Reign of Queen Elizabeth*, Camden Society, n.s. 28 (1880).

[55] *Ibid.*, pp. 115, 117–21.

present themselves arraigned 'amongeste theves and mowderars'.[56]
Here Stow's sympathies are not in much doubt. When, in the
following year, the Marian bishops were removed from their imprisonment in the Tower to more comfortable quarters, Stow records
that the preachers at Paul's Cross and other places fed the flames of
popular prejudice, preaching 'as it was thowght of many wysse men'
'very sedyssyowsly', and he particularly mentions William Baldwin,
the author of the satire *Beware the Cat*, whose sermon had demanded
that the bishops 'and othar papestis' be hanged in Smithfield.
Although he had assisted him in early work on his abridgement of
the *Chronicles*, Stow seems to have taken pleasure in the fact that
Baldwin died of the plague a week after this provocative sermon.
When Sir Thomas Lodge as lord mayor grew a beard, the first to
have done so, it was thought of 'mayny people' very strange':[57]
beards were Protestant things. By now we begin to appreciate that
Stow's 'all men', 'mayny people', 'many wise men', are confession-
ally loaded rhetorical devices, resembling Camden's use of similar
expressions in his *Annales* of Elizabeth.

Stow's account of the Paul's Cross sermons of these years is
strikingly mordant. A lengthy report of a robustly anti-Catholic
performance by William Cole, the archdeacon of Essex, is ironically
prefaced 'Poynts of Devinitie'; another of Cole's sermons, which
likened priests to apes – for both were bald, the priests before, the
apes behind – was headlined 'A Noate of Divinitye'.[58]

Then comes Stow's invaluable and colourful account of the
vestiarian disturbances of 1566 which launched the Elizabethan
puritan movement: Robert Crowley barring the entry of a funeral
into St Giles Cripplegate, 'saynge the churche was his . . . whereof
he wold rule that place and wold not soffer eny suche superstycious
rages of Rome ther to entre'; a radical sermon preached at St
Magnus the Martyr by a Scot, 'wyth very byter and vehement words
agaynst the quene not here to be named'; the same Scot's conformist
capitulation, appearing in a surplice, whereupon 'a sertayne nombar
of wyves threw stons at hym and pullyd hym forthe of the pulpyt,
rentyng his syrplice and scrattyng his face'; the women of St
Margaret's Fish Street shouting 'ware horns!' at the bishop; women
(again) loading the non-conformist preachers with bags and bottles,
sugar and spice, as they passed over London Bridge to custody in the

---

[56] *Ibid.*, pp. 121–2.   [57] *Ibid.*, pp. 126, 127.   [58] *Ibid.*, pp. 128, 133.

country. It is significant that this narrative puts centre stage the gross and radical disorder of 'womanish brabbles'.

And then follows Stow's spin on the actions of those radical Protestants whose response to the vestments crisis was to reinvent the secret, privy churches of Mary's reign: 'About that tyme were many congregations of the Anabaptysts in London, who cawlyd themselves Puritans or Unspottyd Lambs of the Lord.'[59] We know about these people from other sources.[60] They did not call themselves Puritans, and they were certainly not Anabaptists.

There is no more informative account of the divided religious scene which was the sequel to the fires of Smithfield, and it is clear on which side of the fence Stow stood in these still inchoate 1560s. His religion was probably not very different from that of the undertaker and diarist, Henry Machyn, whose Catholic sympathies have never been in doubt.[61] But he was the religious opposite of the great Protestant chronicler John Foxe, who gloried in the repudiation of the religious past, and who suppressed evidence of religious division among Protestants and of those radical tendencies which Stow gleefully exposed. Were Stow's memoranda intended as a riposte to the *Acts and Monuments*?[62]

In the years which followed, if Stow did not become a Protestant, he learned to be discreet. His *Summarie of Englyshe Chronicles*, which began to appear from the press in 1565, contains none of the tendentious observations on the religious events of the mid-1560s which he had privately recorded. His practice in recounting for public consumption events close to his own time was, as with his use of Fitzstephen in the *Survey*, to incorporate other chronicles in his possession, and one of these, now contained in MS Harley 540, was conservative in outlook.[63] It characterized Katherine of Aragon as 'a blysyd lady and a good', and told the story of the punishment of two women who had said that she and not Anne Boleyn was rightfully

---

[59] *Ibid.*, pp. 135–44.

[60] Patrick Collinson, *The Elizabethan Puritan Movement* (London and Berkeley, 1967; Oxford, 1990), part 2, ch. 3, 'London's Protestant underworld'.

[61] J. G. Nichols (ed.), *The Diary of Henry Machyn Citizen and Merchant-Taylor of London, From A.D. 1550 to A.D. 1563*, Camden Society, 42 (1848).

[62] I owe this point to Dr Thomas Freeman.

[63] C. L. Kingsford (ed.), *Two London Chronicles From the Collections of John Stow*, Camden Miscellany 12, Camden Society, 3rd ser. 18 (1910). Stow also employed a chronicle, more Protestant in tone, MS Harley 530, together with MS Harley 194, edited by J. G. Nichols as *The Chronicles of Queen Jane and of Two Years of Queen Mary*, Camden Society, 48 (1850).

queen.[64] Stow omitted these details from his *Summarie*. The early editions of the *Summarie* gave an upbeat account of the accession of Mary Tudor, and of her restoration of the old religion. 'In this tyme the people shewed themselves so ready to receive their old religion, that in many places of the realme, understandyng the quenes plesure, before any law was made for the same, they erected agayne theyr aultars, and used the Masse and latin service, in such sorte as was wont to be in kyng Henries tyme.' These passages too were dropped from later editions.[65]

There is further self-censorship in the *Survey* itself. When Stow quotes the epitaphs inscribed on pre-Reformation tombs, he turns them into theologically innocuous statements, mere monuments, omitting the lines which invite prayers for the dead or refer to the doctrine of purgatory. The full texts can be found in the original MS of the *Survey*, MS Harley 538. Thus, the nine lines quoted from the tomb of John Rainwell, fishmonger, in St Botolph's Billingsgate (1446) end with an 'etc.', omitting five more, where we find: 'Wherfore now agre / To pray unto God that reynethe eternally / His soule to embrace and take to his mercy.' Only in MS Harley 538 do we find these words from the epitaph for Robert Dalusse and his wife, buried in St Martin in the Vintry in the days of Edward IV: 'Pray for us, we yow pray. / Lyke as you would be prayed for another day'; and, from the lengthy epitaph in St Anthony's Budge Row for Thomas Knowles, a former mayor, and his family, the formula: 'We may not pray, hartely pray ye / For our sowles pater noster et ave; / The sonner owre paynes lessed may be, / Graunt vs the Holy Trinitie.'[66]

If there is any sense in which John Stow was converted, if not exactly to a religion known as Protestantism, to the Protestant Church of England, he doubtless underwent, as with so many of his generation, a process of conversion by conformity. There is no evidence that he was ever a recusant and copious evidence on almost every page of the *Survey* to continuing commitment to the fabric and the social and mystical community of London's parishes. But when Stow refers, as he sometimes does, to churches having been recently

[64] Kingsford, *Two London Chronicles*, pp. 7–8.
[65] Stow, *A Summarie of Englyshe Chronicles* (1565), fos. 222v, 224. Stow's version of the spontaneous return of Catholic practice under Mary can be compared with the Yorkshire story told in A. G. Dickens (ed.), 'Robert Parkyn's narrative of the Reformation', *English Historical Review* 62 (1947), 58–83, reprinted in Dickens, *Reformation Studies* (1982), pp. 287–312. It may be no less indicative of where his sympathies lay. Compare later editions of the *Summarie*.
[66] These omissions were noted by Kingsford: Stow, *Survey*, II.309, 326, 327.

rebuilt or refurbished, one should not be misled. In every case it appears that the improvements to which he refers were not at all recent, and had been carried out before the Reformation, a watershed which he probably never ceased to regret.[67] Later editions of his *Summarie of Chronicles* included laudatory obits for Archbishop Parker, whom he calls 'my especiall benefactor', and for Bishop Jewel, 'a most eloquent and diligent preacher, but a farre more painfull and studious writer, as his workes remaining witness'.[68] It sounds as if Stow's library had been reconstructed since Bishop Grindal's chaplain visited it in 1569. However, one is bound to conclude from this investigation of religious opinions and attitudes, expressed and suppressed, that John Stow's *Survey of London* was born out of the old religion and its values, roughly adapted to fit the new suit of clothes which we almost have to call, however anachronistically, Anglicanism.

IV

In 1602, one year before Stow's second edition, another survey was published by a fellow member of the Society of Antiquaries, Richard Carew: *His Survey of Cornwall*.[69] Carew was not unaware that the world is a changeable place. In his Preface he wrote: 'the state of our countrie hath vndergone so manie alterations, since I first began these scriblings, that in the reviewing, I was driuen either likewise to varie my report, or else to speake against my knowledge'. Given what he called 'the ceaselesse revolution of the Vniverse' it would be marvellous if any part of it 'should retain a stedfast constitution'. But having stated the problem, Carew immediately put it behind him, declaring that what he called, significantly, his *'Eulogies'* would plot Cornwall 'as it now standeth'.[70]

So Carew provided a huge present-tense snapshot of his native

[67] Examples in *ibid.*, 1.194 (St Peter Cornhill, 'lately repayred, if not all new builded'), 202 (All Hallows Lombard Street, 'lately new builded'), 297 (St Michael Wood Street, 'a proper thing, and lately well repayred'), 314 (St Peter in Cheap, 'a proper Church lately new builded'). I have been helped with this point by Dr Julia Merritt.

[68] Stow, *Summarie of Chronicles* (1587 edn), pp. 370, 350; John Stow, *The Annales of England* (1592), dedicatory epistle addressed to Archbishop Whitgift. The 1601 edition of the *Annales* included for the first time a generous obit for Archbishop Grindal (pp. 1174-5).

[69] Richard Carew, *The Survey of Cornwall. Written by R. Carew of Antonie, Esquire* (London, 1602). There is a modern, somewhat abridged, edition by F. E. Halliday (1953, repr. 1969). All references here are to the original edition.

[70] Carew, *The Survey*, 'To the Reader'.

county. There is a great deal of historical material in his *Survey*, much more than one would suspect if one relied only on F. E. Halliday's modern abridgement. In particular, Carew's pages are stuffed with genealogy. But for anything in the past Carew was reliant on other authorities, many of whom were of the most shaky kind, and his amateurishness as an antiquarian was an embarrassment even to himself. Making what he confessed to be 'a great leap' from King Arthur and his knights to a man who died in 1507, he admitted: 'which conuinceth me an vnworthy associat of the antiquary Colledge'. He tells us about Conan who conquered Brittany and, having settled it, wrote to Dionethus, king and duke of Cornwall, asking him to send over 'some Maidens' to marry with his people. The result was that St Ursula and her 11,000 virgins were shipped over but on the way miscarried, 'as their wel known history reporteth'. Not that Carew was incapable of the sceptical irony with which the Tudor antiquarians often presented historical myths. Another doubtful detail of Cornish history was not to be questioned 'unlesse you will, withall, shake the irrefragable authoritie of the round tables Romants'.[71]

So there is a past as well as a present tense in Carew, as misty as the sea-fret around Tintagel, which excited him with as much romantic awe as any traveller might have felt in the age of Wordsworth and Walter Scott. But the difference with Stow is that the past was not brought critically to bear on the present, as a better time. Carew too was a nostalgic writer, but his nostalgia was one of celebration of the present, of which he paints a very rosy picture. Take, as an emblem of this upbeat writer, his description of the view from the coastal path at Fowey, well supplied with seats for tired walkers and summer-houses 'for their more priuate retrait and recreation': 'In passing along, your eyes shall be called away from guiding your feete, to descry by their fardest kenning, the vast Ocean sparkled with ships, that continually this way trade forth and backe to most quarters of the world', nearer to home the fishing boats 'houering on the coast', and closer still 'the faire and commodious hauen'.[72] Actuarially speaking, there was no better place to live than Carew's Cornwall. 'For health, 80 and 90 yeres age is ordinary in euery place, and in most persons, accompanied with an able vse of the body and his sences.'[73] He does tell us that Cornish houses were

---

[71] *Ibid.*, fos. 61v, 77.   [72] *Ibid.*, fo. 133r.   [73] *Ibid.*, fo. 63r.

infested with rats, 'a brood very hurtful for deuouring of meat, clothes and writings', but he romanticizes even this nastiness, describing 'their crying and ratling, while they daunce their gallop gallyards in the roofe at night' – from which we gather that these were plague-carrying black rats.[74]

One would never suspect that Cornwall, especially in the 1590s, was full of grinding poverty. To be sure there comes the moment when Carew says: 'We must also spare a roome in this Suruey to the poore', but he then tells us that if it were not for the whole shiploads of Irish poor brought over 'yeerley, yea and daly', there would be no problem. Carew, who was a magistrate and had been sheriff, launches into a conventional diatribe against rogues and vagabonds, complaining that what was given to them was 'robberie of the needy impotent', but on the subject of what he calls honest poor parishi-oners he has nothing else to say, except that no-one in Cornwall needed to starve, since there was always plenty of shellfish available for the gathering.[75]

Rather, 'let me lead you from these impleasing matters, to refresh yourselues with taking view of the *Cornish* mens recreations, which consist principally in feastes and pastimes'. And there follows, after a contrived debate about church ales and feasts, whether allowable or not (and Carew clearly approved of these things), the richest descrip-tion of the sporting life which we have for any part of early modern England: miracle plays and what are called 'three men's songs', 'cunningly contriued for the ditty and pleasantly for the note', football – or rather hurling and of two different kinds, one peculiar to east Cornwall, the other to the west – and Cornish wrestling, 'more delightful, and less dangerous' than hurling, which, when ended, 'you shall see them retiryng home, as from a pitched battaile, with bloody pates, bones broken, and out of ioynt, and such bruses as serue to shorten their daies; yet al is good play, and neuer Attourney nor Crowner troubled for the matter'.[76]

John Stow would have set all this in the past and would have lamented the passing of so much honest manliness. But Carew puts it in the present, which causes problems for the historian of traditional culture. His account of the Cornish miracle play, or 'gwary', to which 'the Country people flock from all sides, many miles off' is not only the best, it is the only description we have

[74] *Ibid.*, fo. 22r.   [75] *Ibid.*, fos. 67, 68r, 31r.   [76] *Ibid.*, fos. 68r–76r.

before more modern times of any play in performance, with the actor followed around the stage by the prompter, or ordinary, who tells him his lines.[77] But was the old drama still alive and well in Cornwall in 1600, when it had been suppressed almost everywhere else? The leading authority on the Cornish play text known as the *Ordinalia* finds it remarkable that in a county which only forty years earlier had been in active rebellion against the new religion, the high sheriff should record the performance of the old religious plays, with all their 'devils and devices', to be sure without much sympathy, but with perfect equanimity.[78]

The problem of the gwary and its fortunes as the sixteenth century turned into the seventeenth is tied up with the fact that the plays were written and performed in the Cornish language, which was itself in terminal decline. Carew's somewhat distant and condescending attitude towards the common people was accentuated by the fact that he himself seems to have known little Cornish (whereas he wrote an essay for his friend Camden on 'The excellencie of the English tongue'),[79] and was not sympathetic towards it, alleging that if a stranger who was lost were to ask the way, he would be told, in Cornish, 'I can speak no Saxonage', which was perhaps all the Cornish the man knew. Carew's Cornish phrase book knows nothing about postillions struck by lightning, but does include the Cornish for 'ten thousand mischiefs in thy guts'.[80]

Yet this did not prevent Carew from supplying the most detailed and knowledgeable accounts of how the Cornish people made their living, including 6,000 expert words on the subject of tin-mining. While the men were down the mine, 'the women and children in the West part of *Cornwall*, doe vse to make Mats . . . which for their warmthe and well wearing, are carried by sea to *London* and other parts of the Realme, and serue to couer floores and wals'.[81] And there were no barriers between Carew and his subject, either linguistic or social, when it came to fish and fishing, which he loved.

[77] *Ibid.*, fos. 71v–2r.
[78] Jane A. Bakere, *The Cornish Ordinalia: A Critical Study* (Cardiff, 1980), p. 14. Bakere suspects (p. 13) that Carew had not himself witnessed the 'gwary' in performance, and that his story is apocryphal. But she draws on town records for evidence of plays (unidentified) in performance in several places (pp. 15–22), as does A. L. Rowse, *Tudor Cornwall, Portrait of a Society* (1941), pp. 435–6. See also Roger Longsworth, *The Cornish Ordinalia: Religion and Dramaturgy* (Cambridge, Mass., 1967), Brian Murdoch, *Cornish Literature* (Cambridge, 1993).
[79] The best modern edition of William Camden's *Remaines of a Greater Worke, concerning Britaine* (1605) is by R. D. Dunn (Toronto, 1984).
[80] Carew, *The Survey*, fos. 55r–56v.   [81] *Ibid.*, fos. 7v–19r.

His model may have been Pliny, but he also wrote from the richest personal experience, from digging lugworms for bait to the netting of pilchards. The particular taking of divers kinds of fishes (and he lists more than thirty), is almost as divers as themselves. 'I will . . . shew you, what they are, when they come, where they haunt, with what baite they may be trayned, with what engine taken, and with what dressing saued.' Fourteen pages on: 'But you are tired, the day is spent; and it is high time that I draw to harbour.'[82]

Carew does not tell us, but a report drawn up in the same decade does, that in many places in west Cornwall the clergy, Protestant preaching ministers, were often the victims of physical assault, afraid to poke their noses out of doors.[83] On matters of religion, Carew was to the right of Lambarde, but a little to the left of Stow, and perhaps close to where Camden stood. It was not from the pope that Cornwall had received its Christianity. Vicarages had been created by the impropriation of benefices by the religious houses 'in more corrupt ages'. If the English bishops would only keep fast to their first institution, they would easily close the mouths of those 'who would thrust vpon vs their often varying discipline'.[84] On the whole, Cornwall, church as well as state, worked very well, and there was no better place to live, especially beside Carew's delightful and ingeniously devised fish pond at his ancestral Antony.

Is it possible to be nostalgic about the present, as well as about the past? The proof that it is is in Carew's *Survey of Cornwall*, which covers its subject with a thick, rich gloss which is just as deceptive as the regretful, nostalgic varnish which Stow applied to London. My exploration of these works of late Tudor antiquarianism, Stow, Lambarde, and Carew, suggests that we should not trust any one of them as a simple description of its subject. All three need to be taken with a healthy pinch of postmodernist salt. But that should not in any way diminish our enjoyment of what Hayden White would assure us are three charming fictions. And if that appears too large a concession to make to postmodernism, perhaps we are entitled to say that Kent, Cornwall, and, above all, John Stow's London were, in Benedict Anderson's phrase, so many imagined communities, the product of three very different imaginations.

[82] *Ibid.*, fos. 28r–35r.
[83] 'The lamentable estate of the mynystry in Cornewall', Westminster Abbey Muniments, Muniment Book 15, fo. 84.
[84] Carew, *The Survey*, fos. 81r–82r.

CHAPTER 2

The reshaping of Stow's 'Survey': Munday, Strype, and the Protestant City

J. F. Merritt

Over the last century, historians and editors have laboured long and hard to recapture the 'real' *Survey of London*. C. L. Kingsford, in his famous and accomplished edition of Stow's *Survey*, saw his task as being to remove the accretions of later editions, to restore what he called 'the true work'. In the introduction to his 1908 edition, he remarked on the strange fact that Stow's *Survey* of 1603 had 'never been accurately reprinted'. In the intervening three centuries there had been many editions of Stow's *Survey*, but these were 'so-called' editions, which according to Kingsford, swamped Stow's text with new additions and elaborations, thereby serving to 'conceal the identity and obscure the meaning' of Stow's original. With the purity of Stow's original scheme restored, the *Survey* could finally receive a proper scholarly appreciation.[1]

All subsequent students of Stow have been heavily indebted to Kingsford's excellent editorial work and it more than fufilled the scholarly task it set itself. But it has been unfortunate that the *Survey of London* itself has rarely been studied beyond its 1603 edition. After all, even for Stow himself the 1603 edition was not intended to be his last word on the subject – he clearly planned to embark on further refinements and elaborations. In addition, we cannot confine ourselves to the 1603 text if we wish to look at the impact of the work on its early modern readers. It must be remembered that few readers of Stow in the seventeenth and eighteenth centuries would have had access to either of Stow's original editions of 1598 or 1603. There were many more so-called 'corrupt' later editions than there ever were of Stow's own *Survey*: the title 'Stow's Survey of London' meant something very different to the people of seventeenth- and eighteenth-century England than it does to us today.

---

[1] Stow, *Survey*, I.xli–xlii.

A study of what one might call the 'after-life' of Stow's *Survey* can also give us some intriguing insights into changing ideas and representations of the early modern capital. Several questions and problems immediately present themselves. For example, if the later editions 'obscured' Stow's meaning (as Kingsford claimed), then what 'meaning' did they replace it with? Two aspects of the 'meaning' of Stow's *Survey* have attracted most attention: its character as a work of urban history, and the role of nostalgia, especially religious nostalgia, within the work as whole. Of course these themes were intimately related within the pages of the *Survey*. The profoundly negative attitudes toward urban change are intimately related to Stow's regret for the passing of the pre-Reformation city, and his religious conservatism in the face of Protestantism.[2] But while the theme of urban development contained within the *Survey* is normally seen as one with relevance for later writing on the city, the relationship of the parallel religious theme to later writing on London has not been explored. If Stow's work was partly an exercise in religious nostalgia, how far did later writers build on this characteristic or reorient the text with new material? How far was Stow's text amenable to updating and reshaping in a way that would neutralize its apparent hostility towards Protestant developments? Did it, in fact, limit the themes and parameters available to his later 'continuators'? Stow's work has often been celebrated for the way in which it situates the individual author and his responses at the heart of the work. But how far did his later editors and updaters seek to place their own ideas, lives, and preoccupations into the text?

This essay is not intended as an exhaustive analysis of the later editions and reshapings of the *Survey*. Instead it aims to recapture the myriad ways in which later writers grappled with the problems of applying a nostalgic, perhaps even crypto-Catholic text to the developing Protestant city. Principal attention will be given to Stow's main 'continuators' – Anthony Munday and the 1618 and 1633 updatings, and the more celebrated and massively expanded edition of the *Survey* produced by John Strype in 1720. In between, we will

[2] See most recently L. Manley, *Literature and Culture in Early Modern London* (Cambridge, 1995), ch. 3; I. Archer, 'The nostalgia of John Stow', in D. Smith, R. Strier, and D. Bevington (eds.), *The Theatrical City: Culture, Theatre and Politics in London 1576–1649* (Cambridge, 1995), pp. 17–34 and the chapter by P. Collinson in this volume. Stow himself drew inspiration and material from a range of sources which included a twelfth-century description of London by William FitzStephen, late medieval city chronicles, and William Lambarde's *Perambulation of Kent* (1576).

note some mid-century reshapings of Stow, which shed fresh light on
how Stow's text of regretful nostalgia could be cunningly redeployed.
We will begin with Stow's first posthumous editor: the infamous
Anthony Munday.

I

Anthony Munday, playwright, pageant-writer, polemicist, and friend
of Richard Topcliffe (the notorious torturer of Catholics) was the
driving force behind the two 'continuations' of Stow's *Survey* published during the seventeenth century. One edition of the *Survey of
London*, as it was called, was published in 1618, while another, vastly
enlarged version finally rolled from the presses in late 1633, just after
Munday's death at the age of seventy-three. Today, Munday is
perhaps best remembered as the author of no fewer than eight lord
mayor's pageants, although he was involved in at least fifteen, all but
one produced during the reign of James I.[3] These were the works of
the mature, respectable Munday, who proudly identified himself as
'that ancient servant to the City'. Munday's youth, however, had
been far more eventful, incorporating a curious period abroad when
he may have worked as a spy, time spent hunting English recusants
at home, and a long career as a hack writer and struggling playwright. Munday's pen was responsible for some of the most vicious
anti-papal polemic of the period, but he also happily translated
continental chivalric romances for an eager English audience. The
late 1580s saw Munday – now in the employ of Archbishop Whitgift
– haunting the shops of London booksellers and other likely venues
in search of those responsible for the puritan-inspired Martin
Marprelate tracts, which so scathingly satirized the hierarchy of the
Church of England. This bare summary hardly does justice to the
variety of Anthony Munday's picaresque career.[4] But it was his work
on the *Survey of London* for which the elderly Munday hoped to be
remembered by posterity. Indeed, the very words on Munday's
tombstone describe him as 'That Ancient Servant to the City, With
His Pen, In Divers Imployments, Especially The Survay of London'
and go on to celebrate 'He that hath many an ancient Tombstone

---

[3] D. M. Bergeron (ed.), *Pageants and Entertainments of Anthony Munday* (1985), p. xi.
[4] See Celeste Turner, *Anthony Munday, An Elizabethan Man of Letters* (1928); Anthony Munday,
The English Roman Life, ed. Philip J. Ayres (Oxford, 1980), pp. xiii–xix; Louis B. Wright,
Middle-Class Culture in Elizabethan England (1935), pp. 380–2.

read / I'th'labour seeming, more among the dead / To live, than
with the living, that survaid / Obtruse Antiquities, and ore them laid
/ Such beauteous colors with his Pen / (That spite of time) those old
are new agen.'[5]

Munday began work on the *Survey* not too long after Stow's death
in 1605 and Munday tells us of Stow that, while still alive, 'much of
his good mind he had formerly imparted to me, and some of his best
collections lovingly delivered me, prevailing with mee . . . to proceed
in the perfecting of a Worke so worthy'.[6] It seems that Munday's
insecurity over his own scholarly credentials also led him to stress the
extent to which he had naturally inherited the mantle of Stow. This
was of considerable importance to Munday, given that the orphaned
apprentice, who had never been near a university, had found his
other works publicly attacked by better-educated writers, who
referred slightingly to Munday's suspect knowledge of languages and
labelled him a 'common writer'. The chance to edit Stow was thus a
golden opportunity.[7]

Munday's work has never enjoyed the esteem of Stow's classic, but
for all his obvious limitations it must be stressed that Munday did
undertake his own research, and sought to set his own personal
stamp on the edition. Just as Stow's *Survey* had been the product of a
personal vision, so Munday periodically inserted himself into the
updated text. In particular, Munday conducted his own visitation of
parishes so that the 'perambulation' would be as much his as Stow's.
In the process, he collected vast numbers of inscriptions and details
of monuments in London's parish churches.[8] In updating the
perambulation of London, Munday recorded himself chatting to
ministers over the dating of a church aisle or the significance of an
ancient stained glass window.[9] Munday praised those parishes where
he found that old documents were carefully conserved or displayed
and he very obviously found it worthwhile to become friends with

---

[5] Munday, *Survey* (1633), p. 869.

[6] Munday, *Survey* (1618), 'The Epistle Dedicatory', sig. 2.

[7] Turner, *Munday*, pp. 2–4, 9–11, 126–30, 159–60. At one time Munday had intended to produce a new *Chronicle of London* that would supersede and update Stow altogether, but he clearly backed away from this more ambitious project. A. Munday, *A Briefe Chronicle of the Successe of Times* (1611), pp. 572–3.

[8] Stow's later editor, John Strype, ever ready to pass caustic judgement upon Munday, admitted that this was probably the latter's most valuable contribution to the *Survey*, see Strype, *Survey*, I, 'The Life of John Stow', p. x.

[9] Munday, *Survey* (1618), pp. 265, 298.

parish officers.[10] At St Katherine Coleman Street, Munday commented that Mr Wright 'the learned parson here, gave me his very gentle furtherance', at All Hallows on the Wall, Andrew Greneway, parson, 'used me very kindly', at St Olave, Hart Street, Munday acknowledged 'the friendly Officers there', while at St Botolph Aldgate, Mr John Bridges, 'the painful and industrious Minister', together with the sexton and the parish clerk 'most lovingly befriended me'.[11] In fact it was probably parish clerks who supplied the snapshot accounts of parish boundaries that punctuate the 1618 volume.[12]

But Stow's personal stamp on the *Survey* did not only derive from his intimacy with the city streets; it also emerged from his own attitude towards the changes of the Reformation period. Given that the religious divisions of Elizabeth's reign had kept Munday's pen busy for many years, it is not surprising to find that Munday was attuned to the religious undercurrents of the *Survey*. As Munday extended the scope of the *Survey* and added new material, he therefore introduced a more positive, forward-looking account of what was now clearly a Protestant city. But how far would it be possible for Munday to provide the necessary Protestant gloss, given the constraints of Stow's original text?

It was within the context of the perambulation of the city's parishes that Munday most often interposed new material attesting to the specifically Protestant virtues of London's citizens. The bulk of this material (in the editions of 1618 and 1633) is quite impressive.[13] By enumerating Londoners' bequests, Munday followed on from Stow's example. Munday, however, was particularly keen to identify notable Londoners whose bequests displayed their 'love to religion', as he constantly terms it. This did not simply reflect Munday's ability to draw upon a later generation of Jacobean benefactors; he also highlighted Elizabethan examples which Stow had passed over. The haberdasher, Thomas Aldersey, is praised for 'his love to religion and the poor', the clothier, Peter Blundell (d. 1599), is noted as a 'very godly and Christianly disposed' man, while the leather-

---

[10] *Ibid.*, p. 387.
[11] *Ibid.*, pp. 298, 336, 261, 237.
[12] *Ibid.*, pp. 290–1.
[13] The 1618 edition of the *Survey* was produced by Munday alone. The 1633 edition seems to have been substantially Munday's work, although several others, including Humphry Dyson and 'C.I.', saw it through the press, presumably as Munday's health failed. Dyson primarily supplied new legal material, see pp. 64–8.

seller Robert Rogers (d. 1602) is shown revealing his 'Care of Religion' by supporting divinity students at Oxford and Cambridge through bequests of £400 and another £150 devoted to poor prisoners 'such as were neither Atheists nor Papists'.[14] In another instance the grocer Thomas Ridge (d. 1599) displayed his 'love to religion' through bequests of £400 for poor preachers and £100 towards a lectureship at St Benet Gracechurch Street. This godly generosity remains unacknowledged in Stow's 1603 *Survey*, although Stow did include other memorials and examples of 'secular' good works dating from as late as 1601. By contrast, Munday not only documents Ridge's charity but also inserts his name into a select list of city worthies first compiled by Stow.[15]

It is also striking how bequests by Londoners to support sermons appear far more often and more prominently in the pages of Munday.[16] In Stow's *Survey*, by contrast, only six bequests for sermons find a place. It is also telling that all of these examples are pre-Reformation, and one of them (in St Michael Cornhill) was no longer performed, according to Stow.[17] It is not that Stow was hostile to sermons as such, indeed he carefully notes the extraordinary feat of one William Lichfield D.D.,who reputedly preached 3,083 sermons during his lifetime and was buried at All Hallows the Great in 1448, and of course Stow also discusses the sermons regularly preached at Paul's Cross.[18] The attention granted to sermons as a special form of religious and charitable activity does not, however, carry the same resonance with Stow as with the more firmly Protestant Munday, who is always eager to provide details of sermons and lectureships. In the case of the lord mayor Sir Wolstan Dixie (d. 1593), a member of the Skinners' Company, Stow merely states that he founded a free school at Bosworth in Leicestershire. Munday, however, more accurately portrays the scope of this great benefactor's charitable activities, which included supporting a lectureship at St Michael Basinghall, bequeathing monies to the poor

---

[14] Munday, *Survey* (1618), pp. 184, 182, 149–50.

[15] *Ibid.*, p. 180, cf. Stow, *Survey*, I.249 (1601 monument of Richard Plat, who founded a free school at St James Garlickhithe).

[16] Munday, *Survey* (1618), pp. 189–99, 255, 368, 744 and Munday, *Survey* (1633), 'The Remaines', *passim*.

[17] This is an approximate calculation, which tallies with the index entries in Kingsford's edition of the *Survey*: Stow, *Survey*, I.110, 167–8, 185, 198, 201; II.178. Stow does note one example of a post-Reformation lecture established through a legacy: I.243.

[18] *Ibid.*, I.167–8, 235, 331.

Protestants of the Dutch and French stranger churches, as well as further legacies to scholars at that breeding ground of puritanism, Emmanuel College, Cambridge.[19]

Munday's insertion of additional sixteenth-century monuments also underlines how his priorities differed from those of Stow. These monuments commemorated prominent Londoners whose deaths occurred sufficiently early for them to have featured in Stow's work. One cannot be sure if their omission by Stow reflected his actual distaste, but the pro-Protestant views expressed on the monuments undoubtedly prompted Munday to ensure that they were included. Verses on the tomb of the foreign painter-stainer John Shute (d. 1563) at St Edmund Lombard Street, for example, refer specifically to his hopes of election, while Munday draws attention to the early word-centred piety of Elizabeth Lucar (d. 1537) by quoting the verses on her tomb at St Lawrence Pountney: 'Reading the Scriptures, to judge the Light from Darke, / Directing her faith to Christ, the onely Marke.'[20] It may be going too far to suggest that Stow *systematically* suppressed important pro-Protestant material, although the nostalgic antiquarianism that shaped his work often had this result. Certainly Stow himself admitted that he sometimes chose not to commemorate those who had themselves defaced earlier monuments.[21]

Undoubtedly, however, the religious presuppositions of Stow and Munday help to explain not only their selection of material, but also the manner in which they framed discussions of prominent Londoners. Munday, for example, lavished several pages on William Lambe (d. 1580), a wealthy member of the Clothworkers' Company, who counted among his friends Alexander Nowell, the staunchly Protestant dean of St Paul's, and the martyrologist John Foxe. Stow mentions Lambe primarily to explain the fate of a former ecclesiastical property – the Hermitage of the chapel of St James in the Wall – which was sold to Lambe after its confiscation by the Crown. For Munday, however, Lambe is used as a springboard to discuss the

---

[19] Munday, *Survey* (1618), p. 206; Stow, *Survey*, I.114–15.

[20] Munday, *Survey* (1618), pp. 382–3, 415–16. Other Elizabeth monuments noted only by Munday include the tomb of Reginald West D.D. (d. 1563), parson of St Margaret Patterns, for 'whose sincere, pure, and godly doctrine, as also his vertuous end, the Lord be Praysed evermore': *ibid.*, p. 395.

[21] R. P. Sorlien (ed.), *The Diary of John Manningham* (Hanover, N.H., 1976), p. 154. E.g. Stow, *Survey*, I.114. Reasons of space also restricted what Stow included and he therefore periodically referred readers to 'my Summarie', for details of large legacies of more modern benefactors.

laudable activities of a great Protestant benefactor.[22] Of course, Munday was also able to include virtually a whole new generation of Protestant Londoners in his pages, and these men and women are richly documented within both his 1618 edition and the 1633 posthumous edition. In general, Munday tends to let the enumeration of acts of godly Protestant charity speak for itself, but other arresting evidence of God's Providence acting through one of His London benefactors is occasionally noted. In the case of the wealthy widow, Alice Elkin, Munday painstakingly records various godly bequests including money towards a fellowship at Emmanuel College, Cambridge, contributions to libraries in both Oxford and Cambridge, and her largesse to poor preachers. This is accompanied, however, with the providential tale of how Alice only just escaped death as a child, when an arrow pierced her hat as she played near a group of archers practising in the fields of Islington. As Munday noted approvingly, it was therefore in the town of her birth that 'she made choise to expresse her thankfulnes to God up on the Altar of her charitable Almes-houses and Schoole'.[23]

So far we have considered how Munday sometimes used the opportunity of updating Stow's parish perambulation to introduce a more Protestant gloss on the recent past. But it is an entirely new section of the *Survey* on church-building that provides the clearest evidence that Munday intended to build in a more specifically Protestant agenda to the *Survey*. 'A Returne To London', which forms a substantial final portion of the 1633 volume, sets out to document a new resurgence in London church repair, rebuilding, and beautification, and it undertakes a parish-by-parish survey of the capital's churches.[24] It is the very separateness of the 'Returne' as a section which draws attention to its message and there is no doubt that it represents the most systematically researched and presented portion of the 1633 *Survey*. This new subject was originally suggested by John King, the firmly Calvinist bishop of London. The bishop urged Munday to include details of the notable revival of church repair as

---

[22] Stow, *Survey*, I.316; Munday, *Survey* (1618), pp. 177–9. Stow tersely alludes to Lambe's 'many other charitable actes'. See also *Dictionary of National Biography* (*DNB*), s.n. 'William Lambe'. Lambe's religious views, however, may not have been straightforward; see Ian Archer, below, p. 111.

[23] Munday, *Survey* (1618), pp. 212–13.

[24] Early Stuart church-building and Munday's survey of rebuilding in the capital are discussed in greater detail in J. F. Merritt, 'Puritans, Laudians, and the phenomenon of church-building in Jacobean London', *Historical Journal* 41 (1998), 935–60.

a way of refuting Roman Catholic accusations that Protestants neglected church fabric and scorned works of charity. Munday presented Bishop King with the dedication of the 1618 edition, but had to confess that he had yet to complete the task.[25] Nevertheless, Munday clearly had been collecting material diligently and when this great survey of London churches did appear in 1633, it documented what was largely a Jacobean and pre-Laudian building programme, although it included material from as late as 1631. In his entries on each parish, Munday usually noted the state of the church in recent years, amounts spent on church-building and repair since *c.* 1603, the means by which the work was funded, names of particular benefactors, a description of handsome new items of church furniture, recently erected monuments, and other notable additions to the church such as armorial glass, tables of parish benefactors, and memorials to the Armada or to King James.[26]

The 'Returne' provided a striking counter to the tales of church desecration and neglect which filled Stow's earlier account. The elderly Stow's own experience of the Reformation era destruction meant that late Elizabethan building work in London churches was still seen by him within an overall pattern of decay. For example, the pre-Reformation rebuilding of the church of St Botolph Aldgate 'builded at the speciall charges of the Priors of the holy Trinity' contrasts starkly with Stow's sour observation that the increase in the number of parishioners in the Elizabethan period has in more recent times led to the church being 'pestered' with new lofts and seats.[27] In Munday's account, however, the building of similar new lofts and galleries elsewhere was happily presented as evidence of Protestants' commitment to their parish churches. One wonders if Stow's ambivalent attitude towards Elizabethan treatment of ecclesiastical buildings may explain why he omits the 1588 monument of Edmund Chapman 'Esquier-Joyner' to the Queen, whose memorial, Munday shows, not only suggested his place among the 'Saints elect', but also commemorated the church furniture he crafted for his own parish church of St James Garlickhithe.[28] Finally, Munday was also able to

---

[25] In addition to surveying church-building in the capital, Munday had also promised to survey the new building of parsonage houses, information that was never forthcoming.

[26] E.g. Munday, *Survey* (1633), pp. 835, 840–2, 850, 859–61, 909.

[27] Stow, *Survey*, I.127.

[28] 'Who to his neighbors (while he liu'd) the fruits of loue exprest / Fine Pewes within this church he made, & with his Armes support, / The Table, and the Seats in Quire, he set in comely sort': Munday, *Survey* (1618), p. 454.

celebrate the undoing of earlier, unsympathetic treatment meted out to a former ecclesiastical building. At St Saviour Southwark, he describes how a very beautiful chapel belonging to the enormous church (actually the retrochoir of this former priory church) had been leased out by the parish as a bakehouse in 1559. However, now Munday is able to report that in 1624 over £200 had been spent on reconverting the chapel as it was 'repaired, renewed, well and very worthily beautified'.[29] The changed context in which Munday wrote also allowed him to illustrate a more recent example of destruction, the demolition of the ancient tower of Austin Friars, which had stood for years as 'so goodly an ornament' to the City. Munday clearly felt able to include this example, where 'private benefit' led to what was virtually an act of vandalism, precisely because of his confidence that this type of destruction no longer typified English Protestantism.[30]

Munday's discussion of the practicalities of church repair also countered another dominant theme in Stow's *Survey*, the triumph of individual greed and ostentation over communal interests and commitment.[31] By contrast, Munday was often at pains to emphasize the collective nature of the enterprise although his account left plenty of room for the heroic efforts of individual donors. Over and over again, he noted that churches were repaired and refurbished at 'the sole cost and charge of the Parishioners' and he particularly singles out for praise the collective efforts at St Olave Southwark, with its large population of aliens and poor people.[32]

A Protestant agenda also underpins Munday's systematic survey of another post-Reformation phenomenon: the erection of monuments to Queen Elizabeth inside parish churches. This material only appears in the 1633 edition, where it stands side-by-side with a discussion of church repair in each parish. The form that each

---

[29] Munday, *Survey* (1633), p. 885. The 'abuse' of the chapel is vividly evoked by Munday, but, interestingly, the desecration is not mentioned by Stow, who does not include a great deal on Southwark in any case. For the complicated history of the parish churches in Southwark at the time of the Reformation see M. Carlin, *Medieval Southwark* (1996), esp. p. 95.

[30] Stow had earlier noted that the steeple of Austin Friars church had been 'ouerthrowne by tempest of wind, in the yeare 1362. but was raised of new as now it standeth to the beautifying of the Citie': Stow, *Survey*, I.177. Munday goes on to add that 'still it might have stood, had not private benefit (the only devourer of all reverend Antiquity) puld it down. Both that goodly Steeple, and all that East part of the Church, hath been taken downe, and houses (for one mans commodity) raised in the place, whereby London hath lost so goodly an ornament, and times hereafter may more talke of it': Munday, *Survey* (1618), p. 339.

[31] E.g. Stow, *Survey*, II.78.

[32] Munday, *Survey* (1633), pp. 853–4, 857, 869, 905, 884.

monument took is described, as are the verses which adorned them. These monuments, which particularly celebrate Elizabeth's defence of true religion, appear to have been constructed during the later 1610s rather than immediately after the old Queen's death. In this context, the desire for a more pro-Protestant foreign policy on the continent might easily find its counterpart in nostalgia for Elizabeth's defence of Protestantism against the forces of continental Catholicism. The monuments were at least an implicit rebuke to the failure of the government's foreign policy to live up to Elizabeth's supposed achievements. By the time of the 1633 *Survey*, the prominence accorded to such material still fed into a puritan and anti-Catholic agenda.[33]

Other miscellaneous material in the 1633 edition, much of it contained in a new appendix, suggests that a 'godly' agenda strongly influenced principles of selection. Whatever the exact character or sincerity of Munday's own religious beliefs, the 1633 *Survey* confronts the reader with descriptions of London that celebrate its godliness, or provide a puritan slant on recent events. The Artillery Yard and the Artillery Company, which promoted a martial awareness among godly Londoners, receive praise in the 1618 edition and yet further discussion in the 1633 volume.[34] This later edition also finds ample space to describe monuments commemorating God's providence (especially in England's struggle against Rome) such as a striking series of windows at St Mildred Bread Street. These windows depicted providential events such as the defeat of the Spanish Armada and the failure of the Gunpowder Plot – all with appropriate explanatory verses. Finally, the 1633 edition tapped into fears of Catholicism by re-printing a popular tract, a graphic account of the so-called 'fatal vesper' of 1623, when a building in Blackfriars collapsed during a clandestine Catholic service, resulting in heavy fatalities and a great deal of Protestant providentialist triumphalism.[35]

Certainly godly Londoners would have found much to edify them

---

[33] The monuments are listed within the entries for each parish in 'The Returne to London' in *ibid.*, pp. 819–86. On Jacobean foreign policy see T. Cogswell, *The Blessed Revolution* (Cambridge, 1989); S. Adams, 'Spain or the Netherlands? The dilemmas of early Stuart foreign policy', in H. Tomlinson (ed.), *Before the English Civil War* (1983).

[34] Munday, *Survey* (1618), p. 320; Munday, *Survey* (1633), pp. 764–5. See also William Hunt, 'Civic chivalry and the English Civil War', in A. Grafton and A. Blair (eds.), *The Transmission of Culture in Early Modern Europe* (Philadelphia, 1990).

[35] Munday, *Survey* (1633), pp. 859–61, 381–7. See also A. Walsham, '"The Fatall Vesper": providentialism and anti-popery in late Jacobean London', *Past & Present* 144 (1994), 36–87.

in Munday's additions of more recent godly epitaphs, accounts of notable events, and celebration of acts of public and private charity. Yet it would be a distortion to suggest that Munday's edition was *simply* seeking to 'Protestantize' Stow's text. The Protestantizing elements were not fully integrated into the text nor consistent in their presentation. Moreover, the Munday editions did not in any way 'censor' Stow's text, and readers would still have encountered apparently anti-Protestant stories, such as that of the iconoclastic curate of St Katherine Cree, whose sermons incited the destruction of the maypole at St Andrew Undershaft.[36] As we have seen, Munday could even afford to identify new examples of sixteenth-century desecration. This was partly because it was situated within a celebration of contemporary church repair and partly because the damage or destruction of religious buildings could be incorporated into a general sense of regret for a piece of London's lost history. The impact of Munday's 'Protestantizing elements' partly lay in the breaking up of the negative juxtapositions that typify Stow's approach, and which had allowed the earlier author to make an implicit condemnation of post-Reformation conditions. The difference in emphasis and cumulative impact is important: while Stow's words are still there, their *context* has been significantly altered. The overall result is a more positive, triumphalist reading of London's present condition and of her immediate past.

This was not a systematic *inversion* of Stow's nostalgic text, then, nor did it seek to denigrate the Catholic past. Instead, it is the continuity of the present with the past, rather than regretful nostalgia or iconoclastic modernity, which is the keynote of Munday's work. Like the pageants that Munday composed, in which the appointment of new lord mayors was celebrated by the parading of medieval mayors, Munday's *Survey* is largely a celebration of the continuity and achievements of London's governors and people.

If there is a triumphalism here, then it is a triumphalism that is based on *continuity* with the past – a glorious civic past which has reached its apotheosis in the present. For this reason, Munday happily adds a limited amount of pre-Reformation material to Stow's text. In particular, he notes with enthusiasm medieval depictions of scarlet-robed aldermen still remaining in stained-glass windows.[37] The continuity of London's leadership was further

---

[36] Stow, *Survey*, I.143–4.   [37] Munday, *Survey* (1618), pp. 265, 298, 459.

promoted by the updating – if not always accurately – of Stow's lists
of London's lord mayors, and the augmenting of this with additional
material about the parentage and place of birth of both pre- and
post-Reformation figures.[38] The 1633 edition was so far expanded as
to include what the dedication describes as 'the splendor of Armes,
and other glorious Engines of Honour' – page after page of coats of
arms attached to London's lord mayors running from the medieval
Fitz-Alwin to the present day. Still more significant was the insertion
of the arms of London livery companies in a series of pages which
included ancient companies along with a number which had only
received incorporation since Stow's second edition of 1603.[39] Recent
improvements to the City also stand side-by-side with the notable
achievements of ancient Londoners. For example, Munday lavishes
praise on the heroic efforts of a contemporary Londoner – Hugh
Middleton – in promoting the New River, describing in great detail
the elaborate ceremony held before the Lord Mayor and aldermen,
associated with its completion.[40]

Such civic triumphalism was already a feature of Munday's 1618
edition, and qualifies the simple image of a 'Protestantizing' editor.
By the 1633 edition, the inclusion of substantial new material on the
legal and political history of the City also reflected the fact that
Munday increasingly drew on the assistance of two other notable
antiquaries of the period, the gentleman scholar, Edmund Howes,
and the public notary and book collector, Humphrey Dyson.[41] The
specialist material they provided not only followed on from many of
Stow's interests (and Howes updated Stow's *Annales* in 1615 and
1631), it also emerged from a context in which legal records –
including those of the City – were being collected, edited, and
organized.[42] Many of these documents concerned disputes over the

[38] Munday, *Survey* (1633), pp. 536–98. Munday thanks his 'deare friend' M. W. Williams for
help in compiling lists of sheriffs, mayors, and aldermen: Munday, *Survey* (1618),
'Dedication', p. 4.
[39] Munday, *Survey* (1633), pp. 599–646. For examples of new companies see p. 629 (Curriers),
p. 631 (Founders), p. 637 (Fruiterers), p. 642 (Woodmongers and Brown-bakers), p. 649
(Apothecaries).
[40] Munday, *Survey* (1618), pp. 20a–b.
[41] *DNB*, s.n. 'Edmund Howes'. Howes's work for the *Annales* meant that he composed detailed
accounts of civic occasions and significant events. For the *Survey*, Howes provided, among
other things, an account of the discovery of Roman coins during the rebuilding of Aldgate
as well as a description of the last courts held by the City in relation to the river Thames:
Munday, *Survey* (1618), pp. 33, 230; *DNB Missing Persons*, s.n. 'Humphry Dyson'.
[42] See P. Cain, 'Robert Smith and the reform of the archives of the City of London,
1580–1623', *London Journal* 13 (1987–8), 3–16.

City's jurisdiction, for example, the periodic quarrels between the lord mayors of London and Lieutenants of the Tower of London.[43] To shed light on these and other topics, Dyson provided copies of Acts of Parliament relating to London as well as Acts of the Common Council.[44] Munday also cites at length various ancient legal precedents and other relevant documents supporting the City's claims in its long-running disputes with the Crown over the jurisdiction of the river Thames, much to the displeasure of Charles I.[45]

If religious and civic triumphalism characterized much of what found its way into the early Stuart editions of the *Survey*, it is pertinent to ask how easily these themes were accommodated. What is partly clear is that by his second attempt to update the *Survey*, Munday was struggling not only with the weight of the material collected but also the very structure of the Stow's original text. These problems were identified by one 'C.I.' (possibly C.J.) who wrote an introductory epistle to the now posthumous volume. 'C.I.' explained that the work had grown 'to this Bulke' over a period of years, also noting that it had been three years 'under the Presse'. But he also acknowledged that the work 'which begun Methodically, hath not beene so well prosecuted', apologizing that 'the desire of inserting all things for the delight of the Reader', had bred 'this want of Method'.[46] These comments are confirmed if one examines the bizarre appendix to the 1633 work entitled 'The Remaines'. This section proudly boasts its own title-page, with the full title reading: 'The Remaines or Remnants of Divers Worthy Things which should have had their Due Place and Honour in this Worke, if Promising Friends had Kept their Words'.[47] Many of these 'worthy things' are either events of topical interest – the recent fire on London Bridge – or curiosities, such as the illustration of the tomb of a Persian

---

[43] Munday, *Survey* (1618), pp. 238–41.

[44] E.g. *ibid.*, p. 313; Munday, *Survey* (1633), pp. 665–83, 769–70. Other similar examples include notes from Edwardian meetings of the Court of Aldermen over the status of Bethlehem Hospital, a 1567 survey of the manor of Finsbury taken from City records, depositions relating to the boundaries of the liberty of St Martin-le-Grand (including a plan produced as recently as 1625), and additional material shedding light on the precinct of the Blackfriars: see Munday, *Survey* (1618), p. 318; Munday, *Survey* (1633), pp. 911–16, 917–22, 375–88.

[45] Munday, *Survey* (1618), pp. 22–45, but especially pp. 32–45; Munday, *Survey* (1633), p. 939.

[46] *Ibid.*, 'To the Reader'.

[47] In slightly smaller type, it continues: 'But they failing, and part of them coming to my hands by other good meanes, they are here inserted, to accompagny my Perambulation foure miles about London.'

merchant, whose burial by his countrymen in ground just outside the churchyard of St Botolph Bishopsgate is described in fascinating detail.[48] In compensation, and 'to prevent Distraction in the Reader', 'C.I.' decided to include various tables and concordances. By using one of these guides, for example, 'hee who boasts his Birth in a Magnificent City (as the Ancients did in Rome or Athens) may with great facility find his Ancestors in their Honours, Almesgiving, Tombes, or other memorable and worthy Actions here recorded'.[49] C.I.'s index also tried to allow for the fact that copious parish material now appeared in two different places because of Munday's separate discussion of church-building.

The 1633 edition of Stow's *Survey*, then, remains an ungainly if fascinating work and it is one which crucially shaped both the information available to later writers on London, and the manner in which they wrote. It may seem easy to dismiss it as an amateurish effort which pales before the originality and unified conception of Stow's famous work, but the difficulties under which its author struggled and his efforts towards a solution are worth noting. First of all, the 1633 volume significantly expanded the topographical coverage of the *Survey*. It did not merely include parishes outside London's walls, but reflected the extent to which areas as far afield as Chelsea, Fulham, Islington, and Bromley might legitimately be thought of in terms of the metropolis.[50] In terms of the organization of material, London's continued expansion in the early Stuart period meant that it was increasingly difficult to continue with Stow's perambulation as well as introducing other material relevant to current affairs. We can see that Munday did indeed take faltering steps towards ordering new material thematically, but he appears to have abandoned this course except in one or two cases. There are many possible reasons for this: lack of time, ill-health, or sheer inexperience in organizing material in a more scholarly fashion. It may also be that Munday was ultimately reluctant to create something entirely new himself. He probably saw the association with Stow – updating him and occasionally 'correcting' him on a point of detail – as an important means of establishing his own scholarly

---

[48] *Ibid.*, pp. 780–2.
[49] *Ibid.*, 'To the Reader'.
[50] *Ibid.*, pp. 783–818. The 'Circuit-Walke foure miles about London', which is presented as another important and discrete section, mostly lists funeral monuments and inscriptions and appears after 'The Remaines'.

standing. Although other seventeenth-century writers might choose to write about the capital in a very different way, Munday's use of Stow's *Survey* as a kitemark of quality was to have important consequences later in the century.[51]

II

Munday's methodological struggles with his edition of Stow may have provided a salutary lesson for other seventeenth-century scholars – certainly no-one else was to publish an edition of the *Survey* for almost another century. Indeed, at the same time that Munday's *Survey* was going to press, one Edmund Bolton was proposing to the London court of aldermen a different work entirely – an enormous new history of London, to be written in Latin and English, with a full complement of maps, and with no reference to perambulations at all.[52] But if no author showed any readiness to update Munday's edition of Stow, this did not mean that Stow's text was simply neglected. Rather, a number of scholars raided the *Survey*, and cannibalized its contents for their own 'views of London'. These were what one might call adaptations of Stow rather than editions, but many are no less interesting for that: rather, the fact that they did not feel bound to reproduce Stow's text in full gave them the scope to tailor their choice of contents to suit their particular purposes.

It was during the Interregnum, for example, that the royalist James Howell produced his own view of the capital, *Londinopolis*, which was published in 1657. For all its author's ostentatious claims of methodological innovation, *Londinopolis* was in fact little more than a *Reader's Digest*-style condensed version of the *Survey*. The perambulation was retained, and a good deal of Stow's text.[53] Nevertheless, for all of the provision of information on new building developments, this was not a simple updating of Munday's work. Howell's text had an unmistakable message for post-Civil War Londoners. Despite being a considerably shorter work than any of

---

[51] For the failure of subsequent generations to distinguish between Munday's continuations of the *Survey* and Stow's own work, see pp. 74–5.

[52] D. R. Woolf, 'Genre into artifact: the decline of the English chronicle in the sixteenth century', *Sixteenth-Century Journal* 19 (1988), p. 337.

[53] James Howell, *Londinopolis; An Historicall Discourse of Perlustration of the City of London* (1657), pp. 47–'340' (irregular pagination).

the Stow editions, Howell still found room to retain and sometimes
to expand upon Stow's accounts of earlier sacrilegious depradations,
either with more emphatic adjectives or with supplementary information.[54] To these he added his own accounts of more recent
iconoclasm. Stow's lament for the destruction of churches now
chimes in with Howell's despair at the more recent demolition of
Cheapside Cross, and the neglect of St Paul's Cathedral.[55] St Paul's,
he lamented, was 'like the hulk of a great weather beaten Ship, that
had crossed the Line eight times . . . and lies rotting upon the
Carine: such is the condition of this stately Church, which is like to
be buried shortly in her own ruines, and so become a heap of
rubbish'. The neglect of St Paul's gave Howell the opportunity to
mount a more general defence of the importance of church-building,
noting how it was revered in the early church, and caustically
observing of more recent developments: 'It may justly be doubted,
whether such sordid poor narrow souls, who so malign the beauty,
the holiness, and decencies of God's House here in the Church
militant, will ever be admitted to behold the glory of the Church
Triumphant.'[56] In the same vein, Howell revisited some of the
desecrations of the Edwardian Reformation. He saw God's providential judgement in the execution of the duke of Somerset after the
latter's sacrilegious seizure of stone from churches and priories to
build Somerset House, and was not afraid to cite Roman Catholic
authors for this point.[57] Where Stow's criticism of Somerset had
been merely implied, Howell spelt out the message directly and
emphatically.

Howell also seized upon opportunities to evoke the beauty of
holiness whose loss he so regretted. His evocative account of the
beauties of Westminster Abbey may mostly have been borrowed
(unacknowledged) from Camden, but the insistence that the Abbey
seemed to 'strike a holy kind of Reverence and sweetness of melting
piety in the hearts of beholders' was Howell's own gloss.[58] Howell
also did his best to insinuate a defence of episcopacy into apparently

---

[54] E.g. St Botolph by Billingsgate (*ibid.*, p. 85; Stow, *Survey*, I.207); the destruction of the Priory
of St John of Jerusalem, Clerkenwell (Howell, *Londinopolis*, p. 346; Stow, *Survey*, II.84–5); the
building of Somerset House (Howell, *Londinopolis*, p. 349; Stow, *Survey*, II.84–5); and the
destruction of the rood in Rood Lane (Howell, *Londinopolis*, p. 86; Stow, *Survey*, I.209).

[55] Howell, *Londinopolis*, pp. 114–15, 399–402.

[56] *Ibid.*, pp. 400, 401–2.

[57] *Ibid.*, pp. 343, 349 (contrast Stow, *Survey*, II.84–5).

[58] Howell, *Londinopolis*, pp. 346, 353–7; William Camden, *Britain* (1637), pp. 428–32.

straightforward passages of description.[59] Other attacks on the political and cultural status quo are littered through the text – condemnations of religious sectaries, the overweaning power of the House of Commons, the larger numbers kept prisoners in the Tower than ever before, and the banning of stage plays.[60]

Howell reads as a sort of Anglican, even Laudian, Stow. Here is the same nostalgic antiquarianism, although now it is a nostalgia for a disappeared Protestant Church of England, its church decoration, its hierarchy, and the political stability that accompanied it. There is the same distaste for destruction and profanity, lent added weight by its thematic continuity with Stow's lament for the impact of the earlier Reformation.

The Dissenter Thomas De Laune's *The Present State of London* of 1681 gave a very different historical perspective to that offered by Howell. Like Howell, De Laune was selective in his treatment of Stow's text, but he chose instead to edit out those passages that were critical of the Reformation.[61] While much of Stow's text was cut, De Laune did, however, find plenty of room to repeat Munday's transcriptions of the verses on the Queen Elizabeth monuments, along with his notes on pre-Laudian church-building.[62] De Laune's more emphatic brand of Protestantism was also manifested in greatly expanded meditations on John Foxe's monument, and the insertion of substantial new sections that attacked Roman Catholics' alleged involvement in the Great Fire.[63] On the Great Fire, he recommended William Bedloe's violently anti-Catholic narrative. After providing lengthy extracts from that work, De Laune concluded that 'all these are enough to satisfie any that will not wink himself blind, that London was burnt by Romish Fire-balls . . . thrown by Romish hands'.[64] He therefore applauded and quoted in

---

[59] See for example the historical account of how bishops of London had often proved the City's 'best friends at a pinch' and had 'done her many signal good services' (Howell, *Londinopolis*, pp. 39–40); the inclusion of the Laudian bishops Wren and Warner (lauded as 'two great Luminaries of the Church . . . of rare excellent knowledge') in a list of famous people who had been born in London (*ibid.*, p. 405); and the importance placed on the role of the clergy within the constitution (*ibid.*, pp. 356–7, 359).

[60] *Ibid.*, pp. 30, 47, 343, 356–7, 360, 399.

[61] E.g. the discussion of the St Andrew Undershaft episode: Thomas De Laune, *The Present State of London* (1681), p. 31 (cf. Stow, *Survey*, I.143–4).

[62] De Laune also studiously avoids mentioning the seemingly crypto-popish Lady Alice Dudley when discussing the rebuilding of St Giles in the Fields: De Laune, *Present State*, p. 76.

[63] *Ibid.*, pp. 69–70, 458–66.

[64] *Ibid.*, pp. 458–61.

full the verses recently inscribed on the Fire Monument which blamed Catholics for the tragedy.[65] The whole work was framed with a very clear religio-political agenda, and with specific reference to the recent upheavals of the Popish Plot. It was dedicated to Sir Patience Ward, the Lord Mayor of London, praising his 'Prudent, Zealous and Couragious Conduct in these Perillous and Menacing Times', commenting that his speeches at the time of his election had 'engaged all True Patriots, and Abhorrers of Foreign and Domestick Vassalage (a thing attempted to be Introduced by those Execrable Mediums of Assassinating the Sacred Person of His Royal Majesty, and Everting His Government)'.[66] The acrostic verses at the front of the work offered an even more daring (if coded) expression of support for the Protestant duke of Monmouth's claim to the throne, over that of the duke of York.[67]

The posthumous second edition of De Laune's work, published in 1690, was an even more blatantly Protestant work which could now celebrate the success of the Glorious Revolution. The new editor dedicated the work to another heroic Lord Mayor who had stood up for 'the truth' (Sir Thomas Pilkington), and praised Pilkington's work in restoring the anti-Catholic inscription on the Fire Monument which had been first engraved during the mayoralty of De Laune's first dedicatee, Patience Ward.[68] The editor even found room in his account of London parish churches for a four-page appeal for the toleration of Dissenters.[69]

De Laune's text, then, presented a full-blooded Protestant city, hostile to the threats of Catholics and glorying in its recent past. This was a triumphalist reading that had been significantly blunted in Munday's work by his more limited ideological objectives and his continued inclusion of the whole of Stow's original nostalgic text.

If the religious agenda within De Laune's and Howell's works is striking, their books are also novel in other ways. Howell sought to compare systematically the qualities and amenities of London with

---

[65] *Ibid.*, pp. 463–6.

[66] *Ibid.*, sigs. A2v–A3r.

[67] 'the Royal Seat / of English Monarchs, whose Succession runs / From Royal Fathers, Lineally to Sons': *Present State*, sig. A5r (the verses also begin with a clear statement that the Great Fire was the work of 'the Papal Crew'). Note also the discussion of the murder of Sir Edmund Berry Godfrey: *ibid.*, pp. 156–7.

[68] *Angliae Metropolis: Or, The Present State of London . . . First Written by the late Ingenious Tho: Delaune Gent. and Continu'd to this present Year, by a careful hand* (1690), dedicatory epistle.

[69] *Ibid.*, pp. 204–7.

those of other capital cities, attempting some rudimentary estimates of the population.[70] These tentative moves towards quantification were followed through with considerably more vigour and methodological innovation by De Laune. De Laune used bills of mortality, amounts of beer brewed, and yield of excise to calculate the city's population, and supplied details of the rates and offices of the Penny Post, and rates and orders of coachmen, carmen and watermen.[71] Vowing to interweave 'things highly useful . . . with delightsom', De Laune abandoned Stow's structure altogether, instead providing a more thematic arrangement.[72] Instead of a perambulation, De Laune supplies a brief alphabetical description of churches, dealing with public structures and the houses of the nobility separately, and rounding the work off with an alphabetical account of carriers that is more reminiscent of almanacs.[73] The Great Fire has also left its mark: De Laune's work gives approving, detailed descriptions of the architectural style and design of new buildings, and the second edition enthuses over the new street lighting and the benefits of the newly available house insurance.[74] Rather than weaving history into the text, a miscellaneous 'Historical Account' of notable events and wonders of London's history is provided as an appendix, which unapologetically follows a 'Miscellaneous Method' rather than a chronological order, the former being 'no less profitable, more Recreative and less Tedious'.[75]

De Laune's work was prophetic of the way in which writings on London developed over the next few decades. Increasingly, the emphasis was on providing practical information in an easily consultable, tabulated form – symbolized by the invariable use of alphabetical listings of parish churches rather than a perambulation through the parishes themselves.[76] Discussion of London's history was minimal, and the chief desire was to provide effective accounts of the post-Fire City. Edward Hatton's *A New View of London* of 1708 presented itself as the first proper replacement for Stow. Hatton

---

[70] Howell, *Londinopolis*, pp. 381–407, esp. pp. 403–4.

[71] De Laune, *Present State*, pp. 6, 345–59, 436–42; *Angliae Metropolis*, pp. 345–8, 356–7, 357–62, 363–4.

[72] De Laune, *Present State*, 'To the Reader', sig. A4r–v.

[73] *Ibid.*, pp. 385–436; *Angliae Metropolis*, pp. 401–44.

[74] De Laune, *Present State*, pp. 20–1, 97–8, 158–9; *Angliae Metropolis*, pp. 20–1, 91–2, 149, 351–3, 365–6.

[75] De Laune, *Present State*, pp. 443–75; *Angliae Metropolis*, pp. 367–400.

[76] See Michael Harris, 'London guidebooks before 1800', in R. Myers and M. Harris (eds.), *Maps and Prints: Aspects of the English Booktrade* (Oxford, 1984).

abandoned the method and structure of Stow's work altogether, preferring to follow the methodology of *A Guide through Paris*, and emphasizing that Stow was now essentially irrelevant: 'what was London in Mr Stow's time is now like another City; the Churches, Houses and the very Situation and Names of some of the Streets being so much altered'.[77]

Hatton offered a 'New View' for a new city, and tried to include (as he professed) material for all types of reader, including architects, painters, and mathematicians.[78] A special section even explained the terms of art employed in the work.[79] Not only did Hatton take a pride in his new method, but he also made a point of distinguishing himself from writers such as Munday. He did not take notice, he loftily informed his readers, 'of such Inscriptions on Monuments and Grave-stones as are not worthy of Remark, as "Here lies A. B. Cordwainer, who died the [blank] Day of [blank] Anno Dom. [blank]" and the like, but all such frivolous Accounts I have passed over without notice'.[80] Despite its pretensions and two volumes, Hatton's octavo-size work in part reflected the new expanding market for pocket guidebooks to London. By the late seventeenth century, a wide audience had access to an ever-growing variety of small and convenient guides to the City as well as to picaresque writing which satirized the same guides via fictional accounts, such as Edward Ward's *London Spy*. In these works, snippets of London history from Stow's *Survey* lived on, but often to supplement what were little more than easy-to-consult street listings.[81]

III

But even as ephemeral guides plundered Stow's *Survey*, and other writers, such as Hatton, asserted the irrelevance of Stow's work for the new city of London, preparation for an enormous critical edition and updating of Stow's *Survey* was also under way. In 1720, the ecclesiastical historian John Strype finally published what was to become a landmark in the writing of London history. Strype's edition of Stow's *Survey* was monumental in every respect: two huge

[77] Edward Hatton, *A New View of London . . . Being a more Particular Description thereof than has Hitherto Been Known to be Published of any City in the World* (2 vols., 1708), I, preface.
[78] *Ibid.*   [79] *Ibid.*, II, pp. 803–13.   [80] *Ibid.*, I, preface.
[81] Harris, 'London guidebooks before 1800', *passim*; Max Byrd, *London Transformed* (New Haven, 1978), pp. 21–3, 29.

folio bound volumes, adorned with high-quality engravings of London landmarks (in contrast to the crude ones included in the works of Nathaniel Crouch), ward maps, the entire text of Stow, with Munday's additions, and a massive increase in new material from the medieval period onwards, all at a princely price of more than six guineas.[82]

Strype's work offered little compromise to popular trends in writing about London. Those who wished to revel in architectural terms were instructed to consult Hatton's work; the virtually obligatory list of carriers was included, but it was twelve years out of date; and the volumes manifestly lacked the portability, tabular style, alphabetical listings, and easily consultable format of the newly fashionable guide-books.[83] The point, of course, is that Strype's *Survey* did not aspire to the status of a pocket guidebook. Instead it belonged to a very different genre, namely that of the updated edition of a celebrated Elizabethan text. The later seventeenth and early eighteenth century had witnessed an explosion of new styles of writing about London, it is true, but the production of collected works and scholarly editions was also an important feature of the publishing of the period. Newly expanded and updated editions of other Elizabethan works of history, such as Camden's *Britannia*, had continued to be published in the later seventeenth century, and it was the editor of the 1673 edition of Camden's work, Richard Blome, who planned in 1694 to produce a new edition of Stow's *Survey* 'with large additions and improvements', although this project ultimately came to naught.[84]

After the failure of Blome's venture, the next person approached to undertake a new edition of Stow was John Strype. Although today we are most familiar with Strype as an early historian of the English Reformation, within the publishing world of his time Strype was

---

[82] Cf. Richard Burton [Nathaniel Crouch], *Historical Remarques and Observations of the Ancient and Present State of London and Westminster* (1681).

[83] Strype, *Survey*, I, preface, pp. vii–viii also refers the reader to Hatton for parish boundaries.

[84] F. J. Levy, 'The making of Camden's *Britannia*', *Bibliothèque d'Humanisme et Renaissance* 26 (1964), 70; John Speed, *The Theatre of the Empire of Great Britain* (1676); Richard Blome (ed.), *Britannia* (1673). Thomas Hearne produced an edition of Camden's *Annals* in 1717. The 1694 proposals were described in a printed broadsheet entitled *The Model of a Design to Reprint Stow's Survey of London* which proposed a whole series of improvements and additions. Strype's later work ultimately absorbed a great many alterations and updating additions which Blome had drawn up for this abortive project, which encompassed sections on trade and the election of aldermen, histories of merchant companies, and some new monuments, as well as (most importantly) a set of new maps: *The Model of a Design to Reprint Stow's Survey of London* (1694); John J. Morrison, 'Strype's Stow: the 1720 edition of *A Survey of London*', *London Journal* 2, 1 (May 1977), 40–2.

already known, not only as an ecclesiastical historian, but perhaps more importantly as an editor of texts and historical documents, including an immensely popular account of Ceylon.[85] The weight of Strype's scholarly reputation should not distract us from the point that this new edition of the *Survey* was no pedantic, old-fashioned work created by an other-worldly academic. On the contrary, it was undertaken as a commercial venture, and was initially dropped by its publishers in 1708 when Hatton's *A New View of London* appeared to pip it to the post. Work was only resumed when it became clear that Hatton's work was far from the scholarly updating of Stow's text that the 1694 projectors had originally intended. Nevertheless, the selection of John Strype as editor inevitably entailed that the new edition of the *Survey* would be a much more sophisticated and scholarly volume than the work of those who had plundered the *Survey* over the years.[86]

Strype's experience as an editor clearly led him to take a keen interest in identifying Stow's original text. Strype explained in his introduction to the work that he wished to return to the uncorrupted Stow because 'since the Author's Death: there having crept in a great number of Errors, as it happens in After-Editions'. In this context it is also important to remember that contemporaries had increasingly tended to conflate versions of the *Survey* produced by Stow and Munday. The 1694 *Model* had even assumed that Stow was himself responsible for the 1633 edition with all its imperfections, suggesting that the 'Remaines' at the end of Munday's edition were things 'which Mr Stow, for want of timely information, was forc'd to throw at the end of his Book'. Thomas Horne, one of Strype's publishers, confessed himself baffled by the whole business of the earlier editions, commenting 'I can give no Account nor ever heard who the persons were. Who are A.M. and H.D.[?]'[87] For this reason, Strype made it a priority to disentangle the publishing history of the

85 John J. Morrison, 'John Strype: historian of the English Reformation', PhD thesis, University of Syracuse (1976), pp. 48–61, 348–52.
86 Despite the fact that Strype's edition was published in 1720, we know that Strype completed most of the work for it between 1702 and 1707. After the publication of Hatton's *New View* in 1708, Strype did not return to the *Survey* for nearly a decade. It was completed during a second phase of work between 1717 and 1720: Morrison, 'Strype's Stow', pp. 44, 46–8.
87 *Model*; CUL, Add. MS 9/292. Even those possessing earlier editions of the text might not always make use of them: John Worthington confessed to Strype that while he had owned his own copy of the 1618 edition for many years, he had not looked at it much 'by reason of my having Access to the Folio-Edition [i.e. the 1633 edition] in Sion-Colledge': CUL, Add. MS 9/290.

Survey, which he did partly by introducing a system of marginal annotations. Nevertheless, Strype planned to fill out areas in the *Survey* where Stow's account was sketchy, 'furnishing it with many more Antiquities and Observations of Places, Men and Things belonging to it in former times'. In addition, Strype also decided to update the *Survey* 'that there should be a Continuation of the History of the City in Stow's Method, down to present times'.[88] Even when supplementing the text, then, Strype considered it important to retain what he saw as Stow's method, and Strype's own additions were clearly identified as such in the margins.

As we have seen, then, for all its attention to Stow's text, Strype's version of the *Survey* amounted to more than just an edition. Furthermore, Strype's own preoccupation with Stow, the man behind the text, can easily disguise the extent to which Strype's edition of the *Survey* was driven by some of the newer preoccupations of the early eighteenth century. The fascination with political arithmetic shines through in page upon page of statistics and tables charting matters such as the volume of livery company charity, amounts spent yearly on the diet of the poor, numbers received into and discharged from the capital's workhouses, and a lengthy account of fire insurance rates, complete with charts to calculate premiums. Similarly, the state of contemporary London's wealth and income and its role at the centre of overseas trade are celebrated, with discussions of trading companies and the Bank of England.[89]

But of course Strype was famous as an ecclesiastical historian of the English Reformation, and therefore the question of how he would choose to approach Stow's *Survey* – a text in which religious and urban preoccupations were often intertwined – presents us with a potentially fascinating scenario. Although there are many aspects of the 1720 edition of the *Survey* that deserve study, this particular issue has never been examined in any depth. For both Stow and Strype, writing about London's recent past necessarily confronted each man with traumatic historical events which had affected the city. For Stow this was the Reformation, while for Strype, as we shall see, the Civil War and Glorious Revolution required cautious treatment. Here it is pertinent to consider briefly Strype's own

[88] Strype, *Survey*, I, preface, p. i.
[89] E.g. *ibid.*, II.v.256–73, 404–8, 445–7. Strype also incorporated parts of a tract defending the Bank of England, written by Sir Nathaniel Tench, one of the Bank's governors who was also a neighbour of Strype's.

background, where it is clear that the religious divisions of the period cast their shadow over both his public and private life.

The son of a Dutch immigrant silk merchant, John Strype grew up in a family with strong non-conformist links. This was particularly true of the family of his mother, Hester van Strype, who is known to have sheltered non-conformist ministers in her London house during the 1665 plague. After the death of his father, the young Strype also came under the influence of his brother-in-law, John Johnson, a dedicated Presbyterian minister. It was Johnson who in 1663 arranged for Strype to transfer from Jesus College, Cambridge, to the more amenable Catherine Hall, where John Lightfoot (who had earlier supported Presbyterianism at the Westminster Assembly) was master.[90] Despite this background, however, Strype ultimately decided to position himself firmly within the ranks of the established church, a decision which alienated him from most of his close-knit family for many years. The family blamed this change in direction on his Cambridge contacts and certainly Strype was deeply influenced by Lightfoot, who had himself conformed in 1662.[91]

If we turn to Strype's public life, we also find a man very much involved in the religious politics of the day. Strype served as minister at Low Leyton, just outside London, from 1668 until his death and it was from here that he supported Henry Compton, bishop of London, even when the latter was suspended by James II in 1686. The following year, Strype's doubts over the policies of James II led him to take part in the dangerous business of clandestine publication. Using his contacts in the book world, Strype arranged for the London publication of a manuscript smuggled out of Ireland which criticized the religious policies of the Catholic monarch. Thereafter, Strype's strong support for the Glorious Revolution led to his formal institution as rural dean of Barking by the grateful Bishop Compton and he was additionally rewarded by a lectureship at the nearby parish of Hackney. In the years that followed, Strype's position as dean of Barking extended his role beyond a merely pastoral one, as he also participated in electioneering for the Essex Church-Tory party.[92]

[90] Morrison, 'John Strype', pp. 21–2, 37.
[91] Ibid., pp. 26–8, 37.
[92] Ibid., pp. 33, 67, 70–3, 284, 287–97. Strype also gave sermons which applauded the Glorious Revolution in providential terms, as 'one of the greatest Blessings and Deliverances that ever God vouchsafed this Nation' (e.g. J. Strype, David and Saul (1696), p. 15).

Although Strype did not seek to play a prominent political role, his ecclesiastical histories, produced from the 1680s onwards, also gave him a reluctant prominence in the religious politics of the time, for example when he was opposed by the high-church supporters of Dr Sacheverell.[93]

An interesting encapsulation of some of the tensions and ambiguities in Strype's public and private religious life can be observed in his treatment of the stranger communities in the *Survey*. Strype condemned the naturalization of alien merchants, and emphasized the need to reserve the revenue and trade of London to freemen of the City, deploring how honest English handicrafts had been undermined by foreign fashions. Nevertheless, he still did his best to defend the rights of the stranger communities to be exempted from the requirements of religious conformity. In part, he did this by emphasizing, not their shared membership of an international Protestant community – as puritans had traditionally done – but rather the degree to which their behaviour echoed that of the established church. At the chapel for French Protestants at St Anne Soho, he noted how 'our Liturgy, turned into French, is used, French Ministers, that are Refugees, Episcopally ordained, officiating. Several whereof are hereabouts seen walking in the Canonical Habit of the English Clergy. Abundance of French People, many whereof are voluntary Exiles for their Religion, live in these Streets and Lanes, following honest trades; and some Gentry of the same nation.'[94]

Strype's religious sentiments – fiercely anti-Jacobite and anti-Catholic, disapproving of Dissenters, and passionately committed to the established church – can also be seen to have found outlets in sections of the *Survey*. For example, while Strype followed Stow in including Fitzstephen's encomium of Thomas Becket at the end of the medieval account of London, Strype followed it with the stinging editorial addition: 'That no modern Ears may be offended with this Language, remember by whom it was writ; a Monk, the Pope's sworn Creature, and when; namely, about 500 Years ago, in the very Depth of Popery.'[95] Strype's handling of the notorious 'Fatal Vesper', when scores of Catholics died while attending a clandestine mass at Blackfriars in 1623, is also instructive. While Munday's edition of the

---

[93] Morrison, 'John Strype', pp. 306–10.
[94] Strype, *Survey*, II.v.294–305; II.vi.85.
[95] *Ibid.*, II, Appendix, p. 15.

Survey had actually reproduced the text of one of the more moderate contemporary pamphlets of the period without further remark, Strype added his own caustic comments denigrating the superstitious martyr-complex of those Catholics who escaped alive. He also reported with some glee the later drowning of other Catholic survivors, including one who, he darkly observed, was embarking on a journey to become a nun at the time.[96] Strype's treatment of the Monument to the Great Fire is also revealing. Unlike later eighteenth-century editors of the *Survey*, who felt obliged to denounce the anti-Catholic inscriptions on the Monument to the Great Fire, Strype was comfortable merely to report these additions to the Monument without comment.[97]

More positively, just as Munday was encouraged by Bishop King to document charitable giving and church repair as evidence of Protestant zeal and charity to use against Roman Catholic opponents, so Strype was urged by Bishop Compton to do precisely the same thing and for the same reasons. Indeed, one of the most notable features of Strype's *Survey* is its massive tables of charitable benefactions and it is interesting to note that the zeal for quantification that characterizes Strype's work is more often dedicated to illustrating religious and moral points than commercial ones.[98] Tables which record details of the many sermons and services available across London, for example, are glossed with the comment 'thus is this City signally blessed, in Respect of the Means and Opportunities of Grace that it enjoyeth'. In this respect Strype's tribute to the capital went even further, noting that what Dr Joseph Hall had observed one hundred years before (1618) was 'much more applicable to it now', that 'there is not a City under the Cope of Heaven so wealthy in spiritual provision . . . Others may exceed you in the Glory of outward Structures, in the Largeness of Extent, in the uniform Proportion of Streets, or Ornaments of Temples: but your Pulpits do surpass theirs, and your Preaching can lift up Cities to Heaven.'[99]

---

[96] *Ibid.*, 1.iii.186–90.

[97] See *ibid.*, 1.ii.181 for a description of the Monument, with an engraving of it on the opposite page. See 1.i.226–40 for discussion of the Great Fire more generally. In the 1754 *Survey*, 'T.S.' inserted a lengthy refutation of Roman Catholic involvement in the Fire, suggesting instead the involvement of 'Dissenters and Republicans': *Survey* (1754), 1.ii.501–2.

[98] Strype, *Survey*, I, preface, pp. ii–iii; 11.v.45–72; Munday, *Survey* (1618), 'To the honourable, and right reverend . . . John King'.

[99] Strype, *Survey*, 11.v.22.

Despite ample evidence of Strype's Protestant convictions within the pages of the *Survey*, it would be wrong to suggest that an over-riding, polemically charged Protestantism drives the work as a whole. Even in his historical writings on the English Reformation, Strype displayed a remarkably balanced and sympathetic approach when describing the churchmanship of such conflicting figures as Grindal, Aylmer, and Parker – an approach which infuriated his friends and enemies alike.[100] His capacity for an empathic response to religious conservatism is also evident, not just in his care to record medieval benefactions, but in his sympathetic account of the life of Stow which is prefixed to the *Survey*. Here, Strype did not attempt to hide Stow's religious conservatism, but sought to explain it with reference to the 'Havock and Destruction' caused 'in his Day' by those associated with the new religion. Strype also cited the by-now-famous account of the Edwardian curate at St Andrew Undershaft in order to explain Stow's anti-Protestantism. Even when he encountered Stow's remark 'that Doctrine is more pure now, than it was in the Monkish World', Strype was prepared to suggest that this might have been meant ironically.[101]

While Strype's work does not reflect a simple confessional agenda, there were nevertheless clear ideological preoccupations lying behind sections of the work. Principal among these was a profound concern with the moral life of the City, encapsulated in his enthusiasm for such contemporary organizations as the Society for the Reformation of Manners. It also seems likely that his own experiences as rural dean of Barking came into play here. Strype introduced a new section to the *Survey* that was specifically concerned with 'the late Endeavours used in the City for the restraining of Vice', which described 'in what State Religion and Good Manners stand here at present' partly by an approving overview of the various Societies.[102] Like Munday and Stow, Strype gave an account of charities and almshouses, but here was no mere catalogue of good works – it was clearly a topic which excited Strype's particular interest. He gave a meticulous account of the workhouse in Bishop-

---

[100] Morrison, 'John Strype', pp. 182, 352–60, 369–71, 381–2.

[101] Strype, *Survey*, i, 'The Life of John Stow', pp. i–xxvii. Strype explains how Stow, 'being a Lover of Antiquity, and the old Religious Buildings and Monuments, he was the more prejudiced against the Reformed Religion, because of that Havock and Destruction those that pretended to it, made of them in his Day'.

[102] *Ibid.*, ii.v.30–52.

gate Street: the training it gave to children, its good work in
removing vagrants and beggars from the streets, and its detection of
'several great Cheats, pretending to be Lame, Dumb and Blind, and
Burned'. A series of case studies, illustrating the frauds as well as the
diligent scholars encountered at the workhouse, followed. One was
Robert Cunningham, brought in during September 1705, who 'went
begging up and down the City, with a paper of Rhimes, pretending
to be Deaf and Dumb . . . and to come from London-Derry, and
that he wanted for a Pension'. The man was soon unmasked as a
fraud and briskly sent off to become a soldier. A more edifying
spectacle was provided by the eleven-year-old John Trusty, 'a poor
Boy belonging to the Workhouse', whose speech to Queen Anne
when she came to dine at the Guildhall in 1702 Strype reproduced.[103] To modern ears, Strype sounds a more enlightened note
in his account of Bethlehem Hospital. Especially praised was its
treatment of lunatics, who found 'a greater Kindness, and better
Usage here than in other Quarters', with 'nothing of Violence
suffered to be offered to any of the Patients'. In support of this view,
Strype quoted at length from Dr Ibbot's spital sermon of 1719, which
urged the importance of compassion towards those who lost their
senses 'since the strongest Brain may so suddenly, and by so many
Accidents be disordered'. The sight of such unfortunates 'should
never be made a matter of Sport, and Pastime, Recreation, and
Diversion, That this would be a barbarous, and Inhumane Abuse of
such sad spectacles'.[104]

It is true that Strype framed his discussion of hospitals and
workhouses with a protestantizing rhetoric, quoting Bishop Hall's
1618 spital sermon which had praised these institutions as evidence
of the good works performed by Protestants, and against 'that lewd
slander of Solifidianism' used by Catholics *against* Protestantism.[105]
But his close attention to the internal workings of these organizations
testifies to a more general concern with the instruments of social
control and moral reform that is very much of its time, and
conspicuously different from the world of Stow and Munday, where
the very fact of the founder's charity claimed most attention.

Needless to say, given this moralizing tone and overwhelming
concern for the maintenance of social order, Strype made little space
in his *Survey* for the discussion of sports and pastimes. As a diligent

[103] *Ibid.*, i.i.197–202.   [104] *Ibid.*, i.i.196–7.   [105] *Ibid.*, i.i.202.

editor, he reproduced Stow's account of 'the customary Sports used in the City', but rather than supplementing this with an updated account of such pursuits, Strype rather oddly chose to append a bloodcurdling account of 'some of their customary Punishments in former Times, of Shame or Pain, or both, for divers Sorts of Crimes and Misdemeanours: Such were Pillorizing, Carting, Riding, Whipping'.[106] The association of the two topics in Strype's mind seems clear. It is hardly surprising that virtually the only allusion which Strype makes to theatrical drama in the capital focuses on the City's attempts under Elizabeth to regulate potentially dissolute players and the 'lewd Matters of plays'.[107]

Another major preoccupation which stalks through Strype's pages is the disruption caused by the Civil War. In a sense, the Civil War period was for Strype what the Reformation had been for Stow – an unsettling period of upheaval which had left an ambiguous legacy. Where Stow rhapsodized over the past, however, and criticized the Reformation with varying degrees of explicitness, Strype's purpose was less nostalgic, and he was therefore all the more anxious to pass over the 1640s and 1650s with as little direct comment as possible. When he was forced to confront the upheavals directly, the result was a carefully constructed and very selective account. Nowhere is this more clear than in a new section which Strype introduced into the *Survey*, which dealt with the thorny issue of relations between the Crown and the City of London. Strype's aim was to assert the essential, historical loyalty of the City to the Crown.[108] One section of the chapter which dealt with 'Honourable Citizens' thus carried the running head 'Their Loyalty'. In a series of what were virtually set pieces, Strype first described how the plots of 'Bigotted Papists' against Queen Elizabeth were ultimately thwarted by the 'Citizens loyalty'. But thereafter, Strype moved quickly from the defeat of the Armada in 1588 to Charles I's carefully stage-managed entry into London in November 1641. Strype dwelt on this event – a false dawn of rapprochement before the Civil War – in loving and extraordinary detail. He provided a full account of the preparations, ceremonies, and the formal speeches given on the

---

[106] *Ibid.*, I.i.257–8.
[107] *Ibid.*, II.v.244–6.
[108] Brewster had recognized the problem of the 'several injurious and disloyal acts & entries . . . made in the Cities books' in the time of the Civil Wars, 'to which the City gave too great encouragement': CUL, Add. MS 8/216.

occasion, including Charles's reassuring comment that 'now I see that all these former Tumults and Disorders have only risen from the Meaner Sort of People; and that the Affections of the better and main Part of the City, have ever been Loyal and Affectionate to my Person and Government'. It does not seem too far-fetched to suggest that Strype found much to commend in such a view of the subsequent Civil War.

After this pleasing account of harmony between City and Crown, Strype then leaps forward chronologically to describe how certain loyal aldermen suffered imprisonment in the Tower rather than publish the Act of Parliament which abolished the monarchy. Another strategic leap forward takes the reader to an account of 'how forward and instrumental the City was in bringing back King Charles the IInd'. It is all the more striking that the only reference to the 'seditious' Acts of the Common Council which took place during the Interregnum appears in an account of their repeal in 1683, with the suggestion that such 'abominable' proceedings would not have occurred but for the violence offered to the government of the City. It was qualifications such as these that allowed Strype to conclude that 'the City is thus Loyal to their Princes; but yet jealous of the Invasion of their Religion and Liberty'. The latter qualification enabled Strype to explain the most recent problematic event in Crown–City relations: the flight of James II and 'the Cause the Citizens so readily received the Prince of Orange'. The question of the City's loyalty is then happily, if somewhat uneasily, concluded with the edifying expressions of devotion addressed to the Prince of Orange by the Lord Mayor, Aldermen, and Common Council.[109]

Of course, it was not just political disruption which the Civil Wars had brought. The religious turmoil of the 1640s and 1650s had also had a significant impact on the capital. Strype seems generally to have been keen to downplay this impact. Nevertheless, his condemnation

---

[109] Strype, *Survey*, I.i.293–303. For the entry of Charles I into London, see V. Pearl, *London and the Outbreak of the Puritan Revolution* (Oxford, 1961), pp. 126–9. It is notable that Strype carefully relegated the awkward matter of the seizure of the royal charters of the City by Charles II to a later section dealing specifically with city charters. Even here, however, while Strype dealt with the matter in considerable detail and his sympathies were clear, his treatment allowed him to applaud the actions of William of Orange, and he slipped in an attack on the 'hot Dissenters, and busie Men' who had been promoted in city government under James II: Strype, *Survey*, II.v.351–4.

of the treatment of St Paul's cathedral during the 1640s and 1650s is emphatic. Strype notes with approval how money was raised for the repair of St Paul's in the 1630s, but thereafter he denounces the seizure of money and materials intended for the repair of the cathedral, the conversion of the building into a horse guard for troopers and the digging of sawpits in parts of the church. He concluded sadly: 'and in this deplorable Condition did this near finished sumptuous Structure continue, until the year 1660'. While his treatment of the destruction of Cheapside Cross is muted, Strype is more outspoken in his condemnation of the pulling down of Paul's Cross, 'which had been for many Ages the most solemn Place in this Nation, for the greatest Divines, and most eminent Scholars, to Preach at'. Yet Strype's concern over sacrilege was never as strong as that expressed by Howell in his *Londinopolis*, although in the same section on St Paul's he did specifically condemn the Act for abolishing bishops, deans and chapters, by which 'the very Foundation of this famous Cathedral was utterly shaken in pieces'.[110] Generally, however, Strype sought to avoid dwelling too long on the religious upheavals of the 1640s and 1650s. In this regard, it is interesting to note that he pointedly ignored Samuel Brewster's suggestion that he include a catalogue of the clergy who were sequestered during the 1640s.[111]

Other omissions in the work appear to reflect Strype's caution when dealing with topics where religion and government intersected. It might seem surprising, for example, that the parish-based construction of the *Survey* did not prompt Strype to discuss developments in parochial government since the time of Stow's writing. In particular Strype seems to sidestep a development of which he was certainly aware – the emergence of powerful vestries in London's parishes. By Strype's time, however, the origins and legality of vestry power had become an extraordinarily vexed and controversial issue. Here indeed was a topic which could only be understood by drawing upon a body of historical evidence, most of which was held by parishes themselves. It seems likely that Strype did not have access to the relevant material, but the complete lack of reference to the topic is striking and may reflect Strype's distaste for the

---

[110] *Ibid.*, i.iii.49, 152.
[111] CUL, Add. MS 8/216. Brewster also suggested the inclusion of a catalogue of London clergy who were deprived at the Reformation, with a similar lack of success.

contemporary, partly Whig-orchestrated, attacks on the capital's vestries.[112]

Strype's ideological agenda can often seem obscured by the extraordinary weight of documentary material that he included. But his selection of material, the emphasis that he placed upon it, and the ways in which he chose to frame it, reveal a complex set of objectives and preoccupations. There were other forces at work, however, in determining the ultimate shape and impact of Strype's volumes. Some of these, as we shall see, were purely practical.

The manner in which Strype's version of the *Survey* was compiled and researched, for example, partly explains both its richness and its sometimes surprising omissions. Relevant research materials were not always easily accessible. It is true that Bishop Compton sent a diocesan letter to London clergymen asking them to provide Strype with additional material for each parish, but the response appears to have been disappointing.[113] The chance enthusiasm of certain clergy and parish officials explains why some parishes, such as St James Clerkenwell and St Botolph Aldgate, were far more fully documented than others, especially for the later seventeenth century.[114] Beyond this, Strype conducted his own personal study of churches, travelling with his assistant 'I.W.' 'from Church to Church, in London and the Suburbs, to view all Sepulchral Monuments', also

---

[112] The topic might have been included either in the discussion of the 'Spiritual' government of London or as part of the parish perambulation. The 1690s through to 1716 saw particularly fierce assaults on London's vestries: S. Webb and B. Webb, *English Local Government from the Revolution to the Municipal Corporations Act: The Parish and the County* (1906), pp. 249–56. See also P. Seaward, 'Gilbert Sheldon, the London vestries, and the defence of the Church' in T. Harris, P. Seaward, and M. Goldie (eds.), *The Politics of Religion in Restoration England* (Oxford, 1990), pp. 49–73. Another controversial religious issue in the City's history was that of tithes, but in this case we know that Strype seems to have ignored the offer of Samuel Brewster to provide a history of London tithes based on Brian Walton's manuscript history of the 1630s, supplemented with 'some Law-cases which have happened since his time': CUL, Add. MS 8/216. While Strype does briefly draw on Walton's work and provides a discussion of tithes which extends to the 1630s, his account stops dead at the end of that decade: Strype, *Survey*, II.v.27–8. Cf. C. Hill, *Economic Problems of the Church* (Oxford, 1956), p. 288.

[113] A copy of the printed diocesan letter, dated 20 December 1702, addressed to 'the reverend the clergy of the city of London, and the suburbs' is to be found in BL, Harleian MS 5946 (60). Strype, *Survey*, I, preface, pp. i–iii; CUL, Add. MS 9/248, 9/279. For the range of scholarly contacts and archivists who also provided Strype with material, see Morrison, 'Strype's Stow', pp. 43–4, 46.

[114] At St James Clerkenwell, for example, a churchwarden supplied Strype with a range of parochial information, including the 1698 revival of an annual feast for natives of the parish, Strype, *Survey*, II.iv.63–9. Clergy at St Botolph Aldgate also sent supplementary material on the parish (including information on its almshouses) directly to Strype: see CUL, Add. MS 9/287; Strype, *Survey*, I, preface, p. iii.

noting tables of donors and gifts in churches (although he does not seem to have consulted parish records such as churchwardens' accounts).[115] Bishop Compton's support did, however, mean that Strype had access to diocesan materials of a type which neither Stow nor Munday had available. Strype relied heavily on the recent 1693 visitation to update the perambulation portion of the *Survey*, while information from an earlier visitation of 1636 helped to fill in gaps about the pre-Fire character of certain parishes.[116]

Strype also grappled with constraints imposed by the City authorities. The Court of Aldermen, for example, passed several orders authorizing Strype to consult its records and make transcripts, but it specified that all his notes should be left with the Town Clerk to be reviewed and examined 'lest some things published from them might be prejudicial . . . to the City, or be judged not so convenient to be known'. That being said, there seems to be little evidence of outright censorship. Although three aldermen were allocated the task of vetting Strype's transcripts, they clearly found them too voluminous to read over. If any censorship took place here, it is far more likely to have been self-censorship on the part of Strype, especially when it came to dealing with City privileges and relations between the City and the Crown. Ultimately, the delays caused in gaining access to his transcripts appear to have loomed far larger in Strype's consciousness than any interference in their content.[117]

Finally, any discussion of content must allow for the constraints imposed by time. Strype researched and wrote the *Survey* in two phases, the first from 1702 to 1707 and a second hectic period from 1717 to 1720. In the final stages of writing, Strype was constantly adding new material, much to the consternation of his publishers. In addition, he received reminders that other portions of the *Survey* had not yet been adequately completed. As late as October 1719, it was

---

[115] *Ibid.*, I, preface, pp. ii, vi. It is also not surprising to find that Strype's own parish of Low Leyton receives more attention than its suburban location might otherwise have afforded it, as does the parish of Hackney, where he held a lectureship: *ibid.*, II, Appendix, 'The circuit walk', pp. 114–17; 122–31.

[116] *Ibid.*, I.iii.17–18. E.g. *ibid.*, I.ii.198 (St John Walbrook); I.iii.9 (St Thomas the Apostle).

[117] *Ibid.*, I, preface, pp. iv–v. While Strype did need to seek permission from livery companies to view their records, there is no obvious evidence that his transcriptions were truly 'screened' for content, *pace* Morrison, 'Strype's Stow', p. 43. There is more evidence to show the pressure exerted to *include* information. The Chamberlain of London, George Ludham, for example, pushed Strype and his publishers very heavily to include a new section celebrating London's new water supply and the healthful benefits that it conferred upon Londoners: Morrison, 'Strype's Stow', p. 48; CUL, Add. MS 9/333, 9/293.

noted that necessary information on nine livery companies was still missing, and in the published version of the *Survey*, three livery companies were left bereft of a brief history, with only their coat of arms provided.[118]

A more fundamental factor in determining the ultimate shape and impact of Strype's work, however, derived from its location in a succession of editions of the *Survey*. This worked in a number of ways. Certainly it helps to explain a few serious gaps and anomalies in historical coverage which can mislead the unsuspecting reader. For example, while plentiful information is provided on Jacobean church-building (from Munday's work), there is virtually no reference to any church-building or decoration in London during the Laudian campaign of the 1630s and surprisingly little on the later seventeenth century.[119] There had, of course, been no shortage of such building, but there had been no Munday around to record it, and Strype made no use of parochial documents to investigate these matters further. A striking example of the misleading gaps that appeared in Strype's *Survey* as a result relates to the church of St Michael le Querne: Strype notes the 1617 building work in the church (derived from Munday) but then simply reports that the church was burnt down in the Great Fire, thereby completely missing the far more important rebuilding of the church in the 1630s.[120] For Munday, the issue of church repair had held a clear ideological message and justified its separate treatment, apart from the perambulation of London's parishes. These themes did not hold the same resonance for Strype. Indeed Strype took the decision to eliminate Munday's consolidated discussion of early seventeenth-century church-building and his survey of Queen Elizabeth monuments. Instead, Strype redistributed this material within the overall entries on each individual parish. In this way an editorial decision reduced the cumulative impact and removed the message behind Munday's work, as well as creating an anomalous lack of information on how building in the period after 1633 compared with the rich information provided for the earlier period.

---

[118] CUL, Add. MS 9/322; Strype, *Survey*, II.v.247.

[119] Strype's brisk reference to each post-Fire church usually mentions a date of completion and perhaps some notable feature. A brief discussion of Queen Anne's Bounty emphasizes church-building as a means of reform among the lower orders, all in a manner quite different from Munday's celebration of the activity, *ibid.*, II.v.52–3.

[120] *Ibid.*, I.iii.191; H. Colvin, 'Inigo Jones and the church of St Michael Le Querne', *London Journal* 12 (1986).

More generally, Strype's text sometimes assumes a strange and incoherent quality precisely because of its position within the *Survey* tradition. Although Strype's *Survey* is vastly more effective than Munday in its command and disposition of information and remarkably thorough in its updating of monuments and inscriptions, in the end it still sacrifices coherence by retaining the text of Stow and Munday and the overall schema of the original *Survey*. It is true that Strype does employ a complex system of marginal annotations to indicate his sources, but this does not completely solve the problem.[121] What Strype's *Survey* manifestly fails to do is to provide an up-to-date guide to London: the description of parish boundaries still follows Munday to the letter (even referring to the houses of people long-dead), Stow's description of the course of pre-Fire streets and buildings is still retained, and the maps are over twenty years out of date.[122]

Perhaps the most striking feature of Strype's edition, however, is the cacophony of editorial voices. The authorial 'I' can be found reporting events witnessed in the 1540s, conversations in the 1620s, or visiting Westminster Hall as a boy in the 1650s in order to see the standards taken at the Battle of Worcester. By this stage, the *Survey* has a multiple personality, switching with little warning from nostalgic Elizabethan antiquary to triumphalist Jacobean pageant-writer to diligent post-Restoration recorder of events and back again. Instead of a perambulation where Stow takes the reader by the hand through the streets, it is now a huge boisterous party – Munday, Dyson, Blome, Strype, and others all coming along, interrupting each other, hailing the new and the old using the same authorial 'I', an 'I' that is sometimes nostalgic and regretful, sometimes enthusiastic and forward-looking.[123]

Strype's edition in many ways looks like a throwback to an earlier age – its curious amalgamation showing the impossibility of reconciling Stow's London with the massively expanding post-Fire metropolis. And yet, it proved remarkably popular – despite its huge bulk, it went through three further editions in the next thirty years. Clearly, there was still a public thirst for the reassuring spatial and

---

[121] These are explained in Strype, *Survey*, I, preface, p. vii.

[122] Strype refers the reader to Hatton's *New View* for contemporary parish boundaries: *ibid.*, preface, pp. vii–viii. For a brief discussion of the maps in Strype's *Survey* see Morrison, 'Strype's Stow', p. 41.

[123] Strype, *Survey*, I.ii.66 (cf. Stow, *Survey*, I.143–4); I.iii.16; II.vi.49.

temporal continuity implied by the inclusion of the Elizabethan
Stow's reminiscences among accounts of early eighteenth-century
building. Perhaps it is not too fanciful to suggest that the preservation
of medieval London in the pages of the *Survey*, where it blended
almost effortlessly (indeed confusingly) with the present, may have
provided a much-needed sense of stability and identity.[124]

It would be appropriate to end, however, with another lasting
legacy of Strype's edition of the *Survey*: its impact on the reputation
of John Stow himself. For Stow is in many ways the hero of Strype's
Survey – with the 'Life of Stow' prefacing the whole work, and a full-
page reproduction of his funeral monument. Sufficiently distanced
from the Tudor past in a way that Munday was not, Strype could
present a rounded, realistic, but above all sympathetic account of
Stow's life.[125] His denigration of Munday served all the more to
heighten Stow's scholarly reputation, in the wake of seventeenth-
century commentators such as the Oxford-based scholar, Thomas
Barlow, who had sneered that 'Stow . . . and such other Cattle are of
little Credit with me.' It was largely John Strype who re-established
Stow as the hero of the metropolis, a Londoner for all seasons, and
who ensured that Stow's *Survey* still continues to capture the imagination a good four centuries after its first publication.[126]

---

[124] The continuing focus on the historic City of London in the *Survey* also served to mask the
degree to which the enormous expansion of the suburbs had reshaped the metropolis. For
perceptions of continuity in the capital, see also the introduction to this volume.

[125] It should be noted that the 1694 *Model* had also proposed a life of Stow as a preface to the
edition, 'which will give occasion and opportunity for many useful Observations upon the
state and condition of learning at that time': *Model*.

[126] CUL, MS Dd/viii/82, p. 25.

CHAPTER 3

The arts and acts of memorialization in early modern London

Ian W. Archer

At the heart of John Stow's *Survey of London* is a ward-by-ward perambulation taking the reader into each of the city's churches and recording the key monuments. One of his primary purposes was the recording of the good works of previous generations by way of providing a 'godly example by the posterity to be embraced and imitated'. Although there is a profound tension in the work between the desire to celebrate the charities of Londoners and a sense that his own generation had done irreparable damage to the fabric of civic life in the iconoclasm of the Reformation, Stow nevertheless takes pride in the achievements of civic philanthropy, noting the contribution of Londoners to the building of churches and civic amenities and the relief of the poor, many of which he catalogued in his 'Honour of Citizens and Worthiness of men'.[1] Londoners' charities were more popularly celebrated in the citizen drama of the same period. Thomas Heywood's *If You Know Not Me You Know Nobody (Part II)*, first performed in 1606, dramatized the life of Sir Thomas Gresham and the foundation of the Royal Exchange. The decisive moment comes when the dean of St Paul's Alexander Nowell invites Gresham and Lady Mary Ramsey (herself a recently deceased benefactor to Christ's Hospital) to view a gallery in his house where portraits of notable benefactors of the city (Sir John Philpot, Sir Richard Whittington, Sir John Allen, and two women, Agnes Foster

I would like to thank Ben Coates for his assistance with some of the research behind this chapter and Professor Robert Tittler and Professor Caroline Barron for commenting on earlier drafts. It has also been given at the Early Modern British History seminar at the University of London, and at the research seminar of the University of Exeter Department of History, and I am grateful to participants for their comments.

[1] Stow, *Survey*, 1.91, 104–17; I. W. Archer, 'The nostalgia of John Stow', in D. L. Smith, R. Strier, and D. Bevington (eds.), *The Theatrical City: Culture, Theatre, and Politics in London, 1576–1649* (Cambridge, 1995), pp. 17–34.

and Avis Gibson) are displayed. Both the spectators are inspired by
the exemplars of charity they encounter:

> LADY RAMSEY: Why should I not live so, that being dead,
>   My name should not have a register with theirs?
> GRESHAM: Why should not all of us being wealthy men,
>   And by God's blessing only raised, but
>   Cast in our minds how we might them exceed
>   In godly works, helping of them that need.[2]

This common theme of commemoration as a spur to further
charity struck a chord with the London reading public and theatre-
goers. The purpose of this chapter is to place this literature in a
wider context of other commemorative media, both visually, orally,
and ritually expressed. I shall treat of the London livery company
halls and parish churches as theatres of memory in which the elite
constantly recalled the charitable acts of previous members of the
ruling group, as a spur to further charitable endeavour, and also in
the process legitimating (with varying degrees of success) a set of
unequal power relations.[3]

Several recent historians, recognizing the vehemence of the
Reformation's assault on established patterns of collective memory,
have shown how the new Protestant authorities sought to establish
new forms of identity and commemoration. David Cressy has
demonstrated how the sermons, bell-ringing, and commensality
associated with the anniversaries of royal accessions and of the
providential deliverances of 1558, 1588, and 1605 established a new
calendar of Protestant celebration, albeit one with critical potential.[4]
Robert Tittler has shown how provincial urban elites responded to
the removal of the pre-Reformation mnemonic forms by refa-
shioning the collective memory of their communities through 'the
design and use of civic regalia, the use of secular mythology, a
reinvigorated concern for the historical record, the identification of
the town with the nation through a shared view of recent events, and
the advent of civic portraiture'.[5] Both suggest that the years after the
Reformation saw the development of collective commemorations

---

2 *The Dramatic Works of Thomas Heywood* (4 vols., 1874), I, pp. 275–9.
3 M. Halbwachs, *On Collective Memory* (Chicago, 1992); P. Nora, 'Between memory and history:
  les lieux de mémoire', *Representations* 26 (1989), 7–25.
4 D. Cressy, *Bonfires and Bells: National Memory and the Protestant Calendar in Elizabethan and Stuart
  England* (1989); R. Hutton, *The Rise and Fall of Merry England* (Oxford, 1994).
5 R. Tittler, *The Reformation and the Towns in England: Politics and Political Culture in England,
  c.1540–1640* (Oxford, 1998), ch. 13.

that were both more secular, and more integrative of local community and nation than the pre-Reformation forms they displaced. But one of the purposes of this paper is to suggest that the commemoration (or memorialization)[6] of benefactors in the post-Reformation period was often expressed in forms which owed much to the supposedly displaced Catholic forms, and that the pastoral demands of encouraging charity through commemoration fostered a popular theology which was fuzzy on the question of good works. The existence of the culture of commemoration provided another of those points of contact with pre-Reformation religious practices which, as Alexandra Walsham has recently reminded us, assisted the acceptance of Protestant ideas.[7]

The urge to catalogue charity was shared by his contemporaries, and Stow's work spawned derivatives. Richard Robinson, the pamphleteer and a member of the Leathersellers' Company, was at work in the 1590s on what he called a 'most rare book' entitled 'London's Memorable Loyalties. Briefly showing the founders and benefactors to the City', but although he referred to it as 'a book worthy publishing one day' it never got into print, perhaps because Stow beat him to it. Another hack writer, William Jaggard, turned out the execrable *View of All the Lord Mayors* in 1601, a series of woodcut portraits accompanied by notes on the charities of the incumbents of the city's highest office. Richard Johnson appended to his tract *The Pleasant Walkes of Moore-Fields* (1607) a list of London charities, and Anthony Munday in 1611 included similar material in his *Brief Chronicle of the Success of the Times*, but paying particular attention to the recent charities of the Merchant Taylors from whom he sought patronage.[8] The later editions of Stow by Munday in 1618 and 1633, expanded on Stow's list of worthy citizens, both bringing the list up-to-date, and including many others whom Stow had overlooked. The 1633 edition was provided with two indexes, one of

---

[6] I use 'memorialization' because, as the chapter will make clear, contemporaries often referred to other media, like funeral sermons or pictures, as monuments or memorials.

[7] A. Walsham, 'The parochial roots of Laudianism revisited: Catholics, anti-Calvinists, and parish Anglicans in early Stuart England', *Journal of Ecclesiastical History* 49 (1998), 620–51. For London, see also D. Hickman, 'From Catholic to Protestant: the changing meaning of testamentary provisions in Elizabethan London' in N. Tyacke (ed.), *England's Long Reformation, 1500–1800* (1998), pp. 117–39.

[8] R. Leitch, 'Richard Robinson and the literature of the City of London, *c.* 1576–1603', MPhil. thesis, University of Cambridge (1997), p. 8; W. Jaggard, *A View of all the Right Honourable the Lord Mayors of London* (1601); R. Johnson, *The Pleasant Walkes of Moore-Fields* (1607); A. Munday, *A Briefe Chronicle of the Successe of the Times from the Creation* (1611).

which the 'concordance of those whose honour in their office, charity in their alms, memory in their moment, hath acquainted posterity with their names', enabled readers to locate entries relating to the civic career, charities, and the funeral monuments of individuals. Although Munday's work is clearly incomplete, and the organization ramshackle, for some parishes (usually with the cooperation of the ministers and parish clerks) he was able to provide a full list of local charities and details of the epitaphs on funerary monuments.[9] It is difficult to be sure about the circulation of these works, but one telling fact, in the light of the rarity with which parishes purchased any books of a secular import, is that copies of Stow's *Survey* were owned by at least six of the thirty parishes whose records I surveyed in preparing this chapter.[10]

As Julia Merritt's chapter in this volume shows, the later editions of Stow saw its gradual appropriation and adaptation by the Protestant mainstream. Stow showed a marked lack of enthusiasm for those who had contributed to the building of the new religion: there was very little on the proliferating parish lectureships of late Tudor London. These omissions were silently corrected by Munday who included among the honourable citizens men of undoubted godly hue who had been left out by Stow, and covered very many more funeral monuments of the Elizabethan period.[11] Indeed, one of the key objectives of the cataloguers of charity in the early seventeenth century was the demonstration of the superiority of Protestantism over the Catholic foe. The most ambitious work in this vein was Andrew Willet's appendix to his vast anti-papal tract, *Synopsis Papismi*, the 1614 edition of which provided 'a catalogue of all such good works as have been done since the times of the gospell especially in this honourable citty', with the intention of proving that

---

[9] J. Stow (ed. A. Munday, H. Dyson and others), *The Survey of London: Contayning the Originall, Increase, Moderne Estate and Government of that City Methodically set downe with a Memoriall of those Former Acts of Charity which for Publicke and Pious Uses have been Bestowed by many Worshipfull Citizens and Benefactors as also all the Ancient and Moderne Monuments Erected in the Churches, not onely of those two Famous Cities London and Westminster but (now newly added) Foure Miles Compasse* (1633), sig. A2.

[10] E. Freshfield (ed.), *Accomptes of the Churchwardens of the Paryshe of St Christofer's in London, 1575–1662* (1885), p. 51; E. Freshfield (ed.), *The Vestry Minute Books of the Parish of Saint Bartholomew Exchange in the City of London, 1567–1676* (1890), p. 98; GL, MSS 1176/1 (CWA, St Margaret New Fish Street), between accounts for 1641 and 1642; 1013/1 (CWA, St Mary Woolchurch), fo. 181v; 645/1 (CWA, St Peter Westcheap), fo. 265; 7673/1 (CWA, St Alban Wood Street), fo. 115. Cf. list of parish inventories at n. 45 below.

[11] See above, ch. 2.

'sixty years of the gospel have brought forth more good works than twice as long of popery'. Willet received the cooperation of the city authorities, as the lord mayor Sir John Swinnerton in 1613 sent out precepts to the livery companies requesting their wardens to give him the information he required. The result is the extraordinary enumeration of charities with detailed information on individual donors, and an attempt at calculations of the amounts given of which W. K. Jordan would have been envious. After capitalizing on the yield of annuities Willet estimated the contribution of Londoners to the charitable resources of the kingdom at £615,000.[12] It was clearly an influential work, and its themes passed into the main-stream of Protestant polemic, as the repetition of its argument by later writers indicates. By demonstrating the flow of metropolitan wealth into provincial England in the form of the charities estab-lished by London merchants, the celebration of the charity of Londoners also had the effect of integrating the nation, and later writers used comparisons with cities overseas to promote London's claims to greatness on the international stage.[13]

Protestant sensitivity on the question of charity reflected their vulnerability to Catholic charges about the destructive impact of the Reformation. The Reformation's attack on purgatory and interces-sory prayer had entailed a traumatic break in the practice of memorialization. As Eamon Duffy has written, 'the language of memory pervaded the cult of the dead' in the pre-Reformation church.[14] Men and women sought to be remembered in the prayers of the living through the foundation of chantries and almshouses if they were wealthy, or through their membership of fraternities if they were poorer. Another favoured means of remembrance was the gift of vessels and ornaments of eucharistic worship. London's livery companies and parishes were profoundly implicated in this cult of remembering the dead. The companies had accumulated extensive endowments for the support of chantry priests and the performance of obits in the city's parish churches; others were managed by groups

---

[12] A. Willet, *Synopsis Papismi* (1614), p. 1219; C[lothworkers'] C[ompany] R[ecords], C[ourt] M[inutes], IV, fo. 126; G[oldsmiths'] C[ompany] R[ecords], Reg. P, fo. 64v. For Willet, see A. Milton, *Catholic and Reformed: The Roman and Protestant Churches in English Protestant Thought, 1600–1640* (Cambridge, 1995), pp. 14–16.

[13] T. Fuller, *The Church History of Britain from the Birth of Jesus Christ Untill the Yeare MDCXLVIII* (1656), Book 10, pp. 64–7; T. Fuller, *The History of the Worthies of England* (1662), pp. 38–9; J. Howell, *Londinopolis. An Historicall Discourse or Perlustration of the City of London* (1657).

[14] E. Duffy, *The Stripping of the Altars: Traditional Religion in England, 1400–1580* (1992), p. 338.

of parochial feoffees. Both companies and parishes possessed rich sets of vestments and plate which had often been given them by members and parishioners. St Mary at Hill maintained seven priests to say masses for the souls of benefactors, and it possessed several sets of very rich vestments given by parishioners. The Merchant Taylors managed funds for the support of nine chantry priests, and a further fourteen obits; their inventory of 1512 shows a very rich collection of plate, much of it with imagery relating to the company's patron saint, John the Baptist. All this was swept away at the Reformation.[15] Seeing which way the wind was blowing, many London parishes had sought to avoid the confiscation of their ornaments in Edward's reign by selling them off themselves and using the funds for projects as varied as loan stocks to parishioners, the building of a conduit, the repair of the church, the building of a vestry house, the support of the poor, and so on.[16] Although they had thus retained the resources for communal purposes, the connection of these projects with the original donors was lost. A comparison of the Merchant Taylors' inventories from 1512 and 1609 shows that most of the company's plate had disappeared, and of course all of its ecclesiastical vestments. Although their very rich tapestries showing scenes from the life of St John the Baptist and a set of cushions with angels bearing the arms of Mr Skevyngton the donor appear to have survived, their connection with the name of the original donor seems to have been lost in the inventory.[17] The memory of several of the donors of the chantries persisted because the company bought back the chantry lands confiscated by the Crown in 1548 and conscientiously maintained the charitable distributions (sometimes of very small sums) attached to them, but others whose memory had been cultivated in the early part of the century had been erased from the record.[18]

[15] H. Littlehales (ed.), *The Medieval Records of a London City Church: St Mary at Hill, 1420–1559* (Early English Text Society, original series, 125, 128, 1904–5); C. J. Kitching (ed.), *London and Middlesex Chantry Certificates, 1548* (London Record Society, 16, 1980), pp. 5–6, 87–8; C. M. Clode, *Memorials of the Guild of Merchant Taylors* (1875), pp. 84–92. Cf. S. Brigden, *London and the Reformation* (Oxford, 1989), pp. 6–12, 33–5, 388–9.

[16] Duffy, *Stripping of the Altars*, chs. 11–13; M. Aston, *England's Iconoclasts: Laws Against Images* (Oxford, 1988); PRO, E117/4/2, 5, 8, 11, 12, 21, 22, 25, 47, 55–62, 67–101 (certificates of sales of church goods).

[17] Clode, *Memorials*, pp. 84–96.

[18] Brigden, *London and the Reformation*, pp. 390–1; M[erchant] T[aylors'] C[ompany] R[ecords], Wardens' Accounts, 1594–5, show payments still being made in respect of charities of Gerard Brayesbroke (2s 3d), Hugh Talbot (14d), and John Churchman (22d) established as part of chantry endowments.

The attack on superstitious imagery had caused great damage to funerary sculpture. The iconoclasts were supposed to spare secular monuments, but the enthusiasm of the reformers carried them beyond the wishes of the government. It took the direct intervention of the privy council to prevent the breaking up of John of Gaunt's tomb in St Paul's in 1552, while in September 1560 Elizabeth found it necessary to issue a proclamation to protect tombs which had been set up with purely commemorative purposes.[19] Benefactors like the grocer Henry Kebyll had their tombs ripped up and replaced by others (in his case even by members of his own company). Stow was horrified by the destruction wrought by the iconoclasts in places like the Greyfriars with an astonishing assemblage of tombs of city dignitaries, peers, and royalty: 'All these and five times so many have bin buried there whose monuments are wholly defaced.' So strongly did he feel on the matter that he omitted mention of some new monuments 'because those men have bin the defacers of the monumentes of others and soe . . . worthy to be deprived of that memory whereof they have injuriously robbed others'.[20]

But the fulfilment of the wishes of the dead remained important in the self-identity of both companies and parishes. The reformers' assault had been qualified; fears that the livery companies would be swept away in the holocaust proved groundless, and companies and parishes retained resources intended for poor relief. Moreover, the reformers, appropriating the cause of the poor in their struggle against the Antichrist, urged the duty of charity on their congregations, and giving, much of it directed through companies and parishes, surged through the Reformation years.[21] Perhaps because of the Reformation traumas, attention to the wills of the dead remained strong. Company members were regularly subjected to 'exellent exhortacions' such as that from Richard Thornhill, warden of the Grocers in 1574 reminding his auditory of the 'carefullnes of our forefathers . . . [who] did not spare to bereve ther childerne and kindesfolke of goodes and landes for the conservacion and maynte-

[19] J. G. Nichols (ed.), *Greyfriars Chronicle of London* (Camden Society, old series, 53, 1852), p. 75; P. L. Hughes and J. F. Larkin (eds.), *Tudor Royal Proclamations* (3 vols., New Haven and London, 1964–9), II, pp. 146–8; Aston, *England's Iconoclasts*, pp. 269–70, 313–15.

[20] Stow, *Survey*, I.253, 316–22; R. P. Sorlien (ed.), *The Diary of John Manningham of the Middle Temple* (Hanover, N.H., 1976), p. 154; cf. J. Weever, *Ancient Funerall Monuments* (1631), pp. 37, 47.

[21] I. W. Archer, *The Pursuit of Stability: Social Relations in Elizabethan London* (Cambridge, 1991), pp. 163–82; S. Brigden, 'Religion and social obligation in early sixteenth-century London', *Past & Present* 103 (1984), 104–5.

nance of this worshipfull companie'.[22] Around 1570 the parish of St
Mary Aldermary made amends for the desecration of Kebyll's tomb
by setting up an inscription on folding tables in the chancel recording
his great generosity to the church, and encouraging others to imitate
him.[23] In January 1565 the Merchant Taylors rejected pleas from the
court of aldermen to sell lands given by Sir John Percival in
Lombard Street which were needed for the new Exchange, arguing
that 'the memoryall, intent, and purpose of so good and liberall a
benefactor shulde shortly perishe, and from whence he was, where
he buylded and planted hymself woulde soon be oute of mynde'.
Although they were forced to give in before the recorder's argument
(formulated after consultation with Bishop Grindal and Dean
Nowell) that 'the deads will myght be as well be performed out with
other lands which they shulde have in lieu thereof', the vigour with
which they pushed this case of conscience to the brink suggests the
seriousness with which they regarded the duties imposed upon them
by their benefactors.[24] Among the points over which an incoming
churchwarden at St Bartholomew Exchange expressed anxiety in
1630 was that the church stock had been 'withhoulden detayned and
converted contrarye to ye will of ye dead', and in the years ahead the
parish sought out a suitable property for purchase in order to ensure
that the wills of the dead were performed. Within four years they
had established their charities on a sound footing, carefully enumerating their obligations in the vestry book.[25]

The decoration of livery company halls combined the expression
of loyalty to the Crown with a strong sense of craft identity and
respect for the benefactors of the past. Coats of arms of the Crown
and the company were found in windows, on screens, hung up in
frames, and painted on banners and streamers which accompanied
the company on processional occasions. But heraldry also celebrated
those who had borne high office in the company or who had proved
donors to it. In 1587, shortly after the re-roofing of their hall, the
Merchant Taylors consulted the heralds about the glazing of their
windows with the arms of benefactors, and invited the brethren of
their company to set up their arms at their own expense. The

---

[22] GL, MS 11588/1, fo. 256.
[23] Stow, *Survey* (1633 edn), p. 267.
[24] MTCR, CM, I, pp. 156–60; C. M. Clode, *The Early History of the Guild of Merchant Taylors* (2 vols., 1888), I, pp. 396–400. Cf. GCR, Reg. Q, fo. 22, Reg. W, fo. 71v.
[25] Freshfield (ed.), *Vestry Minutes of St Bartholomew Exchange*, pp. 102, 109, 118, 119.

Clothworkers' parlour, rebuilt in 1594 at a cost of nearly £1,000, had its windows glazed with the arms of twenty-two members at a cost of 8s each (another two were added in 1597–8).[26] As for pictures of benefactors, depictions in glass seem to have preceded those on boards. In 1573 the Armourers agreed that members of the livery wishing for their pictures to appear in the window should have them made by a painter and delivered to the glazier, provided that two pictures of John Richmond and Richard Laycroft 'be set in the begininge of all the pyctures becawse of there ansientnes and being also good benefactors to this howse'.[27] Few companies owned paintings before 1600, but they proliferated thereafter, sometimes being given by the subject himself, sometimes by executors, but more often being commissioned by the company. Although there was clearly some unease in civic quarters about this form of commemoration (perhaps because portraits were more convention-ally commissioned by the aristocratic elite), its potential was soon realized. Peter Simmonds, mercer, requested in his will of 1586 that his portrait hang in Haberdashers' Hall and in Winchester town hall 'although this may seem to smell of vainglory, yet being better construed it may be thought to a better purpose'. George Swayne, cooper (1607), left to his company 'my picture now remayninge at the paynters', with the condition that the picture be set up con-tinually together with a table showing all the money, linen, and books he had given to the company, 'to this only intent and consideracion that other members of the said company may bee therby incouraged to doe the like and not of any vaine glorious showe or ostentacion but to shewe my good will and affection to that societye'. In 1616 John Vernon, merchant tailor, gave his company a portrait shortly before his death 'to the end his faithful true love borne to the company might be had in remembrance'.[28] Although the current state of research does not allow us to chart the chronology of acquisitions precisely, it seems that the turning point

[26] H. L. Hopkinson, *The History of Merchant Taylors' Hall* (Cambridge, 1931), p. 27; CCR, Q[uarter] W[ardens'] A[ccounts], 1594–5, fo. 26v; 1597–8, fo. 13; GCR, Reg. P, fo. 181v, Reg. Q, fos. 65, 65v; Reg. R, fo. 23v; Reg. S, fo. 177.
[27] GL, MS 12071/2, p. 261.
[28] PRO, PROB11/71, fos. 83–5; 11/107, fo. 114v; MTCR, CM, VII, pp. 244–6. On civic portraiture, see R. Tittler, 'Civic portraiture and political culture in English provincial towns, *c.* 1560–1640', *Journal of British Studies* 37 (1998), 306–29; R. Tittler, 'The Cookes and the Brookes: uses of portraiture in town and country before the Civil War', in G. Maclean, D. Landry, and J. P. Ward (eds.), *The Country and the City Revisited: England and the Politics of Culture, 1550–1850* (Cambridge, 1999), pp. 58–73.

was the 1590s, and that company collections of portraits became substantial in the early seventeenth century. The Haberdashers commissioned portraits of ten leading benefactors in 1596. The Ironmongers who in 1604 had commissioned portraits of benefactors in glass, in 1640 contracted with the painter Edward Cockes for pictures of seven key benefactors as well as of the king and queen. In 1623 the Vintners, embarking on a comprehensive and very expensive redecoration of their hall, commissioned from Richard Greenbury paintings of 'sundry aldermen benefactors to this Company who have borne the office of lord maior', which were to replace the existing painting of the Nine Worthies, although they may have been out-shone by the painting of the 'story of the Marriage of Cana in large shapes after the life' at the end of the hall (the total bill for paintings was nearly £200).[29] No-one seems to have followed the example of the Mercers who had in 1567 commissioned a Dutchman to carve terracotta heads of leading benefactors (including Whittington and Colet) to be set up in tabernacles on the north wall of their hall, between which maidens' heads, the company emblem, were placed. The example was perhaps not a happy one, as Sir Thomas Gresham's bust had to be rejected as not being a true likeness.[30]

When company members assembled in their halls for the purposes of feasting they would have encountered other commemorative media in the form of the company's plate: indeed they might have found themselves drinking out of it. Although the plate of most companies seems to have haemorrhaged in the mid-Tudor period, probably due to the Crown's demands in the 1520s and the 1540s rather than the Reformation per se, extensive collections were soon built up once again, a common bequest being a piece of plate 'in remembrance of the love I bear them'. The plate would be engraved with coats of arms and name of donor, and its form might make some punning reference to the donor's name.[31] Plate was vulnerable

---

[29] J. Nicholl, *Some Account of the Worshipful Company of Ironmongers* (1866), pp. 432–8, 465; GL, MSS 15842/1, fo. 102; 15201/2, pp. 324, 329; 15333/3, accts. for 1622–3; CCR, CM V, fo. 128; VI, fo. 44; GCR, Reg. R, fo. 408.

[30] J. Imray, *The Mercers' Hall* (1991), p. 20.

[31] J. B. Carrington and G. R. Hughes, *The Plate of the Worshipful Company of Goldsmiths* (Oxford, 1926); F. M. Fry, *An Illustrated Catalogue of the Silver Plate of the Company of Merchant-Taylors* (1929); M. A. Greenwood, *The Ancient Plate of the Drapers' Company: With Some Account of its Origin, History, and Vicissitudes* (Oxford, 1930); R. Lane, *The Mercers' Company Plate* (1985); F. D. Keefe, *Catalogue of the Clothworkers' Company Plate* (1969); A. Wickham, *The Plate of the Worshipful Company of Barbers* (1978); I. W. Archer, *The History of the Haberdashers' Company* (Chichester, 1991), pp. 260–3, 266–7.

in times of financial pressure, but the resistance of the Vintners to sales of plate in 1643, in spite of their dire financial situation, suggests again that the obligations to the dead were taken seriously. If it was to be sold, companies were careful to take a note of the benefactors and their coats of arms so that the donors could be commemorated on plate to be purchased in better times. The Goldsmiths, who sold large quantities in 1637 as a way out of the financial embarrassment the rebuilding of their hall had caused, preserved tracings of the rubbings taken from the plate sold, and the court record notes the replacement of much of the plate in the early years of the Restoration, showing that the promises were taken seriously.[32]

Other reminders of the charity of company members were to be found in the tables of benefactors hung about the hall. The Clothworkers paid 40s in 1566–7 'for makyng payntyng and lynynge of the new table wherein is conteyned the gyftes and landes geven of benevolence to this companye', and a few years later they paid to have coats of arms painted into it.[33] Tables such as these might form the basis for the recitation by the clerk of charities in the presence of company members assembled on quarter days. This was standard practice at one of the quarter days of the Merchant Taylors' Company, and it was imitated by the Grocers from 1568, and the Ironmongers from 1608. These oral exercises, a reminder of the overlapping oral and literate cultures, could be very time consuming: 'their charitable and godly devises were openly red and remembred so farr as tyme would permitt, then preparation was made for dinner'.[34]

Most of the media we have been looking at were also a feature of parochial commemorations. The parishioners of St Michael Cornhill set up a 'table of remembrance . . . of the charitable benevolences' in 1608; the churchwardens of St Christopher-le-Stocks had 'one spetiall table conserninge the yerely anewetyes'. Elsewhere boards recorded individual benefactions like the table of Sir Henry Rowe's benefaction at St Martin Outwich.[35] The iconoclasm of the

---

[32] GL, MS 15201/4, pp. 105, 123, 125, 126, 129, 139–40; GCR, Reg. T, fos. 28v–30, 32–33v; CCR, CM VI, fo. 83; Wickham, *Plate of Barbers*, pp. 14, 16.

[33] CCR, QWA, 1566–7, fo. 7; 1573–4, fo. 7; CM IV, fo. 79v. Cf. GL, MS 15842/2, fo. 43.

[34] GL, MS11588/1, fo. 179; MTCR, CM, III, p. 135; VII, p. 68; Nicholl, *Ironmongers*, p. 468.

[35] GL, MS 4072/1 (VM, St Michael Cornhill), fo. 100v; Freshfield (ed.), *Accomptes of St Christofer's*, p. 44; Stow, *Survey* (1633 edn), pp. 835, 887. It should be stressed that these boards often related as much to the assertion of parochial claims as they did to the commemoration of benefactors. At St Christopher-le-Stocks, for example, the parish

Reformation had not completely obliterated the record of earlier donors to the church, as Stow regularly records the arms of key benefactors to pre-Reformation church building: of St Andrew Undershaft, for example, he recorded that 'Steven Gennings, marchant Taylor, sometime Mayor of London, caused at his charges to be builded the whole north side of the greate middle Ile, both of the body and the quier as appeareth by his armes over every pillar graven, and also the north Ile which hee roofed with timber and seeled, also the whole south side of the church was glased, and the pewes in the south chappell made of his costes, as appeareth in every window, and upon the said pewes.'[36] One very rare example of a picture of a donor on a board is provided by a 'picture or memorial of Kelsie who gave the three houses to the church for repairing' at St Mary Magdalen Milk Street. As Robert Kelsey was a fourteenth-century donor this too suggests a clinging on to elements of the pre-Reformation heritage.[37] Pictures in glass might have been more common, and could be incorporated into Protestant forms. Nicholas Crispe paid for a five-light window in the church of St Mildred Bread Street accompanied with explanatory verses. The window depicted the providential deliverances of 1588 and 1605, Queen Elizabeth as the restorer of religion, the plague of 1625 as a warning of the penalties of sin, and finally the donor with his wife and children.[38]

Funerary monuments played a key role within the parish church in communicating the contribution of benefactors. Monuments have been studied primarily from an art-historical point of view, and we have yet fully to understand their social function by looking at the texts and ritual practices associated with them.[39] Taking a sample of

asserted its victory in a lawsuit with William Wotton over lands in 1588–90 by setting up frames with maps of its Fleet Street properties: Freshfield (ed.), *Accomptes of St Christofer's*, pp. 18–20, 23–4.

[36] Stow, *Survey*, I.145.

[37] GL, MS 2597/1 (VM, St Mary Magdalen Milk Street), p. 2.

[38] Stow, *Survey* (1633 edn), pp. 859–60.

[39] M. Whinney, *Sculpture in England, 1530–1830* (2nd edn, 1988); A. White, 'Westminster Abbey in the early seventeenth century: a powerhouse of ideas', *Church Monuments* 4 (1989), 6–53; A. White, 'England, *c.* 1560–*c.* 1660: a hundred years of continental influence', *Church Monuments* 7 (1992), 34–74. For more fruitful historical approaches, see N. Llewellyn, 'Honour in life, death and in the memory: funeral monuments in early modern England', *Transactions of the Royal Historical Society*, sixth series, 6 (1996), 179–200; N. Llewellyn, 'Claims to status through visual codes: heraldry on post-Reformation English funeral monuments', in S. Anglo (ed.), *Chivalry in the Renaissance* (Woodbridge, 1990), pp. 145–60; and work in progress by Peter Sherlock of Corpus Christi College, Oxford.

eighty-seven post-1550 monuments recorded in Munday's 1633 edition of Stow, we find that inscriptions were increasingly written in English (72 per cent English; 22 per cent Latin; 6 per cent mixed), although the civic elite were more likely to use Latin (48 per cent of those who served as lord mayor or sheriff in the period 1601 to 1625 had Latin inscriptions). The inscriptions moved from the bare communication of genealogical information to generalized accounts of virtues, and increasingly recorded specific details of the individual's charities (among other things); we find that 47 per cent recorded little more than bare genealogical information: dates of death, age at death, details of marriages, and children. Where there was a more elaborate inscription, piety and family virtues and the public roles performed by the deceased would be celebrated, but 20 per cent of all the inscriptions make reference to the deceased's reputation for charity; while by the early seventeenth century epitaphs more regularly recorded charities in great detail.[40] This is a point of crucial significance when we recall that many funerary monuments celebrated charities which were distributed in that same church. 'Both rich and poore did like him well / and yet do praise his name / Though he behinde him left no child / Which might declare the same / His weekely almes that is bestowed / Within this parish here / Doth witnesse to the poores comfort / The good will he did beare', declared the inscription to Sir Richard Champion (d. 1568) in the chancel of St Dunstan in the East.[41] Some testators realized the ritual potential of this relationship. Thus Peter Simmonds, mercer, left money for a weekly distribution of bread in Winchester cathedral. His loaves were to be placed on a table beneath a stone memorial slab representing the benefactor in prayer, and they were to remain there throughout the service and sermon which the poor were required to attend. Simmonds may have been unusually attentive to the details of the ritual performance, but in practice many other donors were probably ritually incorporated in the distribution of their benefactions. Sir Martin Bowes required the almsmen of the Goldsmiths' Company along with the assistants to attend an annual sermon in St Mary Woolnoth, where he was buried, his tomb being accompanied by a copy of his will; the

[40] Stow, *Survey* (1633 edn), pp. 125–60, 264–71, 335–89 (sample from inscriptions recorded in wards of Farringdon Within, Tower, Aldgate, and Cordwainer Street); G. E. Cokayne, *Some Account of the Lord Mayors and Sheriffs of the City of London, 1601–1625* (1897).

[41] Stow, *Survey* (1633 edn), p. 139.

company was charged to keep his tomb repaired and to renew the
hatchments every seven years, and it is difficult to believe that the
monument played no role in the celebration of his charity.[42]

As the churches were repaired and beautified in the early
seventeenth century their potential as memorial sites was more fully
elaborated. As Julia Merritt has shown, the repair and beautification
of the city's churches pre-dated Laud's arrival at the see of London,
and commanded widespread lay support, often from across the
spectrum of religious positions.[43] Parishioners contributed large
sums in the various assessments made for the support of the church
fabric, but individuals financed portions of the work for which they
were commemorated. Thus the glazing of windows in St Stephen
Walbrook, St Lawrence Jewry, and Holy Trinity Duke Place was
paid for by wealthy parishioners whose coats of arms and names
were recorded.[44] As the churches were repaired so their ornaments
became more elaborate, and the Jacobean and Caroline inventories
testify to the growing volume of communion plate and cloths for the
communion table and pulpit, often donated by parishioners. A
survey of thirty parishes reveals that over two-thirds had communion
cups or flagons donated by parishioners in the years before 1640.
Individual parishioners developed impressive records as donors to
their churches.[45] Richard Croshawe, goldsmith and parishioner of
St Bartholomew Exchange, for instance, donated an elaborate pulpit
cloth in 1616, paid for a screen at the west end of the church and left

---

[42] PRO, PROB11/71, fos. 83–5; *Parliamentary Papers*, 1823, VIII, pp. 326–8.

[43] J. F. Merritt, 'Puritans, Laudians, and the phenomenon of church-building in Jacobean London', *Historical Journal* 41 (1998), 935–60.

[44] Stow, *Survey* (1633 edn), pp. 147–8, 840–1; GL, MSS 2593/1 (CWA, St Lawrence Jewry), fo. 258r–v; 593/2 (CWA, St Stephen Walbrook), acct for 1613–14.

[45] Parish inventories: GL, MSS 7673/1 (CWA, St Alban Wood Sreet), fo. 115; 819/1 (VM, Allhallows the Great), p. 165; 4051/1 (CWA, Allhallows Lombard Street), fo. 94; 4956/2 (CWA, Allhallows Staining), fos. 204v–5; 1432/4 (CWA, St Alphage London Wall), 1639–40 acct; 1279/3 (CWA, St Andrew Hubbard), p. 198; 2088/1 (CWA, St Andrew Wardrobe), at rear; 1303/1 (St Benet Fink), acct for 1639–40; 1568 (CWA, St Benet Gracechurch), p. 618; 878/1 (CWA, St Benet Paul's Wharf), fo. 252; 942/1 (CWA, St Botolph Billingsgate), fo. 157v; 4241/1 (CWA, St Ethelburga Bishopsgate), p. 356; 6836 (CWA, St Helen Bishopsgate), fo. 151; 590/1 (CWA, St John Zachary), fo. 173; 2593/1 (CWA, St Lawrence Jewry), fo. 258r–v; 1176/1 (CWA, St Margaret New Fish Street), between accts. for 1641 and 1642; 4570/2 (CWA, St Margaret Pattens), p. 386; 11394/1 (CWA, St Martin Outwich), fo. 42; 66 (CWA, St Mary Colechurch), fo. 85v; 5714/1 (CWA, St Mary Somerset), fo. 131; 1013/1 (CWA, St Mary Woolchurch), fo. 181v; 2895/2 (CWA, St Michael-le-Querne), fo. 130; 4825/1 (St Michael Queenhithe), fo. 51v; 4409/1 (CWA, St Olave Jewry), p. 258; 5018/1 (CWA, St Pancras Soper Lane), p. 36; 645/1 (CWA, St Peter Westcheap), fo. 265r–v; E. Freshfield (ed.), *The Account Books of St Bartholomew Exchange* (1895); Freshfield (ed.), *Accomptes of St Christofer's*, p. 86.

a charity of 2s per week to be distributed to the poor on his death in 1631.[46] His window apart, Nicholas Crispe donated £75 to church repair at St Mildred's, provided two flagons, and a new font, while his mother and brother paid for other windows.[47]

Individual donors also had their acts of charity commemorated in funeral sermons, many of them printed as 'this walking monument of him in paper to all the world' (as was said of that of Richard Fishbourne, mercer).[48] Funeral sermons were regarded with some unease by some of the early reformers, but the hostility does not seem to have been widespread even among the godly: the most popular preachers of the 1560s were Gough, Philpot, and Crowley, who were on the left wing of the church.[49] By the 1590s in a populous parish like St Botolph Aldgate between twenty and thirty funeral sermons were being preached each year (suggesting that about 500 funeral sermons were preached each year in the capital at this date).[50] The sermon provided an opportunity for contemplation on mortality, as the themes suggested by Londoners in their wills suggest: 'declaringe what a benefyte yt is to be taken and called from this worlde and vale of myserye by the merciful goodness off Allmightie God and at the last day to ryse agayne to everlasting ioye and comforte to remaine in blysse with him forever'; 'wherein the people may be taught or admonisshed of their mortalitie and further to enstructe them howe they ought to dispose themselves in this life that when the tyme come they may yelde up a good soule into thandes of the lyving god'.[51] The bulk of the sermon would consist of the exposition of some key doctrine, from which the 'testimony' or description of the personal qualities of the deceased would be

---

[46] PRO, PROB11/160, fos. 8v–9; Freshfield (ed.), *Vestry Minutes of St Bartholomew Exchange*, p. 75; Stow, *Survey* (1633 edn), pp. 827–8.

[47] PRO, PROB11/175, fos. 348v–50v; Stow, *Survey* (1633 edn), pp. 859–60.

[48] N. Shute, *Corona Charitatis: The Crowne of Charitie. A Sermon Preacht in Mercers Chapell May 10 1625 at the Solemne Funerals of his Ever-Renowned Friend of Precious Memory, the Mirrour of Charitie, Mr Richard Fishburne, Merchant, and now Consecrated as an Anniversary to his Fame* (1626). For Fishbourne, see I. Doolittle, *The Mercers' Company, 1579–1959* (1994), pp. 47–54.

[49] F. B. Tromly, ' "Accordinge to sounde religion": the Elizabethan controversy over the funeral sermon', *Journal of Medieval and Renaissance Studies* 13 (1983), 293–312; R. Houlbrooke, *Death, Religion and the Family in England, 1480–1750* (Oxford, 1998), pp. 294–330; J. G. Nichols (ed.), *The Diary of Henry Machyn, Citizen and Merchant-Taylor of London, 1550–1563* (Camden Society, old series, 42, 1848).

[50] H. G. Owen, 'The London parish clergy in the reign of Elizabeth I', PhD thesis, University of London (1957), p. 186.

[51] PRO, PROB11/52, fo. 10; 11/53, fo. 22. Cf. PRO, PROB11/68, fos. 276v, 314; 11/83, fo. 304; 11/84, fo. 16v; 11/82, fo. 241; 11/83, fo. 304; LMA, DL/C/359, fo. 185v.

detached. Preachers undoubtedly felt uneasy as they embarked upon these testimonies, all too aware that 'men of corrupt minds . . . must be made saints at their funeralls, and though all their life time they have been tracing downe to hell, yet at their death they are posted from the pulpit in a chariot into Heaven'. They justified the praise of the dead in terms of the provision of a spur to virtue among the living and as a reflection of God's glory: 'by paying a tribute of praise to god's dear servants we advance god's glory, perpetuate their remembrance, and add spurs to the pious endeavours of those who survive'.[52] The testimonies rang the changes on several standard themes: the public service, loyalty to family, and piety (especially as manifested in a good death) of the deceased, but there was usually some treatment of charity. It was often stressed that charity had been exercised during the lifetime rather than being given as conscience money at death, and that wealth had not been acquired by unjust means.[53] Some funeral sermons moved from the generalized invocation of virtue to the specific cataloguing of charitable donations, setting forth the deceased as 'a Mirrour of Charity', or drawing attention to his 'faire banke of charitie'.[54]

Commemorations of individual benefactors in sermons were supplemented by civic occasions of collective commemoration in the Easter Spital sermons. Continuing pre-Reformation practices, on the mornings of Easter Monday, Tuesday, and Wednesday the aldermen processed to the churchyard of the former hospital of St Mary Spital outside Bishopsgate to hear sermons preached by leading clerics appointed in consultation with the bishop of London. Before them were assembled also the children of Christ's Hospital in

---

[52] G. Hughes, *The Saints Losse and Lamentation. A Sermon Preached at the Funerall of the Worshipfull Captaine Henry Waller . . .* (1631), p. 48; N. Hardy, *Divinity in Mortality or the Gospels Excellency and the Preachers Frailty* (1653), p. 25.

[53] For some London examples of the genre: S. Dennison, *The Monument or Tombestone: or a Sermon Preached . . . at the Funerall of Mrs Elizabeth Iuxon . . .* (1620); S. Dennison, *Another Tombestone or a Sermon Preached . . . at the Celebration of the Funerals of Master Iohn Iuxon . . .* (1626); R. Fenton, *A Sermon Preached at the Funerall of Mr John Stokele . . .* (1616); R. Eaton, *A Sermon Preached at the Funeralls of that Worthie and Worshipfull Gentleman, Master Thomas Dutton* (1626); Shute, *Corona Charitatis*; Hughes, *Saintes Losse*; T. Gataker, *Two Funeral Sermons . . .* (1620); T. Gataker, *Christian Constancy Crowned by Christ. A Funerall Sermon . . . Preached at the Buriall of Mr William Winter . . .* (1624); T. Gataker, *Saint Stevens Last Will and Testament: A Funerall Sermon . . . Preached at the Enterrement of the Remaines of Mris Joice Featly* (1638); E. Layfield, *The Mappe of Mans Mortality and Vanity. A Sermon Preached at the Solemne Funerall of Abraham Iacob Esquire . . .* (1630).

[54] Shute, *Corona Charitatis*, p. 34; A. Nixon, *London's Dove: Or a Memoriall of the Life and Death of Master Robert Dove* (1612).

their blue coats: 'a fine sight of charity it is indeed', recorded Pepys in 1662.[55] It became standard practice for the preachers to include a rehearsal of the main acts of charity in the city and to review the state of the hospitals. Joseph Hall, for example, in a Spital sermon of 1618, after warning his auditory that 'covetousness is idolatry' asserted that 'London shall vye good works with any Citie upon earth . . . To the praise therefore of that good God . . . to the example of posteritie, to the honor of our profession, to the incouragment of the well deserving, and to the shame of our malicious adversaries, heare what this yeare hath brought forth.' He then worked through a 'briefe memoriall of all the charitable acts of the city this last year past'.[56]

Thus the charity of benefactors was communicated to parishioners and guildsmen in a variety of ways, exploiting visual as well as written and oral means of communication, and often using them in conjunction. It will also be clear that there was a very strong performative element in acts of commemoration, the very act of distributing charity serving to inscribe the benefaction in the minds of those both distributing and receiving it. The most cursory glance at the accounts of churchwardens and company wardens will demonstrate the degree to which the cycle of office-holding was punctuated by regular acts of charitable distribution. The major benefactors spread their donations widely, ensuring that their memory would be ritually recalled in a variety of locations. Take the example of Robert Dow, the merchant taylor philanthropist and benefactor of John Stow himself. From 1589 until his death at the age of eighty-two in 1612 Dow vested his company with a number of endowed charities. Not only were there a large number of beneficiaries each year from Dow's charities – thirteen merchant taylor almsmen (along with six holding reversions), sixty poor persons in the parish of St Botolph Aldgate, the children of Christ's Hospital

[55] Stow, *Survey*, I.166–8; R. C. Latham and W. Matthews (eds.), *The Diary of Samuel Pepys* (11 vols., 1970–83), III, pp. 57–8; E. H. Pearce, *Annals of Christ's Hospital* (2nd edn, 1908), pp. 217–27; J. Knowles, 'The spectacle of the realm: civic consciousness, rhetoric, and ritual in early modern London', in J. R. Mulryne and M. Shewring (eds.), *Theatre and Government Under the Early Stuarts* (Cambridge, 1993), pp. 178–9.

[56] J. Hall, *The Righteous Mammon. An Hospitall Sermon Preacht on the Solemne Assembly of the City on Monday in Easter-Weeke 1618* (1618), pp. 91, 110, 112. Cf. R. Wakeman, *The Poore-Mans Preacher. A Sermon Preached at S. Maries Spittle in London on Tuesday in Easter Weeke being April 7 1607* (1607); R. Fenton, *A Sermon Preached at St Mary Spittle on Easter Tuesday 1613* (1616); *A Psalme of Thankes-Giving, to be Sung by the Children of Christs Hospitall on Munday in the Easter Holy Dayes . . .* (1610).

for whom he provided a teacher of pricksong, the clergy who
examined the boys in Merchant Taylors' School – but many were
involved in their distribution: the wardens substitute and sixteen
men of the merchant taylors who nominated almsmen, the wardens
of the livery who managed the funds, their clerk and beadle, the
churchwardens, eight to ten of the ancient and discreet neighbours,
the minister, clerk, and sexton of St Botolph Aldgate, the churchwardens, clerk, and sexton of Saint Sepulchre's. These roles were not
token acts, and Dow provided small payments for their performance,
or allowed money for a drinking as he did for the wardens substitute
and sixteen men. Indeed Dow's provisions were detailed to the point
of obsessiveness. His almsmen were to wear gowns embroidered
with a dove (his rebus); they were expected to turn up at the feast
day of the Decollation of St John the Baptist; they were provided
with a form of prayer which they were expected to learn by rote (on
pain of fine) and in which they were invited to praise God 'for the
good estate of the said fellowship, and that it would please God to
raise up more good benefactors'. The distribution to the sixty poor
of St Botolph Aldgate was elaborately choreographed with the
recipients being called by name and placed in the choir aisles
according to the place of residence; the church doors then being
locked they were called into the choir to receive their money, and
then sent into the nave, where they would receive a homily from the
minister on the need for regular church attendance, say the Lord's
Prayer, and lastly say 'God reward all good benefactors and bless the
Company of Merchantailers'. Dow demanded that his orders were
to be read out annually at the vestry immediately following the
election of the churchwardens.[57]

Few Londoners commanded resources such as to provide charity
on this scale, but even the more modest benefactions served ritually
to inscribe the memory of the donor. One of the most popular forms
of benefaction was the distribution of twelve penny loaves to twelve
poor each Sunday: the first examples come from around 1555, but by
the end of Elizabeth's reign there were at least sixty-two separate
distributions every Sunday covering thirty parishes, and the flow of
new benefactions continued into the Stuart period. These distributions often took place at the communion table, itself an act of

---

[57] Clode, *Early History*, i, pp. 159–69; *Parliamentary Papers*, 1826–7, x, pp. 436–9; Nixon,
London's Dove.

considerable symbolic significance in the realization of the christian community, and might be accompanied by a homily 'from some godly preacher to show how the same came by the goodness of God unto christians'.[58]

One can see elements of continuity with pre-Reformation forms of giving and commemoration in several of the phenomena we have been looking at. Although now shorn of their intercessory functions, the distributions of bread remind one of charities like that established by Matthew Ernest alias Mettingham in 1506 for five poor to receive a penny each for turning up each week to pray at his grave in St Dunstan in the East. The dinner, sermon, and distributions to almsmen at Woolwich by the Goldsmiths' Company on behalf of Sir Martin Bowes was being described as his year's mind as late as 1572. Similarly, the recitation of the names of benefactors parallels the reading of the parish bede-roll.[59] Another element of continuity was the development of the commemorative sermon. In the early years of Elizabeth's reign bequests for cycles of twelve sermons at monthly intervals were quite common,[60] but by the end of the reign they had been displaced by the provision of annual sermons, often accompanying charitable distributions, and often insisting that the preacher should mention the donor by name to encourage further benefactions. In some parishes they seem to have enjoyed a certain fashionability in the early seventeenth century, perhaps once the process of popish detoxification was sufficiently advanced for them not to seem ideologically threatening. By the 1620s St Botolph Aldgate had nineteen of these commemorative sermons (as they were called) each year, celebrating twelve individuals, and several of them taking place on the anniversary of the donor's funeral. One of them was established in 1614 by order of the parish vestry on Trinity Sunday not only for the commemoration of William Newton, donor of lands to the parish, but 'at which time [also] shall be nominated all such good benefactors as have done charitable deedes to our parish'.[61] Among the Clothworkers, there were annual sermons (in some cases supplemented by dinners) associated with the charities of

---

[58] *Parliamentary Papers*, 1904, LXXI, pp. 215, 216; GL, MS 4887 (VM, St Dunstan in the East). Data derived from survey of London charities in Archer, *Pursuit of Stability*, pp. 164–6; PRO, PROB11/84, fo. 222v; GL, MS 9171/15, fo. 354.

[59] *Parliamentary Papers*, 1823, VIII, pp. 326–8; *Parliamentary Papers*, 1904, LXXI, p. 214.

[60] PRO, PROB11/52, fo. 162; 11/53, fos. 74, 84v; 11/88, fo. 218v; 11/89, fo. 89v.

[61] GL, MSS 9234/8, fos. 211, 212v, 214, 215, 218, 218v, 219v, 220, 221v, 223, 223v, 226, 227, 230, 230v, 234, 237, 241, 243; 9236, fo. 33v.

John Lute, John Heath, Lady Packington, William Lambe, and Samuel Middlemore.[62] Such sermons were not incompatible with firm Protestant piety. Charles Purrett, draper, making his will in 1634, requested that two sermons be preached each year in Boebrickhill, Bucks., 'in remembrance of me', and that twenty poor persons in St Dunstan in the East should receive 12d each at Christmas 'in remembrance of me', but he also left bibles to each of his godchildren and to each old poor cottager in Bow Brickhill, 'whereby God may be glorified and their soules comforted'.[63] Nor were they necessarily unpopular: in the 1630s as many as fifty-five of the liverymen of the Clothworkers' Company (about half) were attending the sermons established by John Lute.[64]

The commemorative sermon could be given an unquestionably godly spin when associated with the record of England's providential deliverances. The earliest (albeit abortive, as it only seems to have lasted a couple of years because of the hesitations of the donor) was established at St Bartholomew Exchange in 1608. Richard Maplisden, the churchwarden in that year, established a loan stock, the interest from which was to pay for a sermon on 5 November 'in perpetuall remembrance and thankfullness unto Almightie God for his mercyfull protections and memorable delyverances of his Church in this kingdome in Anno 1588 and many other tymes and especially from the late monsterous, unmatchable and most horrid popish practice and trayterous conspiracie of undermyninge the parliament howse . . .'. Better known are endowed sermons established at St Pancras Soper Lane by Thomas Chapman in 1616: sermons were to be preached on 10/12 August, 5 November, and 17 November commemorating the defeat of the Armada, Gunpowder treason, and the accession of Elizabeth. Chapman thus ensured that his name was inscribed in the Protestant ritual calendar, 'a monument of fame to remain longer than those Aegyptian pyramides or that pillar that Absolom reared up'.[65]

It is difficult to disentangle the complex web of motives which informed the acts of commemoration and memorialization we have

---

[62] CCR, Book of Deeds and Wills, fos. 151, 326–8, 348–50.

[63] PRO, PROB11/167, fo. 130.

[64] CCR, QWA, 1630–1, fo. 21.

[65] Cressy, *Bonfires and Bells*, pp. 125, 143; Freshfield (ed.), *Vestry Minutes of Saint Bartholomew Exchange*, pp. 62, 67; T. Gataker, *An Anniversarie Memoriall of Englands Delivery from the Spanish Invasion Delivered in a Sermon on Ps. 48. 7, 8* (1626), to the reader.

been looking at. Protestant reformers sought to remove their association with the Catholic economy of good-works salvation by repeatedly stressing that the charities of Londoners were the 'fruits of faith', manifestations of God's glory. They were keen also to disassociate acts of commemoration from 'vainglory', seeing them rather as encouragements to the living to give generously, 'exemplary to posterity and incitements to God's glory'. The ultimate memorial lay in heaven, for here the 'good works of god's saints shall be had in everlasting remembrance'. Memorialists could gain scriptural warrant from Nehemiah chapter 3, where the building of the walls of Jerusalem was recorded. In Daniel Price's 1616 Spital sermon the 'list of benefactors' to that godly work sounds almost contemporary; 'not onely their families and their tribes but their trades; the marchants and the goldsmiths are twise named, the whole trade and company are named, and one, in the 8 verse, an Apothecaries son is named'. And yet in the midst of all the ringing rhetoric of these sermons it might be difficult to disentangle the distinctively Protestant position on works:

good men . . . are as signets on his finger, starres in his hand, apples of his eye . . . they shall flourish as the bay tree, the olive, the myrrh, the palme, the Cedar of Lebanus . . . their names shall be in heaven (Luke 10:20); their members in his book (Psalm 139:19); their meate commeth from his hand (Psalm 145:15); their bones kept by him (Psalm 34:21); their haires numbred by him (Mathew 10:30); their teares reserved with him (Psalm 56:7).

It was difficult to discuss charity save in the framework of the economy of good-works salvation. Lancelot Andrewes had urged his Spital auditory in 1588 that 'you should be lords, knights, aldermen, masters, wardens, and of the livery in good works, as you be several wards and companies'.[66] When Sir John Harrington sought to persuade the coal baron Thomas Sutton to support the repair of Bath Abbey in 1608 he resorted to arguments in which the Protestant element is diluted: 'You rich men should open your barnes: geve, lend, distribute to the poore, and lay up thresore in heaven'; 'for alms in one's life is like a candle borne before one, whereas alms after death is like a candle carried behind one'; if Sutton were to support the work, 'you should have many good prayers in the church in your lifetime, when they may do you good; and when the time is

[66] D. Price, *Maries Memoriall: A Sermon Preached at St Maries Spittle on Munday in Easter Week being Aprill 1 1616* (1617), p. 60; L. Andrewes, *Works*, ed. J. Bliss and J. P. Wilson (11 vols., 1841–54), v, 17, 36–7, 39, 40.

to make friends of the mammon of iniquity as (Christ bids us), that
we may be received into everlasting tabernacles, to which God send
us'; another supporter of the work, Thomas Bellot, former steward
and now executor to Lord Burghley, he describes as 'saynt billet the
benefactor of this church'. Pastoral requirements stood in tension
with predestinarian theology.[67]

We may suspect that for many of those who sought memorialization, the desire to perpetuate their names and join the community of
honour may have played as much of a role as the pious encouragement of others. Among the preachers there was a palpable sense of
unease about the vainglory that could be fostered. 'Not a window
you have erected but must bear your names', complained Thomas
Adams at Paul's Cross in 1613. Joseph Hall criticized 'those obstrep-
erous benefactors that (like to hens which cannot lay an egge but
they must cackle straight) give no almes but with trumpets'; a few
sought to keep their gifts anonymous; others specifically instructed
the preachers of their funeral sermons not to dwell on their charities.
London merchants were denounced by social conservatives like John
Weever for building monuments on a scale more appropriate to the
nobility, for in some epitaphs 'more honour is attributed to a rich
quondam tradesman or griping usurer than is given to the greatest
potentate entombed in Westminster'. Likewise preachers were all too
aware that the social conventions of funerals could encourage
hypocrisy. As Charles Richardson, preacher at St Katherine's by the
Tower, put it: 'it is like they shall be buried with great state, and
some clawbacke or other, in a funerall sermon will not sticke to
commend them above measure, & to call the niggard liberall, & the
churle bountifull, but in the meanwhile the people will deride
them'.[68]

Posthumous reputations could be as contested as lifetime ones.
Epitaphs, commendations in funeral sermons, and so forth could be
ways of answering those who took a more negative view of the all-
too-often libelled London elite. Not to leave charities, like Ellesmere,
could encourage posthumous attacks, but acts of extraordinary

[67] N. E. McClure (ed.), *The Letters and Epigrams of Sir John Harrington Together with the Prayse of Private Life* (Philadelphia, 1930), pp. 64, 131, 135–6, 381–2.
[68] M. Maclure, *The Paul's Cross Sermons, 1534–1642* (Toronto, 1958), p. 229; Hall, *Righteous Mammon*, pp. 110–11; Hughes, *Saintes Losse and Lamentation*, p. 48; Weever, *Ancient Funerall Monuments*, pp. 10–11; D. Featley, *Clavis Mystica* (1636), p. 575; C. Richardson, *A Sermon Against Oppression and Fraudulent Dealing Preached at Paules Crosse the Eleventh of December* (1615), p. 31.

philanthropy like those of Sir Thomas Bodley or Thomas Sutton might not win universal praise. Both were criticized for their neglect of their kinsfolk, 'all this for a vainglory and shewe of goode deeds', as John Chamberlain acidly remarked of Bodley's library. When Bodley's will became public in 1613, we are told that his 'servants murmure and grumble most, with whom he hath dealt very mecanically', and that the executors struggled against the 'speaches spred of him and his hard dealing'. His autobiography did not help the cause, 'omitting nothing that might tend to his own glory or commendation, he hath not so much as made mention of his wife or that he was married, wherby you may see what a mind he caried, and what account he made of his best benefactors'.[69] Those who were posthumously praised beyond their deserts might even have their funeral monuments made objects of mockery. His fellow literateurs responded to the inflated praise of the minor poet, John Owen, on his epitaph in St Paul's Cathedral by attaching libels to it. Acts of benevolence were open to contested interpretations.[70] The gift of William Killigrew to church works at St Margaret Lothbury in 1618 was recorded with gratitude in the vestry book 'to be had in memory for his own honour and the good example of others', but it was made in the wake of a bitter row over Killigrew's plans to annex part of the churchyard for his garden, and the entry concerning his benevolence was written on a slip of paper pasted over another entry which has been obliterated.[71] Moreover, those mirrors of godly charity may not have been always quite as they were claimed to be. William Lambe became in the pages of Holinshed an exemplar of Protestant piety, but in the life appearing immediately after his death in 1580 by Abraham Fleming, the need to defend Lambe against 'privy whisperings' that he was a papist sympathizer suggests that a man who had begun his career in Henry VIII's chapel may have been as uneasy in the transition to the new regime as Stow himself.[72]

[69] N. E. McClure (ed.), *The Letters of John Chamberlain* (2 vols., Philadelphia, 1939), I, pp. 416–17, 420, 460; *The Life of Sir Thomas Bodley . . . Written by Himself* (Oxford, 1647). For Sutton, see P. Bearcroft, *An Historical Account of Thomas Sutton Esq., and of his Foundation in Charterhouse* (1737), pp. 123–5; *Chamberlain Letters*, I, 323–4, 328–9; *CSPD 1611–18*, p. 188; J. Spedding (ed.), *The Letters and the Life of Francis Bacon* (7 vols., 1861–74), IV, pp. 247–54.

[70] *Chamberlain Letters*, II, pp. 518, 532.

[71] E. Freshfield (ed.), *The Vestry Minute Book of the Parish of St Margaret Lothbury in the City of London, 1571–1677* (1887), pp. 42, 46, 50.

[72] A. Fleming, *A Memorial of the Famous Monuments and Charitable Almesdeedes of the Right Worshipfull Meister William Lambe* (1580); *An Epitaph for William Lambe* (1580); *New Dictionary of National Biography*, forthcoming.

Whatever the rhetoric of charitable endeavour within which it was clothed, it is unquestionable that the memorialization of benefactors also served to legitimate the unequal structures of power within London's companies and parishes. The rituals of charitable distributions and the reiteration of the benefits received from the wealthy in the past served to justify the concentration of power in the hands of the ruling group who now administered those resources. The pageants on lord mayor's day often included the celebration of leading benefactors, while the poor at the head of the procession carried shields with coats of arms of company benefactors.[73] But the elite's self-presentation as models of charitable virtue was not always accepted. Voices were occasionally raised to suggest otherwise. Thomas Lateware, clothworker, excoriated the assistants of his company in 1600 that they were 'pellicans and did sucke out the blood of theire dam and weed out the profitt of the companies landes which of right belongeth and was given to them of the handitrade of this Companie'. The assistants sitting in the parlour filled with armorial glass and the portraits of benefactors might subscribe to a rather different version of the company's history and purpose from those over whom they exercised rule.[74]

But however contested the charities and reputations of the London elite were, there are indications that the culture of memorialization resonated with Londoners. Some like Sir William Craven who had sought to keep his lifetime gift to Christ's Hospital secret found the pressures of publicity too compelling.[75] Andrew Willet confessed that he had enumerated the charities of some living contrary to their wishes, 'to make their secret godly acts publike to the praise of God, and good example of others'.[76] It is difficult, of course, to know what impact the rituals and writings of commemoration had, but Pepys's diary makes it clear that he paid close attention to the texts of funeral monuments and the inscriptions recording charities.[77] When satirizing citizen taste in their play *The Knight of the Burning Pestle*, Beaumont and Fletcher singled out the plays in praise of the citizenry. Rather than plays abusing the city, the grocer demands

---

[73] Archer, *Pursuit of Stability*, p. 54.

[74] CCR, CM, III, fo. 211. Cf. P. Griffiths, 'Secrecy and authority in late sixteenth- and seventeenth-century London', *Historical Journal* 40 (1997), 925–51.

[75] *New Dictionary of National Biography*, forthcoming.

[76] Willet, *Synopsis Papismi*, p. 1231; Shute, *Corona Charitatis*, p. 25.

[77] Pepys, *Diary*, I, pp. 145–6; IV, pp. 59–60; IX, pp. 227–8.

'The Legend of Whittington' or 'The Life and Death of Sir Thomas Gresham, with the building of the Royal Exchange', or 'The Story of Queen Eleanor with the rearing of London Bridge upon woolsacks'. Londoners wanted plays celebrating city heroes and their good works.[78] Memorialization could also foster sociability. In November 1649 one of the wardens of the Goldsmiths linked the failure of members to turn up on the day of thanksgiving on 5 November to a 'lack of sociable meetings of the company', which he suggested might be remedied if the company followed the practice of other companies – he had been impressed at the Clothworkers' Hall – where 'benefactors were commemorated by setting up their armes as formerly and having their names and guifts mentioned in written tables to remain to posterity'.[79] For members of the elite, the arts and acts of memorialization were clearly important elements in the generation of group identities and their self-fashioning as models of charitable virtue. But the acts of commemoration this chapter has discussed served to promote a good-works theology that was probably more in tune with the instincts of the congregations and assemblies in parish churches and company halls, and did so in forms which recalled some elements of the pre-Reformation world-view.

[78] F. Beaumont, *The Knight of the Burning Pestle*, induction. Cf. A. Gurr, *Playgoing in Shakespeare's London* (Cambridge, 1987), pp. 102–4.
[79] GCR, Reg. x, fo. 94.

Space, society, and urban experience

City, capital, and metropolis: the changing shape of seventeenth-century London

Vanessa Harding

Stow's original *Survey* and Strype's edition of it mark two date-points on the trajectory of early modern London's growth: neither the beginning nor the end, but sufficiently far apart for complex and dramatic changes to be visible in the city they describe. London's population had more than doubled; the built-up area had spread widely; the fabric and texture of the built environment had changed. If the city is a text, there is an appropriate analogy in the contrast between Stow's compact, structured account – though itself an historical palimpsest – and Strype's more prolix, discursive work, infilled, interpolated, and asymmetric, reflecting the changed shape and appearance of the cities they describe. In the historiography of early modern London as a built and lived environment, there is an important interplay between verbal description, cartographic mapping, and visual representation, as of course there is in Strype's *Survey* itself. It is this interplay that this chapter will illustrate, considering not only the physical changes to London, but also the way in which material changes affected perceptions and experiences of the capital as a space inhabited and used.

I CHANGING SHAPE

The physical changes to the spread and outline of London were obvious and dramatic. Seventeenth-century London's population more than doubled, from around 200,000 to something over 500,000; the area covered by building increased by a still greater amount.[1] London was not neatly mapped by contemporaries in 1600 and 1700: the major map exemplars for early modern London date

---

[1] V. Harding, 'The population of London, 1550–1700: a review of the published evidence', *London Journal* 15 (1990), 111–28.

from the 1550s and the 1670s and 1680s. For the mid-sixteenth century, a large-scale map-view engraved on copper plates, of which three plates are now known, appears to have been the ancestor of both a large-scale woodcut version and of the reduced version published in Braun and Hogenberg's *Civitates Orbis Terrarum* in 1572.[2] The latter (fig. 1), though compressed and simplified from the original, provides the best single-plate overview of London shortly before 1561 (the date of the destruction of St Paul's steeple). It shows 'London' still largely consisting of the walled city and a narrow ring of suburbs, drawn out towards the west by the separate vill of Westminster; to the south of the river, Southwark consisted of a nucleus of settlement around the bridge head and some ribbon development along the roads leading into Surrey and Kent. The capital was compact, definable, separate from its surrounding agrarian hinterland. While this separation of city and country may well have been exaggerated for visual and rhetorical effect, it is still the case that London was limited in extent and easily apprehended as an entity.

Several new maps of London were surveyed and published in the later seventeenth century, and more or less skilful and truthful derivatives proliferated. By 1680 (fig. 2), 'London' had stretched east and west into a continuous and shapeless metropolis. The city, Westminster, and Southwark had merged into a single built-up area: streets and houses stretched from Piccadilly almost to Limehouse, incorporating south Bloomsbury and Holborn to the west of the city and much of Stepney and riverside Wapping to the east; extensive suburbs in central and east Southwark had begun to mirror the suburban spread on the north bank. Almost all trace of the walls and differentiated settlements that had characterized the mid-sixteenth century capital had disappeared from the cartographic overview. The street-plan of the new metropolis had taken on a form of its own, incorporating but hardly determined by the few ancient suburban streets and roads visible in the 1550s.[3]

We do not know how widely available the contemporary cartographic evidence for the spread of London was, since there are few

[2] All three versions are reproduced in A. Prockter and R. Taylor (eds.), *The A to Z of Elizabethan London* (1979). The third copper plate was discovered more recently and exhibited at the Museum of London in 1998.

[3] Cf. R. Hyde, J. Fisher, and R. Cline (eds.), *The A to Z of Restoration London (the City of London, 1676)* (1992).

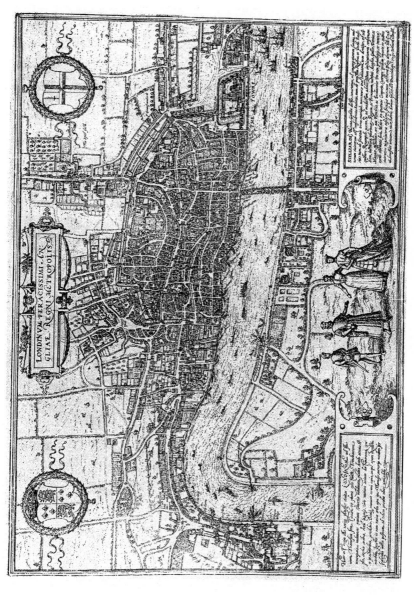

Fig. 1 London in c. 1560, from Braun and Hogenberg's *Civitates Orbis Terrarum* (1572).

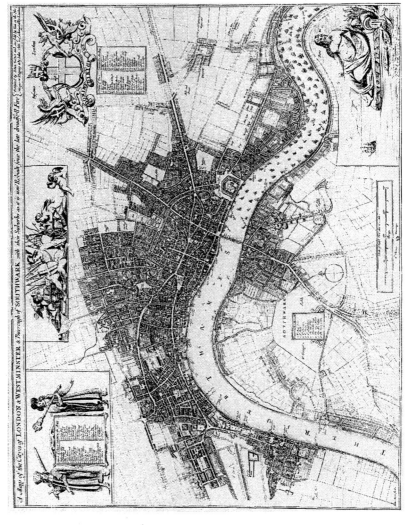

Fig. 2 London *c.* 1680: John Oliver's 'A Mapp of the Cityes of London and Westminster and Burrough of Southwark with their Suburbs as it is now Rebuilt since the late dreadfull Fire'.

surviving versions of any of the early maps. Though it has been suggested that Stow had a print of the Copperplate map when he was writing the *Survey*,[4] this is not wholly convincing; the way in which he described the city seems essentially linear and perambulatory, respecting invisible boundaries and definitions, rather than exploiting a diagrammatic representation. Although his topographical structure reflects the ideology of the map-view (city first and most prominent, satellites and suburbs a long way behind in importance), his account is essentially a tour of the city, proceeding by a series of landmarks and visual cues. 'The next is Brodestreet warde, which beginneth within Bishopsgate, from the water conduit westward on both the sides of the street . . . Next unto *Pawlet* House is the parish church . . . Then next haue ye the *Augustin* Friers church . . . Some small distance from thence.'[5] Nor can we tell how clearly any seventeenth-century Londoners might have had a panoptic, bird's-eye view, image of their city in mind. Some visual images may have gained a wider currency, such as the long views of London from the Thames, but for evidence of awareness of London's changing shape we need to turn to literary and documentary sources, and to what becomes a prominent rhetorical topos.

Stow himself begins the sequence by calling attention to the extent of change and spread that had already taken place by the 1590s. He comments on numerous occasions on the recent sprawl of the metropolis over green fields and pleasant suburbs: he noted how Hog Lane outside Bishopsgate had 'within these fortie years' been a road hedged with elm trees between pleasant fields with a wholesome air; 'nowe within a few years [it was] made a continuall building throughout, of Garden houses, and small Cottages'. Aldgate High Street, once characterized by a few scattered tenements with many gaps between them, was now 'fully replenished with buildings outward, & also pestered with diuerse Allyes', to Whitechapel and beyond.[6] Similarly, from St Katherine's to Wapping 'was neuer a house standing within these 40 yeares' but since then it had become 'a continuall streete, or filthy straight

[4] M. Holmes, 'A source-book for Stow?', in A. E. J. Hollaender and W. Kellaway (eds.), *Studies in London History presented to P. E. Jones* (1969), pp. 257–85.

[5] Stow, *Survey*, I.175–81. Cf. M. de Certeau, *The Practice of Everyday Life* (Berkeley, 1988), pp. 115–30, on the contrast between 'tours' and 'maps' as a way of describing the city.

[6] Stow, *Survey of London*, I.127.

passage . . . almost to *Radcliff*, a good mile from the Tower'.[7]
Munday's editions (1618 and 1633) add some material to Stow's
structure, when describing the spread of London. For example, in
talking of the east end, he gives an account of the usurers or
moneylenders who now inhabit Houndsditch, a description of
Wapping chapel, built in 1617, and an account, with documents, of
the neighbourhood's struggle against an alum works that had been
established there in 1627.[8] The real contrast, however, is with Strype.
Stow's text is embedded in Strype's, and the latter was certainly a
more prolix writer, especially on forms of government, and he
imported a huge amount of documentation; nevertheless the difference in treatment of certain areas of the capital is very marked, and
the work as a whole is at least six times as long. Stow had noted in a
few lines, for example, that in his lifetime the street from St
Katherine's to Wapping had been lined with buildings, but his
implication is that it was no more than that; Strype needed six pages
to describe an area now 'exceeding thick with Buildings, . . . very
populous [and] . . . much improved by human Industry'.[9] Stow
mentions building towards Ratcliff and Shadwell, while Strype
discusses the whole of Stepney and its hamlets including Mile End
New Town 'built with many good Houses'; Spitalfields, 'Now all
built into Streets'; Shoreditch, 'all along a continual building of
small and base Tenements, for the most part lately erected'.[10]

There were other forms and genres of literary comment on
London's physical extension, a number of which are usefully col-
lected in Lawrence Manley's anthology *London in the Age of Shakespeare*.
For the western spread, John Speed in 1611 wrote that

this London, as it were disdaining bondage, hath set herself on each side far
without the walls, and left her west gate (Ludgate) in the midst, from
whence with continual buildings she hath continued her street to the king's
palace, and joined a second city to herself . . . no walls are set about this
city, and those of London are left to show rather what it was than what it
is.[11]

---

[7] *Ibid.*, II.70−1.

[8] [Anthony Munday, H. Dyson, and others], *The Survey of London . . . begun first by the Paines and
Industry of Iohn Stow, in the yeere 1598 . . . And now completely finished by the study and labour of A.M.,
H.D. and others, this present yeere 1633* (1633), pp. 460−8.

[9] Strype, *Survey*, II.iv.37−43, esp. p. 39.

[10] *Ibid.*, II.iv.47, 49−50.

[11] John Speed (1611) in *The Theatre of the Empire of Great Britaine* (1676), excerpted in Lawrence
Manley (ed.), *London in the Age of Shakespeare: An Anthology* (1986), pp. 42−3.

Thomas Freeman in 1614 wrote of London's 'progress' to Islington, and that 'Saint Katherine she takes Wapping by the hand, and Hogsdon will to Highgate ere't be long'.[12] A century later, Strype's contemporary Defoe, speaking of London 'in the Modern Acceptation', pointed out that the old walls and city were an irrelevance, and that London now included 'all that vast Mass of Buildings, reaching from *Black-Wall* in the *East* to *Tot-Hill Fields* in the *West*; . . . and all the new Buildings by, and beyond, *Hannover Square*'. He estimated the circumference of the built-up area at over thirty-six miles.[13] There is also an important shift in emphasis in the account of the metropolis and its size, from a response that is fearful and resistant to change, to one that celebrates size and success. John Graunt and William Petty, in the 1660s, 1670s, and 1680s, calculated London's size and population and compared it with Paris and Amsterdam; their concern was with wealth, manpower, and the outcome of competition on the European stage and in imperial enterprises.[14] It is not unequivocal, this greater appreciation of the virtues of size and modernity, but it is an important development.

Both changes to the extent of London – the spread of buildings over formerly open land, and the accompanying intensification of population densities within the already-built-up area – began to change the shape of London in the sense of the street pattern and urban environment. The chronology and topography of change do not always match, in that sixteenth-century growth may have begun in the near suburbs, been followed by inner-city intensification, and then in the seventeenth century by outer-suburban sprawl. New building and rebuilding were sometimes concurrent, sometimes alternating, and different parts of London had their own particular developmental histories, affected by such factors as landlord enterprise, leasehold terms, and the presence or absence of a controlling local or national authority.

[12] Thomas Freeman, *Rubbe and a Great Cast* (1614), excerpted in Manley, *London in the Age of Shakespeare*, p. 250.

[13] Daniel Defoe, *A Tour thro' the Whole Island of Great Britain* (1724–6; ed. G. D. H. Cole, 2 vols., 1927), I, pp. 316, 318–23.

[14] John Graunt, 'Natural and political observations upon the Bills of Mortality' (1676); Sir William Petty, 'Two essays in political arithmetick concerning the people, housing, hospitals, etc. of London and Paris' (1687); Sir William Petty, 'Five essays in political arithmetick' (1686/7): all reprinted in C. H. Hull (ed.), *The Economic Writings of Sir William Petty, Together with Observations on the Bills of Mortality* (New York, 1963–4), II, pp. 314–435, 501–13, 519–44.

Although the most dramatic and visible aspect of London's early modern growth must have been the spread of building over green fields, the effect on the city centre was probably no less important. The population within the walls rose from perhaps 40,000 in 1550 to *c.* 70,000 in 1631, and could have reached 90,000–100,000 by 1664, so that densities rose from around 100 persons to the acre to an average of nearly 200. The highest densities, on the eve of the Fire of 1666, may have reached 230 persons to the acre in the centre of the city, to the south of Cheapside, and along the waterfront to the west of the Bridge.[15] There was a bit of slack to take up in the mid-sixteenth century, a certain amount of space to play with, as a result of late medieval contraction and population loss, but by the early seventeenth century Cheapside was so densely built up with merchants' houses, shops, and warehouses that there were very few gardens and not every house had even a yard; some used the leads or flat roofs of adjacent properties or warehouses as their only outdoor space. The high property values of the city centre meant, however, that the quality of accommodation was fairly high: the demand was for substantial houses at high rents, not multiple dwellings at lower cost. The inhabitants of Cheapside were paying very much higher rents than were the inhabitants of the city fringes, but they were enjoying a more spacious way of life. Building upwards – houses rose to four, five, and six stories – gave them more rooms per family and fewer families shared houses.[16]

Further from the city centre, the cost of land was somewhat lower, and the potential rent value also low. High densities were achieved here not by building upwards but by crowding more people into fewer rooms, and by converting gardens and garden buildings such as sheds and stables to living accommodation. A property in Harrow Alley outside Aldgate was described in 1637 as 'a great coachhouse divided and inmated'; 'Thomas Sarter a pewterer at Algate built 6 double houses upon a garden platt last summer and in four of these

15 Harding, 'The population of London'. The intramural population was around 80,000 in the 1690s, and all the evidence suggests that it had fallen significantly as a result of the Fire and rebuilding, so it could have been as high as 100,000 on the eve of the plague. Approximate population densities for 1631 can be calculated by ward; for population densities by parish in 1695, see P. E. Jones and A. V. Judges, 'London population in the late seventeenth century', *Economic History Review* 6 (1935), 45–63.
16 D. Keene and V. Harding, *Historical Gazetteer of London before the Great Fire, vol. 1, Cheapside* (microfiche: Cambridge, 1987).

houses 11 inmates dwell'.[17] Although the population was less densely packed than in the centre – perhaps 150 persons to the acre in the mid-seventeenth century – their conditions seem to have been very much worse. After the initial colonization of open spaces, further population increase was accommodated by subdivision and multi-occupancy, so that more people shared the same amount of floor space.

A good example of the way in which development took place is the infilling of the city ditch. The long stretches of land between the wall and the extramural roads of Houndsditch and Minories, which were open and used as tenter grounds and gardens in *c.* 1550, belonged to the Corporation, but were nevertheless let, in fairly large parcels, on leases that permitted building from the 1570s. Stow noted that the ditch 'of olde time was vsed to lie open' but that now it was enclosed and 'the banks thereof let out for Garden plots, Carpenters yardes, Bowling Allies, and diuerse houses thereon builded'.[18] When these first leases fell in, from the 1590s and early 1600s, the area was let in smaller parcels, at higher rents. At first only the street frontage was built up but soon the yards and gardens behind were colonized and the ditch itself covered over; by the late seventeenth century the area was thickly covered with houses, a tight complex of leaseholds and subtenancies (fig. 3).[19] The typical physical form of development in many of the inner suburbs was thus the close or alley, a narrow cul-de-sac leading off from the main street, giving access to several dwellings that may have been formed from the outbuildings of the original street-front house, and that at any rate occupied what was once its yard or garden. These small dwellings generally lacked any private open space, sharing only the semi-public area of the court. Many of the courts and closes that characterized the 'old suburbs' of the seventeenth-century city, and contained some of its worst housing, were probably developed in this way.[20] A survey of tithable rent values in the city in 1638 confirms this impression. It notes in most parishes the presence or absence of

[17] PRO, SP16/359, fos. 92, 94. I am grateful to Derek Keene, Director, Centre for Metropolitan History, for allowing me to use his notes from this source and for a copy of his unpublished paper, 'The poor and their neighbours in seventeenth-century London'.
[18] Stow, *Survey*, I.126.
[19] CLRO, City Lands. A partial reconstruction of the development is in the archive notes of the Centre for Metropolitan History, Institute of Historical Research, University of London.
[20] Compare plates 26 (Houndsditch) and 46 (Pheasant Court, Smithfield) in John Schofield (ed.), *The London Surveys of Ralph Treswell* (1987).

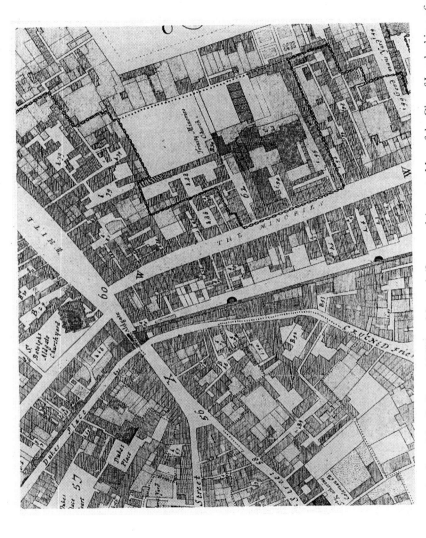

Fig. 3 A section from John Ogilby and William Morgan's 'Large and Accurate Map of the City of London' in *c*. 1676, showing Aldgate, the city wall, and the buildings between the Minories and the wall, infilling the waste space of the city ditch.

what were called rents or tenements, meaning not necessarily single divided buildings, but certainly groups of low-rent units under a single landlord. In the northern and eastern suburbs in particular the returns list numerous tenements, apparently whole alleys of units valued at £1 to £3 rent each. The extramural parish of St Botolph Aldgate contained properties such as Red Lyon Alley, with thirty or more tenements, valued at £60 per annum in all; sixteen tenements in 'Mr Green's rents', valued at £20; and 'Squirrel Alley rents', at £30.[21] These clearly represent the kind of development pictured in fig. 3, and this information confirms their character as low-rent living areas.

It is also arguable that these new ways of accommodating the population militated against a sense of neighbourhood. The medieval streets of the city were narrow, but they formed an effective circulation network. Most houses opened onto major or minor streets rather than lanes and alleys, and there was a relatively free flow of contact and access. As indicated above, the expanded early modern population of the inner city found accommodation in divided houses, higher buildings, and the building-over of back plots; in the immediate fringe beyond the walls, development took the form of closes, narrow blind alleys onto which a dozen or more dwellings opened. In both cases the simple relationship between house and householder, and between house and street, was undermined. The texture of the built environment had become much more dense and congested, and it must have been very difficult to keep a clear sense of all the linked spaces of a neighbourhood. Equally, these new developments made it more difficult to perceive the human community, since the spatial obscurity of such dwellings also obscured the identity of their inhabitants. The tithe survey of 1638 lists thousands of householders by name, but the references to 'rents' or 'tenements' with a number of unnamed occupants suggest that in the eyes of the parish clergy, who returned the information, the occupants of such places had significantly less individuality.[22] These alleys and closes might have their own social life and identity as a micro-neighbourhood, but they were clearly not fully assimilated into the larger parish to which they belonged. The Fire of 1666 obviously had an impact on the texture of the inner city, rebuilt with

---

[21] T. C. Dale, *The Inhabitants of London in 1638* (1931), esp. pp. 211, 217.
[22] *Ibid.*, pp. 203–39.

wider streets and clearer building-lines and plot divisions, but it may
have increased the overcrowding of the nearer suburbs, into which
the dispossessed poured, leading to a still stronger contrast between
an orderly centre and a disorderly and spatially incoherent inner
ring of suburbs.

In addition to intensification of this kind, early modern growth
extended the built-up area well beyond the city's medieval limits. It
is important to note that, despite the proclamations and attempts to
limit growth, there was no physical or jurisdictional barrier that
confined development to within the city boundaries – unlike, for
example, Edinburgh and Paris in the same period, where either
fortifications or a strict limit on urban privileges meant that expansion of population had to be accommodated within existing boundaries and produced high-rise housing all over the city. What this
meant in London, of course, was that the areas of new building were
not so tightly constrained, and could afford to include gardens and
open space, but also that they sprawled further.

Drawn and written surveys of London housing in the mid-
seventeenth century show this graphically and reveal the contrast
between east and west end development.[23] Overall, the new suburban growth was of mixed character; there was poor housing in
both east and west ends, but very little substantial housing in the
east. Towards Westminster especially, the new building included
good-quality housing for gentry and government officials, as well as
the great houses of nobles and court figures. Hollar's map of the
Covent Garden area in c. 1658 (fig. 4) shows not only the extension of
building since the mid-sixteenth century but also that many of the
better houses had clearly been built with reasonably generous
gardens. Houses in High Holborn (Staple Inn) were substantial, with
up to ten rooms, and three-quarters of them had gardens. This kind
of development contrasts with that in the east. Shadwell was a
settlement almost entirely built up after 1600. There had been very
little building here at all in the sixteenth century, but rapid growth
especially from the 1620s and 1630s had by 1650 created a sizeable

---

[23] The principal study of this is M. J. Power, 'East and west in early-modern London', in E. W.
Ives, R. J. Knecht, and J. J. Scarisbrick (eds.), *Wealth and Power in Tudor England. Essays
Presented to S. T. Bindoff* (1978), pp. 167–85. See also N. G. Brett-James, *The Growth of Stuart
London* (1935), esp. pp. 151–213, 366–419; L. Stone, 'Residential development of the west
end of London in the seventeenth century', in B. C. Malament (ed.), *After the Reformation.
Essays in Honor of J. H. Hexter* (Manchester, 1980), pp. 167–212; E. McKellar, *The Birth of
Modern London. The Development and Design of the City, 1660–1720* (Manchester, 1999).

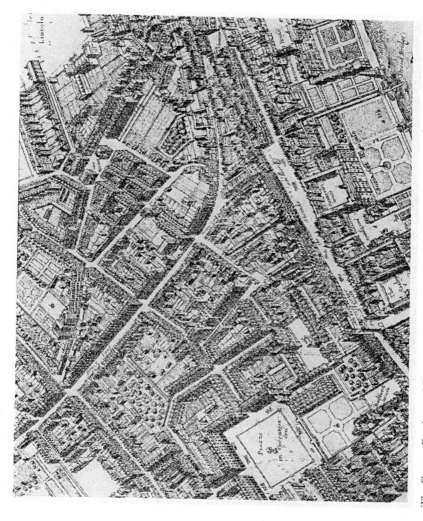

Fig. 4 The Covent Garden and Drury Lane section of Wenceslaus Hollar's map 'Westminster and London', *c.* 1658, showing the substantial houses of the Strand ('the Stronde') and the relatively spacious layout and gardens of this area.

community of 3,500, as large as many provincial towns. This doubled again between 1650 and 1675 and continued upwards thereafter. The development was fairly low density, mostly consisting of small two-storey houses of up to four rooms, nearly half of them with gardens.[24]

There was a big contrast between areas developed by or for landlords and those that spread relatively unchecked. The classic areas of imposed uniformity are of course the large-scale west-end developments, starting with Covent Garden in the 1630s and continuing in the rows of houses round Lincoln's Inn Fields and in St James's and other new squares. But this could also happen on less prestigious estates: under Shadwell's landlord, developers in the 1620s began by building groups of two or three houses, but rapidly moved on to building eight, ten, twelve, at once.[25] This developmental pattern was repeated in other new areas, giving, no doubt, something more of uniformity to their appearance and character than was the case in older-established areas where ownership was fragmented and development took place piecemeal. Where landlord control was weak, or local government control non-existent, the result could be chaotic. Tower Hill, the open space outside the Tower of London, was under the king's jurisdiction, not the city's, and hence presumably a place where civic regulations could be flouted. Nor does royal jurisdiction appear to have been exercised with vigour. Over 200 houses, mostly of poor quality, had been built on the open space here by 1649.[26] Open space in the early modern city could only survive if defined, claimed, and valued as such; unclaimed open space had no defence against encroachment.[27] Other exempt areas like the precinct of St Martin le Grand or the former royal property at Coldharbour on the Thames seem to have become notorious for poor housing, illicit trading, and unchecked crime.[28] One of the worst housing areas may have been New Palace Yard in

---

[24] Power, 'East and west'; M. J. Power, 'Shadwell, the development of a London suburban community in the seventeenth century', *London Journal* 4 (1978), 29–46; M. J. Power, 'East London housing in the seventeenth century', in P. Clark and P. Slack (eds.), *Crisis and Order in English Towns, 1500–1700* (1972), pp. 237–62.

[25] Power, 'Shadwell', 30–2.

[26] Power, 'East and west', p. 170.

[27] V. Harding, 'Gardens and open space in early modern London', in M. Galinou (ed.), *London's Pride: The Glorious History of the Capital's Gardens* (1990), pp. 44–55.

[28] V. Pearl, *London at the Outbreak of the Puritan Revolution* (Oxford, 1961), pp. 25–7, 32; J. L. McMullan, *The Canting Crew. London's Criminal Underworld, 1550–1700* (New Brunswick, 1984), p. 63.

Westminster, where, though rents were high (presumably because of its proximity to the court), houses were small and densely occupied, and the quality of the building was poor. Forty per cent of the houses were described *c.* 1650 as sheds, and they were largely timber-framed as opposed to the more fashionable and durable brick.[29]

II SOCIAL TOPOGRAPHIES

Clearly, the growth of population and settlement of seventeenth-century London was producing a city of greater variation, stronger local characteristics, and social and environmental extremes. While the medieval mix of rich and poor was never wholly eliminated, and almost all areas continued to include dwellings, and inhabitants, of several different kinds, the expansion of early modern London led to a new social topography, and a clearer east/west and centre/suburbs opposition. This has been illustrated by mapping indices of wealth and poverty, health, and social structure across the capital.

The city-wide tithe assessment of 1638 indicates a marked gradient of desirability – if rent value can be taken as a proxy for this – from the city centre to the outlying areas. Both median rents and the proportion of high-value properties were generally highest in the city centre and lowest in the parishes bordering the city wall, both inside and outside. It is not a perfect concentric pattern, because the high-value centre was stretched out east–west along the main axis of the city, while there is some evidence for greater wealth in the western suburb than in the eastern.[30] A contemporary survey of divided and inmated houses also highlights the poverty of the nearer suburbs. Squirrel Alley rents, noted above, contained three aged couples who would work but 'want the means to set themselves to work' and one widower who would not work, with six children between them. Red Lyon Alley contained at least fourteen aged couples and two widows who would work but lacked the means, one aged widow, one man who could not work through age, four poor widows, and one man 'very poor', with twenty-six children between them.[31] The Hearth Tax returns of the 1660s, as well as giving a sense of the size of

[29] Power, 'East and west', p. 170.
[30] E. Jones, 'London in the early seventeenth century: an ecological approach', *London Journal* 6 (1980), 123–34; R. Finlay, *Population and Metropolis. The Demography of London, 1580–1650* (Cambridge, 1981), pp. 70–82.
[31] *CSPD (1637)*, pp. 178–83; PRO, SP16/359, fo. 90v.

houses in different areas of the city, also indicate how many house-holds were exempted, on account of poverty, from paying the tax. In the city centre such non-chargeable households were few; in some of the western suburbs between 20 and 25 per cent of the households were not liable; in Shoreditch, Aldgate, and Shadwell the proportion was 50 per cent, and in Whitechapel 70 per cent of households did not pay the hearth tax.[32] We can probably identify, therefore, scattered but not extreme poverty in the city centre; pockets of poverty in some suburbs, probably representing courts and alleys of small dwellings; and wide areas in some of the eastern suburbs where the majority of the population was poor. Not necessarily destitute, but poor.

We can also identify distinctive living patterns. A survey for the Privy Council in 1637 showed that multi-occupancy, defined in terms of divided houses and lodgers, was much higher in the periphery of the walled city and in the nearer suburbs, the first ring around the city centre, than in the centre itself. Within the walls, multi-occupancy was more likely to entail letting large houses as single rooms: in Silver Street, just within the wall, one house of ten rooms was occupied by '10 several families, divers of which also had lodgers'; in All Hallows the Less, by the river, another house contained eleven married couples, seven widows, and eight other single persons. Outside, 'divided houses' really meant the creation of numerous illicit residential units on the yard or garden of an older house, in the form of rents or alleys, as described above.[33] Later taxes suggest that in the city centre some 107 families were living in every 100 properties designated as single houses, while in the wards outside the walls at least 121 families were doing so.[34] The Parliamentary Surveys of c. 1650 show that both the shed dwellings of New Palace Yard and the much larger houses of Long Acre and Holborn were often occupied by more than one family, though values per room per annum (a plausible measure of demand) were actually highest in Westminster, despite the conditions. Few or none of the small houses in Shadwell, however, were occupied in this way.[35]

[32] M. J. Power, 'The social topography of Restoration London', in A. L. Beier and R. Finlay (eds.), *London 1500–1700: The Making of the Metropolis* (1986), pp. 199–223; Power, 'East and west', p. 181.

[33] *CSPD (1637)*, p. 180; PRO, SP16/359.

[34] Jones and Judges, 'London population in the late seventeenth century', p. 53.

[35] Power, 'East and west', p. 170.

Another feature of seventeenth-century London is the range in family and household size. Apart from underlining the prevalence of the nuclear family in London as a whole – few extended families with resident kin – there was a distinct difference in the size of households in richer and poorer areas. In the city within the walls in 1695 the mean number of persons per household was 6.1; in the city without the walls the mean was 5.1. Further out the proportion falls further; the mean for villages and hamlets was, it is suggested, little more than 4 persons per household.[36] City-centre households were larger because they had more servants and apprentices, not necessarily more resident children, than those in the suburbs: obviously, a prosperous and independent craftsman or trader was in a position to take on the charge, and ultimately the benefit, of one or more apprentices, while the wage earner was not. Even moderately prosperous householders had female household servants, and some had several. Mean household size in some of the poorer areas of London was brought lower by the presence of numbers of widows living alone. They are to be found all over the city occupying single rooms and one-hearth dwellings, but in some areas like Aldgate they appear to have congregated, no doubt attracted by low rents and employment opportunities as landladies, nurses, and so on.[37]

One of the significant ways in which the centre/suburbs relationship changed was in the perception of health and order. A simple contrast was made in people's minds between the prosperous, orderly, if densely packed, centre and the poorer and often unplanned and chaotic suburbs.[38] In so far as much of the new development strained urban services to the limits, this was justified. Water was piped to the richer areas of the town; the weakness of local government in the suburbs meant that street cleaning and environmental regulation were less effective there. The common perception was also justified by the geography of plague mortality,

[36] Jones and Judges, 'London population in the late seventeenth century', pp. 61–2; D. V. Glass, 'Gregory King's estimate of the population of England and Wales, 1695', in D. V. Glass and D. E. C. Eversley (eds.), *Population in History. Essays in Historical Demography* (1965), pp. 183–220.

[37] D. V. Glass (ed.), *London Inhabitants within the Walls, 1695* (London Record Society 2, 1966), pp. xxvi–xxvii, xxxiii; PRO, SP16/359, fos. 89–99. For widows and their work, see P. Earle, 'The female labour market in London in the late seventeenth and early eighteenth centuries', *Economic History Review*, 2nd series, 42 (1989), 328–47.

[38] Aspects of this relationship are discussed in S. Mullaney, *The Place of the Stage. License, Play and Power in Renaissance England* (Chicago, 1988), though there is some confusion between suburbs and liberties.

which shifted from the city centre in the mid-sixteenth century to the outer suburbs in the mid-seventeenth and later. Paul Slack's influential study of plague revealed a marked shift in its topography between the mid-sixteenth and the early seventeenth centuries. In 1563 the ten worst-affected city parishes all lay within the walls, and mostly towards the centre, where population was most dense. The ten parishes least affected (in terms of elevation beyond normal mortality levels) included some city-centre ones but also peripheral and waterfront parishes within the walls, and four of the large parishes outside the walls to east and west. By 1603, the least-affected parishes were those in the city centre, focusing on Cheapside, while the worst mortality occurred in pockets within the walls, including peripheral and waterfront parishes, and in some of the extramural parishes. By 1665, the polarization was complete: all the least-affected parishes clustered in the city centre, and all the worst-affected lay on the periphery of the city, just inside or outside the walls or on the waterfront.[39] While the exact dimensions of this particular shift may not have been apparent to contemporaries, the perception of the suburbs as particularly affected by plague was widespread, because of the currency of the Bills of Mortality. The Bills, listing the number dying weekly of plague and of all other causes, presented an image of London as a collection of parishes, arranged into the city within the walls, the sixteen parishes in the immediate suburbs, wholly or partly under the city's jurisdiction, the outparishes, and the distant parishes. The disparity between the numbers and sizes of parishes in each group exaggerated these distinctions, but without needing to make detailed calculations it was obvious that in the outer parishes the death-toll was extremely high. In 1665, according to the Yearly Bill, nearly 10,000 died of the plague within the walls, but nearly 30,000 in the sixteen parishes, and over 20,000 in the twelve outparishes. Nearly 5,000 died of plague in the parish of St Giles Cripplegate, to the north-west of the city wall, and 6,500 in Stepney parish in east London.[40] Contemporary and popular comment emphasizes how the Bills shaped percep-

[39] P. Slack, *The Impact of Plague in Tudor and Stuart England* (1985), pp. 151–64. For the distribution of mortality in 1665 see also J. A. I. Champion, *London's Dreaded Visitation: The Social Geography of the Great Plague in 1665* (Historical Geography Research Series, 31, 1995).

[40] In all, the Bill for 1665 notes 97,306 deaths, of which 68,596 were attributed to plague: *A Collection of the Yearly Bills of Mortality from 1657 to 1758 Inclusive* (1759); figures also available in Champion, *London's Dreaded Visitation*, pp. 104–7.

tions: they are a major theme of Defoe's account, supplying data for his authorial calculations, but also informing the characters in the narrative and motivating them to action.[41] The Bills circulated widely in London, but were also sent to correspondents in the provinces or even abroad. People who had no personal knowledge of the capital were familiar with the names of parishes and with the varied social topography of London. As James Robertson emphasizes, the Bills must be seen as 'among the earliest and, arguably, among the most influential texts in shaping national views of London'.[42]

III CHANGING PERCEPTIONS OF EXPERIENCED SPACES

In the context of changing perceptions of London as a space inhabited and experienced, the changed importance of formal boundaries within London become important. One boundary that never changed, within this period, and indeed for much longer, was that of the city. The city walls remained standing (though almost submerged by building in some places) and the gates were notable architectural features, but these were not jurisdictional boundaries: the city's irregular and historically contingent boundary encircled the walled city and a further ring of inner suburb. It was marked on the major roads by bars, more or less substantially constructed, at which there was at least at the start of the century still some attempt to take tolls (fig. 5). The boundary did not formally change, though, as has been noted, London's buildings spread far beyond it. In the sixteenth century, City government and Privy Council were reluctant to accept the reality and irreversibility of growth, and consequently slow to consider making changes to existing governmental structures and jurisdictional boundaries. By the time that the need for some response had become pressing, in the seventeenth century, relations between City and central government were seriously strained, and it was impossible to reach terms for an administrative and jurisdictional reorganization.[43] It remained a real boundary in administrative terms, with the area under the mayor and aldermen being more

[41] Cf. N. E. McClure (ed.), *The Letters of John Chamberlain* (2 vols., Philadelphia, 1939), II, pp. 617, 618, 621, 622; Daniel Defoe, *A Journal of the Plague Year* (1986).

[42] James Robertson, 'Reckoning with London: interpreting the *Bills of Mortality* before John Graunt', *Urban History* 23 (1996), 325–50.

[43] Brett-James, *Growth of Stuart London*, pp. 223–47.

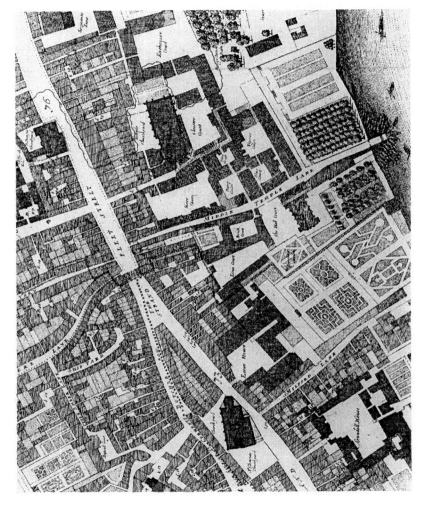

Fig. 5 A section from John Ogilby and William Morgan's map of London in c. 1676. Temple Bar, between the Strand and Fleet Street, stood at the limit of the city's jurisdiction (indicated on the map with a chain) but nowhere near the edge of the built-up area.

effectively governed, with far greater moral and financial resources, than the areas outside, which had a variety of *ad hoc* administrative arrangements. Thomas Freeman made a point of this contrast in 1614, when he characterized the city's spread as 'going to revel it in some disorder, Without the walls, without the liberties, Where she need fear nor Mayor nor Recorder'.[44] This is one of the important and enduring characteristics of early modern London. Local government, national taxes, ecclesiastical surveys, all respected the city boundary; historians have tended to do so too, since the surviving archival sources are structured by administrative divisions.[45] But there were other ways in which the sense of the boundary was weakening. Joseph Ward's recent book emphasizes a growing metropolitan consciousness, exampled by the guilds' attempts to extend their exercise of regulatory powers to areas beyond the city's jurisdiction, and by the city magistrates' interference in the moral regulation of the suburbs.[46] By the end of the century the city's ruling elite no longer necessarily lived in the city. And as Defoe said, London 'in the modern acceptation' went far beyond the old boundaries.

Of the smaller divisions of the urban space, wards – within the city – were probably increasingly meaningless as experienced spaces, as the functions of the wardmote withered, though wards and precincts were still retained as sub-units of taxation.[47] Stow used the wards to structure his account of the city, even though this obscured some features of importance, such as Cheapside itself, which straddled three wards (this particular problem was remedied in the second edition of 1603).[48] Strype also, perforce, took wards as a unit of description, and this gained some added legitimation by the production of ward-maps, a notable feature of Strype's *Survey* and of later works on London.[49]

---

[44] Freeman, *Rubbe and a Great Cast* in Manley, *London in the Age of Shakespeare*, p. 250.

[45] V. Harding, 'From compact city to complex metropolis: records for the history of London, 1500–1720', in M. V. Roberts (ed.), *Archives and the Metropolis* (1998), pp. 83–92.

[46] J. P. Ward, *Metropolitan Communities. Trade Guilds, Identity, and Change in Early Modern London* (Stanford, 1997).

[47] V. Pearl, 'Change and stability in seventeenth-century London', *London Journal* 5 (1979), 25–7.

[48] Stow, *Survey*, I.xxxviii, 264–9.

[49] J. J. Morrison, 'Strype's Stow: the 1720 edition of "A Survey of London"', *London Journal* 3 (1977), 40–54; C. M. Barron and V. Harding, 'London' in C. R. J. Currie and C. P. Lewis (eds.), *English County Histories, A Guide* (Stroud, 1994), pp. 260–1; R. Hyde, *Ward Maps of the City of London* (London Topographical Society Publication no. 154, 1999).

Parishes, however, had both less and more meaning in the
seventeenth century. Certainly the traditional idea of the parish as a
spiritual community that was spatially coextensive with a residential
one had been undermined. The comprehensive and sufficient nature
of parochial worship was a central principle of the Elizabethan
settlement, yet within a century separatism and congregationalism
were openly preached and practised. Only a handful of separatist
and independent churches can be identified before the 1630s, but
they represent a fundamentally different conception of the basis for
church organization: the voluntary, 'gathered' congregation of
saints, rather than the territorially organized parish.[50] The turmoil
of the 1640s allowed many more divergent views on church organization to be voiced. A leading Independent of the time disparaged
parish boundaries as 'that invisible line . . . drawn by the hand of
blindness' in 'times of ignorance and superstition'.[51] The 1650s saw a
range of independent churches flourishing in London alongside a
somewhat lame and incomplete parochial Presbyterian church.[52]
The post-Restoration settlement re-established the parochial, territorial church of England and effectively institutionalized the opposition between parochial and gathered church systems. The latter
had another twenty-five years of fugitive and persecuted existence.
After 1689, toleration restored the civil rights of non-conformists,
but the new churches which they were then able to establish were
seen as direct competitors to the Anglican church, and as before
their congregations ignored parish boundaries.

The map of ecclesiastical parishes in the city of London was
significantly changed in the later seventeenth century as a result of
the Great Fire of 1666, in which eighty-four parish churches were
burnt but only forty-nine of these subsequently rebuilt. The thirty-
five parishes whose churches were not rebuilt (often, but not always,
among the smallest in area and population) were united for ecclesiastical purposes with neighbouring parishes, and thereafter shared
clergy, sacraments and services, and obligations.[53] The registers of
these united parishes show the populations merged for baptism,
marriage, and burial ceremonies; their theoretical congregations

[50] M. Tolmie, *The Triumph of the Saints: The Separate Churches of London, 1616–49* (Cambridge, 1977).
[51] John Goodwin, 1645, cited in Tolmie, *Triumph of the Saints*, p. 100.
[52] Tai Liu, *Puritan London: A Study of Religion and Society in the City Parishes* (1986).
[53] W. G. Bell, *The Great Fire of London* (1920), pp. 299–312, 334–7.

now averaged over 1,000, though there was clearly no expectation, by now, that all would attend. Another important point here is that the suburban parishes were always very much larger in acreage than the city centre ones, and as the major location of new population settlement they became very populous. Several were each as large and populous as a significant provincial town. The parishes that ringed the city walls by 1700 each contained populations of from 2,500 to well over 10,000. Parishes that had been largely open and cultivated land in 1550, such as St Martin-in-the-Fields, now had populations in the tens of thousands. The huge parish of Stepney, which comprised most of east London, had had one smaller parish carved out of it before 1700 but still its population had grown from less than 2,000 to over 40,000 in 1700.[54] For most seventeenth-century Londoners, then, the parish was no longer self-evidently a neighbourhood, an intimate community easily apprehended as a spatial environment and offering personal and direct human contact with fellow-parishioners.

However, parishes gained more meaning from other functions, and indeed in the suburbs it was these functions that constructed the local community and the beginnings of local administration. Parishes were taken over as the basic unit of resource and responsibility for the administration of the Elizabethan Poor Law, and in the long term, the exercise of these powers established the parish as the effective unit of local government and helped to regenerate the parish as a focus for local identity. The Poor Law emphasized the identity of the parishioner as participant (whether benefactor or beneficiary) in a process of redistribution; in some sense it made the parish a miniature commonwealth, by establishing the wealth of richer parishioners as a resource available to support the poorer. It helped to mark the distinction between the local resident poor and the passing stranger in need of relief. Parish poor and parish pensioners, especially when identified by badging, were the visible manifestation of the community's care for its members. There was a very strong territorial aspect to all this. Each parish had its own poor, its own problems, its own resources, its own level of charge, and the criterion for both liability and eligibility was the exact place

---

[54] These figures are based on communicants in 1548 and on numbers of deaths in *c.* 1700: see C. Kitching, *The London and Middlesex Chantry Certificate of 1548* (London Record Society, 16, 1980); *A Collection of the Yearly Bills of Mortality from 1657 to 1758 Inclusive*; and Harding, 'The population of London', for multipliers and methods of calculation.

of residence. The parish boundary marks that now appear as a
quaint survival on city buildings once had a real significance for
local residents. The Act of Settlement of 1662 reinforced the
identification of individuals with parishes, by basing eligibility for
relief on place of 'settlement' – normally the place of birth. In a
geographically mobile society, individuals carried with them through
life their certificates of settlement, and their identity as members of
another parish, unless they could 'gain a settlement' elsewhere
through employment or tenancy.[55]

IV INDIVIDUAL ITINERARIES

Clearly, no seventeenth-century Londoner could know the whole
metropolis, and the worlds of city, east end, and west end were
diverging in character and culture. Stow's *Survey* was written at
about the last date that it was possible to do so comprehensively and
reasonably succinctly. He could indeed survey London with authority and personal knowledge of most of its parts. But as the capital
spread, few people can have had the need or the desire to comprehend it all. An infinite number of individually imagined cities must
have existed. To find their way around, Londoners must have relied
on a mixture of accumulated personal experience and transmitted
information and directions. The later seventeenth century saw the
appearance of street and trade directories and also of readable maps,
whether for the whole metropolis or for wards and parishes.[56]

Only rarely can we trace an individual's mental map of the city.
Nehemiah Wallington offers one example, of a man who moved hardly
at all as far as residence went, but who had contacts and connections
across and outside the city. He was born and brought up in the parish
of St Leonard Eastcheap, apprenticed to his own father, and settled
on marriage in the next parish before moving back to St Leonard's;
he also had a large number of kin resident nearby.[57] He clearly
traversed the city itself, and his business and other occasions took him
to Southwark, Westminster, Blackheath, Romford, and Ipswich.[58]

[55] P. Slack, *The English Poor Law, 1531–1782* (1990), esp. pp. 26–9, 35–9, 61–2.
[56] P. Atkins, *The Directories of London, 1677–1977* (1990). More generally, see L. Picard, *Restoration London* (1997); C. Wall, *The Literary and Cultural Spaces of Restoration London* (Cambridge, 1998).
[57] P. S. Seaver, *Wallington's World. A Puritan Artisan in Seventeenth-Century London* (1985), pp. 69–73, 77.
[58] *Ibid.*, pp. 58, 97–8, 150–1.

His close connections within and outside London, however, were shaped by his membership of the godly community, which brought him distant contacts (extending to the nearby continent and to North America) but perhaps limited the number of geographically proximate neighbours with whom he was prepared to engage.[59] The sophisticated Pepys, on the other hand, who came to London as a young man, travelled constantly for business and pleasure between the court and government at Westminster, his home in Mincing Lane, and places downriver at Deptford and Greenwich. Extremely familiar with the fashionable west end, his excursions there were motivated by tastes and desires that would have been alien and deeply shocking to Wallington.[60] Another, less well-known Londoner was Richard Smyth (d. 1675), who kept an obituary list of his acquaintance in London which allows us to trace his path through the city and reconstruct the geographical, as well as the social and affective, world to which he belonged. Smyth was in a good position to know several parts of London well: as a city law-officer living in Old Jewry, he linked the courts at Guildhall and the Poultry and Wood Street Compters with the legal world of the Inns of Court and with the central Law Courts at Westminster. Once retired to Moorfields, he had leisure to pursue his book-collecting, and indeed was 'constantly known every day to walk his rounds through the shops', though he also had a network of more local friends, acquaintances, and neighbours (fig. 6).[61] Each of these men, however, was only one Londoner among several hundred thousand; undoubtedly others, whether from the prosperous professional and mercantile middle classes or the unsettled and mobile poor, would have had equally idiosyncratic circuits. New foci of activity in the later seventeenth century would have included the coffee houses of Lombard Street near the Royal Exchange, as well as the retail centres and entertainment venues of the west end and the offices of government frequented by Pepys. Women, including Elisabeth Pepys, moved differently round the city and between certain spaces and poles.[62]

---

[59] *Ibid.*, p. 104.
[60] R. Latham and W. Matthews (eds.), *The Diary of Samuel Pepys* (11 vols., 1970–83).
[61] V. Harding, 'Mortality and the mental map of London: Richard Smyth's *Obituary*', in R. Myers and M. Harris (eds.), *Medicine, Mortality and the Book Trade* (Folkestone, 1998), pp. 49–71.
[62] Cf. e.g. Peter Earle, *A City Full of People* (1994), pp. 107–55.

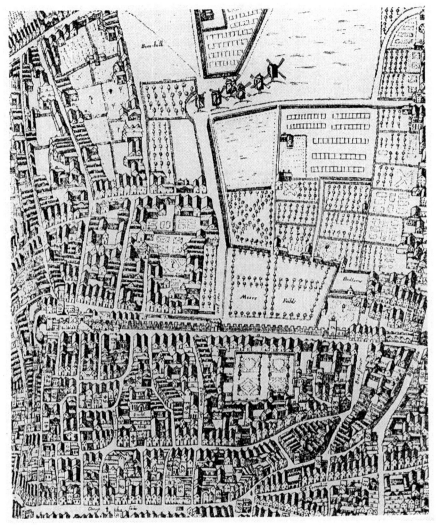

Fig. 6 A section from William Faithorne's 'An Exact Delineation of the Cities of London and Westminster and the Suburbs' of 1658. Richard Smyth lived first in Old Jewry (near 87, bottom centre) and later on the west side of Moorfields (centre), a quite separate neighbourhood, though not more than a few hundred yards away.

There is clearly no possibility of mapping more than a few of these personal itineraries, or of closely relating them to the broader characterizations of London localities made earlier. I will only conclude, therefore, by reiterating the initial analogy between the texts of Stow and Strype and the London they described: compact, integrated, comprehensible, as opposed to extended, amorphous, inadequately underpinned by formal structure. Their attitudes to London contrasted too. Stow saw London as essentially a unity, a concentric city whose history formed a single coherent narrative, though he was uncomfortably aware of the disruptive potential of contemporary forces of change. Strype found his London project almost unmanageably difficult in technical terms, and could not satisfactorily resolve the problem of relating the parts to the whole. In attempting to respect the structure of the original, he accepted a programme not best suited to the London of his day. His difficulties, however, are a reflection of the increasingly complex character of early modern London, incredibly rich and diverse, but beyond comprehension even by contemporaries.

CHAPTER 5

Gendered spaces: patterns of mobility and perceptions of London's geography, 1660–1750

Robert B. Shoemaker

In the 122 years between the first publication of Stow's *Survey* in 1598 and Strype's edition of 1720, the multi-dimensional nature of the metropolis became ever more apparent. At a basic level, this is evident in the titles of their books: Stow offered a survey of *London*, by which it is clear he meant primarily the City of London, though he did include sections on the suburbs and liberties without the walls and on the City of Westminster. By 1720, the title of Strype's edition, like the volumes themselves, had become unwieldy: *A Survey of the Cities of London and Westminster, and the Borough of Southwark . . . Illustrated with Exact Maps of the Cities and Suburbs, and of all the Wards, and, likewise, of the Out-Parishes of London and Westminster, and the Country Ten Miles around London.* As a result of phenomenal population growth, by the early eighteenth century the City of London accounted for only about a quarter of the metropolitan population.[1] London was also becoming socially and culturally fragmented. In a statement that was later echoed by Joseph Addison in *The Spectator*, Thomas Brown wrote in 1702: 'London is a world by itself. We daily discover in it more new countries, and surprising singularities, than in all the universe besides. There are among the Londoners so many nations differing in manners, customs and religions, that the inhabitants themselves don't know a quarter of them.'[2] In his recent book Joseph Ward maintains that, despite the growth of the suburbs in the seventeenth century, which were often perceived as the disorderly

I would like to thank Pascal Brioist, Laura Gowing, Tim Hitchcock, and Lawrence Klein for generously providing me with valuable references and copies of their unpublished and/or published work. I am also grateful for the many helpful comments made by the participants of the 'Imagining the City' conference where this paper was first presented.

[1] Vanessa Harding, 'The population of London, 1550–1700: a review of the published evidence', *London Journal* 15 (1990), 112.
[2] Thomas Brown, *Amusements Serious and Comical, Calculated for the Meridian of London* (2nd edn, 1702) p. 22; Joseph Addison, *The Spectator*, no. 403 (12 June 1712).

antithesis to the well-governed and orderly City, a metropolitan sense of community *was* preserved in the ideas of religious and moral reformers and in institutions such as the guilds. Yet he acknowledges a diversity of attitudes among Londoners: while some thought and acted in terms of 'communities', others treated London like a more diffuse 'society'.[3]

Thus we are confronted with one of the main problems addressed in this volume: how did the residents of this vast metropolis at the turn of the eighteenth century perceive and experience this diverse mass of places and peoples? Did they think and act as if they were residents of the metropolis as a whole? Or did they carve out smaller sections of London as *their* city, the city *they* inhabited? In other words, how large and diverse was the London that most Londoners experienced? If the metropolis was too big and complex for most people to experience it fully, the parish, the unit of analysis adopted by Stow and Strype, was clearly too small. Consistory court depositions reveal that the kind of loyalty to one's parish often found in rural areas was limited in London. Londoners frequently travelled outside the boundaries of their own parish on a temporary or permanent basis and showed little solidarity with their local parish. Although defamation cases attest to the strength of neighbourhood ties, these neighbourhoods were often no larger than a single alley or court.[4] Many Anglicans failed to have much loyalty to their own parish church. When witnesses were asked whether they attended their parish church, it was not uncommon for them to respond, as Elizabeth Hancock did in 1681, that 'she frequenteth her own parish church, but goes oftener to other parish churches'.[5] The large number of dissenters in London further undermined the role of the parish church as a community centre.

As Ward suggests, the boundaries of Londoners' personal experiences were highly variable and thus depended very much on the perspective of the individual, and on his or her occupation, social status, wealth, and cultural attitudes. London meant different things

---

[3] Joseph P. Ward, *Metropolitan Communities: Trade Guilds, Identity and Social Change in Early Modern London* (Stanford, 1997), esp. ch. 2 and conclusion.

[4] Between 1700 and 1709, 79 per cent of the defamation cases brought before the London Consistory Court were between parties living in the same parish: Randolph Trumbach, *Sex and the Gender Revolution*, vol. I: *Heterosexuality and the Third Gender in Enlightenment London* (Chicago, 1998), p. 33.

[5] LMA, DL/C/240, Davis con. Simpson. For other examples, see DL/C/240, E. Field con. W. Holgate and M. Richmond con. W. Holgate.

to different people. We already know from the work of Michael Power that the social composition of various districts of London varied considerably; I have argued elsewhere that one of the consequences of this was that the social dynamics of London neighbourhoods varied considerably – they were, for example, very different in the western suburban parishes (where there were considerable tensions) when compared with the suburbs east of the City (where neighbours were better able to settle disputes informally).[6] These social differences were reflected in the evolving language used to differentiate separate parts of the metropolis (the terms 'east end' and 'west end' used in this chapter are more modern usages). In contrast to the 'City' (used specifically to refer to the separate legal jurisdiction of the City of London), the terms 'Court' and later 'Town' were used to refer to the west end and Westminster. Significantly, a term had not yet evolved for the suburbs east of the City, despite the fact they were at least as populous as the west end: the primarily elite authors who wrote about London at this time imagined a city without the vast districts east of the Tower inhabited by sailors, dock workers, artisans, and labourers – clear proof that perceptions of the metropolis varied according to the point of view of the observer, particularly his or her social class.

In arguing that there are important *gender* differences in perceptions of London, I do not wish to minimize the importance of other social differences, but this important dimension has so far been neglected.[7] Women, of course, are conspicuous by their absence in both Stow and Strype, with the exception of short sections devoted to female benefactors.[8] The essentially corporate focus of both authors rendered women largely invisible, despite the fact that women made up significantly more than half the urban population.[9]

---

[6] M. J. Power, 'The social topography of Restoration London', in A. L. Beier and R. Finlay (eds.), *London 1500–1700: The Making of the Metropolis* (1986), pp. 199–223; Robert B. Shoemaker, *Prosecution and Punishment: Petty Crime and the Law in London and Rural Middlesex, c. 1660–1725* (Cambridge, 1991), ch. 10.

[7] With the important exception of Laura Gowing, 'The freedom of the streets: women and social space in London, 1560–1640', in Paul Griffiths and Mark Jenner (eds.), *Londinopolis: Essays in the Cultural and Social History of Early Modern London* (Manchester, 2000).

[8] Stow, *Survey*, i.116–17; Strype, *Survey*, i.xxx.278–80.

[9] Non-married women (spinsters and widows) in the City of London outnumbered their male equivalents by almost a quarter: D. V. Glass, 'Notes on the demography of London at the end of the seventeenth century', *Daedalus* 97 (1968), 584–6.

Female Londoners were by no means confined to the 'separate sphere' of the home: they were a prominent feature of London's public life – on the streets and in shops, theatres, walks, and gardens.[10] But of course women's experiences and perceptions of urban life were not the same as men's. As Christine Stansell has argued in her study of women in nineteenth-century New York City, the two sexes can inhabit the same spaces on very different terms; city streets can be perceived differently by men and women, who each construct their own distinctive city.[11] But it will become clear quite quickly in this essay that women's experiences were no more homogeneous than those of men. Significantly, Thomas Brown made another comment similar to the one cited earlier explicitly about women in London:

> Nay, how many different nations are there of our English Ladies. In the first place, there is the politick nation of your Ladies of the Town. Next . . . the free nation of the coquets. The invisible nation of the faithful wives . . . The good natur'd nation of wives that cuckold their husbands . . . The warlike nation of intriguing ladies . . . The haughty nation of citizens wives, that are dignified with a title . . . The Strowling nation of your regular visitants.[12]

Even within each gender, the experiences of Londoners were diverse.

In studying the gendered dimensions of Londoners' experiences and perceptions, however, we encounter significant methodological problems, due to serious limitations of evidence. There is little direct evidence of how the vast majority of Londoners thought about their city, and this applies particularly to female Londoners. Literary portrayals, largely written by elite men, reveal some contemporary male preconceptions, but they are confined by prevailing gender

---

[10] Robert B. Shoemaker, 'Separate spheres? Ideology and practice in London gender relations, 1660–1740', in M. McClendon, J. Ward and M. MacDonald (eds.), *Protestant Identities: Religion, Society and Self-Fashioning in Post-Reformation England* (Stanford, 2000), pp. 266–87.

[11] Christine Stansell, *City of Women: Sex and Class in New York 1789–1860* (New York, 1986). For other examples of this approach, see Linda Kerber, 'Separate spheres, female worlds, woman's place: the rhetoric of women's history', *Journal of Women's History* 75 (1988), 36–7 and Lynda Nead, 'Mapping the self: gender, space and modernity in mid-Victorian London', in R. Porter (ed.), *Rewriting the Self: Histories from the Renaissance to the Present* (1997), pp. 167–85.

[12] Thomas Brown, *A Walk around London and Westminster, Exposing the Vices and Follies of the Town*, in *The Works of Mr Thomas Brown* (3 vols., 1707–8), III, p. 72.

stereotypes and do not necessarily reflect how ordinary men and especially women actually experienced and thought about the city. For example, in the passage by Thomas Brown just cited the major factors by which Brown differentiates women are their sexual behaviour and marital status. This is typical – printed discussions of women in public places in this period rarely venture far from sex: women are portrayed as either virtuous or as whores, and the women in certain parts of the town are inevitably portrayed as the latter. Although such perceptions may have actually limited women's worlds – unaccompanied women may have been reluctant to travel in certain parts of town at certain times of day for fear of being treated as if they were prostitutes – this presents an undoubtedly limited portrayal of female Londoners and their experiences.

Owing to these problems of evidence, we have to take a different approach. Instead of examining their thoughts, which were rarely recorded, we have to examine their behaviour, the extent to which they moved about the city, both over the course of their lives when changing residences, and in their day-to-day activities, including their work and social engagements. From this evidence we can identify the geographical limits of Londoners' experiences of their city, see how this varied by gender and other factors, and consider what implications we can draw from this evidence about perceptions of London. We can determine whether men and women roamed freely across the entire metropolis or restricted their activities to certain parishes or districts. Now, of course, we have too much evidence, for just about any source that documents the comings and goings of Londoners could be useful. There are a few surviving diaries, notably of course that of Samuel Pepys, but they were all kept by elite men. For the day-to-day conduct of a larger number of people we can look at different types of sources: the stories of disputes over marital and sexual conduct recorded in consistory court depositions; narratives of violent disputes found in the *Old Bailey Proceedings*; and the places of residence of the sureties which defendants provided when they were bound over by recognizance. For life-cycle mobility we can look at the potted biographies that witnesses were asked to give in consistory court depositions (they were asked to identify where they were born and all the places they had lived in the past five or ten years) and in bastardy and settlement examinations (where a limited narrative of where the deponent had previously lived was necessary in order to enforce the provisions of the poor law).[13] Although what follows is based on limited samples from these voluminous sources, the fact that a range of different types of sources yielded similar patterns provides some confidence in the conclusions reached.

Because Londoners' experiences differed so profoundly depending on their social position, it is necessary to structure our discussion according to social class. While gentlemen, as well as (for the most part) ladies, ranged widely across most (but not all) of the metropolis, gender differences in patterns of mobility were greater lower down the social scale. Many middle- and lower-class men were more rooted in their local neighbourhoods than their wives or unmarried female counterparts, who both lacked the institutional links which tied men to specific places and needed to move about more in order to support themselves. Surprisingly, it is these women who turn out to have the most identifiably 'metropolitan' identity in preindustrial London.

Among the gentry, male and female Londoners clearly travelled widely in the metropolis, facilitated by their easy access to coaches, sedan chairs, and water transport. Together, married couples journeyed outside their immediate neighbourhoods to the theatre, pleasure gardens, and leisure activities in places like Hampstead or Kensington on the periphery of the metropolis. One of the best sources for Londoners of this status is of course Pepys's diary. Pepys travelled all over London, from government offices, the court, and the theatre in Whitehall and Lincoln's Inn Fields to his house near Tower Hill (and City shops and the Royal Exchange in between); eastwards to the docks; south of the river to pubs and pleasure gardens and for sexual dalliances; and west of the metropolis for similar purposes.[14] Pepys experienced the full geographical extent of the metropolis. Although unfortunately no diary survives for his wife Elizabeth, many of her movements were recorded by Samuel. Often travelling separately, she also journeyed widely, but not quite so widely: there is little evidence of her going to the east end, and unsurprisingly unlike Samuel she did not visit the fleshpots of Drury Lane (though she did go to the theatres) or the secret rural

---

[13] I have consulted the Chelsea settlement exams in a transcript generously provided by Tim Hitchcock. These have now been published in Tim Hitchcock and John Black (eds.), *The Settlement and Bastardy Examinations of St Luke, Chelsea, 1733–1766* (London Record Society, 33, 1999).

[14] R. Latham and W. Matthews (eds.), *The Diary of Samuel Pepys* (11 vols., 1970–83).

rendezvous in Lisson Green, Acton, and Lambeth Marsh where Samuel went with his mistresses such as Elizabeth Burrows and Betty Martin. Samuel had more freedom of manoeuvre than his wife, who not only travelled less widely but was not allowed to stay out as late: on one occasion he was unhappy that she visited her father at his residence in Long Acre, a place 'among all the bawdy-houses', and on another he was 'vexed' when she did not come home until 10 o'clock in the evening.[15] Pepys, however, may have been unusually protective, as there is evidence of elite women travelling freely around London, if not quite as freely as the men. When, in 1712, young aristocratic hooligans (the 'Mohocks') terror-ized the streets of the west end, a newspaper noted that the resulting panic led 'the Ladies . . . constantly [to] lock themselves up before eight; Punch's theatre is entirely deserted; and the Gentlemen of the October Club are forced to break up by twelve'.[16] While this suggests that the men stayed out later than the women (who were frequently targeted in the attacks), note that the women themselves chose not to go out: it was not their husbands who prevented them.

Over the course of this period, men of Pepys's standing may have adopted a more constricted range of travel, as the mercantile concerns of the City were increasingly differentiated from the more refined sociability of the gentry in the west end. The fictional main character of *The Tatler*, a magazine that helped create polite socia-bility, was Isaac Bickerstaffe. As Lawrence Klein has pointed out, although Bickerstaffe was 'an avid pedestrian', he walked primarily in the west end, not the City: 'in the Haymarket, on the Mall, at various spots within St. James Park'.[17] While some real-life gen-tlemen still moved about frequently between the City and Westmin-ster, others followed Bickerstaffe's lead and concentrated their activities in the west end. While a student at the Inns of Court, Dudley Ryder often visited coffee houses, taverns, meeting houses, shops, and friends in places ranging from Westminster Hall to Cornhill. The scientist Robert Hooke concentrated his activities within the City, where he was based at Gresham College, though his

---

[15] *Ibid.*, v, p. 50; vII, pp. 204–5, 240; vIII, p. 376.

[16] *The Medley*, no. 8 (24–28 March 1712). For the Mohocks, see Daniel Statt, 'The case of the Mohocks: rake violence in Augustan London', *Social History* 20 (1995), 179–99. For evidence of elite women travelling widely around London, see William Matthews (ed.), *The Diary of Dudley Ryder* (1939), *passim*.

[17] Lawrence Klein, 'Politeness and cultural reorientation in England, 1660–1715: the case of urbanity' (unpublished paper), pp. 29–30.

favourite coffee house, Garway's, was in Westminster. The Virginian plantation owner William Byrd, however, although constantly moving about like the other diarists, travelled far less widely during his extended visits to London between 1717 and 1719. He moved primarily around the west end, going to coffee houses, the theatre, parks and gardens, and visiting friends. Occasionally he did go 'into the City' to visit coffee houses, the Royal Exchange, and friends, but he very rarely visited any other parts of the metropolis.[18] None of these gentlemen visited the east end. A man of Pepys's status living fifty years later was unlikely to live even on its border, as Samuel did.

A more geographically restricted sociability among the gentry is also evident in the patterns of residence of the defendants for whom they acted as sureties.[19] Although gentlemen, more than many other men, often acted as sureties for people living outside their parish (thus suggesting a wide range of contacts), they were less likely than some to extend these contacts outside the general region of London in which they lived, which was of course most commonly the west end. Thus a gentleman living in St Giles in the Fields served as a surety for a coachman living in St James, or a gentleman living in St Clement Danes was surety for a widow in St Martin in the Fields, but in this sample from 1723 there were no cases of gentlemen in the west end serving as sureties for people living in the City or the east end. Unfortunately, since few women acted as sureties and few female defendants were identified by their parish of residence, it is not possible to use this source to compare men's social contacts with those of women. Nonetheless the somewhat more circumscribed gentlemen's mobility at the end of this period suggests that the men of this class were not significantly more geographically mobile than their female counterparts.

There is parallel evidence that tradesmen and merchants living in the City were unlikely to venture into Westminster. According to the

---

[18] Matthews, *Diary of Dudley Ryder*; Pascal Brioist, 'Hooke et Pepys: deux espaces-vécus de Londres du XVIIe siècle', in C. Petitfrère (ed.), *Images et Imaginaires de la Ville a l'Epoque Moderne* (Tours, 1998), pp. 19–23; Louis B. Wright and Marion Tinling (eds.), *William Byrd of Virginia. The London Diary (1717–21) and Other Writings* (New York, 1958).

[19] Sureties guaranteed the appearance of the defendant in court, by pledging to forfeit £10 or more if the defendant failed to turn up. Although they were not necessarily close acquaintances of the defendant, they needed to be sufficiently well known to them for them to be willing to assume a financial liability as a means of guaranteeing appearance in court: Shoemaker, *Prosecution and Punishment*, pp. 107–9. The following discussion is based on an analysis of the sureties on all 282 recognizances issued to attend the April 1723 Middlesex Sessions: LMA, MJ/SR/2402.

1728 edition of the pamphlet *A Trip Through London*, no matter how hard they try to emulate the gentry and nobility, City men in 'St James' cannot 'erase the impressions that a counter, a leather-apron, or a livery, has left upon a man's manners' – tradesmen, one is led to believe, were made to feel unwelcome in polite circles.[20] Nonetheless, there is evidence that the more prosperous of this class of men and women travelled widely around London, once again often by coach, and often separately. As Cesar de Saussure commented, London merchants 'sometimes' had two coaches, 'one for the master of the house and one for the mistress'.[21] For a variety of reasons, however, women of this class seem to have travelled more widely than the men. Because it was more acceptable (indeed prestigious) for middle-class wives to live genteelly than it was for their husbands (who had businesses to run), such women were less out of place in Westminster.[22] And whereas many businesses, run primarily by men, were still based at home, women's responsibility for organizing household consumption took them shopping, 'a time-consuming and labor-intensive' activity in this period. As Margaret Hunt has argued, 'despite the pervasive belief that women should stay close to the home . . . many middling women consumers may well have spent less time at home than their husbands did'.[23]

Recent research suggests that many middle-class women also engaged in trade, often in partnership with other women, running businesses as milliners, haberdashers, drapers, victuallers, and similar types of shopkeeping. This extended women's geographical mobility into wholesalers' warehouses, alehouses (where business transactions were negotiated), and gentlemen's houses (where some sales took place), and Hunt suggests that since women's trades involved more distributive activities than men's, such women 'may have been less tied to their homes than their husbands were'.[24] Nonetheless, women who ran their own businesses could be geogra-

20 *A Trip Through London: Containing Observations on Men and Things* (8th edn, 1728), p. 12.
21 Madame van Muyden (ed. and trans.), *A Foreign View of England in 1725–29. The Letters of Monsieur Cesar de Saussure to his Family* (1995), p. 135.
22 Daniel Defoe complained that both tradesmen and their wives had taken up genteel activities, but he was less concerned about the latter, whose activities were far less likely to undermine the family economy: *The Complete English Tradesman* (London, [1726], 1987), esp. chs. 9, 10, 21.
23 Margaret Hunt, 'Wife beating, domesticity, and women's independence in eighteenth-century London', *Gender and History* 4 (1992), 12.
24 Margaret Hunt, *The Middling Sort. Commerce, Gender, and the Family in England, 1680–1780* (1996), ch. 5, quote from p. 128.

phically constrained: Betty Martin, another mistress of Pepys, was a linendraper with a stall in Westminster Hall, and Pepys's contacts with her were almost entirely confined to a narrow circle of places in Westminster – unlike his contacts with Elizabeth Knepp. An actress and friend of Pepys, Knepp frequently travelled in London without her husband, and encountered Samuel (both on his own and with Elizabeth Pepys) in locations all over London, from Pepys's house and office near Tower Hill, to the New Exchange off the Strand, shops and places to eat in the City, the theatres in Westminster, and places on the urban periphery like Chelsea and Kensington.

While middle-class men, of course, did venture out of their home and neighbourhood to go to alehouses and coffee houses, conduct business, and shop, evidence from diaries and sureties suggests they did not travel as much or as far as their wives. Christopher Knepp, Elizabeth's husband and a horse dealer, only encountered Pepys in the City. Although Pepys's diary offers a limited window into Mr Knepp's movements, it is clear that Christopher's contacts and outside interests were much more limited than his wife's.[25] Similarly the diary of Peter Briggens, a Quaker merchant who lived in Bartholomew Close in the early eighteenth century, indicates that, with the exception of family trips to resorts on the urban periphery, his activities were largely confined to the coffee houses and businesses of the City.[26] Much the same could be said for the lawyer and book-collector Richard Smyth, whose activities have been analysed in Vanessa Harding's contribution to this volume.[27]

Because tradesmen and master craftsmen were likely to possess long leases and because they needed a stable location where customers could be certain of finding them, they tended to live for a long time in one place. Peter Earle's analysis of the London Consistory Court depositions for the first decade of the eighteenth century shows that, although there was considerable turnover among younger residents, 'the length of continuous residence of the older householders is quite striking, with over 40 percent of those in their forties and nearly half of those over fifty having spent at least fifteen years in the same parish'.[28] Even the emerging separation of

[25] Latham and Matthews, *Diary of Samuel Pepys*, *passim*.
[26] Eliot Howard, *The Eliot Papers* (Gloucester, 1894), II, pp. 32–67 and *passim*.
[27] See above, ch.4.
[28] Peter Earle, *The Making of the English Middle Class. Business, Society and Family Life in London, 1660–1730* (London, 1989), pp. 240–1.

home and work did not necessarily extend geographical horizons:
when John Fossey, a goldsmith of Wood Street, bought a second
house so he could live separately from his work, it was located on
nearby Lombard Street.[29] The overall impression that men of this
class did not travel extensively is confirmed by the sureties evidence.
Like gentlemen, tradesmen rarely acted as sureties for people who
lived outside the district of the metropolis in which they lived.

As Earle argues, these long periods of continuous residence
suggest that the middle class must have been well tied into local
networks. Such ties, however, were clearly gendered, affecting men
much more than women. It was middle-class *men* who participated in
parish government and frequented the largely homosocial environments of local alehouses and coffeehouses.[30] Although consistory
court depositions show that women spent considerable time (often
with their husbands) talking to their neighbours, we have seen that,
more than their husbands, women's shopping, business, and leisure
activities drew them further afield. There is some evidence, however,
that middle-class men were also stimulated to move more widely
during this period, owing to the increasing popularity of clubs and
voluntary societies. These were all men-only in this period, and, by
appealing to those with a specific interest or agenda (whether
religious, intellectual, economic, or political), they attracted men
from wide geographical areas.[31] Dudley Ryder, for example, travelled to different parts of London to hear non-conformist sermons and
attend the various clubs (based in taverns or coffee-houses) of which
he was a member. It is possible that the growing popularity of such
class-specific organizations served to undermine local neighbourhood ties in parts of London: there are more church-court depositions in the early eighteenth century than before where neighbours
testify that they knew each other only 'by sight'.[32] By the end of our
period, middle-class men may have been less rooted in their local

29 LMA, DL/C/273, D. Walker con. J. Walker.
30 For coffee houses and alehouses, see Shoemaker, 'Separate spheres?', pp. 282–3.
31 Peter Clark, *Sociability and Urbanity: Clubs and Societies in the Eighteenth-Century City* (H. J. Dyos
    Memorial Lecture, Victorian Studies Centre, University of Leicester, 1986); Jonathan Barry,
    'Bourgeois collectivism? Urban association and the middling sort', in J. Barry and
    C. Brooks (eds.), *The Middling Sort of People: Culture, Society and Politics in England, 1550–1800*
    (Basingstoke, 1994), pp. 84–112. For the gendered dimensions of clubs and societies, see
    Hunt, *Middling Sort*, ch. 4.
32 LMA, DL/C/262, Merchant con. Ingram; 272, Flowers con. Gregory; Karl Westhauser,
    'The power of conversation: the evolution of modern social relations in Augustan London',
    PhD thesis, Brown University (1994), p. 380.

neighbourhoods than they had been at the Restoration. This particularly applies to those men, such as excisemen and informers, who were expected to conform to new standards of objectivity and rationality while carrying out their duties all over the metropolis.[33]

That the Londons of women's experiences were often geographically more extensive than the Londons experienced by men is more evident in the movements of the lower classes. Because they did not own property, or have secure accommodation, lower-class men were more mobile than their middle-class counterparts, but they tended to remain within the same district of the metropolis. This is well illustrated by the recent histories of two witnesses to a church-court case in 1724: John Townshend, a fruiterer, and John Thompson alias Newman, a shoemaker, had both lived in a number of different places, but all the locations were within close proximity, indeed often within a stone's throw, of one another, centring on the parish of St Giles in the Fields. Townshend's description of his movements, as summarized by the clerk, is worth quoting in full:

for above 6 months he hath lodged in a cellar at a glovers over against the golden ball in Queen Street by the Seven Dials, and before then in a back room upon the ground floor at Mr Casy's a salesman at the gold ball in Monmouth Street about fifteen months, and before that in the cellar at Mr Fisher's a shopkeeper at the half moon in the same street for several years.

Newman's movements were only slightly more wide ranging: he had lived in Peter Street in Old Soho, Monmouth Street, and, as an apprentice, in Feather's Court in Holborn.[34] The fact that these movements were almost all within the same parish of residence is consistent with the fact that the thirteen tailors and shoemakers who acted as witnesses in a sample of consistory court cases all witnessed the insulting words in their parishes of residence.[35]

While these men worked in their own shops, other craftsmen travelled around London in the course of their work. This helps to

---

[33] For excisemen, see Miles Ogborn, *Spaces of Modernity: London's Geographies 1680–1780* (1998), ch. 5. For informers, see Shoemaker, *Prosecution and Punishment*, pp. 240–4. Work in progress by John Beattie indicates that over the course of this period respectable householders in the City of London increasingly refused to act as parish officers. Towards the end of the eighteenth century, middle-class Londoners were spread out over the metropolis, thereby encouraging geographical mobility if they were to attend the leisure activities they held in common: L. D. Schwarz, 'Social class and social geography: the middle classes in London at the end of the eighteenth century', *Social History* 7 (1982).

[34] LMA, DL/C/262, E. Johnson con. M. Larkin.

[35] LMA, DL/C/240, 243, 255, 262, 272, 638 (1679–81, 1689–93, 1715, 1724–5, 1738–40, 1749–52).

explain why, of those who acted as consistory court witnesses, two of
the four labourers, the woodmonger, the two painters, two of the
three sailors, a man who looked after horses, one of the two
bricklayers, the two joiners, and the chairman all happened to be
away from their parish of residence when they heard the insulting
words. Similarly, the labourers who were bound over to appear at
quarter sessions often chose sureties who lived in different parts of
the metropolis, and similarly labourers acted as sureties for defendants who lived in different parishes. But the geographical range of
the activities of these men was constricted: working men moved
about in searching for and carrying out their work, but these
movements rarely took them outside the immediate district of the
metropolis in which they lived. Thus, to take a typical example of
mobility within this class, John House, a labourer who lived in Old
Soho, became involved in a defamation case in Bloomsbury because
he had worked with a neighbour (a bricklayer) of the victim and the
two happened to be drinking in a Bloomsbury alehouse after work –
but this activity did not take him outside the west end.[36]

Once again, women who were involved in similar trades to men
had similarly restricted patterns of mobility. A married couple of
painter stainers who lived in Aldersgate became caught up in a
defamation case in a yard off Fleet Street because they happened to
be painting the victim's coach in front of the victim's home when the
insults were made. Once again the distance between the two places,
both of which were in the City, was not great.[37] The same point can
be made with respect to places of residence: Alice Newby, a widow
button maker of St Katherine by the Tower, testified to the
consistory court that she had lived in a number of different places in
the past year, but they were all within a small area around East
Smithfield, just like the concentration of residences of the St Giles
fruiterer and shoemaker discussed earlier.[38] On the other hand, the
wives of sailors, although typically based in the east end, could be
found further afield, presumably in search of employment. One
based in Clerkenwell witnessed an insult which took place in
Wapping, and two others, one from the Minories (near Tower Hill)
and the other from Stepney, witnessed an insult in Leighton, Essex.
The last, Anna Smith, told the court that she maintained herself by

[36] LMA, DL/C/272, S. Speed con. W. Sterry.
[37] LMA, DL/C/240, M. Richmond con. W. Holgate.
[38] LMA, DL/C/262, M. Rees con. E. May.

nursekeeping, washing, and scouring.[39] Such activities were frequent sources of employment for lower-class women, and in the course of their work they needed to travel widely.[40]

More substantial evidence of the geographical mobility of lower-class women comes from domestic service, an occupation they frequently followed during their late teens and early twenties.[41] Because they were hired on short-term contracts and demand for their services fluctuated, and also because they sought to maintain their independence, servants frequently served in a succession of short-term posts, often widely distributed over the metropolis. This was particularly true of female servants, who were more numerous than their male counterparts and typically served less prosperous masters, where employments were shorter and less secure. Mary Tipper, a 25-year-old servant, testified to the consistory court that she could 'not recollect the different places she hath lived for ten years past'.[42] There is plenty of evidence of similar mobility in the Chelsea settlement examinations: Catherine Price, the mother of a bastard child born in Chelsea in 1733, had previously been a cook in a house in Hanover Square, and subsequently, when out of a place, took up lodgings in St James.[43] Such places of residence were often separated by considerable distance, but they were of course not randomly distributed; servants had a habit of returning to places where they had previously found employment. Ann Miles, a servant who was only nineteen, reported to the consistory court that she had lived, in succession, in Paul's Wharf in the City, in Rosemary Lane just northeast of the Tower, in Mansfield Street, in Nightingale Lane again near the Tower, and then back to Paul's Wharf. She was currently living in nearby Lambeth Hill.[44]

As Patty Seleski has commented in her study of female servants in late eighteenth- and early nineteenth-century London, 'the frequent changes of service, with time spent in and out of place, might mean

---

[39] LMA, DL/C/255, A. Anderson con. Blew and Bolton, A. Marlow con. J. Bruce.

[40] P. Earle, 'The female labour market in London in the late seventeenth and early eighteenth centuries', *Economic History Review*, second series, 42 (August 1989), 339.

[41] *Ibid.*, pp. 343–4.

[42] LMA, DL/C/272, A. Flowers con. A. Gregory. See also P. Seleski, 'Women, work and cultural change in eighteenth- and early nineteenth-century London', in T. Harris (ed.), *Popular Culture in England, c.1500–1850* (Basingstoke, 1995), p. 149; D. A. Kent, 'Ubiquitous but invisible: female domestic servants in mid-eighteenth century London', *History Workshop Journal* 28 (1989), 120.

[43] Hitchcock and Black (eds.), *Settlement and Bastardy Examinations*, case 12.

[44] LMA, DL/C/262, M. Rees con. E. May.

that a servant knew people all over London, and that she was firmly embedded in [several different] local networks of working people'.[45] When in post, masters and mistresses sought to confine servants as much as possible to the daily drudgery of household work and limit their opportunities outside the house (except when accompanying their masters or mistresses), but Seleski argues that servants were able to subvert such controls, particularly when they ran errands and during their time off, and their social contacts were obviously facilitated by the fact that they had often previously lived in other parts of the city. She provides examples of servants walking in the fields, drinking tea, frequenting alehouses, and visiting family, often outside the neighbourhood of their employers. In an attempt to maintain some control over such geographically mobile women (of whom local knowledge was often minimal), register offices were set up in the 1750s to provide employers with lists of servants with good characters who were looking for work.[46]

In the course of carrying out their assigned duties, male servants probably ventured outside the home more often than their female counterparts, but usually they were in the company of their masters or mistresses. Tom Edwards travelled all over London with Samuel and/or Elizabeth Pepys. But masters attempted to limit the opportunities of male as well as female servants for independent travel, and Samuel Pepys could get quite angry when he felt Tom spent too long away from his house.[47] In any case, male servants changed jobs less often than their female counterparts, and the wider range of job opportunities for men meant they often left service earlier for jobs which did not involve such frequent geographical mobility. Whereas eight out of the twenty (40 per cent) female servants who acted as witnesses in a sample of defamation cases happened to be in a different parish than the one they resided in when they heard the insulting words, this applies to only two of the nine (22 per cent) male servants who acted as witnesses.[48] The men in the Chelsea settlement examinations who started their careers as servants reported subsequent employment as husbandmen, gardeners, and a labourer. In taking up these new posts they had not travelled far, coming as they

[45] Seleski, 'Women, work and cultural change', p. 152.
[46] *Ibid.*, pp. 152, 154; Ogborn, *Spaces of Modernity*, pp. 211–19.
[47] Latham and Matthews, *Diary of Samuel Pepys*, VII, p. 19; VIII, pp. 176, 202.
[48] In some of these cases the servant had changed positions (and thus residences) since the incident took place.

did to Chelsea from nearby Kensington, Richmond, and Battersea, all from the same region of London's western periphery.[49]

The poorest Londoners of both sexes needed to travel most, in search of employment, sources of poor relief, or new accommodation (since their lodgings could be as insecure as their jobs). Although poor men could be quite mobile (those who were had been pauper apprentices tended subsequently to move all over the metropolis),[50] women's lives were more insecure and consequently they moved around London even more. If a woman's husband died or abandoned her, a crucial source of support was lost and she was often forced to move. A widow at the age of twenty-four, Rachel Marlow told the consistory court that her recent residences were in Goodman's Fields in Whitechapel (where she was employed doing chores); Plaistow in West Ham (where she lived with a Gentlewoman); and near the church of St Christopher on Threadneedle Street (where she worked for a Notary Public).[51] Unmarried women who became pregnant were also extremely mobile, often testifying before the Justices of the Peace in Chelsea that they had become pregnant in one parish, and given birth in another, before coming to Chelsea where they were examined by the poor law authorities. Thus Elizabeth Simonds told the Chelsea justice in 1734 that she became pregnant in the parish of Kensington, and gave birth in the workhouse of St Margaret Westminster.[52] As this case suggests, in most of the Chelsea cases such women's movements inside the metropolis were confined to Westminster and the west end. Whether this was because the western suburbs were closest or because they offered the best prospects of employment (as servants) is impossible to say. In any case, single women and widows were more likely than married women to have connections with people in other parts of the metropolis, and this is reflected in the geographical distribution of their sureties.

In the public mind, single women were associated with illicit sex, and without accepting this stereotype it is of course true that many women did engage in sex for money at some point in their lives as a way of making ends meet. Owing to the contemporary disapproval of extra-marital sex, those who chose to engage in it were often

[49] Hitchcock and Black, *Settlement and Bastardy Examinations*, cases 23, 42, 49, 52, 58.
[50] See, for example, *ibid.*, case 60. Men who were poor and/or bound over for vagrancy offences like playing unlawful games were also more likely to have sureties from far away.
[51] LMA, DL/C/273, D. Walker con. J. Walker.
[52] Hitchcock and Black, *Settlement and Bastardy Examinations*, case 9. See also cases 12, 34, 38, 48.

forced to go outside their normal geographical haunts, not only to avoid recognition (and possible condemnation) but also to be certain of finding willing partners. As we have seen, in order to cover up his illicit liaisons Samuel Pepys travelled to places in and around the metropolis, such as parts of Drury Lane and the rural haunts of Lisson Green and Acton, where his wife did not go.[53] Yet Pepys may have been unusually secretive: since male sexual promiscuity was far less scandalous than women's, men tended to travel less far to find it. Randolph Trumbach suggests that men 'seem to have gone to whores in one of the bawdy house areas near to home' – and because there were several such districts, they did not need to travel far.[54] When Dudley Ryder sought a prostitute, he simply 'wandered about the streets till I found one to my mind' while on his way home.[55] The geographical mobility induced by illicit sex affected the lives of those who made their living in this way – the women – much more than their customers. Mistresses were regularly dumped by their patrons, prostitutes fell out with their bawds, bawds were forced to leave by neighbours or parish officers, streetwalkers were 'moved on' by constables and the watch: all were frequently forced to relocate. Mary Bowles, whose husband left her in the early 1740s when she was only twenty-two, tried to support herself by taking in plain work and going into service, but she ended up as a prostitute. First she was kept by a gentleman in a house on Lemon Street, Goodman's Fields in Whitechapel (an area full of brothels); later she moved to Thompson's Bagnio in Charing Cross. Such geographical mobility from east end to west end was rare in the records I have examined, and seems to have been encouraged by the fact that she was earning her living by prostitution.[56]

The answers to the questions posed at the start of this paper are thus varied and complicated. On the one hand, their immediate neighbourhood was very important to Londoners, as indicated by the numerous disputes over reputations which erupted between people living on the same street which were deemed of sufficient importance

[53] Latham and Matthews, *Diary of Samuel Pepys*, VII, p. 72. See also LMA, DL/C/273, D. Walker con. J. Walker.
[54] Trumbach, *Sex and the Gender Revolution*, I, p. 99.
[55] Matthews, *Diary of Dudley Ryder*, p. 331.
[56] LMA, DL/C/273, D. Walker con. J. Walker. For similar stories, see Trumbach, *Sex and the Gender Revolution*, I, pp. 131–2, 147, 166. See also Tony Henderson, *Disorderly Women in Eighteenth-Century London: Prostitution and Control in the Metropolis, 1730–1830* (1999), p. 123.

to be brought before the courts. On the other hand, Londoners of both sexes frequently moved outside their parish and neighbourhood to conduct business, find new accommodation, see friends and family, and participate in leisure activities. But on the whole, they did not move very far: in general, Londoners' movements were confined to the districts in which they lived, such as the west end, City, or east end. Judging by the evidence examined here, there was not a lot of movement across the metropolis, from east end to west end or Southwark to north London, except among the highest and lowest social classes. In this sense, there was not much metropolitan-wide identity revealed in Londoners' behaviour at this time, though this is not to say that such people did not necessarily identify with the metropolis as a whole. But each person's area of London was defined differently, and this depended on individual characteristics such as level of wealth and occupational demands as well as gender. Whereas servants were likely to find jobs all over the metropolis, and gentlemen and ladies travelled widely (but rarely to the east end), artisans and business people of both sexes tended to move in more limited circles. Miles Ogborn was thus correct to characterize eighteenth-century London as consisting of 'a variety of geographies'.[57]

For the most part we can only speculate on how these distinctive patterns of mobility were reflected in Londoners' perceptions of their city. But the diaries of elite Londoners such as Pepys, Ryder, and Byrd provide some intriguing hints. As more than one analyst has commented, Pepys was 'impervious' to his immediate surroundings – he fails to describe the street scenes he passed through so often, and his immediate neighbourhood apparently meant little to him, except during the unique circumstances of the Plague and the Great Fire. Instead, Pepys saw London through the lens of two preoccupations: his search for sexually available women, and, more consistently, his ambitions for social advancement. As John S. Pipkin noted, 'Pepys has a sharp eye . . . in picking out those "of quality" from the anonymous mass.' His London is geographically a relatively undifferentiated whole from which he selected those people with whom socializing would advance his interests.[58] Ryder and Byrd's

[57] Ogborn, *Spaces of Modernity*, p. 235.

[58] John S. Pipkin, 'Space and social order in Pepys's Diary', *Urban Geography* 11 (1990), 153–75, quote from 164; Brioist, 'Hooke et Pepys', p. 28. For Pepys's use of sociability for social advancement, see Karl E. Westhauser, 'Friendship and family in early modern England: the sociability of Adam Eyre and Samuel Pepys', *Journal of Social History* 27 (1994), 517–36.

Londons were similarly topographically vague, with little detail in their diaries of the streets (even, in Byrd's case, their names) and parishes through which they travelled. Although all three frequently travelled on foot, the propensity of elite Londoners (of both sexes) to travel by coach or chair may have encouraged their inattention to the details of local street life, but the real reason for the limited scope of their vision was their social preoccupations. As suggested earlier, middle-class male Londoners may have paid more attention to their local streets, neighbourhood, and parish, but it is likely that at the very bottom of the social scale the 'modern' beggars on the major thoroughfares, discussed by Tim Hitchcock in this volume, shared a similar lack of local identity with upper class Londoners.[59]

Unsurprisingly, given prevailing patterns of mobility, there is evidence in this period of an emerging vocabulary of regional difference within the metropolis. While there is little evidence of this in Pepys, Byrd always noted when he travelled from his west end home into 'the City', and also, more idiosyncratically, he denoted a small section of the west end (around Parliament and Whitehall) as 'Westminster', where he went to visit alehouses and testify at the House of Lords. This was a far smaller area than that actually encompassed by the City of Westminster, which in fact included most of the area covered in his daily rounds.[60] Similarly, Ryder used the term 'Westminster' to refer only to his visits to the Houses of Parliament.[61] This was the time when social distinctions between the west end and the City of London crystallized in gentry discourse into that between the polite 'Town' and the commercial 'City', a distinction which had important gender dimensions in that the mercantile 'City' was seen as essentially masculine, while the 'Town' was thought to be inhabited by gentlemen and women, with their refined, polite, and sociable lifestyles.[62] Perhaps it is the more sociable and feminine aspects of perceptions of the west end which explain why the area was not often labelled as 'Westminster', despite the fact most of the parishes west of the City of London fell within its jurisdiction as a city. As a place name, Westminster seems to have had primarily legal and political connotations and was therefore narrowly applied to the Houses of Parliament.

[59] See below, ch. 6.
[60] See, for example, Wright and Tinling, *William Byrd of Virginia*, pp. 53, 79, 217.
[61] Matthews, *Diary of Dudley Ryder*, pp. 58, 171, 180.
[62] Klein, 'Politeness and cultural reorientation in London'.

Beyond this basic distinction, the gendered dimensions of perceptions of London are far more difficult to document. Whether, for example, female inhabitants of the City actually perceived it as 'masculine' is unknown. There are, however, strong reasons to suggest that women of all social classes viewed London differently from their male counterparts. Whereas, in an effort to avoid being tainted by vice, upper-class women may have travelled somewhat less extensively than their husbands, those lower down the social scale had wider geographical horizons than men. We have seen this in particular in the shopping, trading and leisure habits of middle-class wives (in comparison to their stay-at-home businessmen husbands, with their ties to formal and informal local institutions), and in the extensive movements of female servants, deserted wives, and prostitutes all over London (in comparison to the more locally based movement of male labourers and craftsmen). This is important because it illustrates just how publicly visible women were in the metropolis, and how in some ways they were more knowledgeable about and more acquainted with London as a whole than their male counterparts. Female Londoners may have been more likely than men to adopt a metropolitan-wide idea of London, even if, like Pepys, their viewpoint was confined by their particular social aspirations and economic needs. This provides further evidence of the way in which urban life opened up new opportunities for women, and in doing so potentially undermined traditional expectations of gender roles. In another respect, it supports the notion that London women were the 'first modern individuals'.[63]

The experiences and attitudes of female Londoners thus flew in the face of prevailing expectations, embodied in the advice literature, that a woman's place was in the home, and this, together with the fact so many women in public were from the lower class, helps explain why so much of the literature about London at this time was so misogynist in its tendency to label women in public places as prostitutes or adulterers. For example, consider the series of pamphlets published in the early eighteenth century with titles like *A Trip*

---

[63] Ogborn, *Spaces of Modernity*, pp. 73–4; Nancy Armstrong, *Desire and Domestic Fiction. A Political History of the Novel* (Oxford, 1987), p. 8. By contrast, women in medieval towns faced far greater constraints on their geographical mobility: Barbara A. Hanawalt, 'At the margins of women's space in medieval Europe' in her *'Of Good and Ill Repute': Gender and Social Control in Medieval England* (Oxford, 1998), pp. 81–4. Gowing suggests that women's sense of space in early modern London was 'fairly circumscribed': Gowing, 'The freedom of the streets'.

Through London: Containing Observations on Men and Things (1728) or *A Trip Through the Town, Containing Observations on the Humours and Manners of the Age* (4th edn, 1735), which sought to instruct newcomers in the ways of the town and to entertain resident Londoners with accounts of their foibles. These pamphlets (of which there were many similar titles) document, and implicitly or explicitly censure, women's widespread presence in London public life. As *A Trip Through London* of 1728 put it, 'to make feasts, and sit at the upper end of the table, seems to have been the utmost ambition of our great-grandmothers; they said their prayers in their closets, and seldom went to churches and playhouses'. Now, they 'expose their bosoms', insist on pin money, and go out on the town; in short, 'woman . . . now triumphs over her master man'.[64] The response to this new female public presence was to describe women encountered in public places, whether in parks, public gardens, theatres, coffee houses, alehouses, or simply on the streets, in terms of sexual licence: women in public are labelled as whores. To be a 'public woman' was to be a whore. For example, the pamphlet *Hell Upon Earth: Or the Town in an Uproar* (1729), which purported to give an hour-by-hour account of life on the streets of London, described the pedestrians on the 'principal streets' at eight o'clock in the evening in terms of the following groups: 'whores, shoemakers, butchers, joiners, and all sorts of handicraft tradesmen'. The only women the author of this pamphlet could see were whores – all others were invisible to him.[65] This attitude is evident in Ryder's account of his visit to the music and dancing house at Lambeth Wells, where he complained that 'the women seemed to be all whores and of the meanest sort, not one dressed like a gentlewoman', despite the fact 'the men that were there . . . seemed to be men of fashion'.[66]

Thus women in public, who were quite common in London, were condemned using the oldest insult in the book. Although the association of women's spatial freedom with sexual licence was nothing new,[67] the repetition of such stereotypes in eighteenth-century descriptions of London's streets can be interpreted as a reaction against women's very visible public presence. Of course such portrayals did not keep women off London's streets, though this

---

[64] *A Trip Through London*, pp. 17–20.
[65] *Hell Upon Earth: Or the Town in an Uproar* (8th edn, 1729), p. 10.
[66] Matthews, *Diary of Dudley Ryder*, p. 57.
[67] Gowing, 'The freedom of the streets'.

suspicion that every woman in public could well be a whore must in some ways have served to limit women's geographical freedom. To avoid being accosted by lewd men, or harassed by other prostitutes trying to protect their 'beat', or arrested by reforming constables or informers, women, especially single women, needed to dress respectably and avoid certain streets, especially at night.[68] But we should not exaggerate the extent to which these stereotypes actually constrained women's activities. It is striking that neither the presence of prostitutes in Drury Lane – a street where Samuel Pepys once 'took two or three wanton turns' – nor Pepys's own concerns about her reputation kept Elizabeth Pepys from attending theatre performances on the same street without him, though usually she went in the afternoon.[69] This is a good example of how the same physical spaces could be experienced and perceived differently by Londoners, depending in part on the time of day.

In sum, just as elite men's language of description of London often failed to recognize the vast, largely working-class districts of the east end, it also failed to account for the many dimensions of women's metropolitan-wide activities in London, the details of which are documented in diaries and judicial records. Paradoxically, perhaps it is precisely because many women in their day-to-day lives tended to be *more* metropolitan than men that published portrayals of women in the metropolis tended to minimize or censure their activities. It is to be regretted that so few first-person female accounts of the metropolis have survived to provide a different perspective.

[68] Robert B. Shoemaker, *Gender in English Society, 1650–1850: The Emergence of Separate Spheres?* (1998), pp. 272–3; Paul Griffiths, 'Meanings of nightwalking in early modern England', *The Seventeenth Century* 13 (1998).
[69] Latham and Matthews, *Diary of Samuel Pepys*, V, p. 246; VII, p. 72; IX, pp. 14, 246.

CHAPTER 6

The publicity of poverty in early eighteenth-century London

Tim Hitchcock

It is a commonplace familiar from the writings of almost all eighteenth-century commentators that the streets of London were crowded with beggars. In the 1690s the Grand Jury found 'their being suffered to begg in great numbers up & downe the streets of this city';[1] while a few years later Misson was able to affirm that the 'Town is Crowded with beggars'.[2] The irritation that these suppliants caused to the wealthier inhabitants of London is also clear. At mid-century Henry Fielding could complain:

there is not a street which does not swarm all day with beggars and all night with thieves. Stop your coach at what shop you will, however expeditious the tradesman is to attend you, a beggar is commonly beforehand with him; and if you should not directly face his door, the tradesman must often turn his head while you are talking to him, or the same beggar or some other thief will pay a visit to his shop.[3]

It was largely this perception of a ubiquitous social problem that drove the process of social policy reform and innovation that characterized the first half of the eighteenth century and which resulted in the passing of several new Vagrancy Acts, and the development of a whole panoply of institutions, from hospitals to workhouses.[4] But, while the story of the response to begging and

I would like to take this opportunity to thank John Black, Stuart Hogarth, Robert Shoemaker and Sonia Constantinou for their help and advice with this chapter.

[1] Quoted in Stephen Macfarlane, 'Social policy and the poor in the later seventeenth century', in A. L. Beier and Roger Finlay (eds.), *London, 1500–1700: The Making of the Metropolis* (1986), p. 260.

[2] *M. Misson's Memoirs and Observations in his Travels over England*, trans. Mr. Ozell (1719), p. 221.

[3] Henry Fielding, *A Proposal for Making an Effectual Provision for the Poor* (1753), p. 10.

[4] New vagrancy acts were passed in 1714, 1740, and 1744, superseding Elizabethan and early Stuart legislation. See 'For Reducing the Laws relating to Rogues . . . and Vagrants into one Act . . .' (13 Anne c.26); 'For amending and enforcing the Laws relating to Rogues, Vagabonds and other idle and disorderly Persons . . .' (13 Geo. II c.24); and 'To amend and make more effectual the Laws relating to Rogues, Vagabonds . . .' (17 Geo. II c.5). The

disorder has attracted generations of historians, the impressions and reactions of elite commentators and social policy reformers represent only half the story.[5] The other half is found in the lives and strategies of the poor themselves. This chapter will examine the depiction and reality of poverty in early eighteenth-century London from the perspective of the lonely beggar and street urchin who plied their trades on the margins of metropolitan society.

In some respects the beggars of eighteenth-century London seem remarkably timeless. Women with children soliciting alms are again a common sight; while the sellers of the *Big Issue* bear a marked resemblance to the ballad sellers so frequently depicted in early modern prints. And while the hungry and the homeless are less frequently missing limbs, or infested with vermin, than were their eighteenth-century counterparts, and while a cardboard sign has replaced a cry in this more literate age, the parallel is nonetheless self-evident.[6] Squeegee merchants have replaced link-boys and shoe-blacks, but their function in the urban environment is frighteningly unchanged.

We should not, however, fall victim to the kind of ahistorical observation that, not only are the poor always with us, but that they are always the same. Despite their modern and in all probability medieval and sixteenth-century counterparts, the beggars of eighteenth-century London had their own culture and perspective and, as important, a specific and complex relationship with authority and social policy. They were not the passive objects of social policy reform that institutional historians have sometimes painted them, but were instead active participants in the rituals and rites of exchange, of which the elite formed only one part.[7] More than this,

Middlesex Bench and London Common Council also regularly revised their policy on vagrancy and begging in this period.

[5] The literature on the social policy of this period is extensive. Some of the best recent literature includes Donna Andrew, *Philanthropy and Police: London Charity in the Eighteenth Century* (Princeton, 1989); Hugh Cunningham and Joanna Innes (eds.), *Charity, Philanthropy and Reform From the 1690s to 1850* (1998); Norma Landau, *The Justices of the Peace, 1679–1760* (Berkeley, 1984); Lynn Hollen Lees, *The Solidarities of Strangers: The English Poor Laws and the People, 1700–1948* (Cambridge, 1998); Paul Slack, *From Reformation to Improvement: Public Welfare in Early Modern England* (Oxford, 1999).

[6] The use of signs as a part of the beggar's kit first emerged in the latter half of the eighteenth century, and was primarily restricted to disabled servicemen.

[7] For two recent explorations of the nature of this relationship see M. J. D. Roberts, 'Reshaping the gift relationship: The London Mendicity Society and the suppression of begging in England 1818–1869', *International Review of Social History* 36 (1991), 201–31; and Deborah Valenze, 'Charity, custom and humanity: changing attitudes towards the poor in

they made use of the built environment in ways which were peculiar to their occupations, and responded to the changing fabric of London in ways that both subverted the intentions of architects and transformed the meaning of the spaces they occupied.

There were essentially three kinds of beggars on the streets of eighteenth-century London. They can be characterized as the 'stationary public beggar'; the 'itinerant domestic beggar' and the 'beggarly self-employed'. These were not, of course, clear divisions. Many people practised all three forms of begging, depending on the time of year and personal circumstances. Age, physical condition, the day of the week, or the ability to raise a penny or two in capital, could from day to day or month to month change the strategy adopted. It was even possible that a change of gender would impact on how one chose to beg. Strype noted a 1708 example of 'a man drest in woman's cloaths, begging and counterfeiting himself lame'.[8] Each of these three forms of begging had their own techniques, and their own place within the perceptions of elite commentators. More than this, the actions of each responded and contributed to the transformation of urban social policy which characterized the late seventeenth and early eighteenth centuries. By describing a few of the techniques and behaviours which were practised by the men and women and children who begged on the streets of London this chapter will suggest some of ways in which these peculiarly public signs of poverty contributed to the creation of a new regime of urban social policy.

The most important of these three categories of the public poor was the 'stationary public beggar'. Under this rubric can be placed all those men and women (frequently with small children) who chose a pitch and solicited alms from the passing crowds. This practice comprised the most public form of urban begging and was deeply irritating to the middling sort and the elite.

Joseph Price, a common beggar, said he chose to beg at the 'corners of streets', because he could be assured of finding large numbers of people, and because he could employ himself as a sweeper.[9] The author of *A Trip Through Town* was accosted in the

---

eighteenth-century England', in Jane Garnett and Colin Matthew (eds.), *Revival and Religion Since 1700: Essays for John Walsh* (1993).

[8] Strype, *Survey*, 1.197.
[9] Quoted in Peter Earle, *A City Full of People: Men and Women of London, 1650* (1994), p. 232.

Strand and in Covent Garden.[10] Lincoln's Inn Fields was a particularly noteworthy location in which to beg. Thomas Brown suggested that beggars had already begun to take up their positions in Lincoln's Inn by seven in the morning,[11] while Steele in *The Spectator* noted a beggar he dubbed 'Scarecrow' as being a regular inhabitant of the Fields.[12] John Gay warned that urban pedestrians should beware of crossing Lincoln's Inn Fields at night for fear they would be knocked down with the crutches of beggars who had spent the day soliciting charity.[13] The Royal Exchange was similarly full of 'Mumpers, the halt, the blind, the lame, your venders of trash, apples, plumbs, your raggamuffins, rakeshames, and wenches [who] have justled the greater number of . . . [merchants] out of the place.'[14] Likewise, John Sharp, one of the City of London's most active vagrant catchers regularly patrolled London Bridge in search of beggars.[15] Beyond these locations, beggars could be found in the Haymarket, Temple-bar, Smithfield, and the city gates.[16] They could be found at both Mew's Gate[17] and Warwick Street[18] in Charing Cross, at St Paul's[19] and on Tower Hill,[20] in Grays Inn's Walk,[21] at Temple Stairs,[22] and Westminster Hall.[23] In other words, they could

[10] *A Trip Through Town. Containing Observations on the Humours and Manners of the Age* (4th edn, 1735), p. 11.

[11] Thomas Brown, *The Works of Thomas Brown, Serious and Comical, In Prose and Verse in four volumes* (2nd edn, 1720), I, p. 171.

[12] *The Spectator*, no. 6.

[13] John Gay, *Trivia: Or, The Art of Walking the Streets of London* (1716) in Vinton A. Dearing (ed.), *John Gay: Poetry and Prose* (1974), p.164, Book III, lines 133–8.

[14] *The Spectator*, no. 509.

[15] See for example the examinations of Thomas Ossier, 3 May 1738, Abraham Cartwright, 31 March 1738 and 3 May 1738, and Mary Johnson, 19 September 1738, all apprehended by Sharp on London Bridge: CLRO, 'Vagrant Books, together with 5 loose pages and a bill of mortality, 1738–1742', Misc. MS 322.5.

[16] *Low-Life: Or One Half of the World, Knows Not How the Other Half Live* (2nd edn, 1749), p. 97.

[17] See [Isaac Bickerstaff], *The Life, Strange Voyages and Uncommon Adventures of Ambrose Gwinett. Formerly Known to the Public as the Lame Beggar: Who for a Long Time Swept the Way at the Mew's Gate, Charing Cross* (4th edn, c. 1770).

[18] *The Spectator*, no. 454.

[19] *Pastorals, Choice Fables and Tales, with other Occasional Poems . . . To which is added The Adventures of a Farthing, Or, the Humours of Low-life* (1785), p. 61.

[20] [Ned Ward], *The London Spy* (Folio Society edition, Chatham, 1955), pp. 231–2.

[21] *The Spectator*, no. 269.

[22] See Abraham Mondius, 'A Frost Fair on the Thames at Temple Stairs', c.1684. Reproduced in Mireille Galinou and John Hayes, *London in Paint: Oil Paintings in the Collection at the Museum of London* (1996), pp. 58–9.

[23] An early eighteenth-century image of Westminster Hall with a beggar in the foreground is reproduced without attribution in [Ward], *The London Spy* between pages 152 and 153.

be found in most of the 'public' streets and major thoroughfares of the centre of the capital.

From the perspective of the beggar who solicited alms from unknown pedestrians and from the occupants of coaches as they alighted, the sites listed above provided the perfect venues at which to beg. All of them were locations where the pedestrian traffic was likely to be dense, and to contain a reasonable variety of social classes. Before the Embankment changed the shape of pedestrian London, the Royal Exchange, St Paul's, Temple Bar, The Strand and Covent Garden, and finally Charing Cross formed a natural corridor which drew pedestrians from east to west and from west to east, and was part of the traditional processional route which had helped to define ritual London for centuries. Beggars soliciting farthings and half-pence on these streets knew that they would have a reasonable selection of consciences to work upon. At the same time Lincoln's Inn Fields, perhaps the most frequently mentioned site for begging, was conveniently located on the walking route between the prosperous suburbs of the north-west of town and the courts. These were not the backwaters of St Giles's or St Martin's, these were not the areas in which the poor actually lived; instead they were positions from which a 'stationary public beggar' could make a living.

Beyond your choice of thoroughfare, you also had to be in the right place on the street. On a relatively narrow pavement you were unlikely to be very successful if you forced pedestrians to 'give up the wall'.[24] At the same time a pitch sited in a doorway simply encouraged the householder to move you on. What was needed was that perfect compromise, a location which allowed you to force yourself on the limited charity of passers-by and yet avoided attracting too much negative attention. For the great number of people missing legs, or paralysed, or suffering from serious epilepsy, the choice of a pitch was particularly difficult. For someone like Henry Buxton, a 26-year-old beggar from Lincolnshire, this question was particularly fraught. Having broken his back and injured his bowels in a violent fall and been discharged from St Thomas's Hospital as incurable, he was in no condition to do more than sit

---

[24] For a comprehensive and enjoyable discussion of eighteenth-century street etiquette see P. Corfield, 'Walking the city streets: the urban odyssey in eighteenth-century England', *Journal of Urban History* 16 (1990), 132–74.

passively at the roadside.[25] For him a truss of straw brought in the morning and set down by a post on the street away from the pavement, or just around the corner from a shop and up against a wall, formed a more useful pitch.[26] Alternatively, in places like Covent Garden where the way was wide enough to avoid being run over, beggars set up in the road itself, next to the arches.[27] And, according to John Gay, in 'the publick square[s] . . . all besides the rail, rang'd beggars lie'.[28] Of course, many places were taken by shoe-blacks and ballad sellers, so that those unable to stand had to claim their pitch very early in the morning.

As important as the ability to attract attention was the ability to avoid the wrong sort. The choice of pitch and of street was in part determined by the level of policing, which in turn was influenced by the sense of ownership and responsibility that individual house-holders felt for these particular sites within the townscape. In a society in which hue and cry and personal prosecution formed the backbone of the policing system, it is little wonder that public locations tended to fall through the net.[29] Although there was a system of officers paid to apprehend beggars, their effectiveness is open to doubt.[30] During one of the few periods for which we have complete figures, only about ten people a month were apprehended by these men in the whole of the City of London.[31] Also, throughout our period private prosecutions of vagrants and beggars are extremely uncommon. Of a sample of 42 commitments for loose, idle, and disorderly behaviour to the Westminster house of correction for which the prosecutor is known, 32 prosecutions were instigated by

[25] See Henry Buxton's examination dated 12 June 1738: CLRO, 'Vagrant Books, 1738–1742', Misc. MS 322.5.

[26] For references to the truss of straw beggars sat on, see *A View of London and Westminster: Or the Town Spy, &c.* (1728), Part I, p. 42 and *Low-Life*, p. 32.

[27] A beggar is depicted in this position in Samuel Scott's 'Covent Garden Piazza and Market' *c.*1749–58, reproduced in Galinou and Hayes, *London in Paint*, p. 122.

[28] Gay, *Trivia*, p. 156, Book II, lines 461–2.

[29] For a comprehensive discussion of the policing of petty crime in the capital see Robert B. Shoemaker, *Prosecution and Punishment: Petty Crime and the Law in London and Rural Middlesex, c.1660–1725* (Cambridge, 1991) and for a recent account of the development of the Night Watch see Elaine Reynolds, *Before the Bobbies: The Night Watch and Police Reform in Metropolitan London, 1720–1830* (1998).

[30] For a more positive assessment of the impact of the system of policing vagrancy in the period see Nicholas Rogers, 'Policing the poor in eighteenth-century London: the vagrancy laws and their administration', *Histoire sociale-Social History*, 24, no. 47 (May 1991), 127–47.

[31] The Lord Mayor's vagrancy records for the period 1738 to 1742 are incomplete, but do cover fifteen full months. In total only 153 individuals were examined in this period: CLRO, 'Vagrant Books, 1738–1742', Misc. MS 322.5.

constables, and 4 of the remainder by JPs, overseers, and officers. Only 6 prosecutions were identifiably the result of the activity of private citizens. While this is a pattern that can be found both before and after our period, it does suggest that the policing of vagrancy and by extension begging was particularly inefficient.[32] More than this, it suggests that the public spaces which beggars occupied were not substantially policed by the general populace. The very nature of a busy thoroughfare encouraged an attitude towards the street which made begging easier. In a very real sense, because the street was everyone's business, it was no-one's business. And as long as the poor avoided shop fronts, or the doorways of private houses; as long as they remained in obviously 'public' spaces, they were relatively unlikely to be arrested by private citizens, and were in only a small danger of being picked up by the constables.

While choosing your pitch was of supreme importance, there was much more to the process of soliciting alms than simply being in the right spot. Once you had set up your straw truss and you had settled yourself down for the day, having dragged yourself, or hobbled on crutches from the outskirts of town, or the squat or 'bulk' in which you had spent the night,[33] you then had to adopt the right attitude and language. If you had one, an upraised right hand and suppli-cating cry were now required.[34] Elite commentators waxed eloquent on the tone of voice used. The author of the 1735 *Trip Through Town*, described the process as follows:

a beggar asks you to exert [your pity] . . . for Jesus Christ's sake . . . He represents to your view the worst side of his ailments and bodily infirmities; in chosen words he gives an epitome of his calamities, real or fictitious; and while he seems to pray to God, that he will open your heart, he is actually

---

[32] These statistics are derived from the database of 'Westminster House of Correction' records included in Tim Hitchcock and Robert Shoemaker, *Economic Growth and Social Change in the Eighteenth-Century English Town* (TLTP, History Courseware Consortium) CDRom, ver.1.0, Glasgow, 1998).

[33] References to sleeping in abandoned houses and in the bulks are common. The anonymous author of one 1749 pamphlet suggested: 'Houses which are left open, and are running to ruin [are] filled with beggars . . . [while] Black-guards . . . are sleeping in the bulks of houses.' See *Low-Life*, p. 5. Mary Saxby, on first running away from home also slept under a 'bulk' in order to avoid the attentions of the watch. See [Mary Saxby], *Memoirs of a Female Vagrant Written by Herself* (1806), p. 6.

[34] For examples of beggars depicted in this attitude see Hogarth's 'The Morning', from his series 'Four Times of the Day' (1738). This image is reproduced in David Bindman, *Hogarth and His Times: Serious Comedy* (1997), p. 98. See also the early eighteenth-century image of Westminster Hall with a beggar in the foreground reproduced without attribution in [Ward], *London Spy* between pages 152 and 153.

at work upon your ears; the greatest profligate of them flies to religion for aid, and assists his cant with a doleful tone and a study'd dismality of gestures: But he trusts not to one passion only, he flatters your pride, with titles and names of honour and distinction, your avarice he sooths with often repeating to you the smallness of the gift he sues for and conditional promises of future returns, with an interest extraordinary beyond the statute of usury, tho' out of the reach of it. People not used to great cities, being thus attached on all sides are commonly forc'd to yield and cannot help giving something tho' they can hardly spare it themselves.[35]

Stephen Badhem, a common beggar hanged in 1740, 'always used a great many scripture words with great success';[36] while according to another author, a sedentary beggar 'tunes his voice [and] raises his pipe to a pity-drawing pitch, and a shower of copper falls into his lap'.[37]

Not all 'stationary public beggars' were immobile. Many women with small children begged from a single pitch, but were at the same time more than capable of following a likely individual down the street. If you were able to spend a long day standing, finding a good pitch was much easier. It mattered much less if you were moved on and it was a simple matter to keep out of the way of more aggressive users of the pavement. Similarly, if you had a baby in your arms you could not very well be accused of prostitution. But your approach had to be tuned to your circumstances – for an able-bodied woman like Mary Maremore, who went out begging with her two children, four-year-old Isaac and two-year-old Charles, in early June 1742, the apparently common (or at least commonly complained of) strategy of exposing amputated stumps and putrefying wounds was inappropriate.[38] And while many commentators believed that children could be rented out for four pence a day either from parish nurses, or, more fancifully, a baby rental agency in St Giles,[39] women necessarily appealed when begging to 'the usual rhetorick of a sick . . . husband at home, [and] three or four helpless little children all starving with cold and hunger', and rewarded any benefaction with 'blessings and acclamations'.[40] Being able to move, even if encum-

[35] *Trip Through Town*, pp. 11–12.
[36] Quoted in Earle, *A City Full of People*, p. 191.
[37] *View of London and Westminster*, Part I, p. 42.
[38] See the examination of Mary Maremore, 5 June 1742: CLRO, 'Vagrant Books, 1738–1742'. Misc. MS 322.5.
[39] See for example *The Tatler*, no. 25; and for the baby rental agency, *Trip Through Town*, p. 11.
[40] *The Spectator*, no. 232.

bered with children, meant that people coming out of coaches could
be more easily approached, while the ebb and flow of the city crowd
could be allowed to dictate which squares and corners should be
targeted at particular times of day.

Stationary public beggars engendered a huge degree of distrust
and fear. The literature is full of accounts of their tricks and
perfidy.[41] Their wounds were supposedly fake, and their stories the
imaginative inventions of work-shy charlatans. And while there was
clearly a hierarchy of beggars, which resulted in women in particular
becoming disproportionately subject to the system of removal under
the vagrancy laws, and whereby obviously disabled beggars were
more likely to establish themselves as regular members of their
community, there was a clear antipathy to all forms of this sort of
public begging. But not all supplicants were viewed in this entirely
negative light. There were two other sorts of beggars whose activities
shaded into, but were distinct from, that of the roadside supplicant.
The first of these was the 'itinerant domestic beggar' who went from
door to door asking relief; and the second, the 'beggarly self-
employed' – the army of link-boys, shoe-blacks, and ballad sellers
who filled London's streets.

Misson complained that in London: 'Among the customs of those
gentlemen [beggars] it is one with them to knock at peoples' doors as
boldly as if they were the masters of the house, when they beg alms',
and went on to suggest that they really should follow the French
custom of 'never giving above one knock and that a soft one, at the
doors of a superior'.[42] Despite the assertiveness that this kind of
begging required, it appears to have been viewed with a large of
degree of tolerance. Perhaps the most powerful single image
reflecting social attitudes to itinerant domestic begging can be found
in Hogarth's 'The Industrious Apprentice out of his Time &
Married to his Master's Daughter'. In this print the weaver's house
in the middle of the city is being serenaded by the musicians who
traditionally marked London weddings. The significant figure
however is the poor woman at the door to the house, on her knees,

---

[41] See for example, *The Spectator*, no. 430; 'I looked out of my window the other morning
earlier than ordinary and saw a blind beggar an hour before the passage he stands in is
frequented, with a needle and thread thriftily mending his stockings: My astonishment was
still greater when I beheld a lame fellow whose legs were too big to walk within an hour
after, bring him a pot of ale.'

[42] *Misson's Memoirs*, p. 221.

with a baby strapped to her back, accepting broken food from a servant into her apron. As this is an image of the virtuous behaviour of the industrious apprentice, her presence reflects an elision between relief in kind dispensed on the doorstep and neighbourly concern. It is an appeal to an older ideal of hospitality.

In 1677 St Martin's decided to allow paupers 'to aske and receive broken meate only and not to beg of coaches or of people going in the streets, and the hours of asking at doores allowed are from one to foure in the afternoon and noe longer, and none are to aske at doores without a badge', reflecting again a real division between this kind of domestic begging and its more public forms.[43]

Most accounts of itinerant domestic begging are set in a more rural context. The autobiography of Bampfylde Carew, the king of the beggars, for instance, while of uncertain authorship, gives numerous examples of the process of begging from door to door in southwest England.[44] But it is much more difficult to find any urban, or specifically London, examples. A related activity which was definitely common in town was begging at the church door. As with going from door to door, this was a traditional form of begging that had been common throughout the Christian history of London, and was more or less acceptable at different periods. In the seventeenth century, for instance, distributing alms to the poor in churchyards on the occasion of a funeral was a common practice. In the eighteenth century the tolerance for this kind of supplication, while greater than for the 'stationary public beggar', was showing real signs of decline. Several commentators suggested that the church door was simply a favoured pitch and in no way reflected a less professional approach to the practice of begging. One writer even suggested that 'small bribes [were] bestowed on beadles of parishes by common beggars, for liberty to ask money at the church doors when the sermon is over'.[45]

The 'beggarly self-employed' is the final group of people I want to discuss briefly. Any account of the streets of London would be

---

[43] Quoted in Jeremy Boulton, 'Going on the parish: the parish pension and its meaning in the London suburbs, 1640–1724', in Tim Hitchcock, Peter King, and Pamela Sharpe (eds.), *Chronicling Poverty: The Voices and Strategies of the English Poor, 1640–1840* (1997), p. 33.

[44] See for example *An Apology for the Life of Bampfylde-Moore Carew (Son of the Rev. Mr. Carew of Bickley.) Commonly Known through the West of England by the Title of King of the Beggars and Dog Merchant General* (1749), p. 88.

[45] *Low-Life*, p. 54.

incomplete without some acknowledgement of the sheer numbers of street vendors who populated the public spaces. At the bottom end of the economic spectrum, however, it is important to note that these itinerant salespeople were little more than beggars, and were frequently considered as such by the wealthier users of the street. Gay devotes some sixty lines of *Trivia* to an account of how a beggar child might be set up as a shoe-black. Starting off as a 'beggar brat' who 'know all the pray'rs and whines to touch the heart', this young boy is given 'the strong bristles of the mighty boar', 'a tripod . . . to raise the dirty foot, and ease his toil', and 'a vase with fetid oil', before being sent off to his post: 'where branching streets from Charing Cross divide; / his treble voice resounds along the Meuse, / and White-hall echoes – Clean your honour's shoes.'[46] Link-boys, too, were considered little more than beggars. One author described how 'Link boys who have been asking charity all the preceding day, and have just money sufficient to buy a torch, take their stands at Temple-bar, London-bridge, Lincoln's Inn Fields, Smithfield and the City Gates, and other open publick places.'[47] Gay, again, warned his readers about the dangers of trusting a link-boy: 'Though thou are tempted by the link-man's call, / yet trust him not along the lonely wall.'[48]

Ballad singers, likewise, inhabited that grey area between legitimate salespeople and common public beggars, or possibly prostitutes. Most ballad singers appear to have been women, although the occasional blind man is also reported.[49] Frequently, they were depicted as having young children with them, as in Hogarth's 'The Enraged Musician' of 1741, and to be singing ballads of seduction and female ruin. Hogarth's ballad singer is selling a tune entitled 'The Ladies Fall'. Our one legitimate account of the life of an itinerant eighteenth-century ballad singer suggests that this connection to both begging and prostitution reflects the reality of many people's lives. In her autobiography Mary Saxby recalls having made her living as a ballad singer in the late 1740s and early 1750s. She was frequently accosted by men who assumed she was sexually

---

[46] Gay, *Trivia*, pp. 147–9, Book II, lines 141, 143, 158, 160, 161, 162, 214–16.
[47] *Low-Life*, p. 97.
[48] Gay, *Trivia*, p. 164, Book III, lines 139–40.
[49] Ned Ward describes 'a blind ballad-singer, who was mournfully setting forth the wonderful usefulness of a godly broadside proper to be stuck up in all righteous and sober families'. See [Ward], *The London Spy*, p. 77.

available and on at least one occasion she was the object of an attempted gang rape. She also interspersed her ballad singing and selling with begging at doors and on the streets.[50]

A torch, a tripod and rag, a handful of ballads, a flute, a few broken pieces of food; these were all the equipment the beggarly self-employed needed to inhabit the streets of London. By equipping themselves in this way beggars could more easily avoid the unwanted attentions of the constable and smooth the initial approach to a reluctant contributor. Whether in retrospect one wishes to lump these people with common public beggars is problematic, but it is clear that eighteenth-century commentators frequently did so. The repeated orders of the Middlesex Quarter Sessions for the suppression of the vendors of 'oysters, oranges, decayed cheese, apples, nuts, ginger bread & other wares' which were sold from wheelbarrows, supposedly as an enticement to gambling for 'unwary passengers & children', reflect elite ambivalence to street hawkers in general.[51] And while many men and women made use of the light provided by link-boys and the services of shoe-blacks, it is also clear that the elite did not trust the providers of these services.

In one way or another, the members of each of these groups were part of a larger category: the public poor. These were individuals whose main impact on the historical record was restricted to their presence in the public sphere. The halt and lame who peopled the streets of London were never placed in the context of a family, or of a household, or of a community, and to this extent appear to us as uniquely 'modern' individuals. They were targeting people who were unknown to them and the descriptions of their behaviour which we possess indicate they worked outside of the patriarchal household. And while the fanciful literature concerned with gypsies and the king of the beggars which the eighteenth century inherited from the sixteenth continued to be published, no-one suggested that the public beggars of London formed an organized sub-culture. Ned Ward did include a 'Beggars' Club' in his *History of the London Club*, but it is perhaps the least credible of any of his creations. He ridiculously suggests that in their spare time beggars went about trying to fool each other by acting out their individual public roles:

---

[50] [Saxby], *Memoirs of a Female Vagrant*, pp. 7–9, 11.
[51] See 'Orders of Sessions against wheelbarrows, 1707': LMA, Acc 1268/uncat.

'they all act their dissembling parts as much to the life as if they were really at their respective posts in the city, one halting about the room cap in hand as if he was at the arse of a miserable alderman'.[52]

At least superficially, therefore, the public poor appear uniquely free of the constraints of community, and hence one of the first groups of 'modern' individuals. More than this, their financial relationship with the people from whom they earned a living was likewise uniquely modern. 'Modern' both in the sense that it was almost entirely made up of an exchange of money encouraged by public advertising, and to the extent that it was an exchange between individuals who did not apparently know each other in any other way.[53]

But, at the same time, we must be careful not to replace historical reality with elite perception. There are a number of reasons to suggest that this apparent lack of community links is misleading. For one thing, the mob frequently supported beggars at the expense of the elite. Richard Steele recounted one incident in which he

was listning to a new ballad, [when] a ragged rascal, a beggar who knew me, came up to me, and began to turn the eyes of the good company upon me, by telling me he was extreme poor, and should die in the streets for want of drink, except I immediately would have the charity to give him six-pence to go into the next ale-house and save his life. He urged, with a melancholy face, that all his family had died of thirst. All the mob have humour, and two or three began to take the jest; by which Mr Sturdy carried his point.[54]

Likewise, if we look at the legal settlement of vagrants actually prosecuted for begging, they appear to be much more strongly connected to the local community than elite commentary might suggest. Of a sample of 153 individuals apprehended for begging and loitering in the City of London between 1738 and 1742 almost half, 75, had a legal settlement in the metropolitan London area. Only 18 were identified as having a settlement elsewhere in the country, while no legal settlement was identified for the other 60 examinees. A full two-thirds of the 76 women examined had a London settlement, and three-quarters of the children. Indeed, the only group of people of

[52] [Ned Ward], *The History of the London Club, Or the Citizens Pastime* (1709), p. 7.
[53] The interrelationship between the rapidly changing supply of money, particularly small coinage, and the new publicity of begging is beyond the scope of this chapter, but would bear much further analysis.
[54] *The Spectator*, no. 454.

whom a majority could have had a settlement outside of the metropolitan area was adult men – approximately 60 per cent of whom were either not examined as to their settlement, or were named as being settled elsewhere in the country.[55]

Also, we need to remember that many of the public poor were lame. When the only way you have to get around is to drag your partially paralysed body along the streets, or to hobble on crutches, when, like William Sindrey, you were discharged onto the cold November streets of London, 'incurable with lameness from St Bartholomew's Hospital', it is difficult to believe that you had much choice but to remain in the same locality for as long as you could.[56] As a result, these beggars inevitably became a part of the local scene. Hogarth's use of figures like the well-known crippled ballad singer 'Philip in the Tub' as a bit-character in one of his prints reinforces the extent to which the public poor could never be entirely anonymous, or entirely separate from the communities in which they worked.[57] Indeed, there is a suggestive disparity between the visual and literary depiction of beggars and the image which emerges from vagrancy examinations. The disabled, and disabled men in particular, are extremely prominent in literary and visual sources, while the population examined by the Lord Mayor prior to removal was dominated by apparently able-bodied women. This at least implies that disabled men were able to make a place for themselves on the streets of eighteenth-century London.

More than this, the changing pattern of migration which characterized the late seventeenth century inevitably had an effect on this population. Long-distance migration became less frequent, while short-distance and intra-London migration became more

[55] *Place of settlement by gender of vagrants examined by the Lord Mayor of London, 1738, 1741, 1742*

	London	Unknown	Other	Total
Female	42	27	7	76
Male	24	33	8	65
Child	9	0	3	12
Total	75	60	18	153

Sample: 153. Source: CLRO, 'Vagrant Books, 1738–1742'. Misc. MS 322.5.

[56] See William Sindrey's examination, 16 Nov. 1741. CLRO, 'Vagrant Books, 1738–1742'. Misc. MS 322.5.

[57] 'Philip in the Tub' is mentioned in notes on 'The Industrious Prentice out of his time' in Joseph Burke and Colin Caldwell, *Hogarth: The Complete Engravings* (New York, n.d.), n. 208.

common.[58] The poor population of London therefore became both less likely to live in their parish of birth and probable settlement, and at the same time, more likely to have relatives, connections, friends, and a parish of settlement within a reasonable distance. In sum, as the evidence of the settlement examinations suggests, the public poor of early eighteenth-century London had more links to the variegated communities of the capital than their sixteenth-century predecessors, or indeed their twentieth-century inheritors. They were, to all intents and purposes, similar to the 'deserving' poor who received their weekly or monthly collection from the parish officers.

We can now turn to the development of social policy in order to assess some of the ways in which the changing nature of public poverty interacted with elite perceptions. London was the test bed for both private and public social policy initiatives throughout the eighteenth century. If anywhere in Western Europe can be said to provide evidence for the growth of Foucault's carceral archipelago, it is London. In Corporations of the Poor and parochial workhouses, in infirmaries and foundling hospitals, institutions for the incurable and for the merely irritating, Londoners created a series of largely residential institutions designed to house and to control individual members of the labouring poor. The last substantive charitable initiative designed to relieve the poor in their homes was the King's Letter fund established in 1688. For the next hundred years, the social policy of London and of Britain as a whole would be characterized by institutions which plucked the poor from their homes and their communities and placed them, naked of friends and relations, in the bureaucratic maw of the prison and the workhouse. The rest of this chapter will suggest that the existence of a peculiarly visible public poor helped make this response to poverty possible.

The sense of physical revulsion which Swift managed to evoke in his description of Gulliver's reaction to the public beggars of Brobdingnag can stand in for elite response in general:

[58] There is now substantial literature on migration. See for example Peter Clark and David Souden (eds.), *Migration and Society in Early Modern England* (1987); Malcolm Kitch, 'Capital and kingdom: migration to later Stuart London', in Beier and Finlay, *London 1500–1700*, pp. 224–51; John Wareing, 'Changes in the geographical distribution of the recruitment of apprentices to the London Companies, 1486–1750', *Journal of Historical Geography* 6 (1980), 241–9; and most recently David Souden and Peter Clark, *Migration and the Early Modern English Town* (TLTP, History Courseware Consortium) CDRom, ver. A 1.4, Glasgow, 1998.

the beggars watching their opportunity, crouded to the sides of the coach and gave me the most horrible spectacles that ever an . . . eye beheld. There was a woman with a cancer in her breast . . . full of holes . . . There was a fellow with a wen in his neck . . . And another with a couple of wooden legs . . . But the most hateful sight of all was the lice crawling upon their cloaths . . . It perfectly turned my stomach.[59]

In a very real sense the convenient stories of faked wounds, of expert make-up, and artistically constructed fictional narratives of woe reported by elite commentators allowed the wealthier inhabitants of London to dismiss the suffering experienced by the tide of humanity which confronted them in every public street. But, at the same time, these convenient fictions of the rich about the public poor made the creation of a social policy which would correct these self-evident evils all the more urgent. And in our period there were two interrelated changes occurring simultaneously which together re-sulted in the creation of both the new types of institution mentioned earlier, and new types of behaviour on the part of the poor. First, the nature of parochial relief changed. As Jeremy Boulton has demon-strated for the parish of St Martin in the Fields (in part, confirming a trend which Paul Slack has identified nationally), the overall amount of parish relief available grew substantially in the last decades of the seventeenth century.[60] More than this, the balance between pensions and casual relief – that is, between money given to individuals as regular weekly doles and that distributed as one-off payments – changed.[61] A growing proportion of parochial relief in London came to be spent on the casual poor, perhaps on the very beggars who have formed the major topic of this chapter. As a result the casual poor (who were nonetheless probably relatively local and hence not particularly threatening) came to take a higher priority in the financial concerns of the parish; a trend which was reinforced by the growing administrative burden created by the Law of Settlement.[62]

---

[59] Jonathan Swift, *Gulliver's Travels*, ed. Harold Williams (Oxford, 1965), pp. 112–13.
[60] For the figures for St Martin's, see Boulton, 'Going on the parish', p. 24, figure 1.4. For the national picture see Paul Slack, *Poverty and Policy in Tudor and Stuart England* (1988), ch. 8, 'The growth in social welfare'.
[61] See Boulton, 'Going on the parish', p. 25, figure 1.5.
[62] The best overview of the evolution of the Law of Settlement is still Philip Styles, 'The evolution of the law of settlement', reprinted in Philip Styles, *Studies in Seventeenth-Century West Midlands History* (Kineton, 1978), pp. 175–204. There is also a growing literature on the laws' impact and implementation. See for example J. S. Taylor, 'The impact of pauper settlement 1691–1834', *Past & Present* 73 (1964), 61–2; K.D.M. Snell, *The Annals of the Labouring Poor: Social Change and Agrarian England, 1660–1900* (Cambridge, 1985); K. D. M. Snell, 'Pauper settlement and the right to poor relief in England and Wales', *Continuity and*

Also, as part of the same process, the vagrancy legislation which had been created to deal with public poverty seems to have become more confused and narrowly focused. From 1699 the removal of vagrants to their parish of settlement was handed over to county officials and paid for from a county rate, encouraging overseers to pass paupers as vagrants, if possible, and effectively confusing the line of demarcation between the two.[63] In a sense, the creation of a sophisticated legal notion of settlement with its certificates and system of removal ensured that the sharp division between the vagrant and the parish pauper, which had lain at the heart of the parallel development of legislation throughout the sixteenth century, no longer seemed so clear. The public poor, the beggars and supplicants whom the rich confronted in the street, became confused with the deserving poor.

At the same time, the physical make-up of the city itself provided another source of change. The rebuilding of the City after the fire and the subsequent development of the West End created a series of increasingly 'public' spaces. Wide clear streets, open squares, and mile after mile of formal railings created poorly policed public areas which made excellent sites for stationary begging, but which discouraged itinerant domestic begging and undermined the sense of ownership and responsibility which less grandiose cityscapes engendered. If one simply considers that ubiquitous piece of eighteenth-century street furniture, the cast-iron rail, its likely impact is clear. At one and the same time it closed off traditional areas of communal activity, like the churchyard, and effectively separated elite houses from the street. When in 1714 it was decided to spend £11,000 on a cast iron palisade to encompass St Paul's, not only was a traditional site for political rabble rousing and community politics lost to Londoners, but one of the more traditional and acceptable pitches for begging was lost to the poor.[64] As a result stationary public begging became increasingly detached from tradi-

    Change 6 (1991), 375–415 and Norma Landau's reply in the same volume, 417–39; Norma Landau, 'The Laws of Settlement and the surveillance of immigration in eighteenth-century Kent', *Continuity and Change* 3 (1988), 391–420; Norma Landau, 'The regulation of immigration, economic structures and definitions of the poor in eighteenth-century England', *Historical Journal* 33 (1990), 541–72.

[63] 11 William III. c.18 (1699). For a discussion of these changes see Sidney and Beatrice Webb, *English Local Government: English Poor Law History: Part* 1. *The Old Poor Law* (1927), pp. 378–83.

[64] See Dan Cruickshank and Peter Wyld, *Georgian Townhouses and their Details* (London, 1975), p. 211.

tional notions of Christian charity; becoming more obvious, possibly more offensive, and probably more centralized on newly 'public' spaces. At the same time it became less clearly the responsibility of individual householders and parish communities.

Collectively, these forces had two interlinking influences. Firstly, they ensured that the 'public poor' became more obvious as a social problem. And secondly, they made these 'public paupers' less threatening, less obviously the vicious vagrants who seemed so profoundly to affect the imaginations of late sixteenth-century social policy commentators.[65] Now, instead of being in a separate category, the 'public poor' had become just one more outpost of poverty in general.

One way to think about the social policy developments of eighteenth-century London is as a simple response to the new publicity of the beggarly poor. The poor relief initiatives of the 1670s and 1680s, designed to relieve the poor in their own homes, gave way in the 1690s to institutions whose object was the homeless and unsettled.[66] For the next four generations, in Corporations of the Poor and workhouses, in foundling hospitals and in infirmaries,[67] the object of attention was the individual beggarly pauper, the supplicant who sat by the roadside with no obvious home and no apparent connection. That the poor, even the beggarly poor, were never, or very seldom, without either connection or family, without a domestic hinterland, ensured that the mismatch between need and provision would grow. It ensured that the institutions that formed the bulk of these new initiatives would always be hated by the poor themselves. More significantly, it ensured that social policy throughout the period would act as a vicious corrosive to the domestic and settled lives of the poor half of the population of London, splitting up families, and driving households in need of a

---

[65] For the most comprehensive discussion of sixteenth and early seventeenth-century vagrancy and elite and government response to it, see A. L. Beier, *Masterless Men: The Vagrancy Problem in England, 1560–1640* (1985).

[66] I refer specifically to Thomas Firmin's employment scheme established in 1677 and to the 'King's Letter' fund of 1688, with which Firmin was also associated. See Macfarlane, 'Social policy and the poor', p. 259.

[67] For recent accounts of these various London initiatives see Macfarlane, 'Social policy and the poor'; Tim Hitchcock, 'Paupers and preachers: The SPCK and the parochial workhouse movement' in Lee Davison, Tim Hitchcock, Tim Keirn, and Robert Shoemaker (eds.), *Stilling the Grumbling Hive: The Response to Social and Economic Problems in England, 1689–1750* (Stroud, 1992); and Andrew, *Philanthropy and Police*.

bit of temporary help into penury and total dependence.[68] As importantly, because beggars are always seen as a nuisance, because their faults and their social infractions seem to loom unreasonably large within our view of them even when their poverty is admitted, social policy which was meant to relieve the suffering of the deserving poor became increasingly punitive in its intent.[69] What had changed was not simply the content and intent of elite views of the poor in general, but the very object of social policy itself. By the early eighteenth century that object had quite simply ceased to be the elderly cottager, or overburdened young family, and had become that modern representation of poverty, the individual beggar, with all his or her faults. By the middle of the century Fielding could accurately observe: 'They starve, freeze and rot among themselves; but they beg and steal and rob among their betters.'[70] The problem was that by this time their betters could see no further than the begging. So, in 1716, when four men, including Henry Hoare, discussed poverty in London from their comfortable seats in St Dunstan's Coffee House, they could claim without hyperbole that:

Notwithstanding the provision settled by our laws and the collections made by the charity of well disposed Christians for the relief of the poor it is obvious to anyone that *walks the street* [my italics] that the same is not sufficient to preserve great numbers of them from beggary, to the great grief of all good men and the no small reproach of our religion and country.[71]

Their solution was the Westminster infirmary and hospital, one of the earliest non-parochial residential institutional establishments, and the first of a series of similar foundations which were to characterize London social policy for most of the rest of the century.

---

[68] For an account of some of the ways in which the structure and organization of workhouses interacted with the lives of the poor see Tim Hitchcock, ' "Unlawfully begotten on her body": Illegitimacy and the parish poor in St Luke's Chelsea' in Hitchcock, King, and Sharpe (eds.), *Chronicling Poverty.*

[69] The classic statement of the broad European trend towards institutional and punitive treatment of the socially undesirable is Michel Foucault, *Discipline and Punish: The Birth of the Prison* (English translation, 1977).

[70] Henry Fielding, *A Proposal for Making an Effectual Provision for the Poor* (1745), p. 10.

[71] Quoted in J. G. Humble and Peter Hansell, *Westminster Hospital, 1716–1974* (2nd edn, 1974), p. 6.

CHAPTER 7

'To recreate and refresh their dulled spirites in the sweet and wholesome ayre': green space and the growth of the city

Laura Williams

In Stow's *Survey*, Elizabethan Londoners seeking 'to recreate and refresh their dulled spirites in the sweet and wholesome ayre' might clamber over stiles to access the bounding fields of the city. And yet increasingly these spaces, in this instance the fields beyond Bishops-gate, had been 'within few yeares made a continuall building throughout'.[1] Stow was clearly anguished by the engulfing of open land by the swell of the city. Numerous attempts were made to restrict the extent of new building within the cities of London and Westminster and beyond the city gates by the Elizabethan govern-ment, but, ultimately, these proved futile. From 1565 to the turn of the century it is estimated that the population of London grew from around 85,000 to 180,000, including suburban developments. But in the century that followed, the sprawl of the city that had so concerned Stow became even more accentuated, and the pressures on urban green space increasingly intense. By 1700 London's residents numbered in the region of 575,000, and 675,000 by 1750, accounting for 11 per cent of the total English population.[2] This expanding urban fabric, increasingly congested through infill and sprawling bounds, imagined as both splendid and alarmingly over-grown, is portrayed as simultaneously compromising and fuelling the desire to find solace in open and airy green space.[3]

Stow's stress on the importance and value of open space for urban

---

[1] Stow, *Survey*, I.127.

[2] Penelope Corfield, *The Impact of English Towns, 1700–1800* (Oxford, 1982), pp. 10, 7–8; Vanessa Harding, 'The population of London 1550–1700: a review of the published evidence', *London Journal* 15 (1990), 111–28; E. A. Wrigley, 'A simple model of London's importance in changing English society and economy 1650–1750', repr. in P. Abrams and E. A. Wrigley (eds.), *Towns in Societies* (Cambridge, 1978), p. 215.

[3] Laura Williams, 'Rus in urbe: the greening of English towns, 1660–1760', PhD thesis, University of Wales (1998), esp. chs. 1, 2, and 5.

residents, alongside anxiety that access to this fresh air and greenery was being compromised, represent concerns expressed with increasing fervour alongside the inexorable growth of the city. This chapter studies the ways in which tensions generated by the exceptional growth of the city were in part met by recourse to nature, and in particular a series of measures that sought to domesticate nature within an urban setting. The ordering, portrayal, and use of urban green space reveals a great deal about contemporary perceptions of the built and natural environment. By focusing on how green space was absorbed within the growing city, and on representations of these spaces, this chapter explores the imagined relationship between urban greening and the physical and moral welfare of the individual and urban society.

The key trend, in the character of London's green space from Stow to Strype, is the shift of focus away from peripheral open fields, meadow, and pasture for walking and recreational use, and towards more ordered and formal sites. Stow's grievance over the infringement of common rights and loss of recreational access to private interests forms a part of his lamenting changes to the city of his youth, and reaction to the push of the bounds of the city over the fields. As a result of the pestering of 'filthy cottages', alleys, and the like, the common fields north of Whitechapel, 'all which ought to lye open & free for all men', and 'being sometime the beauty of this city on that part', no longer provided any 'faire, pleasant or wholsome way for people to walke on foot'.[4] The suburbs to the north and east of the city did indeed experience marked population growth between 1560 and 1600.[5] In part, these suburbs were being swelled by those who were keen to avoid (or were excluded by) the legislation and controls imposed by the city, but who wished to remain within London's orbit. Out to the west, Westminster had been expanding with the personnel of the royal court and the influx of service-providers to meet the consumer needs of this entourage.[6] And yet in spite of Stow's anxious recording of creeping urbanization, the bulk of his fellow Londoners still lived within and immediately without

---

[4] Stow, *Survey*, II.72.
[5] Roger Finlay and Beatrice Shearer, 'Population growth and suburban expansion', in A. L. Beier and Roger Finlay (eds.), *London, 1500–1700 The Making of the Metropolis* (1986), pp. 44–5.
[6] Gervase Rosser, 'London and Westminster: the suburb in the urban economy in the later Middle Ages', in John A. F. Thomson (ed.), *Towns and Townspeople in the Fifteenth Century* (Gloucester, 1988), pp. 47–51, 53–4.

the city. This would not remain the case for long. From the turn of the century the rate of growth of the suburbs began to accelerate until it outstripped that of the city, so that, conversely, by 1680 three-quarters of Londoners lived in the suburbs, and only a quarter in the city.[7]

So what impact did the pace and scale of these developments in the city and suburbs have on London's open spaces? Where did pockets of greenery survive, and why? Certainly, barely any green space survived the pressures of population growth and filling of gaps with new building within the city walls, bar a few private gardens and green churchyards.[8] The development of the suburbs was generally more piecemeal and less densely packed than expansion within and around the City, preserving some open space valued for recreational use on the fringes and within walking distance of the centre. There were other pressures on the open fields and pastures about the city, however. Some of the land which Stow records as lost to common access was being enclosed for intensified market gardening, to feed the burgeoning population.[9] Stow was well aware that the enclosing of common ground was no new development, sympathetically recounting how in the reign of Henry VIII the infringement of rights of access to the common fields provoked Londoners into destroying the hedges and ditches that impeded their recreational walking and archery practice. And yet he finds the current situation 'in worse case than ever'. It is not just tenements and cottages that Stow records as spreading across the open ground around the bounds of the city, but also 'inclosure for Gardens, wherein are builded many fayre summer houses', rather scathingly dismissed as 'not so much for use or profite, as for shewe and pleasure, bewraying the vanity of mens mindes'.[10] Both the copperplate map and 'Agas' woodcut of London in the mid-sixteenth century reveal a good number of private ornamental gardens within and around the city.[11] Some of London's larger houses evidently had sizeable adjoining formal gardens, such as Salisbury House, Ely

---

[7] Finlay and Shearer, 'Population growth', pp. 42-4.
[8] Vanessa Harding, 'Gardens and open space in Tudor and Stuart London' in Mireille Galinou (ed.), *London's Pride: The Glorious History of the Capital's Gardens* (1990), pp. 44-55.
[9] Rosser, 'London and Westminster', pp. 52-3; see Rosemary Weinstein, 'Feeding the city: London's market gardens in the early modern period' in Galinou, *London's Pride*, pp. 80-99.
[10] Stow, *Survey*, II.78.
[11] See Adrian Prockter and Robert Taylor, *The A to Z of Elizabethan London* (London Topographical Society no. 122, 1979).

House, and Somerset and Arundel House along the Strand fronting
the Thames, clearly depicted on Ogilby and Morgan's city map of
1676.[12] The *Survey* relates how Thomas Cromwell extended his own
garden plot at the expense of that of Stow's father, shifting his
garden-house back 22 feet on rollers.[13] In the City, Companies such
as the Carpenters and Drapers retained their gardens, but, into the
seventeenth century, it was the new houses edging towards Westminster that could afford to have adjoining gardens.[14]

Open fields still separated the City and Westminster at the time of
Stow's *Survey*, punctuated by the corridor of the Strand with its
large houses and formal gardens. The area that would later be
developed as Piccadilly and Soho was similarly unbroken ground.[15]
The push west was characterized by less crowded housing, making a
virtue of a more open and airy situation to contrast with the closely
packed city and the eastern flank along the Thames. John Macky
remarked that Holborn had 'many Ornamental Streets towards the
Fields for People of Quality'.[16] Strype finds 'good gardens' belonging
to the houses at Spring Garden at Charing Cross, and notes areas
like Peters Court, Hunts Court, and Stretton Street, in the Parish of
St Martin-in-the-Fields, with 'small gardens behind them'. The large
houses of Bedford Row were fronted with enclosed 'little Garden
Plots, adorned with handsome Flower Pots, and Flowers therein'.[17]
Montague House had 'a fine garden and Terrace behind, and a
noble Prospect to the adjacent Country', whilst Buckingham House
celebrated in its famous 'Rus in Urbe' inscription a prospect out over
open country from its garden.[18]

Horticulturists like the Tradescants, John Rose, and later George
London, Henry Wise, and Robert Furber both encouraged and
catered to local demand for plants and seeds, whilst Evelyn acknowledged that the atmosphere of London offered a particular challenge
to the gardener.[19] By the time of Strype's *Survey*, gardening was

---

[12] See Ralph Hyde, *The A-Z of Restoration London (The City of London, 1676)* (Lympne Castle, Kent, 1992).

[13] Stow, *Survey*, I.179.

[14] M. J. Power, 'The east and west in early-modern London', in E. W. Ives, R. J. Knecht, and J. J. Scarisbrick (eds.), *Wealth and Power in Tudor England. Essays Presented to S. T. Bindoff* (1978), p. 173.

[15] *Ibid.*, p. 169.

[16] John Macky, *A Journey through England* (2 vols., 1714–22), I, p. 277.

[17] Strype, *Survey*, I.iii.254; II.vi.77–8.

[18] Macky, *Journey Through England*, I, p. 173.

[19] John Evelyn, *Fumifugium: or The Inconveniencie of the Aer and Smoak of London Dissipated* (1661),

becoming firmly established as an urbane leisure pursuit among the aspirational middle classes, accompanied by an ever-growing number of nurseries, catalogues, and flower shows.[20] Thomas Fairchild, owner of a nursery at Hoxton, produced the first gardening text directed specifically at the urban market, professing that he wished to 'cultivate this innocent pleasure among my fellow citizens'.[21] Newly built town houses such as those around Grosvenor Square on the fashionable Grosvenor Estate in Mayfair were afforded sizeable back gardens formally styled with walks and flower plots.[22] However, by the middle of the eighteenth century Pehr Kalm was recording that in every little town house yard the people 'had commonly planted in these yards and round about them, partly in the earth and ground itself, partly in pots and boxes, several of the trees, plants, and flowers which could stand the coal smoke in London'. The reason for this Kalm attributed to the fact that they 'sought to have some of the pleasant enjoyments of a country life in the midst of the hubbub of the town'.[23]

If the developments of the West End were characterized as more open, airy, and refined, then it was a tone set by the broad sweep of royal parkland. Stow found 'divers fayre houses lately builded before the Parke' of St James's, a foretaste of the rash of fashionable development that characterized the area from the late seventeenth and into the eighteenth century.[24] Hyde Park and St James's Park had originally been drained and set aside as royal hunting grounds by Henry VIII. Limited public access for recreational use, temporarily interrupted by the Civil War and the neglect of the Commonwealth, was resurrected by the restoration of Crown rights and

p. 7. For more on London's horticultural trade see Robert Todd Longstaffe Gowan, 'The London town garden 1700–1830. The experience of nature in the eighteenth-century city', PhD thesis, University of London (1989), esp. ch. 6; Neil Burton, 'Town gardens' in D. Cruickshank and Neil Burton (eds.), *Life in the Georgian City* (1990); John Harvey, *Early Nurserymen* (1974); John Harvey, *Early Gardening Catalogues* (1972); Brian Halliwell, 'Flowers and plants in the seventeenth century' in Galinou, *London's Pride*, pp. 66–77; Todd Longstaffe Gowan, 'Gardening and the middle classes 1700–1830' in Galinou, *London's Pride*, pp. 122–33.

[20] Keith Thomas, *Man and the Natural World. Changing Attitudes in England 1500–1800* (Harmondsworth, 1984), pp. 224–6; N. McKendrick, J. Brewer, and J. H. Plumb (eds.), *The Birth of a Consumer Society. The Commercialization of Eighteenth-Century England* (1982), pp. 10–11.

[21] Thomas Fairchild, *The City Gardener* (1722), p. 8.

[22] Burton, 'Town gardens', pp. 195–7.

[23] Pehr Kalm, *Kalm's Account of his Visit to England on his way to America in 1748*, trans. J. Lucas (1892), p. 85.

[24] Stow, *Survey*, II.101.

advent of grand landscaping projects that fashioned the parks as
London's most fashionable promenades. In the months and years
following the Restoration, Charles poured large sums of money into
fashioning St James's park as a reinstatement of natural sovereign
order.[25] Thomas Rugge toured the park in October of 1660 and
found 'about 300 men are every day employed in his majesty's worke
in makinge the River'. A year later he recorded that parts of the park
had been levelled, large ditches filled in, and 'grass seed sowed to
make pleasant walking'. The old trees were taken down and replaced
with trees planted in straight walks.[26] Hyde Park formed the western
flank of a green corridor stretching from Whitehall to Kensington.
Free access granted to the royal domain from the 1630s was cut short
by its sale into private hands by the Long Parliament in 1652, but the
park survived to be reclaimed by the Crown upon the Restoration.
The famous Ring within the park, a fenced enclosure resorted to by
the beau monde in order to ride in full view of each other,
encapsulated the imagined appeal of the West End, combining the
taking of fresh air with chic sociable display.

The more spacious, open feel to the building developments of the
West End was enhanced by the laying out of squares, as landowners
and developers identified and exploited the kudos of open space to
contrast with the densely packed courts and alleys of poor-man's
London. Bloomsbury Square set a precedent in the 1660s, to be
followed by the likes of St James's, Leicester, Red Lyon, King,
Hanover, Grosvenor, and Golden Squares.[27] Many of these 'fine
open spaces' featured central gardens of 'flowers, trees and paths'.[28]
London's four Inns of Court, Lincoln's Inn, Gray's Inn, and the
Inner and Middle Temples, provided further pockets of green
singled out in portraits of the cityscape. The benchers of Gray's Inn
enclosed and laid out their back plot of land, facing across the fields
towards Hampstead and Highgate, towards the end of the sixteenth
century, and thereafter it was often frequented and commented on

---

[25] For commentary on the political agenda behind the renovation of St James's Park see Mark
Mcdayter, 'Poetic gardens and political myths: the renewal of St James's Park in the
Restoration', *Journal of Garden History* 15, no. 3 (July–Sept. 1995), 135–48; and Mark Jenner,
'The politics of London air. John Evelyn's *Fumifugium* and the Restoration', *Historical Journal*
38 (1995), 535–51.

[26] 'The journal of Thomas Rugge' (BL, Add. MS 10116), fos. 210 (October 1660), 448
(September 1661).

[27] John Summerson, *Georgian London* (new edition 1962), pp. 39–42.

[28] Cesar De Saussure, *A Foreign View of England in the Reigns of George I and George II. The Letters of
Monsieur Cesar de Saussure to his Family*, ed. M. Van Muyden (1902), p. 70.

for its tree-shaded walks and prospect to the north. Strype thought the Inn's 'chief Ornament' to be its spacious garden, 'much resorted unto, by the Gentry of both sexes'.[29] In spite of losing some land to the developers, Lincoln's Inn retained a large garden with statues and formal walks, which, Strype observed, gave 'a delightful prospect to the Inhabitants'. The Temple Gardens, fronting the Thames, provided a similarly formalized garden lay-out, styled by Strype as 'very well-kept, with delightful Walks'.[30]

Although the pastures of Spitalfields were built over, to the north of the city lay the open ground of Moorfields. Drained and levelled in the sixteenth century, archers and walkers shared access to this City-owned land with grazing animals and drying laundry. The emphasis shifted more in favour of leisured use from the early seventeenth century, with the planting of tree-lined walks in the years 1605 to 1607. South of the River, the St George's Fields and Lambeth marshes that stretched away from Southwark at the time of Stow's *Survey* were still recognizable in Strype's day. *The Foreigners Guide* to London of 1729 noted that leaving the Borough of Southwark 'you come into the Meadows called St George's Fields, which reach as far as Lambeth . . . [and that] here are pleasant Walks and places of great resort, particularly Cupids Garden, Spring Garden, Lambeth Well'. Spas and pleasure gardens struck a potent chord in the urban imagination, providing a significant recreational facility for London from the 1660s, situated for the most part around the fringes.[31] Sites like Sadler's Wells, Islington Spa, St Pancras and Lambeth Wells, Mulberry, Marylebone, Cupers, Vauxhall, and Ranelagh Gardens, with their cultivated enclosed garden plots bounded by fields, were presented as packaging the pleasures of a countrified air, al fresco eating, and pleasing prospects without straying too far from, or sacrificing, the sociability of the city. The pre-eminent example, the Vauxhall Gardens, which opened as the New Spring Gardens in 1661, were progressively developed to present London's company with a resort of groves, wildernesses, and 'Rural Downs', a turfed area 'where Lambs are seen Sporting', and avenues extending out into what a mid-eighteenth-century promoter described as 'a View into the adjacent Meads; where Haycocks, and Haymakers sporting, during the mowing Season, add a Beauty

[29] Strype, *Survey*, I.iii.253.
[30] *Ibid.*, I.iii.278.
[31] Warwick Wroth, *The London Pleasure Gardens of the Eighteenth Century*, new edition (1979).

to the Landskip'.[32] The development and significant financial
investment in recreational sites like Vauxhall Gardens, St James's
Park, and Moorfields, and in private domestic gardens, attests to the
growing premium placed on urban green space apparent not just
in London but in a raft of towns across England.[33] Stow's survey of
late Elizabethan London details the use of fields around the peri-
meters of the city as the recreational space that served citizens
seeking to 'recreate and refresh their dulled spirites'. By the time of
Strype's *Survey*, London's green spaces had become more formally
delineated and self-consciously incorporated into the urban fabric,
in the form of parks, gardens, and walks. But why was this
happening? What does it tell us about contemporary perceptions of
city and country?

One of the most significant influences on shifting perceptions of
the urban environment was the stress on habitat as a key factor in
determining health, an emphasis which gathered steam from the
second half of the seventeenth century. This coincided with increasing confidence in the control and malleability of the natural world.[34]
This was a confidence built around scientific observation of flora and
fauna, climate, population, and topography as steps towards understanding and control of the environment. And yet the urban
environment presented particular challenges within the imagined
framework of improving society. Whereas on the one hand the city
was pitched at the core of civilization, as the hub of progress, on the
other hand it appeared to encapsulate the blighting of health and
moral degeneracy. London was unequivocally associated with high
mortality rates, unsanitary conditions, and overcrowding, concen-
trating the dregs as well as the assets of society. The demographer
John Graunt's analysis of mortality in seventeenth-century London
concluded that the capital's shorter life spans were attributable to

---

[32] John Lockman, *A Sketch of the Spring-Gardens, Vaux-Hall. In a Letter to a Noble Lord* (n.d. [1750/
2]), pp. 20, 2.

[33] For example, Exeter's town council financed the creation of a tree-lined walk with seating
along the town walls at Northernhay from 1612; Shrewsbury's Quarry, open green land
skirting the town walls, was set with tree-lined gravelled avenues from 1719; and in Bath a
combination of corporation and privately backed initiatives led to the development of the
Gravel Walks, Harrison's Walks, the 'Ring', the Parade Gardens, and Spring Gardens as
outdoor leisure facilities for the company. See Williams, 'Rus in urbe', ch. 4, 'Proprietors
and promenaders'.

[34] See James C. Riley, *The Eighteenth-Century Campaign to Avoid Disease* (Basingstoke, 1987);
Andrew Wear, 'Making sense of health and the environment in early modern England', in
Andrew Wear (ed.), *Medicine In Society. Historical Essays* (Cambridge, 1992).

the fact that its 'Smoaks, Stinks and Close Air, are less healthful than that of the Country'.[35] Even laudatory guides were forced to acknowledge that there was a problem: 'In the Winter indeed, the Town is not altogether so pleasant in itself: The thick Air, proceeding from the Moistness of the Weather, and the Smoak from the great Quantity of Coals burnt, render it Obnoxious to many Constitutions.'[36] Daniel Defoe noted a commonplace recognition of this in the capital, describing the 'smoke and dirt, sin and seacoal (as it was coursly express'd) in the busy city'.[37]

By the mid-eighteenth century Thomas Short's observations on urban mortality were unequivocal in pinpointing density and over-population as contributing factors to the inherent unhealthiness of the built environment: 'The closer Towns and Villages stand, the more pent-up the Houses, the lower and closer the Rooms, the narrower the Streets, the smaller the Windows, the more numerous the Inhabitants, the unhealthier the Place.'[38] But plague and fire had already fixed the notion. The plague represented one of the city's most devastating causes of mortality up until the last outbreak in 1665–6, which killed more than 80,000, with Londoners acutely aware that infection rates were at their highest in the poorest and most overcrowded areas.[39]

To help counter this threat, those with the means chose residences in open, spacious, and leafy parts of town, layering environmental patterns with a social zoning whereby the poorer citizens were left in the least salubrious areas. The problems of close streets and houses, human and animal waste disposal, spread of disease, and smoke pollution from the burning of sea coal were real enough, but these aspects of urban life were compounded in the imagination by the spectacle of profligacy, of wealth and time and youth mis-spent on food and drink, fashion and display, and idleness. The city embodied excess, or at least the capacity for it. The Scottish physician George Cheyne judged that moral and physical infirmity multiplied in

[35] John Graunt, *Natural and Political Observations . . . upon the Bills of Mortality* (1676), quoted in Wear, 'Making sense of health and the environment', pp. 130–1.

[36] Anon., *The Foreigners Guide: Or, a Necessary and Instructive Companion Both for the Foreigner and Native, In their Tour through the Cities of London and Westminster* (1729), p. 132.

[37] Daniel Defoe, *A Tour through the Whole Island of Great Britain* ed. G. D. H. Cole and D. Browning (2 vols., 1962), I, p. 168.

[38] Thomas Short, *New Observations on City, Town and Country Bills of Mortality* (1750), quoted in Wear, 'Making sense of health and the environment', pp. 130–1.

[39] Paul Slack, 'Metropolitan government in crisis: the response to plague', in Beier and Finlay, *London 1500–1700*, pp. 61–3.

proportion with increasing wealth and the move towards an urban existence consumed with luxury, 'the Wealth and Abundance of the Inhabitants (from their universal Trade) the Inactivity and Sedentary Occupations of the better Sort (amongst whom this Evil mostly rages) and the Humour of living in great, populous and consequently unhealthy Towns, have brought forth a Class and Set of Distempers, with atrocious and frightful Symptoms, scarce known to our Ancestors'.[40]

It was framed within this imagery of pollution that nature in the city gained its potency, heading off these ills and keeping society on the right track. The distinction between urban and rural forms a powerful current in medical thinking. The further humankind slips away from a simpler and hardier existence rooted in honest labour and exercise, clean living and cleansing surroundings, the greater the imbalance, manifested in disease and disorder. Recourse to nature was thus considered fundamental in correcting these deficiencies. Added to this, the associations drawn between a dense, claustrophobic, and overcrowded urban environment, a lack of physical exertion on the part of the town dweller and ill health were compounded by medical theories on the importance of circulation. Here, the key idea was that good health was vested in movement as opposed to stagnation, applicable not just to circulation within the body of the individual, but the body of the town itself. Conceptions of the city as organism draw clear parallels between the human and urban body, exemplified in the descriptions of town parks and gardens as the lungs of a city that were commonplace from the nineteenth century, but in currency well before this. Simon Schama explores the theme of circulation in antiquity, noting that Plato compares currents within the natural world and the human body.[41] Richard Sennett emphasizes William Harvey's 1628 scientific treatise, *Du motu cordis*, on the circulations of the body as having a significant effect on notions of public health allied to ideas of circulation in the city.[42] Tom Brown wrote of London, 'The Streets are as so many *Veins*, wherein the People Circulate.'[43] The unobstructed flow of blood, air, and water was a prerequisite for a good

---

[40] George Cheyne, *The English Malady*, ed. Roy Porter (1991), preface, p. ii.
[41] Simon Schama, *Landscape and Memory* (1995), pp. 247, 256–63.
[42] Richard Sennett, *Flesh and Stone. The Body and the City in Western Civilization* (New York, 1994), pp. 23, 256–63.
[43] Tom Brown, *Amusements Serious and Comical, Calculated for the Meridian of London* (1700), p. 23.

constitution. Motion was a sign of vitality. This stress on free-flow and movement promoted the case for open space as crucial to the functioning of the otherwise congested city. Use of green space in and around the town emphasized the physical exercise factor, stretching the limbs and getting the blood flowing. Furthermore, it is not accidental or on purely aesthetic grounds that most town parks and gardens were developed around flowing water, rivers and streams and spas, and in elevated sites with clear, unhampered airflow.

Physical exercise such as walking was vaunted as promoting circulation of the blood and, given the appropriate environs, the respiratory circulation of good air. Dr Cheyne's essay on health of 1724 was of the opinion that 'Of all the Exercises that are, or may be used for Health . . . Walking is the most natural' whilst riding was more manly, and good for shaking the body into healthy internal action. With its stress on the cleansing ritual and function of exercise, this activity required a non-polluting atmosphere. As Cheyne put it, 'being in the Air, contributes much towards the Benefit of Exercise'.[44] A London Guide of the 1720s advised 'Those that take delight in the Walking-Exercise, have nowhere a greater Opportunity, than in the several fine Meadows and Fields, which surround the Town, and lead to the many agreeable Villages full of fine Houses, Gardens, Walks, and Places commendable for the good Air.'[45] It did little good to walk in the street, a potentially dirty, congested, unsafe, and morally dubious domain. Accordingly, carriages delivered their passengers to the gates of St James's Park. In the comedy *St James's Park* of 1733, Lady Betty is carried right onto the Mall and set down.[46] One did one's walking in designated promenades. Walking was certainly a defining characteristic of these open-air sites. The promenade was no coffee-house or assembly room to idle in. The use of the city's parks and gardens was very much tied up with keeping in motion. Walking in these gardens frequently involved following a circuit along laid-out walkways, often incorporating particular vistas. In this respect the act of viewing nature was not passive, but hinged around movement. In the St James's Park comedy, Mrs Loll bemoans the vogue for constantly promenading, 'if it were not for the odious custom of keeping

[44] George Cheyne, *An Essay of Health and Long Life* (1724), pp. 94–5.
[45] Anon., *Foreigners Guide*, p. 126.
[46] P. Q., *St James's Park: A Comedy* (1733), p. 10.

continually upon one's Feet, this Park would be a perfect Heaven'.[47]
The company long to fling themselves down on the grass but such
languor is not in keeping with the accent on healthy activity.

As already indicated, in the context of what was, or was perceived
to be, a claustrophobic, smoky, contagious urban atmosphere, clear,
flowing air was at a premium. The general consensus on the
importance of air to health was lent scientific gravitas by enquiries
like that by the physician John Arbuthnot, who published *An Essay
Concerning the Effects of Air on Human Bodies* in 1733, the physicist
Robert Boyle's investigation of the atmosphere, and the demographer Thomas Short's assertions that the healthiest places were those
with 'a free, pure, open Air'.[48] City air suffered for being enclosed,
and subject to the concentrated exhalations and noxious emanations
from waste, decomposing matter, and the sickly. In 1620 a sickly
merchant taylor of London, one Robert Holloway, was 'advised to
walke foorth of London into some fresh and sweet ayer', and so
'presumed to walke into your Ma.ts garden commonlie called the
Spring Garden neere to Whitehall'.[49] John Evelyn's Restoration
treatise, *Fumifugium*, was concerned with improving the atmosphere
in the capital, and related the quality of air to both physical and
mental well-being: 'as the Lucid and noble Aer, clarifies the Blood,
subtilizes and excites it, cheering the spirits and promoting digestion;
so the dark, and grosse (on the Contrary) perturbs the Body,
prohibits necessary Transpiration for the resolution and dissipation
of ill Vapours, even to disturbance of the very Rational faculties,
which the purer Aer does so far illuminate'.[50]

In recognition of the problems with the city's atmosphere, Evelyn
propounded the notion that natural elements introduced into or in
close proximity to the town could *actively* purify the air. This meant
that the value of parks and gardens lay not *just* in being self-
contained pockets to retreat to for draughts of fresh air. Rather, in
being drawn into the city, nature could extend a positive influence
over the urban environment as a whole and help cleanse the
atmosphere. At around the time of the Restoration a number of
horticultural enthusiasts were theorizing the merits of planting to

[47] *Ibid.*, p. 5.
[48] Riley, *Eighteenth-Century Campaign*, pp. 20–6; Wear, 'Making sense of health and the
environment', p. 135.
[49] G. Gater and W. Godfrey (eds.), *L.C.C. Survey of London* (London, 1940), XX, p. 58.
[50] Evelyn, *Fumifugium*, p. 3.

'rectify and purify the ayre of all the neighbouring countrey, both for health of body and mind'.[51] Evelyn was certainly the most notable figure amongst those promoting garden schemes for the improvement of body and soul, but he was engaged in a ready dialogue with a group of like-minded contemporaries, and scientists researching the properties of air.[52] In 1659 John Beale, a gentleman gardener, relayed to Evelyn his ideas concerning the use of scented flowers to purify the air. These proposals were, in his opinion, of great potential value within London as a 'sweet and easy remedy' to its pollution.[53] It was this concept that Evelyn advocated in the publication of *Fumifugium* two years later, which was explicit in linking and promoting plantations as a natural foil to urban pollution. Evelyn held that the actual siting of the capital was naturally good, but that this advantage was spoiled by the polluting of the air, principally by the industrial burning of sea coal in and around the city 'so universally mixed with the other wise wholsome and excellent Aer, that her Inhabitants breathe nothing but an impure and thick Mist . . . disordering the entire habit of their Bodies'. By contrast, pure air was that which was 'cleare, open, sweetely ventilated and put into motion with gentle gales and breezes; not too sharp, but of a temperate constitution'. Removing this air pollution would render the city 'one of the sweetest, and most delicious Habitations in the World'. His proposed solution to this problem was two-fold; that the offending industries be removed several miles out of the city, and that bands of trees, shrubs, and flowers be planted in the environs of the city to perfume the air. The character of the plantations proposed, Evelyn pointed out, was 'not much unlike to what his Majesty has already begun by the wall from old spring-garden to St James's in that Park; and is somewhat resembled in the new Spring-garden at Lambeth'. This is to say that these open spaces were the closest London came to a template for natural purification of the town. The plantations themselves were to be planted 'with such Shrubs, as yield the most fragrant and odoriferous Flowers, and are aptest to tinge the Aer upon every gentle emission at a great

---

[51] The gardener John Beale in a letter to John Evelyn, 30 September 1659, quoted in Graham Parry, 'John Evelyn as Hortulan saint' in Michael Leslie and Timothy Raylor (eds.), *Culture and Cultivation in Early Modern England. Writing and the Land* (Leicester, 1992), p. 140.

[52] Jenner, 'The politics of London air', 535.

[53] Beale's letter to Evelyn, 30 September 1659, quoted in Parry, 'John Evelyn as Hortulan saint', p. 141.

distance'. Amongst the scented plants and flowers that might be used, Evelyn recommended roses, rosemary, lavender, and lime trees as suitably 'odiferous and refreshing'. The result of these aromatic plantings, fanned by breezes, would be that 'the whole City, would be sensible of the sweet and ravishing varieties of the perfumes, as well as the most delightful and pleasant objects, and places of Recreation for the Inhabitants'.[54] The project may not have come to fruition in the grand manner conceived, and at any rate Evelyn also had a political agenda in the wake of the Restoration, but the work helped promote the sense that areas of greenery actively generated pure air that could then waft improvingly across the cityscape.

Optimistic appraisals of the healthiness of the city built upon this faith, countering the imagery of a contaminated atmosphere by playing up ease of access to fresh air in and about town. *The Foreigners Guide* rhapsodized: 'This City . . . has the Advantage of being sweetened on one Side by the fresh Air of the River, and on the other by that of the Fields.'[55] Both Stow and Strype articulate the value of London's green space in terms of wholesome activity and clean air. Stow is scathing about the shift of recreation away from what he sees as healthy and useful archery to gambling at dice and bowls, 'by the meane of closing in the common grounds'.[56] Strype re-asserts the benefit of encircling 'rich and pleasant fields' in relation to 'The pleasant, profitable, and healthful Situation of the City', and applauds efforts 'taken for preserving the Wholesomeness of the Air of the City'. To this end, he notes, there are the 'open and airy gardens' of the Inner and Middle Temple, laid out in 'delightful walks', Lincoln's Inn Fields, a 'spacious Place, with an excellent Air', and the Moorfields, 'pleasant walks set with trees' and 'no mean cause of preserving Health, and wholesome Air to the City'. The siting of the New Bethlam Hospital fronting Moorfields, providing grounds for patients 'to walk and air themselves in', articulated faith in and reinforced the association between health and green space.[57] Round about the capital, the villages of Hampstead and Highgate, Hackney, Stratford, Marylebone, and Kensington provided semi-rural excursions, and were peppered with weekend retreats, to 'go

---

[54] Evelyn, *Fumifugium*, pp. 5, 2, Dedication, 24–5.
[55] Anon., *Foreigners Guide*, p. 2.
[56] Stow, *Survey*, I.104; II.79.
[57] Strype, *Survey*, I.i.2; I.iii.70, 64.

on a Saturday in the afternoon to take the pleasure of the Country Air'.[58]

It is clear from these portraits of the city that increasing value was being ascribed to proximity to green space and fresh air within the urban environment. The question now is, what impact did this growing conviction of the physiological benefits of urban greenery have on the cultural representation and social worth of these spaces? Was there any discernible interplay between urban greenery and social status? Descriptions of city housing articulate one aspect of the relationship between the city, its inhabitants, and open green spaces. Increasingly, the promotion of spacious and elevated green sites as the most airy and refined within the urban body, compared with narrow, enclosed yards and alleyways, rendered the occupation of these healthiest, most ventilated plots an indicator of one's refined constitution.[59] The attraction of these lofty, airy sites keyed into and was reinforced by Addison's stress on the importance and value of an unfettered perspective, 'a spacious Horison is an Image of Liberty, where the Eye has Room to range abroad', the pertinence of which was not lost in the close-packed streets and alleys of the city.[60] In this environment, social climbing meant exactly that, to clamber above the urban scrum and flag one's elevated status. The height of good taste and social advantage was advertised in the fine view one commanded over natural environs from an elegant upper-storey window.

In his surveying of residential London, Strype time and again bears witness to the association drawn between the healthiness of a district and its social character. He describes Great Russell Street, especially the north side, 'as having Gardens behind the Houses: and the Prospect of the pleasant Fields up to Hamsted and Highgate. Insomuch that this Place by Physicians is esteemed the most healthful of any in London.' Accordingly, it was 'graced with the best Buildings in all Bloomsbury, and the best inhabited by the Nobility and Gentry'.[61] Exclusive developments like Grosvenor Square were portrayed as enjoying a location 'at the farthest Extent of the Town, upon a rising Ground, with the Fields on all Sides;

[58] Anon., *Foreigners Guide*, pp. 142, 128.
[59] M. J. Power, 'The social topography of Restoration London', in Beier and Finlay, *London 1500–1700*, pp. 199, 209–10.
[60] *The Spectator*, ed. Donald F. Bond (5 vols., Oxford, 1987), III, no. 412, p. 541.
[61] Strype, *Survey*, II.iv.85.

which, with the fine Air it thereby enjoys, renders the Situation delightful'.[62] The building developments of the first half of the eighteenth century 'towards the Fields in the Liberty of Westminster' were described as 'where most of the Nobility and Gentry now live, for the Benefit of the good Air'.[63] Queen Square, in London, flaunted 'very fine Houses, which the Prospect into the Park, renders more agreeable'. Cavendish Square was 'commendable for its fine Situation, enjoying a clear Air, and open Prospect over the Fields'.[64] Thomas Fairchild, author of *The City Gardener* of 1722, was very particular about the importance of the prospect into the garden square from the surrounding properties. Accordingly, obstructions such as tall trees planted on the outside of the square were not to be tolerated for, once matured, 'they must stand in our Way, and resist our Sight, and rob the Gentlemen of that View which they have by their Expence endeavour'd to gain'.[65] The duke of Buckingham kept his wall in the gardens of Buckingham House deliberately low so as 'to admit the view of a Meadow full of cattle just under it (no disagreeable object in the midst of a great city)'.[66] Strype describes Lincoln's Inn Fields as 'a very curious spacious Place, with an excellent Air, and therefore garnished with three Rows of very good Houses, very well inhabited'.[67] Southampton House enjoyed 'a curious Garden behind which lieth open to the Fields enjoying a wholsome and pleasant Air'.[68] The elegant houses of St James's Place, inhabited by gentry, received 'a fresh Air out of the Park', whilst large plots like that of Burlington House exploited a location on the fringe of the city fronting the fields, and 'from thence receives a fresh and wholesome Air'.[69] The houses of Berkeley Street faced the garden of Berkeley House, 'which renders them very pleasant and airy, and occasions the Street to be better inhabited'.[70] Similarly, it was 'the Enjoyment of so good a Prospect and free Air' from the houses of Arlington Street, with their gardens backing down to the wall of St James's Park, that 'makes them to be taken up by Persons

---

[62] Anon., *Foreigners Guide*, pp. 10, 122.
[63] *Ibid.*, p. 2.
[64] *Ibid.*, pp. 26, 120.
[65] Fairchild, *City Gardener*, pp. 13, 42.
[66] Quoted in Peter Coats, *The Gardens of Buckingham Palace* (1978), p. 37.
[67] Strype, *Survey*, II.iv.75.
[68] *Ibid.*, II.iv.84.
[69] *Ibid.*, II.vi.78 (St James's Place), II.vi.83 (Burlington House).
[70] *Ibid.*, II.vi.78.

of Quality'.[71] The large houses at the upper end of Downing Street were 'fit for Persons of Honour and Quality; each House having a pleasant Prospect into St James's Park, with a Tarras Walk'. The back windows of the fine houses along Duke Street overlooked the park, 'and many of the Inhabitants have the Favour of a Door out of their Garden into the Park, which is no small Benefit, by Reason of the Enjoyment of such good Walks'. Likewise, the 'very good Houses' of Park Street fronting St James's Park, enjoyed 'the conveniency of Doors out of their Gardens into the same'.[72]

This private access to the Royal Park was a keenly prized liberty and declaration of superior status. In 1668 the enlarged St James's Park was enclosed with a new brick wall.[73] The preservation of a regulated boundary was obviously deemed crucial in stemming the unchecked flow of the people into the park. When part of the boundary wall collapsed in 1742, the keeper ensured that temporary fencing was erected on the same day 'to keep the Deer in, & people out'.[74] The number of gates and doors leading into the park was initially reduced in 1665 for fear of the safety of Charles II on his walks around the estate.[75] Further anxiety over the king's safety around 1678 led to nineteen doorways being blocked off.[76] A process of selective access ensued. In 1681 it was noted that unregulated entry occasioned 'many inconveniences by affording passage and retreat to lewd and disorderly persons', and that therefore a number of access points should be stopped up.[77] However, petitions for the re-opening of old and construction of new private doorways into the Park continued to be granted to large residences occupied by nobility and gentry around the perimeter.[78] For example, in 1686 and 1687 Sir Edward Hales, Lord Jeffreys, the earl of Scarsdale, and the countess dowager of Plymouth were all granted private access from their respective properties along the wall 'for convenience of ingress and recreation

[71] *Ibid.*
[72] *Ibid.*, II.vi.63–4.
[73] *CSPD (1667–8)*, p. 35 (22 April 1668).
[74] PRO, Works 1/2, 6 and 12 October 1742, fo. 59.
[75] Jacob Larwood, *The Story of the London Parks* (1873), p. 335.
[76] In 1678 it appears that access was limited in direct response to an assassination attempt on the king whilst walking in the park. Christopher Wren, Surveyor General of the Works, was charged with 'shutting and walling up certain doors and passages going into St James's Park' numbering some nineteen: *CSPD (1678)*, pp. 466, 493, 497 (18, 29, 31 October 1678).
[77] *CSPD (1680–1)*, p. 209 (11 March 1681).
[78] *CSPD (1678)*, p. 580 (20 December 1678); *CSPD (1680)*, p. 447 (24 April 1680).

in the park'.[79] Furthermore, new building projects around the edges
of St James's, constructing 'Substantial Houses fit for the Reception
of Persons of Fortune & Distinction', were allowed to open up
passageways leading directly from these streets into the park.[80]

The new residential squares of the West End exemplify this
arrangement of private access to land that was ostensibly public.
The importance of the planned square lies in the ambiguity of a
'public' space reserved for private consumption. Simon Varey notes
that the railing of city squares enshrined the politics of keeping
distance.[81] The image of the open urban square as a place of free
public concourse was matched in reality by the sectioning off of
these spaces to serve the interests of the immediate residents, and to
enhance the repute of the developer. Richard Sennett makes the
observation that the squares incorporated within the Bedford and
Bloomsbury developments in London were 'not filled with people
but with shrubs and trees'.[82] Planting out these squares not only
improved the visual appeal of otherwise empty space, but stamped it
with gardenesque associations of health, cultivated taste, and harmonious order. It also established a stark contrast between leisured
and pointedly non-productive garden, and communal ground that
might be used for play and sport, trading, the grazing of animals,
collecting of firewood, and so on. The enclosed garden square
became recognized as emblematic of residential areas of distinction.
Macky notes how Leicester Square has 'several Houses of abundance of the first Quality. The Middle is planted with Trees and
railed round, which gives an agreeable Aspect to the Houses.'
Likewise Golden Square, planted and railed, was the residence of
'many great People of Quality'.[83] What Saussure refers to as
London's fine open spaces, planted with flowers and trees, were

---

[79] *CSPD (1686-7)*, pp. 241, 262 (15 August, 12 September 1686); 345, 428 (19 January, 19 May 1687).
[80] PRO, Works 6/17, IV, fos. 141, 148. The approved petition of James Mallors, builder, to open up a new passageway leading from his new street directly into the park forms a part of his project to enhance the location and appeal of his properties by securing their ease of access. A similar provision of private access for the nobility is also observable at Hyde Park. The anonymous author of *The Foreigners Guide* of 1729, commenting on the noble character Grosvenor Square, remarks 'By the Favour of his late Majesty, a Passage was granted into Hyde-Park, for the better Conveniency of the Nobility in this Quarter to take the Air therein' (p. 124).
[81] Simon Varey, *Space and the Eighteenth-Century English Novel* (Cambridge, 1990), p. 200.
[82] Richard Sennett, *The Fall of Public Man* (Cambridge, 1974), p. 54.
[83] Macky, *Journey through England*, I, pp. 168-9.

actually 'shut in by railings of painted wood'. The square of St James's, surrounded by 'handsome houses belonging to wealthy noblemen' was surrounded by iron balustrades.[84] Strype described Red Lyon Square as 'inhabited by Gentry and Persons of Repute . . . The middle of the square is inclosed from the Streets, or passage to the Houses, by a handsome high Palisado Pail, with Rows of Trees, Gravel Walks, and Grass Plots within: all neatly kept, for the Inhabitants to walk in.'[85] Fairchild devoted a good deal of attention to the subject of the planting out of squares in what he called 'a rural manner'. Such leafiness would in his opinion, 'contribute much to the ease of those, who by their being Great and Noble, are inhabitants of such places'. For these inhabitants, the prospect of open but private and well-ordered space, preferably planted out, was a key part of the attraction of these new developments. Accordingly, garden planting in squares had to take into account the season when the occupants were in residency, and so the challenge was 'how to make it look well in the Winter, and that Part of the Spring, when Persons of Distinction are in Town, or else the main Foundation of the Design will be lost; for they will not pay for a Thing that they have no Benefit of, or Pleasure in'.[86]

Measures aimed at restricting access to the city's green spaces, in the form of railings, walls and policed gates, codes of behaviour and admission charges, endeavoured to preserve the supposedly refined air of these sites.[87] Commendations of nature in the city relied on the notion of free-flow as a positive and improving characteristic. However, since miasmatic theories also associated air flow with contagion, as diseases were identified as spread by airborne particles, the corrective value of London's parks and gardens was vested in their being free of the contaminating bodies that threatened the welfare of the city as a whole. It was deemed to be in the welfare interests of select residents and visitors that such grounds be preserved from the encroachments of urban contaminants. At this point conceptions of physical and moral welfare collide, as the medical metaphor of contagion spread to portray the dangers of unfiltered social contact, too. The unpolluted air made so much of in

---

[84] Saussure, *A Foreign View of England*, p. 70.
[85] Strype, *Survey*, I.xii.254.
[86] Fairchild, *City Gardener*, pp. 13–15.
[87] Williams, 'Rus in urbe', ch. 6 'Keeping off the grass' discusses the means by which access to open space was restricted and the reasons behind this.

accounts of parks and gardens became fused with an imagery of
social refinement, a purity that could be tainted or infected through
too close a contact with the wrong bodies. In both *Sylva* and
Fumifugium Evelyn suggested that eyesore settlements and uncivilized
people ought to be removed from prime green sites, since they
seriously diminished the inherent value of the natural environment.
For example, 'poor and nasty cottages' around the capital, and
notably around St James's Park, 'disgrace and take off from the
sweetness and amoenity of the Environs of London', and so thwart
their potential for 'Health, Profit, and Beauty'.[88] Those living within
the dense body of the town, perhaps in cramped and unhygienic
conditions, were seen as dangerously prone to the contaminating
influences of the urban environment, with the resulting physical and
moral dissolution representing a form of contagion in itself. This
fuelled reactions against too crowded and indiscriminately mixed a
company. Movement, physically and socially, was desirable and
healthy as long as it was within the right environment, and undesirable elements were excluded. This idea of a 'moral miasma' was
particularly prevalent in the nineteenth century, informing attempts
to clean up the breeding grounds of filth and immorality, focusing on
the activities of the working classes.[89] But, given the role accorded to
parks, gardens, and walks in nurturing physical and moral well-
being, the concept of social contagion underpinned efforts to police
access to them from the early eighteenth century.

The idea of contamination of the rarefied air of the city's parks
and gardens is clearly drawn out in literary accounts. The self-
important Mrs Straddle seeks to banish common city workers from
St James's Park as unsuited to breathing its air. Furthermore, to the
question 'what sort of Constitutions art thou willing to allow the
liberty of this place?', the response is 'To none but sound ones.' The
physically, as well as socially, unfit cannot be suffered to taint the
refined atmosphere of the Park, 'The Sick ought to be sent to
Kensington Gravel-Pits, Hampstead, or Highgate, and not be
suffer'd among the polite World, to infect our Gaiety by looking on
their Languor.'[90] The benefits of the Hyde Park Ring for airing are
lost in the dust kicked up by the hordes resorting there, more
concerned with exhibition than constitution, the outcome of which

---

88 John Evelyn, *Sylva, or A Discourse of Forest-Trees* (1664), p. 112; Evelyn, *Fumifugium*, pp. 25–6.
89 Elizabeth Wilson, *The Sphinx in the City* (1991), pp. 37–9.
90 P.Q., *St James's Park*, p. 32.

is that 'the Wealthy and the Great repair, / To draw Contagion from polluted Air'.[91]

Of course, the desire for virtuous sociability stressed by some, emphasizing the importance of keeping company that polished rather than tarnished, and the representation of London's parks and gardens as oases of polite order, did not automatically translate on the ground. The gulf between the ideal and the actual opened up ripe territory for satirists to mine. As one author remarked, St James's Park was favoured and frequented 'because it carries so much the appearance of Innocence, yet at the same time has all the opportunities of Vice'.[92] The disjunction between the ideal of what these sites stood for and how they were actually used was mercilessly exploited. However, exposing the vice and vanity that carried on under the guise of virtue provided means by which to distinguish between those of true substance and those unable or unwilling to engage in the site with the required gravitas.

The emphasis, in all these accounts, is on the public and sociable aspect of London's parks, gardens, and walks, locating them squarely within the city's rapidly expanding panoply of urbane leisure facilities. So were the city's formalized and sanitized green spaces now no more than outdoor assembly rooms? For a start, the continued investment in planting, and in particular the increasing vogue for a more 'rural' outlook and arrangement suggests that the setting remained very much part of the appeal of these venues. But what really distinguished urban parks, gardens, and walks, and lent them particular appeal and kudos within the seventeenth- and early eighteenth-century cultural landscape, was their capacity for drawing on landed and rural associations at the same time as invoking urban civility and sociability. One of the virtues of this dual identity was that urban parks and gardens could be portrayed as green oases, proffering a physical and psychological abstraction from the cloying city, and marking out space in which to elevate oneself above the smoke, scrum, and sin of the city. As an extension of the potential imbalances that the built environment created, the risk that urban excess posed to health was also believed to undermine the moral well-being of

---

[91] [Joseph Browne], *The Circus: Or, British Olympicks* (1709), p. 13.
[92] P.Q., *St James's Park*, pp. 57–8.

those who resided in towns and cities, or who came into contact
with them. The characterized worldliness of the city, its emphasis
on public display and interaction, its business, luxury, indulgence,
and vice, stood in stark contrast to the imagined delights of rural
innocence, honest labour, peace, virtue, beauty, and a closeness to
God through harmony with his creation. But, as already indicated,
this did not translate into unambiguous anti-urban sentiment. For
all its attractions, the marking of one's detached superiority and
exorcizing of the taint of the worldly in rural retirement had its
down side in that it entailed a retreat from urbane sociability. Life
on a country estate could be awfully dull, rural gentry socially
inept, and the countryside dirty and rude. It was far preferable if
the appeal but not the inconvenience of a natural setting could be
incorporated within a commodious and civilizing environment. In
line with the prevailing model of constitutional governance, it was
a question of striking a balance. Urban green space provided a
convenient middle ground. Parks, gardens, and walks, both public
and private, were imagined to be capable of correcting these
deficiencies and maintaining and symbolizing rural qualities within
an urban frame, embodying retreat, spirituality, harmony, and
virtue. In this way, the city's parks and gardens represented the
spatial embodiment of this balance, seeming to offer a form of
removal and a contemplative, virtuous setting at the same time as
remaining public and sociable space. Conveniently, this emphasis
on the 'natural' associations of virtue, innocence, and order that
characterized parks, gardens, and walks might be deployed to
offset fear and criticism of the expanding leisure trade as opening
the door to moral corruption.

The idea of the garden as idyllic paradise retreat, to contrast with
urban dissolution, has an infinitely long lineage. Retirement from
the world to the simple pleasures of green groves crops up in the
literature of any period you care to choose, as Raymond Williams
exemplified.[93] The Roman and Renaissance tradition of retirement,
and cultivating of groves of wisdom within the city, was strong and
influential.[94] The theme of retirement to the countryside was as
pertinent and pervasive in the eighteenth century, as Maynard Mack

[93] Raymond Williams, *The Country and the City* (1st publ. 1973, 1993).
[94] John Dixon Hunt and Peter Willis (eds.), *The Genius of the Place: The English Landscape Garden
1620–1820*, new edition (Cambridge, Mass., 1990), p. 11; see also John Dixon Hunt, *Garden
and Grove: The Italian Renaissance Garden in the English Imagination 1600–1750* (1986).

elucidates in his work on Pope.[95] In full eulogistic mode, the garden was represented as a sanctuary, a protected enclave harbouring natural truth and virtue, and a haven in which to wash away the stains and temptations of the city. As temporary respite from the urban environment, the garden could offer an experience unhinged from time and dislocated in space, a way to cope with urban disease. A correspondent in *The Tatler* reminded the reader of the 'delicious Retirement' afforded by a garden, 'the Beauties and the Charms of Nature and of Art court all my Faculties, refresh the Fibres of the Brain, and smooth every Avenue of Thought'.[96] Meanwhile, Addison had written that the garden, as mankind's first and natural home, was 'naturally apt to fill the Mind with Calmness and Tranquility, and to lay all its turbulent Passions at rest'.[97] To retreat to the garden was to recognize and attempt to recover this natural state, a literal re-creation of innocence lost.

It is clear that positive representations of London's green spaces make play of a steeped tradition of garden retirement. Drawing on a classical discourse of retreat from the city, Edmund Waller drapes Charles II in the enlightening and ennobling olive and laurel and, in his depiction of the king alone and deep in thought in St James's Park, summons up the authority of kings of old who 'by frequenting sacred Groves grew wise; / Free from th'impediments of light and noise / Man thus retir'd his nobler thoughts imploys'. The trees and groves stand as wise and elevated spaces away from the city and its diversions. Here the king will find the perspective and clarity he needs to exercise good government, 'free from Court compliances He walks / And with himself, his best adviser, talks'.[98] The principal champion of Vauxhall's charms, John Lockman, assiduously promoted the notion of these most public gardens as an idyllic rural retreat, 'Retir'd from Town, Life's idle Cares forgot, / How have I hail'd (with Extasy!) my Lot'. Indeed, were Homer and Virgil to visit they would sing, 'What different Pleasures here are found! / Now wand-ring lonely, up and down / The lofty Trees, which shade us round / Waft us in Fancy, far from Town'.[99] In lines cribbed from

[95] Maynard Mack, *The Garden and the City: Retirement and Politics in the Later Poetry of Pope, 1731–1743* (Toronto, 1969).

[96] *The Tatler*, ed. Donald F. Bond (3 vols., Oxford, 1987), II, no. 179, p. 477.

[97] Bond, *Spectator*, IV, no. 477, p. 192.

[98] Edmund Waller, *A Poem on St James's Park as Lately Improved by His Majesty* (1661), pp. 6–8.

[99] Lockman, *Sketch*, pp. 22–3.

Alexander Pope's account of the contemplative solitude and tranquillity provided by gardens, the Druids Walk in Vauxhall was described as suited to those 'whose minds are adapted to contemplation, it seems devoted to Solitude', on the strength of the certitude that 'there is certainly something in the amiable simplicity of unadorned nature, that spreads over the mind a more noble sort of tranquillity'.[100] Tyers himself calculated and played upon the appeal of a 'rural retreat' to Londoners flocking 'from this large and populous City (especially in hot and sultry weather)'.[101] This presentation of the garden as a recreational retreat moderating life in the city echoes Sir Thomas More's Utopian vision of a cityscape in which urban residents have gardens to resort to in the summer.[102] Fairchild promoted gardens for urban residents 'in order to increase their Quiet of Mind, to be fix'd in a right Notion of Country Happiness'.[103] In the context of a city of London's unmatched scale and pace, purification through occasional retreat restored one's sanity. A French commentator noted that St James's Park was 'the Place where People go to get rid of the Dirt, Confusion, and Noise of this great City'.[104] Despite the extensive programme of works carried out, carving the rectilinear Mall and Canal out of its irregular parkland, innumerable accounts play up its rural air. The Frenchman de Muralt described it as 'a fine Country-like Place', finding it 'the more agreeable . . . because it has neither Art nor Regularity', so that 'Its great Beauty consists in bringing (as it were) the Country into the City.'[105] An observer of 1710 noted 'some of the finest English Cows' grazing, and Kip's view of London centred on the park at the heart of the West End contrived to depict the city in the manner of a vast landed estate, picking out features like the milkmaids who would serve promenaders with a glass drawn straight from the cow.[106] A turn in the gardens of Lincoln's Inn restored

---

[100] Anon., *A Description of Vaux-Hall Gardens* (1762), p. 41, lines cribbed from Pope's essay in the *Guardian*, 1713.

[101] Museum of London, Wroth scrapbooks, vol. III, newspaper advertisement, 1736 (source not cited).

[102] Sir Thomas More, *Utopia*, 1st publ. 1516, quoted in John Dixon-Hunt, *Gardens and the Picturesque; Studies in the History of Landscape Architecture* (Cambridge, Mass., 1992), pp. 305–7.

[103] Fairchild, *City Gardener*, pp. 8, 43.

[104] Beat Louis de Muralt, *Letters Describing the Character and Customs of the English and French Nations* (1726), p. 77.

[105] *Ibid.*

[106] Z. C. Von Uffenbach, *London in 1710, From the Travels of Zacharias Conrad Von Uffenbach*, ed. W. H. Quarrell and Margaret Mare (1934), p. 12; Tom Brown, *Amusements*, p. 67.

'usual Temper and Serenity of Soul', and enabled one to retire 'having passed away a few Hours in the proper Employments of a reasonable Creature'.[107] Ned Ward's urban observer, troubled with worldly cares and humane wrongs 'turn'd my back upon the noisy Town' and 'stroll'd into the Fields'.[108] The London Spy, strolling by the water in St James's Park, felt that 'nothing inhabited this watery place but peace and silence'.[109]

This chapter has explored some of the images associated with the representation of green space within London's urban landscape. In the first instance, attention was drawn to the changes in the character of these spaces, simultaneously under pressure from and given emphasis in response to the rate of the city's growth. From Stow to Strype, portraits of nature in and around the city, and its recreational use, reflect the shift from open fields to more formally demarcated and ordered urban parks, gardens, and walks. As the sense of a conflict and distancing between capital and country grows in response to increasing urbanization, the desire to preserve and blend greenery with the urban fabric becomes increasingly self-conscious. Here the representation and use of nature in the city can be located within the wider framework of the concept of constitutional balance, in which nature is the absolute standard from which the true order of things might be divined, and equilibrium achieved. Applied to the city, nature was imagined to have a positive and moderating influence. But the selective portrayal of urban green space as corrective and redemptive conveyed in guides and surveys, maps, prints, medical treatises, and literary accounts of London does not signal an anti-urbanization per se. The complexity of the relationship between the city and the country creates a picture more ambiguous than one of blessed rurality and cursed city. Rather, part of the significance accorded nature in the city during this period, before the accelerated urbanization and industrialization of the later eighteenth century, lies in the confidence vested in getting the balance right, harmonizing the best aspects of city and country and fashioning a refined urban environment, physically, socially, and morally. Incorporating selective elements of the natural world within the make-up of the city was conceived as vital in crafting this

---

[107] Bond, *Tatler*, II, p. 114.
[108] [Edward Ward], *The Field Spy: or, The Walking Observator. A Poem* (1714), pp. 1, 3.
[109] Ned Ward, *The London Spy*, ed. Paul Hyland (East Lansing, 1993), p. 139.

balance. The engravings included in Strype's edition of the *Survey* focus on and highlight a spacious and green aspect to the city, in portraits of the Temple gardens, Lincoln's Inn, Gray's Inn, and Charterhouse, Somerset House, and St James's House, and the Bethlehem, Hoxton, and Greenwich Hospitals. These sites are portrayed as emblems of an easy harmony between nature and the city.

This notion of harmony links in with and was in turn reinforced by the notion of nature as physician to the body of the city and the body of the city-dweller. This extends the concept of nature as a form of control, naturalizing the city, and neutralizing the potentially destabilizing effects of urbanization. Without some exterior standard to check and naturalize the evolution of the physical urban environment, the body of the city and of the city dweller was portrayed as prone to disfunction – disease and disorder. Natural elements were portrayed as cleansing the physical make-up of the city dweller and the fabric of the city. In particular, the corrective role assigned to London's green spaces, as purgative of bodily and urban excess, fixed on the benefits of good air, circulation, and exercise. Obviously, faith in these corrective properties draws heavily upon benevolent imagery of nature, but this does not mean that the natural world was conceived as wholly benign. While acknowledging the wild and danger of the natural environment, the period witnesses an increasingly confident and scientific enquiry into the workings of nature that underpins the conviction that the environment can be worked upon and improved, fitting within a general culture of improvement. By this reading, nature becomes a pliable tool deployed according to will. In shaping the human habitat to best advantage, efforts are made to expunge those elements of nature identified as undesirable, and to play up those aspects deemed conducive to human comfort and welfare. And so, for instance, dark, low-lying, dense, and stagnant environments posed threats that were countered by emphasis on elevated, airy, spacious grounds. Subsequent attempts to cleanse and control what was perceived as dangerous territory and to appropriate the higher ground clearly had a moral as well as physical dimension. The appropriation of green space in the city as informed by the notions of physical superiority discussed here was a theme explored in the final section of the chapter.

The latter section of this chapter flagged the conflation of physical and moral well-being, fashioning the social agenda that accompanied the development and ordering of urban parks, gardens, and walks. What become apparent here are the ambiguities inherent in the representation of urban green spaces as public and yet private, sociable and yet removed, and the tensions over access to and use of urban green space that simmer beneath the façade of unanimity. On the basis of the appropriation of natural imagery as emblematic of superior quality and harmonious order, the deployment of greenery and the marshalling of such environmental criteria as good air and water emerged as influential factors in the social organization of space within the city. The most desirable residential districts became the leafy, airy, spacious parts of the city, capitalizing on the associated moral and physical advantages suggested. Residents enjoying close proximity to gardens, tree-lined walks, parks, and green squares fancied that they were able to abstract themselves from the self-absorption of the city. To step into these natural enclaves was imagined as embracing something beyond economic self-interest, beyond the tarnish of the everyday, to connect with something timeless, even spiritual. This represents a modelling of parks, gardens, and walks in the classic image of garden as retreat, made more pointed as spaces of retirement from the surrounding urban bustle. In this private and contemplative capacity, the city's green oases are imagined as islands of spirituality in a sea of worldliness, harbouring natural harmony and virtue against a crashing tide of sin, luxury, and excess. That parks and gardens, as playgrounds of the wealthy, idle, and dissolute, can simultaneously embody what they are imagined to counter is part of the ambiguity of these spaces within the urban environment. By playing up this aspect of ageless order they also served as excellent devices in offsetting the realities of rapid change, especially reassuring during a period of marked urbanization and the attendant upheavals caused by demographic expansion and population influx, economic growth, and intensified building. In this way these representations of nature in the city traded on what Denis Cosgrove calls the 'inherent conservatism' of the 'landscape idea, in its celebration of property and of an un-changing status quo, in its suppression of tension between groups . . . conservatism in presenting an image of natural and social harmony'.[110] Green sites nourished this impression of cohesion by

---

[110] Denis Cosgrove, 'Prospect, perspective and the evolution of the landscape idea', *Transactions of the Institute of British Geographers* 10 (1985), 58.

rooting it within a natural order, soothingly proclaiming that everything was as it should be, calm, controlled, virtuous, and tasteful. Of course it was not. Nor were parks and gardens truly models of respectability. The play-off between vice and virtue is the core ambiguity of the garden. The city's green spaces could be dangerously wild and sexual places, fear of which motivated attempts to bridle their darker side. But, on the arcadian side, for pleasing associative imagery of peace and inherent order, natural spaces in the city provided the ideal screen upon which to project the illusion of a well-regulated and harmonious urban society.

The capacity of these green sites to provide a buffer zone between the individual and urban society and environment is a recurrent theme in portraits of the city, but the public dimension to these spaces is central to their representation within the urban physical and cultural landscape. The development and frequenting of public space helped to offset disquiet at what was perceived to be the increasingly individualistic and materialistic character of the city, and to foster a sense of collective interest and social harmony.[111] The evolution of this enlightened ideal, of the declaration of public spirit over private interest, was significantly reinforced by the use of parks, gardens, and walks as urban public forums. Squares and collective residential gardens were of particular value in this respect, in that they managed to communicate an impression of communality and public good while remaining private and enclosed spaces. The ambivalence between the public and private function and use of these sites, and other public parks and gardens, lies not just in their simultaneously providing private and contemplative space and accommodating urbane sociability, but also in their representing a public sphere actually constructed around a delimited notion of public. Their virtue and appeal was largely vested in their signification of social/moral and physical superiority and refinement, and this was patently compromised by the unchecked passage of the wrong elements. Some form of filtering was therefore considered desirable to preserve this refinement and the kudos that access to these sites was imagined to lend. It is this that fuelled the appropriating of space and introduction of excluding measures such as gates, sentinels, subscriptions, and behavioural orders, deployed to hedge

---

111 See R. S. Neale, *Bath 1680–1850. A Social History or A Valley of Pleasure, Yet a Sink of Iniquity* (1981), pp. 8, 11.

the reputation of the city's parks, gardens, and walks, and perpetuate the impression of inherent well-being. Whilst being deployed as a means of articulating social distinction, parks and gardens were projects that could be represented as very much in the public, or general interest, improving the physical and moral constitution of the town and the town dweller. Playing on these fused conceptions of physical and moral superiority, the city's green spaces served as excellent devices in imagining a controlled and harmonious society, and a benign urban environment.

Inversion, instability, and the city

From Troynouvant to Heliogabulus's Rome and back: 'order' and its others in the London of John Stow

Peter Lake

Inevitably, a volume inspired by Stow's *Survey of London* is going to spend a considerable amount of time dwelling on the language of celebration – sifting and analysing that language, while checking Stow's elegiac descriptions of the city and its customs against what passes amongst social historians for reality. Such enquiries are necessary because, as Kevin Sharpe has reminded us, in early modern England compliment could very often double as (implicit) criticism. Thus, the plaudits of contemporary commentators were often meant to call attention to the gulf separating what the person or entity being praised was actually like from what it (or they) ought to be.[1] Sensitivity to such nuances is doubly appropriate in a volume partly dedicated to Stow, since, as many of the chapters in this book show, Stow himself was not above using the carefully burnished image of what the city had been, contained in the *Survey*, adversely to comment upon what the city had become.

Where Stow made his point with historicizing subtlety, other commentators plunged in, at one turn, praising the city to the skies and, at another, denouncing its sins and corruptions in equally fervent and extreme language. These seemingly wild oscillations between praise and blame should not surprise us. As the richest, largest, and fastest-growing concentration of persons in England, London was never going to attract only plaudits and awed wonder. Moreover, as Stuart Clark and others have repeatedly reminded us, early modern English people tended to view the world in terms of binary oppositions. Accordingly, what passed for 'order' was often both affirmed and criticized through threatening evocations of disorder. The result was a species of inversion whereby images of

[1] K. M. Sharpe, *Criticism and Compliment: The Politics of Literature in the England of Charles I* (Cambridge, 1987).

perfect order were repeatedly confronted with negatively symme-
trical (inverted) images of disorder.[2]

The resulting images and tableaux of chaos and disorder might be
taken to represent a potentially disturbing and destabilizing 'return
of the repressed'; here were so many screens upon which could be
projected the emotional and discursive materials through the exclusion and repression of which order had been created and maintained
in the first place. One view of such transactions holds, of course, that
far being threatening or dangerous, such exercises in inversion
represented crucial means whereby the structures and assumptions
of order could be strengthened and reaffirmed. After all, the
outcome of these ritualized encounters between order and its
opposites was, for the most part, boringly predictable; order tri-
umphed again over disorder, and the forces of chaos and disorder
were once again dispelled. Moreover, the texts and performances in
which these transactions were enacted were, as often as not,
produced for the delectation and edification of paying audiences or
readers, who, having been vouchsafed a brief glimpse into an
alternately fascinating and frightening abyss of chaos, disorder,
violence, and unregulated desire, could, as it were, return home to
their quotidian mental world and daily round, safe in the knowledge
that all was well with the world. If what was at stake here was indeed
some sort of 'return of the repressed', we might conclude that it was
a distinctly tamed and commodified version thereof that was being
allowed to return.

But was it? After all, as we shall see below, oftentimes the negative
and positive images created in the course of these transactions were
so intertwined, linked at so many emotional and discursive levels,
that it might be difficult to see where one ended and the other began.
Or, to put the matter differently, the transition from one to the other
was not always achieved by switching between obviously opposed
moral polarities, from the black of corruption, decay, and chaos, to
the white of virtue, order, and control. Rather the transitions from
order to disorder, from positive to negative, and back, were often
effected through an exercise in what Quentin Skinner has reminded
us was the rhetorical form of paradiastole. By this means essentially
the same quality or action was relabelled as a vice or a virtue through

---

[2] For two seminal articles on this theme see S. Clark, 'Inversion, misrule and the meaning of
witchcraft', *Past & Present* 87 (1980) and 'King James' *Daemonologie*: witchcraft and kingship'
in S. Anglo (ed.), *The Damned Art: Essays in the Literature of Witchcraft* (1977).

the application to it by a skilled rhetor of a negative or positive evaluative term or label. Thus, as many a godly preacher complained, the profane and the ungodly were only too adept at repackaging drunkenness and gluttony as good fellowship or hospitality, at relaunching greed as prudence and proud and wasteful conspicuous consumption as the fitting display of status and wealth.[3]

Thus, while it is no doubt true that many of the texts and performances that we shall be discussing below were designed as controlled exercises in the 'return of the repressed', we should surely at least entertain the possibility that such inversionary exercises and texts had effects other than the simple reaffirmation of a calmingly ordered status quo ante. On occasion, at least, they may have been just as successful at evoking and presenting order's disorderly other as they were at controlling and dispelling it. What struck or remained with the reader/spectator of the texts and performances discussed below might well have been not only the anodyne and conventional picture of order with which they conventionally opened and closed, but also (or even more so) the interestingly titillating, anxiety-producing deviant bits in the middle.

I do not want to enter here into another round of the seemingly endless subversion/containment pas de deux first set in motion in the 1980s by new historicist commentators on the literature and culture of the period.[4] Like the similar binary oppositions between order and disorder, consensus and conflict, order and crisis, beloved of revisionist historians of the same vintage, I would argue that these either/or dichotomies represent false choices. Indeed, a good deal of the subsequent scholarship and debate has shown only too clearly that to accept such binaries as setting the terms within which we are to conduct our own analyses of early modern English politics and culture is to condemn ourselves to a series of entirely circular exchanges between what were and are two sides of the same inversionary coin; in other words, it is not so much to study contemporary ideological assumptions and discursive forms as to remain trapped within and interminably to reproduce them.[5]

[3] Q. Skinner, *Reason and Rhetoric in the Philosophy of Hobbes* (Cambridge, 1996), pp. 142–53, 156–80.
[4] S. Greenblatt, *Renaissance Self Fashioning: From More to Shakespeare* (Chicago, 1984) and *Shakespearean Negotiations: The Circulation of Social Energy in Renaissance England* (Berkeley, 1988).
[5] See the introduction to K. Sharpe and P. Lake (eds.), *Culture and Politics in Early Stuart England* (1994).

Rather than plumping either for sedition or containment, consensus
or conflict, order or crisis – as the dominant characteristics of
contemporary culture, the central motifs or ends of the textual and
performative practices under review here, I want to suggest a more
modest goal: to use what one might term the underside of order, to
get at what alternately threatened, fascinated, titillated, and disturbed contemporaries about their social and cultural world. Or, to
put the matter somewhat less cryptically, to see what, even as they
praised the place, frightened and alarmed contemporaries about
London.

I

And praise it they most certainly did. For Thomas Dekker – at least
when he was writing in celebratory mode – London was Troynouvant, new Troy. London, he declaimed, in a pamphlet of 1604, was
'Europe's jewel; England's jem; / sister to great Jerusalem; Neptune's
minion ('bout whose waist / the Thames is like a girdle cast,) / thou
that but health canst nothing want, / empress of cities, Troynouvant.'[6] Like Stow, Dekker sang the praises of the city's built
environment, hailing London's 'lofty towers' 'whose pinnacles were
tipped with gold, / both when the sun did set and rise, / so lovely
wert thou in her eyes'.[7]

London in foreign countries is called the queen of cities and the
queen mother over her own. She is the king's chamber royal, his
golden key; his store house; the magazine of merchandise; the
mistress of sciences; a nurse to all the shires of England. So famous is
she for her buildings that Troy hath leaped out of her cinders to
build her walls. So remarkable for her priority and power that hers is
the master wheel of the whole kingdom. As that moves, so the main
engine works.[8]

In a scene from his *Britannia's Honour* (a series of pageants designed
to celebrate the inauguration as Lord Mayor of Richard Deane in

[6] F. Wilson (ed.), *The Plague Pamphlets of Thomas Dekker* (Oxford, 1925), pp. 89–90, from *News
from Gravesend* (1604). On the origins of the myth of London as the new Troy see L. Manley,
Literature and Culture in Early Modern London (Cambridge, 1995), pp. 182–3. On the impact of
plague and contemporary responses thereto see Paul Slack, *The Impact of Plague in Tudor and
Stuart England* (1985).
[7] Dekker, *Plague Pamphlets*, p. 90.
[8] F. Bowers (ed.), *The Dramatic Works of Thomas Dekker* (4 vols., Cambridge, 1968), IV, p. 82.

1628) called 'new Troy's tree of honour', Dekker represented London as a 'lady' 'in a rich Roman attire with an ornament of steeples, towers and turrets on her head ... in her left hand she holds a golden truncheon ... to show that she's a leader and conductress of a mighty people: her right hand ... takes hold of a tree out of which spread twelve main and goodly branches' (which represent 'the twelve superior [London] companies'). Around her in her bower are represented 'peace, religion, civil government, justice, learning, industry and, close to industry, honour. For as all these are golden columns to bear up the glories of the city, so is the city an indulgent and careful mother, to bring them up to their glories. And as these twelve noble branches cover these persons (as it were with the wings of angels) so these persons watch day and night to defend the twelve branches.'[9] Here then is the ideal London; London as a new Troy or a new Rome, rich, populous, powerful and yet a repository of honour, industry, piety, and good government; the very epitome of prosperity and order combined.

Nor was this picture of London confined to such inherently venal and self-serving occasions as mayoral inaugurations when pens like Dekker's were hired to tell both the elite and populace if not what they wanted to hear, then at least what they were supposed to believe. Preaching at Paul's Cross in 1616, Sampson Price compared the glories of contemporary London to those of ancient Rome. London was the most populous city in the world, he exclaimed; Londoners had 'the sea for your ramparts' and enjoyed the services of 'as many learned and religious teachers to instruct as any one church since the apostles times ... you have goodly houses to receive you; pleasant shades to cool you; all delicates of sea and land to feed you'.[10]

In his mayoral pageants, Dekker played such celebratory rant straight. But there was another side to the discourse of praise. The initial verse quotations from Dekker cited above are, in fact, taken from *News from Gravesend*, one of his plague pamphlets and the passage from Price is excerpted from a virtual jeremiad, one of a series of such denunciations of the sins of the city preached from Paul's Cross by a variety of preachers throughout the period. Many of these were occasioned by outbreaks of the plague; one of them

[9] *Ibid.*, pp. 86–7.
[10] S. Price, *Ephesus' Warning Before her Woe* (1616), pp. 70–2.

(cited below) by the same plague of 1604 that prompted Dekker's pamphlet. In texts like these, the glories and blessings of the city had no sooner been evoked than they were dismissed, to be replaced by an equally lurid tableau of the city's sins. All of Dekker's plague pamphlets performed this inversionary trick, flipping over from the city as Troynouvant to the city as Golgotha, a plague pit, a place of fear, disease, death, and putrescence. Here the city under plague became one vast memento mori, a great leveller before which the wealth, pretensions, and displays of the rich and powerful were brought low and the very social fabric of the city broke down, with those who could running away to the country, leaving their less fortunate erstwhile neighbours, the poor and indigent, behind to die.

In the same vein, in a Paul's Cross sermon of 1604, Richard Jefferay took his auditors on a tour of

the buildings enlarged by Achab's cruelty, the coffers enriched by Achan's thievery: the states maintained by Gehesies policy; all these are seen; all these are sin . . . Those that make widows a prey, the fatherless a spoil, the friendless a prize, receive not Christ; many store houses sorted with wares, many warehouses filled with store, many cupboards filled with plate, many wardrobes furnished with gorgeous apparel show that we receive not Christ as we should do; those biting usurers that devour the needy and feed upon the flesh of them that are fallen into their nets receive not Christ.

All this was done to contrast the fineness of the city itself with the corruption of its inhabitants. Of the citizens, some, Jefferay claimed,

were cruel as lions, to wit merciless, prejudicate, bribe-taking magistrates; some greedy as tigers, the simoniacal, illiterate, soul-starving ministers; some fierce as dragons, the extortive, state-spoiling, money mongers; some changeable as chameleons, the political informant, time-serving, state-mongers; some deceivable as foxes, the privy bookers, subordinate scribes and crimping gamesters; some ravenous as wolves, the city sergeants, county bailiffs, corrupt officers; some lascivious as goats, the brothel haunters, sap suckers and soakers; some filthy as swine, the lazy, licentious, inordinate task masters; some proud as unicorns, the rising courtier, standing lawyer, falling merchant; some inhumane as vipers, the unnatural children, ungrateful friends, unfaithful servants.

London, in short, was outstanding amongst the cities and nations of the world, even in its sins: 'in Flanders never was such drunkenness, in Italy more wantonness, in France more dissimulation, in Jewry more hypocrisy, in Persia more curiosity, in Barbary more cruelty, in Turkey more impiety, in Tartary more iniquity than is practised generally in England, particularly in London', Jefferay almost triumphantly concluded.[11]

In Dekker's works, then, we are confronted by two radically different, indeed symmetrically opposite, visions of the city, as new Troy and a plague- and sin-ridden charnel house. The link between the two was provided, of course, by the sins of the city. For, as both pamphleteers like Dekker and myriad preachers at the Cross and elsewhere were at pains to insist, the cause of the plague was not dirty streets or noisome or infected air but human sin. On this view, the plague represented the response of a just but merciful God to the sins of the city, and it was that inevitable transaction between human sin and divine mercy and justice which provided the hinge or link between the city as new Troy and as plague pit. The only way in which that hinge could be turned back to its original position and the world thus thrown upside down righted, was through repentance and then reform. But if the city's repentance should prove short lived and the consequent reformation a chimera, then the city would remain mired in the cycle of human sin and divine judgement of which the plague was so central and spectacular an instrument and sign. Not that the consequence of repeated refusals to reform was a return to a static or cyclical status quo ante. On the contrary, the parallels between London and, say, Jerusalem or Ephesus, around which such claims were habitually organized, led to yet more sinister and extreme outcomes. For the wages of sin repeated in the face of divine judgement and warning were either complete destruction of the sort visited upon Jerusalem by Vespasian or the loss of the gospel like that visited upon Ephesus by the Turks. Or so the preachers loved to insist, in long pages of evocative rant describing the siege of Jerusalem or the fate of Sodom and Gomorrah.[12]

The difficulty here was that at least some of the sins – greed, pride, ambition, luxury, conspicuous consumption, and vainglorious display – that brought down the judgements of God upon the city

---

[11] R. Jefferay, *The Son of Gods Entertainment* (1605), pp. 30–1, 28.

[12] The tenor and tone of these sermons can be gleaned from some of their titles: see for instance F. White, *Londons Warning by Jerusalem* (1619); Price, *Ephesus' Warning Before her Woe*; A. Hill, *The Cry of England* (1595). On this same genre now see A. Walsham, *Providence in Early Modern England* (Oxford, 1999), ch. 6; Walsham's work draws heavily here on P. Collinson, *The Birthpangs of Protestant England* (Basingstoke, 1988), ch. 1, 'The protestant nation' and 'Biblical rhetoric: the English nation and national sentiment in the prophetic mode' in D. Shuger and C. McEachern (eds.), *Religion and Culture in the English Renaissance* (Cambridge, 1997). See also Manley, *Literature and Culture*, pp. 309–10.

were arguably merely different, negative rather than positive, evaluations of the impulses and activities that produced the wealth, the
architectural, sartorial, and gastronomic finery and display, that
prompted encomia on the glories of the city of the sort quoted
above. On this basis, it was possible, as it were, at the flick of a
switch, to convert conventional accounts of the positive attributes
and achievements of London into symmetrically negative denuncia-
tory accounts of the sins of almost all the ranks and estates that
made up the social body of the city. Discoursing at the Cross on the
all but universally deleterious effects of what he termed hypocrisy,
Thomas Adams gave a bravura demonstration of just this trick.

Most of our professions (thanks to ill professors) are so confounded with
sins as if there were not a pair of shears between them. Nay, they can scarce
be distinguished; you shall not easily discern between a hot, furious
professor and an hypocrite; between a covetous man and a thief; between a
courtier and an aspirer; between a gallant and a swearer; between an
officer and a bribe taker; between a servitor and a parasite; between
farmers and poor-grinders; between gentlemen and pleasure-lovers;
between a great man and a mad man; between a tradesman and a
fraudsman; between a monied man and a usurer; between a usurer and a
devil.

In large part what we are observing in passages like these are the
moral and rhetorical results of contemporaries' lack of a morally
unambiguous, univocally affirmative language with which to describe and praise the pursuit, attainment, and display of commercial
wealth. In the absence of such a language or world-view contemporaries remained trapped in the moral universe of Thomas Adams, a
place in which, wherever the pursuit and display of wealth was in
evidence, lust and covetousness, whoredom and usury, could not be
far behind. For, as Adams explained, hypocrisy was both 'a stalking
horse for covetousness' and 'a complexion for lust'.[13] This was a
both striking and significant elision that reveals the way in which for
contemporaries the sins of the flesh, of carnal desire and sexual
pleasure (what John Bossy has termed the sins of concupiscence),
remained indelibly associated with, indeed in some sense could be
made to stand for and comment upon, the sins of the marketplace,

---

[13] T. Adams, *Works* (1630), pp. 44, 49, from *The White Devil*, a sermon preached at Paul's Cross,
7 March 1612. On the lack of an explicit and coherent language of praise for mercantile
wealth see L. C. Stevenson, *Praise and Paradox: Merchants and Craftsmen in Elizabethan Popular
Literature* (Cambridge, 1984), *passim* and esp. ch. 6.

covetousness, envy, and ambition (central elements in what Bossy has termed the sins of aversion).[14] All of which ensured that, when contemporaries came to take moral stock of the city, its achievements and dominant attributes, they remained doomed to oscillate from praise to blame and back, their propensities in that direction increased by the irruptive force of divine judgement in the shape of the plague that intermittently invaded and laid waste to the city throughout the period.

II

Of course, much of all this was conventional, indeed formulaic. It was, of course, the job of preachers to denounce the providential judgements of God against the sins of a fallen humanity and to descry and decry sin wherever in the social order it occurred. Nor was clerical complaint at the greed, pride, and luxury of the city novel in the early modern period. Thus, if we want to pursue these themes further we must turn to another body of texts, equally obsessed with the sins of the city, but concerned to put them to rather different rhetorical purposes from those espoused by the preachers. I refer to what might best be termed crime pamphlets and plays, relatively cheap texts and performances, which tried to sell to a socially heterogeneous (popular?) audience moralized accounts of the latest enormities culled from the London streets.[15]

The events retold in such texts tended to be extreme; extreme either in the ghastly and ghoulish nature of the crimes themselves or in the social locales in which they occurred or in both. Thus while the social locale of the crime recounted in the play *Two Lamentable Tragedies* was ordinary enough, involving the murder of a prosperous grocer Beech and his boy servant by his envious neighbour, Thomas Merry, the crime itself was outlandish. Both Beech and his boy were done in by multiple hammer blows to the head; Beech's body was dismembered and distributed about the city. The boy survived miraculously for days with the hammer still sticking out of the

---

[14] J. Bossy, *Christianity in the West* (Oxford, 1985). As we shall see, many of the texts with which we shall be concerned below in fact collapsed or elided lust into covetousness and covetousness into lust in just such a way.

[15] On this sub-genre of cheap providentialized print see P. Lake, 'Deeds against nature: protestantism, cheap print and murder in early seventeenth-century England', in Sharpe and Lake, *Culture and Politics*. On providentialized news pamphlets more generally see Walsham, *Providence in Early Modern England*.

gaping wound in his head, until he was able to discover the identity
of his assailant, at which point he gave up the ghost.[16] In other
accounts the crimes themselves might be commonplace enough –
armed robbery, ending in murder, infanticide by a prostitute desperate to rid herself of an unwanted child – but the persons who
committed them were very frequently culled from the social extremes: either masterless men and prostitutes from the London
backstreets, or gentle rakes and patriarchs run berserk.

In the rake or patriarch run amok and the whore, readers were
confronted with the absolute opposites, the symmetrically perfect
anti-types, of those two pillars and personifications of order, the
dutiful wife and the virtuous household patriarch. Some sense of the
sort of perfect inversion of social and moral norms at work here can
be gleaned from an archetypal sin, one pictured, in several of the
pamphlet narratives, as common to both whores and patriarchs –
infanticide. For child-murder represented the complete inversion of
the normal ties, feelings, and obligations of human society described
in the pamphlets. Infanticides were presented, as the title of one
pamphlet had it, as 'nature's cruel stepdames or matchless monsters
of the female'. Theirs were the ultimate 'deeds against nature', as
the title of another infanticide pamphlet termed them. The paradoxical image of the 'pitiless mother' (to quote yet another pamphlet
title) seemed to sum up the inverted moral order of the London
backstreets as these texts described it.[17]

Remarkably, for all that infanticide was statistically a predomin-
antly female crime and was presented in many a pamphlet as
perhaps the perfect expression of the unnatural depravity of the
masterless or rebellious woman, not all the infanticides described in
the pamphlets were women. At least two gentry patriarchs, one Mr
Calverley of Calverley and John Rous, are shown slaughtering their
offspring. Both were provincial gentlemen of ancient lineage, heads
of gentry houses, who, having ruined themselves morally and
financially in London, through lives of sexual excess, conspicuous
consumption, and heedless gambling, killed their offspring in order
to save them from the lives of poverty and dishonour to which their
own actions would otherwise have doomed them.

---

[16] Robert Yarrington, *Two Lamentable Tragedies* (1601).
[17] *Deeds Against Nature and Monsters by Kind* (1614); H. Goodcole, *Nature's Cruel Step-dames or Matchless Monsters of the Female* (1637); *A Pitiless Mother, that Most Unnaturally at One Time Murdered Two of her Own Children* (1616).

In the story of John Rous, the decline into murder and death started with an act of adultery with a maid servant. The upset following that affair sent his first wife to an early grave. Rous married again, all the time continuing his liaison with the maid. Next, he left his second wife to live a life of debauchery in London with his mistress. Defrauded of his property, he went abroad for a time. At last, ruined, he returned home to his wife and children. But there

the devil still tempting him to mischief and despair, putting him in mind of his former better estate, comparing pleasures past with present miseries and he revolving that he had been a man in that town ... that he had friends, lands, money, apparel and credit, with means sufficient to have left for the maintenance of his family and that now he had nothing left him but poverty and beggary and that his two children were like to be left to go from door to door for their living.

In this devil-induced despair he killed both his children, to save them, as he thought, from a life of beggary and shame.[18]

His story parallels almost exactly the similar descent into debauchery, debt, despair, and child murder described by Mr Calverley of Calverley. This last was a particularly infamous crime which occasioned at least two pamphlets, a ballad, and two plays. One of these, *A Yorkshire Tragedy*, followed very closely the pamphlet accounts, and concentrated entirely on the tragic events in Yorkshire, while the second, *The Miseries of Enforced Marriage*, invented a whole narrative and social background to Calverley's fell deeds, set almost entirely in the fleshpots of London. Certainly in both the pamphlets and the plays Calverley is presented as stark mad, driven out of his wits into a world of delusion, anxiety, and violence by the intensity of his own sin and depravity.[19] Rendered desperate by his debts, he blames his wife. 'That mortgage fits like a snaffle upon mine inheritance, and makes me chew upon iron', he rages at one point. 'I hate the very hour I chose a wife, a trouble trouble, three children like three evils hang upon me, fie, fie, strumpet and bastards, strumpet and bastards.' He lurches from lamenting his gambling-induced poverty to forcing his wife to liquidate her

[18] John Taylor, *The Unnatural Father or a Cruel Murder Committed by one John Rous ... upon Two of his Own Children* (1621).

[19] *Two Most Unnatural and Bloody Murders: The One by Master Calverley a Yorkshire Gentleman* (London, 1605); *A Yorkshire Tragedy* (1608, Malone Society reprints no. 116, 1973); G. Wilkins, *The Miseries of Enforced Marriage* (1607).

dowry lands so that he can continue to dice away his remaining resources.

At one point, he seems finally to have been called to a sense of his own sins by news of his younger brother who, having stood as surety for Calverley's debts, is now paying the price of his elder brother's profligacy in prison. This information seems about to bring Calverley to his senses. 'I never had sense till now, your syllables have cleft me', he tells the messenger who has brought him this news. Certainly his brother's suffering induces in Calverley a sense of the enormity of his sins and the extent of his responsibilities as the head of an ancient family of honour and renown. 'Down goes the house of us, down, down, it sinks. Now is the name a beggar, begs in me that name which hundreds of years has made this shire famous in me and my posterity runs out. In my deeds five are made miserable beside myself, my riot is now my brother's jailor, my wife's sighing, my three boys penury and mine own confusion.' The result of this sudden flash of insight, however, is not genuine repentance and amendment of life but a desperate attempt to slaughter his children in order to protect them from the lives of beggary and dishonour to which his own extravagance and riotous misrule have condemned them. As he tells his eldest son, 'thou shalt not live to ask an usurer bread, to cry at a great man's gate . . . no, nor your brother. Tis charity to brain you', which, of course, he then proceeds to do.[20]

As the other play based on the case, *The Miseries of Enforced Marriage*, makes clear, Calverley's descent into sin-induced desperation and infanticide took place in London, as a direct result of hanging out in gambling dens and ordinaries with the whores and pimps who surround Sir Francis Ilford and his rakish cronies. An arrested version of the same moral decline is experienced by the gallant Matheo in Dekker's play *The Honest Whore* and (albeit to a lesser extent) by Malheureux in Marston's *The Dutch Courtesan*. The main plot line of that play involves two young gallants, Freevill and Malheureux. Freevill, about to marry the virtuous Beatrice, is in the process of disentangling himself from his attachment to the beautiful whore, Franchesina. Malheureux enters the action attempting to persuade his friend, Freevill, out of his lustful, whore-addicted ways (I, i, 57–60). Freevill defends his nocturnal habits only to be told

---

[20] *A Yorkshire Tragedy*, sigs. A4r–Br, Cr, C2r–v.

sternly that 'the most odious spectacle the earth can present us is an immodest, vulgar woman'. When Freevill persists, Malheureux only agrees to accompany his friend to meet his Dutch whore because 'the sight of vice augments the hate of sin' (I, i, 146–7, 152). But once in the whore's presence, Malheureux, to Freevill's huge enjoyment, falls desperately in love with Franchesina himself. Since Freevill is about to throw her over in order to marry Beatrice, Malheureux's determination to enjoy Franchesina's favours – 'Soul, I must love her [I, i, 137]' – seems easily and conveniently enough arranged. The whore must merely swap the custom and affections of one gentleman about town for another. Franchesina, however, will have none of it. When she learns of Freevill's impending marriage and her impending abandonment she goes berserk and vows revenge. Thus, when Malheureux declares his love for her, she requires him to kill his friend Freevill in order to secure her sexual favours for himself. Her intentions here are doubly, indeed trebly, vicious, since she intends then to denounce Malheureux to the authorities, thus sending him to the gallows, while discovering Freevill's previous liaison with her to Beatrice, thus breaking her heart twice over. Here she is, revelling in what she takes to be the imminent success of her schemes. 'Now ick shall revange. Hay, begar, me sal tartar de whole generation! mine brain vork it. Freevill is dead; Malheureux shall hang; and mine rival, Beatrice, ick sall make run mad.' 'Now sall me be revenge. Ten tousant devla! Dere sall be no Got in me but passion, nought but rage, no mercy but blood, no spirit but the deval in me. Dere sall noting tought good for me, but dat is mischievous for others' (IV, iii, 29–31, 42–5). Here then is the whore as the epitome of sheer willful malevolence and evil; a perfect gendered image for what happens to the fleshly aspects of a fallen human nature when it is removed from the controlling constraints of patriarchal authority. Franchesina's pure malevolence, her wilful determination to do damage echoes the equally destructive frenzy experienced by Calverley or Rous, male authority figures driven to the end of their tether by total surrender to the lusts and demands of the flesh (for the delusional, diseased, and corrupting pleasures of which whores like Franchesina provided perfect symbols or figures).[21]

Very often the sinful both carnal and criminal unions between

---

[21] I quote from Keith Sturgess (ed.), *The Malcontent and Other Plays* (Oxford, 1997).

whores and rakes were pictured as taking place in the dicing houses, brothels, taverns, and ordinaries of the backstreets of London. This was a milieu described by George Whetstone in the most lurid of terms. The second half of his tract, *A Mirror for Magistrates of Cities*, was devoted to 'exposing the dangerous mischief that the dicing houses . . . and other like sanctuaries of iniquity do daily breed within the bowels of the famous city of London'. Here, in the 'taverns, common tables, victualing houses, stews and brothel harbours' of the city – locales he described as 'filthy places', the 'foul ulcers of the commonweal' – were to be found 'the swarm of unthrifts which live upon shifts in and within the city of London'. Such people were 'the scum of the city, I mean ruffians, bawds, brokers, cheaters, shifters and others'. Here 'dice, drunkenness and harlots' 'consumed the wealth of a great number' both 'of ancient gentlemen' and of unwary young men at the Inns of Court; 'the bravery of the company, the glee and revel that they keep were able to bring a staid man unto their society but are sure to enchant a light young man which cometh (rawly) out of the country'.[22]

Here was a milieu in which the social extremes met as the producers and consumers of the city's sex and leisure industries. On the one hand, this world reached upward to the landed class and even to the court, as young gentlemen of good birth and estate played the role of the gallant and man about town learning from their social inferiors how to gamble, swear, whore, and spend and consume beyond their means. This was a process with which Whetstone, who claimed to have been himself its victim, was obsessed. Moreover, other plays and pamphlets depict the same phenomenon. Thus in the pamphlet, *The Lives, Apprehension, Arraignment and Execution of Robert Throgmorton, William Porter, John Bishop, Gentlemen*, the descent into moral depravity, theft, and then murder of three young men of good birth is described as taking place in and through the delights and temptations of London. All three young men are presented as having been born 'of an honourable, ancient and worthy family'. All three could lay claim to 'dignity in birth, admiration of wit and height of courage'. But all three abused these gifts, plunging, in London, into a life of overt indulgence and

---

22 G. Whetstone, *A Mirror for Magistrates of Cities* (1584), pp. 4b–5a, 27a, dedicatory epistle 'to the young gentlemen of the Inns of Court'. On Whetstone's authorial strategies see Manley, *Literature and Culture*, pp. 315–18.

debauchery. For while their claims to nobility were derived from their origins in the provinces, their 'native country', their descent into debauchery, theft, and murder was located explicitly as taking place 'within the city of London whither the concourse and inundation of all states, degrees, sects, faculties, humours, nay almost whatsoever in this kingdom hath moving doth, as falling rivers, fall into that main ocean'.

The pamphlet goes on to describe their moral decline in the most florid terms. 'These three gentlemen' 'lived together, not according to the rule of virtue . . . but according to their appetites, distemperate passions and the frantic errors of headstrong and unbridled youth'. They proceeded to act as 'though that excess and riot were not the consumptions of reputation but rather ladders and scales to advancement, holding the worst maxim that ever folly brought forth which is that unnecessary expense begets the best means for spending'. In short, they began 'to think that thirst could not be quenched without drunkenness, the body not be kept warm without satin and velvet, the heat of the blood not cold without change of courtesans nor the stomach filled without it belch back the superfluity of their surfeits'. Thus inflamed, they rapidly began to live beyond their means (or rather their parents' allowances) and 'many times wanting money to supply the baseness of their appetites, they began to put on a resolution to relieve their licentious appetites by any preposterous course whatsoever, were it by cosenage, theft, nay, as it appeared by view of their actions, even by murder itself or the most loathed massacre'.

Desperate for money, one day they set out on a ride towards Bagshot with no fixed intention except to 'take any man's purse they met with'. Meeting two citizens of London and a merchant from Southampton on the road they proceeded to rob them. The two Londoners parted readily enough with their money, but the Southampton merchant, one Smith, put up a fight and actually managed to worst young Bishop. Fearing for his life Bishop called to his mates Throgmorton and Porter for help and, as Smith turned to escape, 'rising from the ground and gaining his sword' (lost in his earlier scuffle with Smith) Bishop 'ran the merchant side ways through the body'; 'showing', as the anonymous author editorialized, 'more cruelty in the bloodiness of his revenge than unnatural and dishonest covetousness to be possessed of the goods to which he could never justly pretend any title'. Thus was a scion of the ruling class brought

low by a life of depravity and whoredom in London. Not only had
the three been reduced to theft and murder, Porter, having been
worsted in a fair fight by a mere merchant, had been reduced to
finishing off his intended victim with a cowardly stab in the back
entirely unworthy of a gentleman of honour.[23]

The tendrils of such metropolitan and elite corruption did not
merely link the scions of the provincial ruling class to the dregs of
the city, they also reached up to the court itself. In the play, *A
Warning for Fair Women*, the seducer, adulterer, and murderer Brown
reveals himself in his speech from the gallows as another perfect
exemplar of this style of metropolitan/elite corruption and depravity.

> Vile world how like a monster come I soiled from thee?
> How have I wallowed in thy loathsome filth,
> drunk and besmeared with all thy bestial sin?
> I never spake to God, unless when I have
> blasphemed his name with monstrous oaths.
> I never read the scriptures in my life,
> but did esteem them worse than vanity.
> I never came in church where God was taught.
> Nor ever, to the comfort of my soul,
> took benefit of sacrament or baptism.
> The sabbath days I spent in common stews,
> unthrifty gaming and vile perjuries.
> I held no man once worthy to be spoke of
> that went not forth in some strange disguised attire,
> or had not fetched in some vile monstrous fashion,
> to bring in odious detestable pride.
> I hated any man that did not do
> some damned or some hateful, filthy deed,
> that had been death for virtuous men to hear.
> Of all the worst that live, I was the worst.
> Of all the cursed, I the most accursed.
> All careless men be warned by my end,
> and by my fall your wicked lives amend.

But if that is Brown's definitive verdict on his own life and
character, the text in fact contains a good number of other estima-
tions of him that serve to place him in a dense and detailed socio-
cultural context or locale. He is introduced as a military man who

---

[23] *The Lives, Apprehension, Arraignment and Execution of Robert Throgmorton, William Porter, John
Bishop, Gentlemen* (1608), *passim*.

has served the Crown in Ireland and done well for himself; he enters the action telling tales of Dublin society and first preens himself before a decidedly unsmitten Ann Sanders by offering to use his pull at court on her husband's behalf. Ann's initial take on him is as socially precise as it is dismissive: 'These errand-making gallants are good men, / that cannot pass and see a woman sit / of any sort, alone at her door, / but they will find excuse to stand and prate, / fools that they are to bite at every bait.'

Something of a gallant, if not a courtier, then certainly known at court, with friends and contacts in very high places, Brown clearly both dressed and acted the part. He committed the murder dressed, we are told, in 'a doublet of white satin and a large pair of breeches of blue silk'. As for his manner, we can guess at that from a conversation between two officers. Told that 'divers lords are come from court to day, / to see the arraignment of this lusty Brown', the second officer replies scornfully, 'Lusty? How lusty? Now he he's tame enough, / and will be tamer. Oh a lusty youth, / lustily fed, and lustily appareled, / lusty in look, in gate, in gallant talk, / lusty in wooing, in fight and murdering / and lustily hanged, there's th'end of lusty Brown' [sig. H3v]. Thus, when the bodies of the slain Sanders and his man John Bean are discovered, that repository of plebeian common sense 'Old John' concludes, 'this is the deed of some swaggering, swearing desperate Dick. Call we them cavaliers, mass they be cannibals, that have the stab readier in their hands than a penny in their purse. Shame's death be their share.'

Significantly, other on-lookers in the play perceive Brown very differently. One calls him 'a goodly man, believe me, too fair a creature for so foul an act'. Another tells him that 'I know you well, your fortunes have been fair, as any gentleman's of your repute.' One of the Lords of the Privy Council, no less, goes so far as to admit that 'we are sorry for your fall, / you were a man respected of us all / and noted fit for many services'. Brown, then, like Throgmorton and his mates is presented as a man of parts, of birth, breeding, and connection, who had been corrupted by the city; his real gifts and capacities turned to evil courses through the conspicuous consumption, lascivious display, and fleshly delights of London.[24]

But if the milieu of the London backstreets stretched up to the

---

[24] *A Warning for Fair Women* (1599), sigs. I3v–4r, B3v, F2v, Hr, H3v.

landed class, the Inns of Court, and even to the fringes of the court, it also reached down into the very dregs of the social order, the masterless men, the thugs, pimps, and whores who made their living on the streets of the city. Henry Goodcole, the ordinary of Newgate, made something of a speciality of describing the low-life denizens of this milieu in a series of short, cheap crime pamphlets. In these notes from the London underground we meet a variety of infanticidal prostitutes, vicious murderers, and lustful old men. In Goodcole's pamphlet of 1635, *Heaven's Speedy Hue and Cry after Lust and Murder*, those ideal types of masterlessness and disorder, the thug and his moll, the murderous prostitute, and the casually violent, entirely ruthless masterless man, come together in a peculiarly threatening partnership in crime. In this pamphlet Goodcole described the careers and capture of Country Tom and Bess of Canberry. Bess was a prostitute and Tom, her accomplice, a violent thief; together they lured unwary men into the fields and open spaces around London and then killed and robbed them. The woman, of course, was the bait, what Goodcole termed 'the setter', who

set on such a brazen face that upon a man unknown to her she searcheth in the open streets and with her deceitful smiles and salutes so enchants and incaptivates and leads him unto slaughter. Like a decoy duck she alone is going abroad but not alone returning . . . the bargain she strikes up and goeth before to a secret appointed place upon whom, unawares to the seduced person, attendeth a merciless strong thief and most barbarous cruel murder that at once strikes and stays, of whose cunning practises, secret snares and subtle wiles I labour to give all people a light and true insight.

Bess and Tom continually trawled the city streets, Goodcole explained, looking for suitable marks, 'both hunting for one prey and frequenting and watching such places and houses for persons fitted for their occasion and to make use of'. To this end they haunted 'playhouses', 'taverns', 'inns', 'ale houses', 'the open streets', and 'the fields', everywhere searching for 'one that had that day been too busy with the pot'. Meeting her victims in such bustling, quintessentially urban, indeed metropolitan, locales, Bess then lured them into the various open spaces that dotted the city, no doubt on the promise of some fleeting sexual encounter under the stars but in fact to meet their doom at the hands of her accomplice, Tom, and the 'short truncheon' or 'bastinado' 'of iron' which he carried under his cloak.

III

Elsewhere in the same pamphlet Goodcole distributed the forces of disorder sketched in this and his other pamphlets across the social and physical topography of the city. Thus he recounted the deaths of Rowland Holt in Clerkenwell Fields, of Thomas Claxton in Grey's Inn, and of Michael Low who was fatally wounded by 'Lady Hatton's wall' at Newgate. But Goodcole went further than supplying his readers with the topographical specifics of the particular crimes under discussion. He appended to his pamphlet 'intimation of such places in and about the city of London that harlots watch their opportunities to surprise men' just as these had been 'confessed by this malfactor':

First at West Smithfield within the rails and Dutch lane end; second and thirdly by the taverns at Smithfield and cooks shop in Pye corner and Clothfair a great harbour for such; fourthly, by Smithfield pond and sheep pens; fifthly, by the little conduit in Cheapside in the evening; sixthly, St Antholins church when the shops are shut up; seventhly and lastly remember London bridge over which you must necessarily travel into the southern parts. Beware you go not by night with a cloakbag but in your hand nor behind you on horseback lest you be justled against the wall by a cutpurse in the habit of a gentleman and so lose it. Beware likewise of your hat and purse in a fray stirred up purposely in the street to allure people into concussions, in plain to speak pickpockets, deceit, and cosenage. In Middlesex towards Pancras church in the fields, at Cow Cross towards the butchers at Bloomsbury, in St Giles in the Fields beware of such like offenders.[25]

Goodcole's text thus conjures up an urban landscape dotted with places of danger and depravity; the city looms over his text as a both wonderful and threatening place through which only the practised local can move without danger. Not only, as in Whetstone's vision of the city, were the dicing houses and brothels, the taverns and ordinaries pictured as being mixed in amongst the dwellings of the respectable and the wealthy, but amidst the densely packed buildings of the city were fields and open spaces, which, at certain times of day and, more particularly, of night, could become threatening sites of sin and depravity, symbols and carriers of the corruption, disorder, and sin pressing in on the structures of order and the

[25] H. Goodcole, *Heaven's Speedy Hue and Cry after Lust and Murder* (1635).

denizens of respectable society that made up metropolitan society proper.[26]

On this view the city contained, within its midst, the very sites of corruption, the social types and malfactors that threatened the moral standing, social stability, and spiritual health of the metropolis. We can gain a heightened sense of how this worked from the detailed social profile and locale conferred upon the thief, murderer, and hit man, Blackwill, in the play *Arden of Faversham*. He is presented there as the archetypal masterless man; an ex-soldier who, having served in Henry VIII's French campaigns at Boulogne in the 1540s, is now, in the 1550s, wandering from Kent to London and back in a restless search for an easy mark. He is, in short, a figure solidly based in the social reality of the 1550s, when the play was set and the actual Arden murder had taken place, but also familiar from the recent social experience of the play's audience during the war years of the late 1580s and early 1590s, when the play was, in fact, first written and performed.

But Will is more than an ex-soldier turned sturdy beggar, ruffian, and thief, a point the play makes clear by associating him not only with the world of the tramping poor and the desperate, demobilized soldier, but also with the equally threatening, amoral, and violent milieu of the London backstreets. Thus, at one point, his prowess as a desperate killer called into question by yet another failed attempt to finish off Arden, Blackwill brags,

thou knowest Greene, I have lived in London this twelve years, where I have made some go upon wooden legs for taking the wall on me; divers with silver noses for saying 'there goes Blackwill'. I have cracked as many blades as thou hast done nuts . . . The bawdy houses have paid me tribute; there durst not a whore set up unless she have agreed with me for first opening her shop windows. For a crossed word of a tapster I have pierced one barrel after another with my dagger and held him by the ears till all his beer hath run out. In Thames street a brewer's cart was like to have run

---

[26] For the distribution of bawdy houses through both the infamous suburbs and the city itself see I. Archer, *The Pursuit of Stability: Social Relations in Elizabethan London* (Cambridge, 1991), pp. 211–15, see esp. the map at p. 212. This voyeuristic tendency (alternately comic and threatening) to present the city as the site of a variety of more or less sinister and threatening criminal sub-cultures all but impenetrable to the unwary outsider who therefore needed some sort of native guide if he were safely to negotiate the city, reached its apogee in the famous rogue and cony-catching literature produced from the 1590s on. For the comments of various social historians on the veracity of this literature see for instance Paul Slack, *Poverty and Policy in Tudor and Stuart England* (1988), pp. 24–5, 102–5 and most pertinently for my current purposes Archer, *The Pursuit of Stability*, pp. 204–37.

over me: I made no more ado but went to the clerk and cut all the notches off his tallies and beat them about his head. I and my company have taken the constable from his watch and carried him about the fields on a colstaff. I have broken a sergeant's head with his own mace and bailed whom I list with my sword and buckler. All the ten penny ale houses would stand every morning with a quart pot in their hand, saying, 'will it please your worship drink?' He that had not done so had been sure to have his sign pulled down and his lattice born away the next night. To conclude, what have I not done? (sc. XIV, I.11–28)[27]

A very specific geographical, social, and cultural milieu is being assigned to Blackwill in this passage. Associated with London low life, a world of whores, ten-penny ale houses, of casual interpersonal violence, and crime, Blackwill's is a life lived entirely at odds with the behaviour patterns and values of the respectable middling sort and their servants, in the midst of whom he lived. This is a group represented in the passage quoted above by the tapster and the brewer's clerk, the ale-house keepers and the ordinary citizens passing in the street, all variously assaulted and terrorized by Blackwill. But Blackwill's was also a career lived in open conflict with the stock symbols of authority, hierarchy, and the law again represented in the passage cited above by the constable, the sergeant, and his mace.

Now at first sight this might all seem bad and threatening enough. However, to the extent that the forces of sin and disorder could be restricted to the dicing houses, brothels, and taverns of the city, relegated to the social extremes represented by the masterless man, the whore, and the gentry rake, the resulting image of disorder was at least as comforting as it was threatening. It left untouched the orderly households of ordinary respectable citizens and the structures of government and authority in and through which the city elite and middling sort in fact maintained order. Indeed, it is tempting to see the pamphlets and plays we are discussing here as processing extreme versions of the sins and crimes of the city for the delectation of a middling and better sort of city audience, an audience that remained safe in its sense of itself as having little or nothing in common with the criminal underworld, the rakes, whores, and infanticides being paraded before them on the way to

---

[27] I quote from the New Mermaid edition of *Arden of Faversham*, edited by Martin White (1982). On the resort of discharged soldiers to the city and their status as a source of disorder and crime see Archer, *The Pursuit of Stability*, pp. 156, 210–11. On the problems of masterlessness, vagrancy, and crime more generally see *ibid.*, pp. 205–9.

the gallows. They might live amongst such people, but they most definitely were not like them; the threat came from outside, it might be close, but it was safely other.

Certainly if the sort of systematic moral and social apartheid outlined above could be maintained, then the rhetorics of social criticism, condemnation, and blame being levelled in these texts at the sins, abuses, and corruptions of the city, could be rendered not merely compatible with but also supportive, indeed, in some sense, constitutive of, the rhetorics of praise deployed by the likes of Dekker as they hailed London as Troynouvant, the new Troy. We can gain some further sense of how this worked by watching as authors like Goodcole and Whetstone, having separated out these contrary images of the city, then proceeded to set the one against the other. Thus, the very title of Henry Goodcole's pamphlet of 1619, *London's Cry Ascended to God and Entered into the Hearts and Ears of Men for Revenge of Bloodshedders and Burglars and Vagabonds*, pictured the city as a battleground between the forces of disorder and violence, evoked in the pamphlet's title and exemplified by the crimes described, and the forces of order, embodied in the person of Sir Edward Sackville, the London justice to whom Goodcole dedicated the tract and the grand and trial juries of both London and Middlesex, whose names he listed along with those of 'the honourable and worshipful benchers and justices in this sessions for the city of London and county of Middlesex'.[28] We can see the same binary opposition in George Whetstone's tract, *A Mirror for Magistrates of Cities*. On the one hand, Whetstone outlined the forces of virtue and control, personified by the Lord Mayor and aldermen, to whom he dedicated the book, and inscribed in a series of almost absurdly draconian measures for the moral control of the city. These, he claimed, were based on similar ordinances allegedly passed by the emperor Alexander Severus in ancient Rome. Over against this fantasy of order and control, Whetstone set an image of London/Rome as a city where 'cosenage was esteemed lawful merchandise, and dicing fair pastime; lechery was held no sin, nor chastity virtue; ruffians were honoured, the gods despised, the mouth of virtue was locked and vice spake through a trumpet'.

On this view, the hinge between these two visions or versions of

---

28 H. Goodcole, *London's Cry Ascended to God and Entered into the Hearts and Ears of Men for Revenge of Bloodshedders and Burglars and Vagabonds* (1619).

the city, London as the corrupt den of iniquity, of Rome under Heliogabulus, and London as the reformed and virtuous Rome of the reformer Alexander Severus, was relatively easily turned. All that was needed to effect that transition was a magistracy committed to the cause of order, determined personally to view the sins of the city and to visit justice and condign punishment on its 'taverns, dicing places and brothel houses', its 'shifters, bawds and brokers'. Or so Whetstone and indeed many a Paul's Cross sermon claimed.[29]

IV

But the overall purport of these texts was, in fact, nowhere near as straightforward or reassuring as such reforming panaceas might be taken to imply. To begin with, the basic sins being excoriated, and the crimes the discovery and punishment of which were being depicted in these texts, could not plausibly be relegated to or contained within the backstreet milieu to which authors like Whetstone or Goodcole tried, in the main, to restrict them. Pride, covetousness, ambition (impulses grouped by Whetstone under the rubric of 'envy'), the lustful and/or avaricious pursuit of fleshly pleasure and gain, could not be portrayed as the preserve of any one social group. Not only were they the ubiquitous spiritual stigmata of a fallen humanity, they were precisely the faults to which the inhabitants, even the most respectable and substantial inhabitants, of a city whose wealth was based on commerce and trade, might well fall subject.

And, in fact, many of the crimes described in these pamphlets and plays took place in quite commonplace, what one might, somewhat anachronistically, term, entirely respectable locales – the households of merchants and artisans. Here wives and their lovers killed husbands, husbands killed wives, parents killed children, and children or (more often) servants killed parents or masters. They did so, moreover, prompted by the most commonplace and obvious of motives – lust, greed, adultery, revenge, envy.

Accordingly, the pamphlet and play texts under discussion did not only work to distance the reader from the awful crimes and shocking sins that formed their central subject matter. On the contrary, they

[29] Whetstone, *Mirror for Magistrates*; Thomas Lodge, *An Alarum against Usurers* (1584), in Edmund Gosse (ed.), *The Complete Works* (4 vols., Glasgow, 1883), I.

worked on their readers in two linked but apparently contradictory ways. On the one hand, the extremity of the crimes committed in these narratives – typically murder, often, as we have seen, of the most gruesome and shocking sort – served to distance them from the immediate experience of the average reader. We can watch the pamphlets taking advantage of this fact the better to present the reader with a safely enjoyable titillatory tableau of sex and violence, of miraculously providential discovery and deserved punishment, of the good or bad deaths acted out by felons on the gallows.

On the other hand, the morally improving, providential frames which these texts sought to impose upon this material, the overarching edificational purposes which some of these texts (at least notionally) set themselves, worked in precisely the opposite direction. On this view, in at least some of the pamphlets, the stories being told became extreme exempla of central spiritual truths about the condition of fallen humanity; truths about the nature of sin, the relationship between sin and God's providence, between sin, providence, punishment (both human and divine) and true repentance and between repentance and salvation; truths which applied to all those who wanted to be saved. On this basis we might argue that far from distancing the reader from the material being so luridly evoked, at least some of these texts were attempting to induce their readers to inhabit morally, to apply to their own experience and circumstances, the moral lessons, the providential and salvific narratives inscribed within these bitter and disgusting little stories.

Of course, a cynical observer might claim that the prime purpose of the second function was to legitimate the first, allowing readers their voyeuristic pleasures without disrupting, indeed while positively enhancing, their sense of their own moral respectability and (relative) spiritual safety and social distance from the felons whose acts and fates were being so luridly described. (Given the nature of the evidence, such claims must remain mere speculation, since we can penetrate neither the intentions of the writers and printers who produced these texts nor the responses of the readers who consumed them.) In any case, we can surely conclude that the crimes and sins at the centre of these texts were being presented in ways that were designed not merely to engage the voyeuristic attention of the reader, but also to stimulate and exploit his or her anxieties, impulses, and (surreptitious) pleasures. If the repressed really was returning in these texts it was surely doing so not merely as a spectacle to be consumed from a safe distance before being dismissed from view, but as a reminder of contradictions and areas of tension and anxiety in the experience and assumptions of the viewer/consumer.[30]

The lines of emotional, moral, and psychic force at work here emerge yet more clearly once these stories and their readers are inserted into an explicitly metropolitan context. To develop the point, we need to return to George Whetstone's *Mirror for Magistrates of Cities* and Thomas Lodge's *An Alarum against Usurers*. Lodge and Whetstone were not concerned only to attack the London demi-monde of dicing houses, taverns, ordinaries, and brothels. What went on there merely provided him with a synecdoche for a wider process whereby what Whetstone took to be the representative sins of the city – 'covetousness and usury' – undermined the moral and financial standing and independence, of the landed class. Since it was on the moral probity and military service of that class that the stability, independence and strength of the commonwealth as a whole rested, Whetstone argued that this was a most serious state of affairs, one which, he contended, called for immediate and draconian executive action; an outline for which he then proceeded to provide in the remainder of the pamphlet in what was, in fact, a scheme to reform the corruptions of the whole commonwealth through the reformation of the metropolis. As Whetstone explained the situation, the emperor Alexander Severus had found 'the outward wounds of the weal public' to be 'pride, prodigality, dicing, drunkenness, lechery, usury, covetousness etc.', sins which abounded in, indeed typified, the city of Rome/London. And certainly it was on the denizens of the city that Whetstone/Severus placed the blame for the resulting moral and social corruption and decay. 'If there were no brothel houses, shame would delay lechery. But for taverns and tippling booths, drunkards should be sober against their wills. But for ordinary tables, dicers should (many times) be idle or better occupied then in swearing and consuming their patrimony.' If Whetstone had had his way all these establishments would have been suppressed and swingeing punishments dealt out to all those who either ran or frequented them. His was a fantasy of order and control severe enough to satisfy even Recorder Fleetwood and the most puritanically inclined of the London aldermen and magistrates to whom the tract was dedicated.

[30] On this point see Lake, 'Deeds against nature', *passim* but esp. p. 283.

Whetstone and Lodge's was an extreme vision and, on the whole, other authors did not follow them in producing a structural version of London's corrupting influence on the moral economy of the whole country.[31] But other texts did continue to point out that the artisans and merchants of the city were deeply implicated in the impulses and exchanges through which moral corruption spread (particularly but not only into the landed classes). To cite but one example, in the play *Eastward Ho!* the apprentice Quicksilver tells his master Touchstone that his keeping company in dicing houses and taverns with young men about town is entirely in his master's interest. 'And by God's lid, 'tis for your worship and for your commodity that I keep company. I am entertained among gallants, true; they call me cousin Frank, right: I lend them moneys, good; they spend it, well. But when they are spent, must not they strive to get more? Must not their land fly? And to whom? Shall not your worship ha' the refusal?' In other words, Quicksilver claimed to be spending and lending his master's money out so that Touchstone himself could benefit in the end by calling in the accrued debts of various gentry spendthrifts, thus enriching himself at their expense. This was a practice that Quicksilver (here, of course, echoing Whetstone) presented as an age-old method whereby denizens of the city had battened off the follies and indiscretions of the landed class; 'how would merchants thrive, if gentlemen would not be unthrifts? How could gentlemen be unthrifts if their humours were not fed?' This analysis provokes a tirade of middling-sort moralizing from Touchstone who, in fact, soon dismisses the young ne'er-do-well, Quicksilver, from his service, but the basic point has been made (I, I, 26–47).[32] Indeed, as Dekker made plain through the shopkeeperly complaisance of the linen draper Candido in his play *The Honest Whore*, the merchants and shopkeepers of the city did not need to espouse Quicksilver's credo to remain complicit in the luxury trades, the buying, selling, and lending processes, whereby their pockets were lined, their clients and customers cut a dash in the world and moral corruption and sin spread throughout the commonwealth.

Indeed, in many of the so-called city comedies of the early seventeenth century we are shown London tradesmen and gentry

---

[31] Whetstone, *Mirror for Magistrates*, pp. 9a–b, 20a. On Lodge and Whetstone see Manley, *Literature and Culture*, pp. 315–18.

[32] I quote from The Revels edition of *Eastward Ho!*, edited by R. W. Van Frossen (Manchester, 1999).

rakes, gallants, and men about town all engaging in elaborate schemes and stratagems of mutual exploitation and antipathy, as each group vies to outdo the other in the depth of its corruption and dishonesty. Very often, of course, the resulting densely choreographed intrigues and exchanges take on a sexual form, as gentlemen plan to cuckold the tradesmen who are trying, just as intently, to cozen them. Sometimes, as Douglas Bruster has pointed out, merchant husbands are pictured as pimping for their wives, selling their sexual services for pecuniary gain or social advantage; sometimes they are shown being cuckolded against their will. Here the moral and social breakdown of the external world of getting and spending invades the domestic sphere, as heads of households and husbands who have so signally failed to discharge their moral and social duties in the wider world are undermined and ridiculed at home. Social disorder and moral decay goes domestic, and sins and corruptions initially expressed in terms of covetousness, ambition, and envy, turn sexual. The moral, sexual, and monetary economies are folded into one another, each reflecting and commenting upon the corruption of the other.[33]

We can gain a heightened sense of how these complicities and connections were conceived and figured in these texts if we turn our attention for a moment to the contemporary resonance of the term 'whore'. As both Laura Gowing and Faramerz Dabhoiwala have observed, 'whore' operated during this period as far more than a synonym for prostitute. Dabhoiwala argues that the word was used to refer to someone engaged in a whole spectrum of unchaste sexual behaviour, that might include or culminate in various sorts of bought sex but which, in fact, included a whole range of other forms of behaviour, including adultery, promiscuity, the co-habitation of the unmarried, all of which fell a good way short of what the modern observer would regard as prostitution proper. Gowing's analysis of the language of defamation confirms these claims. For she finds the appellation 'whore' to have been the single most common and serious allegation/epithet that could be levelled against any woman.

---

[33] For an early farce-like example of this see William Haughton's play of 1598, *Englishman for My Money or A Woman Will Have Her Will*. For a later more sophisticated reworking of such themes, see, for instance, Dekker and Webster's play of 1607, *Westward Ho!* These matters are discussed in Stevenson, *Praise and Paradox*, ch. 5. See also D. Bruster, *Drama and the Market in the Age of Shakespeare* (Cambridge, 1992), esp. ch. 4. On the public/private distinction see L. C. Orlin, *Private Matters and Public Culture in Post-Reformation England* (Ithaca, 1994).

Accordingly, the word's potential area of reference far exceeded full- or even part-time workers in the sex industry of the day, to encompass any element or hint of sexual looseness or untoward display or immodesty that might attach to a woman's conduct or appearance or to the company she kept. Moreover, thus broadly conceived, 'whores' were regarded as persons who undermined not merely the emotional and sexual, but also the monetary household economy: siphoning off – either through their own finery of dress and outward display, or through the gifts and payments lavished upon them by their often married male clients – material resources that should otherwise have been expended on the prosperity and standing of the household viewed as a patriarchally defined unit of affect, production, consumption, edification, and control.

The whore, then, was the symmetrically perfect reverse image or inversion, the polar opposite, of the dutiful, sober, and honest wife and mother. But paradoxically this did not mean that the two figures were separated by a vast moral and social gulf, but rather that they were connected by a finely graded chain of incremental moral infractions and failures, that could lead modest and virtuous matrons, wives, and mothers into a moral condition that amounted to whoredom.[34] Accordingly, many of these texts show respectably married matrons being transformed into whores through extravagance, inordinate sartorial, and hence sexual or at least sexualized, display, slatternly conduct, or loose and lewd speech. In *Arden of Faversham* the well-born and once loving and loved wife, Alice Arden, is transformed, through her passion for the low-born Mosby, into a lustful, utterly wilful adulteress and murderer, the moral equivalent, employer and, in the end, partner-in-crime, of that ultimate figure for disordered masterlessness, Blackwill. Similarly, in *A Warning for Fair Women*, Ann Sanders is transformed from a loyal and virtuous wife into a besotted adulterer and husband murderer by the blandishments of the gallant lusty Brown and his accomplice Mistress Drewery. On this view, even the most respectable, ordered, and loving marriage and household could be overturned through one of the chains of sins that lead in the pamphlet narratives from pride, lust, greed, or envy to theft, adultery, murder, and death.

---

[34] F. Dabhoiwala, 'Prostitution and police in London, *c*.1660–*c*.1760', DPhil thesis, University of Oxford (1996); L. Gowing, *Domestic Dangers: Women, Words and Sex in Early Modern London* (Oxford, 1996). On the 'social reality' of prostitution in early modern London, see Archer, *The Pursuit of Stability*, pp. 211–15, 231–3, 249–54.

The initial moral infraction, the sinful incision, which offered Satan his chance in these narratives was often small enough. In *A Warning for Fair Women*, the event that leaves Mistress Sanders vulnerable to the approaches of Brown and his go-between, Drewery, is a spat with her merchant husband over the purchase of a pair of gloves and some lace, luxury goods, indeed mere fripperies, and, as such, perfect types for the sort of (feminine) vanity and pride that was likely to lead the unsuspecting into soul threatening sin. In *Two Lamentable Tragedies*, the moral equivalent to Ann Sanders' pride and petulance is Merry's covetous envy of his older and more established neighbour, Beech's, economic success. While the former lapse leads Sanders into adultery and murder, the latter leads Merry into attempted theft and murder.

Thus, if the whore and whoredom stood as gendered synecdoches for what would happen to the carnal fleshly aspects of a fallen human nature once that nature was removed from the controlling structures of social, political, and patriarchal control and order, the significance of that symbolism was not restricted to the realms of the household, gender relations, and sexual sin. On the contrary, as we have seen, in the view of the world under discussion here, no such hard and fast divisions existed.

Whoredom, after all, was not merely a sin of the flesh, it was also a (corrupt and unnatural) commercial transaction. As such, contemporaries often connected and compared it to a variety of corrupt financial or economic practices and exchanges, the most corrupt and corrupting of which was that other quintessentially urban sin: usury. Just like the whore, in this moral universe, the usurer played the role of an extreme anti-type at the end of a spectrum of linked tendencies and failings. (In the case of usury, contemporary commentators organized those failings and temptations under the sin of covetousness; in the case of the whore, of course, they organized them under the sin of lust.) Just like the whore, the usurer represented unnatural and immoral forces that, once embraced, would undermine or consume from within the structures of order and normality upon which society was founded. Thus, Thomas Adams explained at the Cross in 1612, usury

is a teeming thing, ever with child, pregnant and multiplying: money is an unfruitful thing by nature, made only for commutation, it is a preternatural thing it should engender money: this is monstrosus partus, a monstrous birth . . . The nature of it is wholly devouring . . . the usurer is like the worm we call the timber worm, which is wonderful soft to touch but hath teeth so hard that it eats timber, but the usurer eats timber and stones too.[35]

The whore perverted procreative sexual relations into money relations, while the usurer profited from his equally unnatural capacity to make money itself procreate and reproduce itself. As Orlando explains to Matheo in *The Honest Whore*, he scorns to lend his money out at interest since 'I cannot abide to have money ingender. Fye upon this silver Lechery, fye!' (Second part, 2, 1, 93–4).[36] The whore and infanticide either did away with the products of their own unnatural and unlawful (because venal) reproductive processes, or, at the very least, as Bellafront explains to some of her erstwhile clients in *The Honest Whore*, gave as 'interest on the principle' only 'a filthy loathed disease'. 'That usurie's worst of all, / When th'interest will eate out the principall' (First part, 3, 3, 63–4). For his part the usurer hoarded, equally unnaturally and illegally, the proceeds of his illegally engendered monetary progeny.

As we have seen, while the whore represented an extreme moral anti-type, the route to whoredom led incrementally through any number of seemingly trivial or minor temptations and lapses. So, in turn, we might imagine usury as located at the end of a chain of economic sins that might start innocently enough with the sort of over-enthusiastic pursuit of economic success or envy of the more prosperous of one's neighbours, of which even the most honest, indeed godly, young tradesman (like Thomas Merry) might be guilty. But, again as the case of Merry showed, once started such concatenations of temptation and sin could lead to the most dreadful of crimes and fates. In his *Alarum against Usurers*, Thomas Lodge tried hard to distinguish between the general run of merchants who 'to public commodity' 'bring in store of wealth from foreign nations' and those who 'degenerate from the true name and nature of merchants' and 'by their domestical practises' 'not only enrich

---

35 Adams, *Works*, p. 55 from *The White Devil*. On the social reality of money lending, see N. Jones, *God and the Money Lenders* (Oxford, 1989), ch. 3; R. Ashton, 'Usury and high finance in the age of Shakespeare and Jonson', *Renaissance and Modern Studies* 4 (1960); M. K. McIntosh, 'Money lending on the periphery of London, 1300–1600', *Albion* 20 (1988); B. A. Holderness, 'The clergy as money lenders in England, 1550–1700', in F. Heal and R. O'Day (eds.), *Princes and Paupers in the English Church, 1500–1800* (Leicester, 1981); C. Muldrew, 'Interpreting the market: the ethics of credit and community relations in early modern England', *Social History* 18 (1993). For complaints in London against usury, particularly as a means of oppressing the poor, see Archer, *The Pursuit of Stability*, p. 53.

36 I quote from Dekker, *Dramatic Works*, II.

themselves mightily by others misfortunes but also eat our English gentry out of house and home'. But that distinction kept breaking down under the weight of the general assault on the sin of covetousness towards which the moral argument of his tract was always tending. 'Since we see', he concluded, 'that much hoarding cannot be without sin, much getting, without grief, much profit, without pain, much increase of goods, without decrease of virtues, I cannot but conclude, with the philosophers, that the hoarding up of riches maketh many impressions of vices'. In texts like Lodge's, we are seeing the term usury and the figure of the grasping usurer operating not so much as caricatures or characterizations of particular persons or practices but rather more as extreme anti-types for a whole set of metropolitan and commercial values and practices which may not, in themselves, have been technically or legally usurious but which were fatally tainted with covetousness and which might well, therefore, be taken as stepping-stones on a road that led inexorably towards usury and which might hence be sensibly organized and discussed under the sign of usury. In short, we are confronting, once again, the logical, moral, and rhetorical consequences of that lack of an unambiguously positive contemporary language for the description and praise of commercial wealth, with which we started.[37]

Again, in many of the texts under discussion, both whore and usurer were pictured as battening off the unsuspecting young scions of the ruling class; the one by seducing inexperienced young men into fleshly liaisons and affairs of the heart, the other by inveigling them into debilitating contracts and loans. This tendency reached its apogee in Lodge's *An Alarum against Usurers*, where the usurious merchant, his gentle broker, and their natural ally, the whore, combine to part the unsuspecting young gentleman from first his money and then his land. The general tenor of Lodge and Whetstone's analysis was still being endorsed from the pulpit in the next century by preachers like Thomas Adams. 'The usurer', Adams claimed,

wounds deeper with a piece of paper than the robber with a sword; many a young gentlemen, newly broke out of the cage of wardship, or blessed with the first sun shine of his one and twenty goes from the vigilance of a restraining governor into the tempting hand of a merciless usurer . . . Many a man that came to his lands ere he come to his wits or experience of

---

[37] Lodge, *An Alarum against Usurers*, pp. 13, 14, 41.

their villainy is so let blood in his estate by usury that he never proves his own man again.[38]

Interestingly, as the work of Laura Stevenson and Norman Jones might have led us to expect, in many of these texts, the figure of the usurer was nowhere near as prominent as that of the whore. Since the statute of 1571, if not before, social reality had fallen increasingly out of line with the pronouncements of many of the preachers and moralists. Usury always had been, and was now even more, a rather slippery moral quantity, and given (at least on some definitions) its prevalence in, indeed centrality to, the financial dealings in the city, it was perhaps rather too close to home. The whore provided a more safely marginal and comfortingly gendered (i.e. female) image for the peccant impulses and mechanisms of corruption and decay, of covetousness, pride, envy, and lust, being adverted to in these texts. Thus, even in Lodge's *Alarum against Usurers*, it was the whore – ('Mistress Minx'), 'an old beaten dog and maintainer of the brothel house brotherhood, a stall for young novices and a limb of satan himself' – who was the main agent who introduced the young ingenu to the desires and lusts of the flesh, addiction to which effected his final ruin at the hands of her ally the usurious merchant. 'This minion so traineth our seduced youth in folly as not only himself is at her command but also his substances remaineth to her use, this high prised commodity is employed to the courtesans bravery and she, which makes him brutish in behaviour, doth empty his replenished purse. Thus the eye of reason is closed up by sensuality and the gifts of nature are diminished by the disordinate visage of beastly venery.'[39]

On the basis of passages such as these it is tempting to see in the whore a figure if not for the city itself, then certainly for its corrupt alter ego, brazenly selling its often corrupting commodities and loans, things which, on the outside, seemed eminently desirable, but which, on the inside, were riven with consuming corruption and disease. On this view, then, the texts we have been discussing were so anxious to relegate the whore, her masterless accomplices in crime, and her well-born young clients, to the moral, social, and topographical margins, precisely because the sins and impulses being

---

[38] Adams, *Works*, p. 58.
[39] Stevenson, *Praise and Paradox*, ch. 5; Jones, *God and the Moneylenders*; T. B. Leinwand, *Theatre, Finance and Society in Early Modern England* (Cambridge, 1999), esp. chs. 1 and 2; Lodge, *An Alarum against Usurers*, pp. 17, 19.

thus excluded and excoriated were, in fact, central to many of the (potentially or actually usurious?) economic activities and transactions which conferred on the city the wealth, power, and beauty which the likes of Dekker were so anxious to praise in their visions and tableaux of London as the new Troy.

It was, of course, upon the resulting moral and social ambiguities and ambivalences that many a so-called city comedy fed and commented; staging the moral complicities that united solid citizens and tradesmen with the whores, pimps, and rakes of the London backstreets. (And from the perspective adopted here, of course, it is no accident that Dekker himself should have been so prolific a producer of precisely such plays.) Sometimes, most famously in Jonson's plays *The Alchemist* and *Bartholomew Fair*, the either puritan or patriot 'busy controllers' who not only presented themselves as immune from the market-based and market-disseminated corruption which surrounded them, but also claimed, if given their head, to be able to reform and control that corruption, were held up to derision as well. Such performances were, of course, put on for the amusement and moral edification of city audiences who were themselves as implicated in the cycles and exchanges of corruption being portrayed on stage, as were the playwrights who were, after all, selling the resulting ludic texts and performances to paying customers.[40] These, of course, were ironies out of the exposure of which Ben Jonson extracted both money and laughs. But arguably all that Jonson was doing in plays like *The Alchemist* and *Bartholomew Fair* was elevating to new and dizzying levels of self-consciousness and self-reflexivity the ironies and contradictions that ran throughout virtually all of the texts with which we have been concerned here.

[40] On this see Bruster, *Drama and the Market* and Leinwand, *Theatre, Finance and Society.*

CHAPTER 9

Perceptions of the crowd in later Stuart London

Tim Harris

The scenario is a familiar one. An Englishman, somewhat the worse for alcohol, is knocked down in the streets by a foreign national. Despite being one o'clock in the morning, the victim's cries prompt a crowd of his compatriots to assemble quickly in large numbers to avenge the injury, threatening violence to the property and persons of those foreigners they take to be implicated in the crime, before the riot squad eventually arrives to restore order. Those who read the sports pages of the English press might be forgiven for thinking that I am referring to the types of violent outbursts that occurred when England played their games in the World Cup Finals in France in the summer of 1998, which were held shortly before the conference at which this paper was first presented took place. In fact, the incident I am alluding to happened in London in November 1668, when the Dutch ambassador's footman created a good deal of unnecessary trouble for himself when he knocked down a drunken man he came across in the streets with no more than 'a gentle push'.[1]

Those in the media have always had a schizophrenic attitude towards the crowds of people who follow England's national sport. The hooligan element – even though they show up week-in, week-out, spending what little money they have going to matches – are not real football supporters; they are drunken yobbos, criminals, thugs. Our genuine English fans, on the other hand, are the best in the world. To quote an internet article by Alec McGivan, the campaign director for England's 2006 World Cup bid, on the behaviour of English football supporters during *Le Coupe du Monde* in France: 'England's real fans were well-behaved and a credit to us, creating a level of passion and support inside the stadiums unequalled at any

---

[1] *CSPVen (1666–8)*, pp. 320–1.

other matches during France 98. We cannot allow the thugs', 'the minority of hooligans', 'to destroy our game'.[2] There is nothing new here. We can detect a similar ambivalence towards the London crowd in the early modern period. Londoners, contemporaries thought, were prone to riot at the slightest provocation.[3] The hooligan element of the metropolis was a national disgrace. Foreigners, one English pamphleteer reminded his readers in 1621, regard 'the baser sort of people in England, to be more rude and barbarous' than 'the canaly of any Countrey'.[4] Talking of the Shrovetide tradition of sacking bawdy houses, the same author noted how the 'rude multitude' acted, at times, as if they were 'turned starcke mad; and as though the City were without lawes and magistrates'.[5] John Strype deplored the fact that 'the Apprentices of London . . . have sometimes made themselves formidable by Insurrections and Mutinies in the City', though he insisted that they were 'commonly assisted, and often egged on and headed by Apprentices of the Dreggs of the Vulgar, Fellows void of worthy Blood, and worthy Breeding; yea, perhaps not Apprentices at all, but forlorn Companions, masterless Men, and Tradeless, and the like'.[6] During the revolutionary upheavals of the Stuart century, the repeated attempts by ordinary Londoners to intervene in politics – whether through petitions, demonstrations, or riots – were routinely condemned in the most forthright terms. The voice of the people was the voice of the devil, one early seventeenth-century pamphleteer proclaimed.[7] 'The multitude judg weakly', another contemporary observed.[8] 'All Popular Longings are Phantastical, and Impetuous', the government's licenser of the press, Roger L'Estrange, insisted in April 1685; 'The People are . . . Mad, for they know not What.'[9]

Yet the London crowd could also be venerated. One seventeenth-century balladeer enjoined people to sing praise to the Shrove Tuesday rioters, 'these bold prentices', 'Who thus intend to bring to

---

[2] Alex McGivan, 'How we will bring football home in 2006', 14 Jul. 1998, http://www.soccernet.com/english/news/ENG-NATIONAL – 2243–61498.HTM.

[3] *CSPVen (1669–70)*, p. 29.

[4] D. N., *London's Looking-Glasse; Or, The Copy of a Letter, Written by an English Travayler, to the Apprentices of London* (1621), p. 8.

[5] *Ibid.*, pp. 25–6.

[6] Strype, *Survey*, II.v.332–3.

[7] D. N., *London's Looking-Glasse*, p. 21.

[8] *The Diary of the Reverend John Ward, 1648–1679*, ed. Charles Severn (1839), p. 223.

[9] Roger L'Estrange, *The Observator in Dialogue* (3 vols., 1684–7), III, no. 35, 29 April 1685.

end / All that is vile and bawdie'.[10] A tract from 1647 spoke of 'the glory' which London 'hath by her Prentices accrew'd', and not only lauded those 'brave Prentices' who rioted against brothels, but also boasted about that 'kinde of a supernatural Sympathy and a generall Union, which knits their hearts in a bond of fraternall affection', so that 'if any (either reall or supposed) wrong, or vyolence be offered to anyone, the rest . . . doe imediatly (and commonly without examination of the quarrell) engage themselves in the rescue, afrighting the adversary with this terrible sentence, Knock him down, he wrongs a prentice'.[11] We can even find members of the political elite praising the political interventions of the London crowd and encouraging collective political agitation themselves. As the duke of Newcastle was famously to remark late in life, recalling the mug-house riots of 1715 and the loyalist gangs who took to the London streets to express their opposition to the Jacobite cause: 'I love a mob. I headed a mob once myself. We owe the Hanoverian succession to a mob.'[12]

How do we explain such divergent attitudes? Part of the answer is that it depends on the type of riot and who is doing the describing. There were some types of disorder, no doubt, that no-one would seek to defend – though as historians we must be wary of arguing from the absence of evidence, since we can never be certain that the voices of sympathizers have simply not been preserved for posterity. There were other types of collective agitation that might be condemned by some but condoned by others, perhaps reflecting the different political or even psychological attitudes to varying forms of crowd activity harboured by different types of individuals. For certain people, perhaps, a riot was a riot and never justifiable, no matter what the mitigating circumstances. Others, however, might be more willing to allow themselves to see the justice of a crowd's cause, even to the point of turning a blind eye to the injustices perpetrated by the mob. Let us consider, for example, how contemporaries chose to describe the riots that broke out in London at the time of the Glorious Revolution. On 11 December 1688,

---

[10] 'A Ballad in Praise of London Prentices and What they did at the Cockpitt Play-House, in Drury Lane' in Charles Mackay (ed.), *A Collection of Songs and Ballads Relative to London Prentices and Trades* (1841), p. 97.

[11] *The Honour of London Apprentices: Exemplified, in a Briefe Historicall Narration* (1647), sigs. A1v, A4v.

[12] James L. Fitts, 'Newcastle's mob', *Albion* 5 (1973), 41.

following the flight of James II in the face of William of Orange's invasion, gangs of Londoners, many of them adolescent males, went on the rampage through the metropolis, not only destroying Catholic meeting houses (which had been erected in violation of the law, albeit with the sanction of the Catholic monarch), but also attacking the residences of a number of foreign ambassadors where mass was known to have been held.[13] The Whig cleric, Gilbert Burnet, a Williamite activist who had come over with the Dutch Stadtholder in November and who had already authored a number of pieces urging the English to resist the illegal actions of their Catholic king, used temperate prose in his account of these disturbances in his famous *History*. 'The apprentices and the rabble' fell upon 'all suspected houses, where they believed there were either priests, or papists', making 'great havoc of many places', he wrote. 'But 'none were killed, no houses burnt, nor were any robberies committed', he added (even though the furnishings and other valuables in the houses attacked were burned or otherwise destroyed), going so far as to conclude that 'never was so much fury seen under so much manage-ment'.[14] Many others, however, were shocked by the acts of mob violence. 'All sober people', one eye-witness wrote concerning the attack on the Spanish ambassador's residence that occurred that night, 'are extraordinarily concerned at this horrid violation of the laws of nations'. 'He must be degenerated from common Humanity', the author of a pro-William pamphlet that appeared in January 1689 conceded, 'that will justifie any such base and villainous Actions'. The Tory historian Laurence Echard, writing in the early eighteenth century, described in condemnatory tones 'the sudden Eruptions of the Mob, that Scum of a Nation that . . . readily mounts in a storm', and complained how 'common Rogues' joined with 'the less de-signing Apprentices' to take the 'opportunity to rifle and plunder'.[15]

---

[13] For these disturbances, see William L. Sachse, 'The mob and the Revolution of 1688', *Journal of British Studies* 4 (1964), 23–40; Tim Harris, 'London crowds and the Revolution of 1688', in Eveline Cruickshanks (ed.), *By Force or By Default? The Revolution of 1688–89* (Edinburgh, 1989), pp. 44–64.

[14] Gilbert Burnet, *History of His Own Time: From the Restoration of King Charles the Second to the Treaty of Peace at Utrecht in the Reign of Queen Anne* (1850), p. 505.

[15] *The Ellis Correspondence: Letters Written During the Years 1686, 1687, 1688, and addressed to John Ellis, Esq.*, ed. George Agar Ellis (2 vols., 1829), II, pp. 351–2; *A Dialogue Between Dick and Tom, Concerning the Present Posture of Affairs in England* (1689), p. 8; Laurence Echard, *The History of England* (3 vols., 1707–18), III, p. 932. I am unconvinced by Deborah Stephan, 'Laurence Echard – Whig historian', *Historical Journal* 32 (1989), 843–66, which seeks to redefine Echard as a Whig.

Yet there is more to it than this. It is not just that some riots were
acceptable and others not, or that some individuals would defend
certain types of collective agitation whilst others never could bring
themselves to do so. Rather, we can often find the same people both
condemning and praising the very same type of crowd activity.
During the Exclusion Crisis of the late 1670s and early 1680s, for
example, Tory propagandists could condemn the rabble-rousing
activities of the Whigs and yet write proudly of the exploits of the
crowds who supported their cause. The London crowd could be
both loathed and revered, hated and loved, by the same people.
What I want to do in this chapter is try to make sense of this
schizophrenic attitude. I shall focus on political crowds, which
became a prominent feature of the metropolitan landscape during
the upheavals of the Stuart century, because it is with regard to these
that the schizophrenic attitude is most apparent and in need of
explanation. As English politics became increasingly polarized over
the course of the seventeenth century, partisans on both sides saw an
advantage in trying to appeal to public opinion, to encourage
demonstrations or other manifestations of support for one's side
amongst the population at large. This was particularly so during the
Exclusion Crisis, when both Whigs and Tories actively cultivated
support amongst the London masses. Yet if one were going to court
the crowd, it became very important to be seen to have the right sort
of people on one's side. Hence the ambivalence, this essay will
suggest; support from the crowd could be highly prized, but only if it
could be made to appear that the support was of the right kind and
for the right reasons.

It would be unprofitable here to get drawn into the controversy
about the relative stability or instability of early modern London.
Although London may have been much governed, well regulated,
and fundamentally stable, we nevertheless need to recognize the
reality of the underlying social tensions in the metropolis, and that
the threat of disorder was never far below the surface.[16] Moreover,
the size of the capital – and the population continued to grow at an
alarming rate over the seventeenth century, from about 200,000 in

[16] Ian W. Archer, *The Pursuit of Stability: Social Relations in Elizabethan London* (Cambridge, 1991),
esp. ch. 1, has the balance right, in my mind, in contrast to the more optimistic view found
in Steve Rappaport, *Worlds Within Worlds: Structures of Life in Sixteenth-Century London*
(Cambridge, 1989).

1600 to nearly half a million by the end of the century[17] – meant the potential for large crowds (in the hundreds or even the thousands) which could be very difficult to police. Roger Manning has calculated that there were at least 96 insurrections, riots, and unlawful assemblies in London in the period 1517 to 1640, and 35 outbreaks of disorder in the 22 years from 1581 to 1602 (that is, an average of three riots every two years). He counted some 15 riots and unlawful assemblies in the two years from May 1626 to June 1628 alone, to protest against the policies of the duke of Buckingham.[18] This was nothing, of course, compared to the scale of collective agitation we see in the capital in the 1640s. Although scholars may be correct to stress the relative order in the capital during the disorders of that decade – there was certainly not the bloodbath that the French ambassador expected would have occurred in Paris, if similar events had happened there[19] – the huge crowds that besieged Lambeth Palace or marched on parliament demanding justice against the earl of Strafford were intimidating enough. My researches for the Restoration period have revealed at least 62 riots for the 18 years from 1661 to 1678 – and this is before we get to the period of heightened agitation out-of-doors associated with the Exclusion Crisis in 1679 to 1682 or the violent attacks on places of Catholic worship during the reign of James II. It was the seeming volatility of the metropolitan populace, 'the readiness of the people to revolt' as the Venetian ambassador put it in 1669, that particularly alarmed contemporaries.[20] For example, when two apprentices were put in the pillory in Cheapside in late March 1664, for having beaten their master, 'a great body' of apprentices assembled (more than 4,000, according to one account) 'and with stones and sticks roughly handled the officers of justice and released their two companions', breaking the pillory to pieces. A new one was speedily erected, and a second, successful attempt was made to carry out the sentence, after which the two guilty youths were whipped through the City. 'Where-

---

[17] Roger Finlay and Beatrice Shearer, 'Population growth and suburban expansion', in A. L. Beier and Roger Finlay (eds.), *London, 1500–1700: The Making of the Metropolis* (1986), pp. 38–9, 48.

[18] Roger B. Manning, *Village Revolts: Social Protest and Popular Disturbances in England 1509–1640* (Oxford, 1988), p. 187.

[19] Valerie Pearl, 'Change and stability in seventeenth-century London', *London Journal* 4 (1979), 5; J. S. Morrill and J. D. Walter, 'Order and disorder in the English Revolution', in Anthony Fletcher and John Stevenson (eds.), *Order and Disorder in Early Modern England* (Cambridge, 1985), p. 142.

[20] *CSPVen (1669)*, p. 29.

upon the apprentices appeared again', we are told, in even larger numbers, and proceeded to deface the house belonging to the master of the punished men, threatening to pull down the houses of the magistrates who signed the sentence.[21] The speed with which a highly explosive situation could develop is well illustrated by an incident that happened in the spring of 1686, when a local constable refused to allow a troop of soldiers in James's newly expanded standing army to quarter in Aldgate, on the grounds that the warrant which they had shown him was valid only for Middlesex and not for the City itself. The soldiers seized the constable 'and threatened him with all kinde of military punishments', whereupon the local inhabitants, many of them butchers and seamen, gathered together in a great concourse, armed with meat cleavers and other hand-held weapons, ready to have a go at the soldiers. The lord mayor, sheriffs, and several London magistrates rushed to the scene, only to be told by the soldiers 'that they were cuckolds and should be so made by them, that they would quarter in their houses and turn them out of Guild Hall . . . that they were not worthy to kiss their arses, and that not the civill officers but the soldiers were the keepers of the peace of the kingdome'. It took considerable negotiating skill on behalf of the lord mayor to defuse the situation and prevent a potential bloodbath.[22]

Lacking a full-time, professional police force, the government often found it difficult to prevent or quell disorder. The regular constables and even the trained bands were often no match for urban crowds; sometimes, indeed, they might sympathize with the rioters and refuse to act, whilst heavy-handed policing, or sending in the troops, might prove an inflammatory gesture that would only further inflame the situation. For these reasons, the authorities were often forced to negotiate with the crowd, grant concessions, or hold back from using the full force of the law against those who had acted in violation of it. This has led to the view that there were some types of disorder that were more likely to be tolerated than others. Indeed, several historians have embraced the notion of 'licensed misrule'. Youth unrest could be excused on the grounds that boys will be boys.[23] Or, so long as crowds restricted themselves to attacking groups or activities that were marginal to city life (riots against

---

[21] *HMC, 7th Report*, p. 575; *CSPVen, 1664–66*, p. 10.
[22] Dr Williams's Library, Roger Morrice, Ent'ring Book, Q, pp. 109–10.
[23] Rappaport, *Worlds Within Worlds*, pp. 10–11.

brothels and foreigners would both fit this model), and did so on certain designated days (holidays), but did not directly criticize those in power, the authorities could afford to show a certain amount of leniency.[24] If such an explanation has any validity, then it can perhaps explain some of the ambivalence we see towards the London crowd.

It is not clear, however, how well the theory fits the evidence. Paul Griffiths has pointed out that historians of England have tended to use the notion of licensed misrule rather uncritically; we are never told exactly who is doing the allowing or where the official permission is coming from. In fact, Griffiths is convinced there was no licence afforded from above: 'we search in vain in the records of central and city government', he has stated, 'for even a gesture of support for the actions of the Shrovetide sackers'.[25] My own researches confirm that mob violence was not liked, whatever guise it took, and that the civic authorities in early modern London usually did whatever was in their power to stop it breaking out. The Common Council Journals and the Repertories of the Court of Aldermen contain innumerable mayoral precepts issued in anticipation of holiday unrest, ordering masters to keep their apprentices at home or the doubling of the watch, in the hope of preventing trouble. If trouble nevertheless did break out, the authorities did not just turn a blind eye. When 'a multitude of the Rabble', numbering some 'Two, or Three thousand, or more', proceeded to pull down bawdy houses in the Moorfields area at Easter 1681, civic leaders did not shrug their shoulders and say, 'oh well, boys will be boys'. Instead, Sheriff Cornish went in with a strong detachment of trained bands and did what was necessary to disperse them; tragically, in the ensuing scuffles three people (two apprentices and one law-enforcement officer) lost their lives.[26]

Besides, is it really possible to maintain a distinction between riots which did or did not challenge magisterial authority? All riots implicitly challenged magisterial authority, because they exposed the civic elite's inability to keep order, which was one of their main jobs. Even when crowds were recalling the elite to the performance of their duties, such as their responsibility to enforce the laws against

[24] Archer, *Pursuit of Stability*, p. 5.
[25] Paul Griffiths, *Youth and Authority: Formative Experiences in England 1560–1640* (Oxford, 1996), pp. 152–4.
[26] *Loyal Protestant Intelligence*, no. 13, 19 April 1681.

vice or against the encroachment on civic privileges by aliens, they were still nevertheless challenging the authority of those in power. As a pamphlet of 1595, written about the apprentice food riots of that year, asked: 'shall boies, shall servants, that are subjected under meane subjectes, presume against the higher powers, be law-makers that know not the law, be institutors of orders, and will not themselves be ordered'?[27] When apprentices and other young men rose in Easter week 1668 to pull down bawdy houses, the ringleaders were tried and executed for high treason; by intending to carry out a public reformation, the judges decided, they were usurping the king's authority, which was tantamount to levying war against the king.[28]

It was not, then, that some forms of misrule were deemed acceptable. Misrule, by definition, could not readily be tolerated by those whose job it was to rule. Indeed, one might go further and suggest that all forms of mass political activism – whether riots or violent outbursts, or more peaceful demonstrations and marches – were worrying to the authorities, because of the potential for trouble. Certainly, it was not uncommon for demonstrations that started peacefully to end in violence. Having said this, if the crowd appeared to have grievances shared by broad cross-sections of the population, and, above all, appeared to be composed of respectable types rather than hooligan elements, then those in authority found they had to act circumspectly. What was crucial, therefore, was how the crowd came to be represented.

Let us start, then, by asking who comprised the crowd? The first thing to get straight is that it would be wrong to assume that the London crowd always comprised the meaner sort. It is true that one of the few ways in which the lower orders, who were otherwise disenfranchised, could make their voices heard was by engaging in collective agitation, and that they often did so to powerful effect. We have plenty of evidence of people of humble origin in early modern London coordinating their own riots, demonstrations, rallies, or petitioning campaigns. But crowd activity could also be engaged in by the more well-to-do and the politically enfranchised. Sir Samuel Barnardiston, who in later life was to be an MP and deputy-governor of the East India Company, as a young citizen 'had put himself at

---

[27] *A Students Lamentation that hath Sometime Been in London an Apprentice* (1595), sig. B2.
[28] Tim Harris, 'The bawdy house riots of 1668', *Historical Journal* 29 (1986), 537–56.

the head of the city tumults' in 1641.[29] The Whig MP Sir Edward Norton headed a riotous mob in November 1681 that celebrated the release of the earl of Shaftesbury from prison (after an abortive attempt by the government to indict the earl for high treason) and took retaliatory measures against local Tories.[30] Even when we are told that crowds were composed mainly of apprentices, we should not assume that they were the rabble. There were apprentices from privileged as well as lowly backgrounds. 'I conceave you [apprentices] to be of two sortes', a tract of 1621 stated: 'Gentlemen or welthy mens sonnes, whose parents have bin able to give better education unto you, then have the parents of the other', and 'the ruder and baser sort', no better than carmen, 'whose *Summum bonum* is the Alehouse'. Apprenticeship, of course, was a temporary stage in the life-cycle; many apprentices went on to become freemen and hold civic office. As the author of the same tract put it: 'I esteeme you, as being the upgrowing youth of the chiefe Citty of our Realme of England, and the future Citizens of that Noble and Famous Citty; so as out of you are to ensue the Honorable Magistrates, the Worshipfull Chiefes of Companyes, and Office-bearers in the sayd Citty.'[31] Moreover, although we can find tinkers and carmen (at one extreme) and MPs and future civic leaders (at the other) taking part in crowd action, we inevitably find a heavy contingent of the middling sort involved in collective agitation in the capital. Given the participatory nature of local government in early modern London, these would be the very types who would serve as trial jurors, parish constables, nightwatchmen, or in the trained bands. Hence it was often difficult to police the crowd if the crowd's grievances were widely felt to be legitimate; constables or members of the trained bands, as members of the same community and social class as those who comprised the crowd, would often sympathize with or share the same grievances, and refuse to act.[32]

This ambiguity concerning the status and composition of the members of the crowd lay at the root of the elite's schizophrenic attitude towards the London crowd. Those in positions of authority

---

[29] Samuel Parker, *History of His Own Time*, trans. Thomas Newlin (1727), p. 134.

[30] *CSPD, 1680–1*, p. 583; Basil Duke Henning (ed.), *The House of Commons, 1660–1690* (The History of Parliament Trust, 3 vols., 1983), III, 158–9.

[31] D. N., *London's Looking-Glasse*, pp. 4, 39–40.

[32] Tim Harris, *London Crowds in the Reign of Charles II: Propaganda and Politics from the Restoration until the Exclusion Crisis* (Cambridge, 1987), pp. 15–22.

could scarcely condone mob violence, and for that reason might feel the need to distance themselves from collective unrest, especially when engaged in by the more disreputable elements of metropolitan society. At the same time, they could scarcely turn a blind eye to the protests of honest and respectable inhabitants. As England became increasingly polarized politically as a result of the political and religious upheavals of the seventeenth century, partisans on both sides came to appreciate the value of courting public opinion out-of-doors. They had to do so, however, without allowing themselves to be seen to be engaging in rabble-rousing tactics or countenancing unruliness on behalf of the lower echelons of society. This explains why this schizophrenic attitude is particularly noticeable with regard to political crowds, and particularly at times of heightened partisan conflict.

It is well known that both the parliamentary opposition to Charles I in the early 1640s and the Whig opposition to Charles II in the late 1670s and early 1680s sought to appeal to those out-of-doors in order to bring pressure to bear on the government. What is less clearly understood is why they should choose to do this. Was it simply to intimidate the government into giving them what they wanted, by holding up the prospect of civil unrest or even popular rebellion if they did not? Some partisans of the parliamentarian or Whig causes no doubt genuinely believed that power lay radically in the people, as one anti-Whig tract of 1679 put it,[33] and that the people had the right to call their rulers to account when they violated their contract with their subjects. Yet if this alone explains the logic of their appeal to those out-of-doors, there was clearly no moral ground to be won here, since the king and champions of royal authority certainly did not subscribe to such views. As the Tory propagandist, Roger L'Estrange, put it shortly after the accession of James II: 'the People neither ever Had, nor ever Can have, nor Ought to have, Any Right, Power or Faculty of Government'.[34]

However, even the most uncompromising champions of royal authority accepted, as L'Estrange himself did, that government was 'an Ordinance of Provision for the Common Good'. The 'mobile' (as these crowds were termed) could not call the sovereign to

---

[33] *A Letter to a Friend. Shewing from Scripture, Fathers and Reasons, How False that State-Maxim is, Royal Authority is Originally and Radically in the People* (1679). Cf. T. L., *The True Notion of Government* (1681), pp. 8, 12.

[34] L'Estrange, *The Observator*, III, no. 5, 19 Feb. 1684/5.

account, but 'the Force, the Will, the Reason, and All the Capacities of the Multitude, are Virtually, and by the Order, and Appointment of Providence, Lodg'd in the Supreme Governor, for the Good of the Community'.[35] Or, as John Nalson put it in 1677: 'the Prince cannot be . . . happy whilest his People are really miserable'.[36] This was where the moral weight of having the crowd on one's side lay. If thousands of people were regularly taking to the streets in protest – and not just carmen and tinkers, but more respectable types, middling and even upper sorts, or youths from good families who would one day go on to rule the city themselves – the government could hardly claim that it was acting for the common good. And if the government lost the support of these types, it could find it very difficult to keep law and order in the capital, as Charles I found out to his cost in the early 1640s, and as Charles II was beginning to find out to his cost in the late 1670s. Hence we see attempts by supporters of the Crown – in the 1640s but most dramatically and successfully during the Exclusion Crisis – to win back public opinion, to show that they had the people on their side, even to the point of encouraging loyalist demonstrations and addresses (and in the process, one might add, promoting more disorder in the capital, since rival groups often came into violent conflict). Yet if they wanted to show that they had the people on their side, it had to be the right sort of people. Thus partisans on both sides sought to represent the crowd in such a way so as to legitimize the efforts of their own supporters and delegitimize those of their opponents. We see this in the 1640s, hence the contradictory representations of the same crowds by different observers as being either a rabble of mean, dissolute persons or as citizens of good estates.[37] We see the same again during the Exclusion Crisis, which is what I want to focus on for the rest of this chapter. I should add that I am going to include all forms of collective activity out-of-doors, not just riots, but also demonstrations and petitions.

What, then, determined whether a crowd was legitimate or not? One factor was breeding. If, in the view of contemporaries, the vulgar had neither the education nor the intelligence to understand politics, the same could not be said of those youths and apprentices

---

[35] *Ibid.*

[36] John Nalson, *The Common Interest of King and People* (1677), p. 109.

[37] Brian S. Manning, *The English People and the English Revolution* (1976, new edn, 1991); Keith Lindley, *Popular Politics and Religion in Civil War London* (Aldershot, 1997).

who were the sons of gentry. Thus Tory writers repeatedly spoke of
the lowly social status of those who comprised Whig crowds. Those
who participated in pro-Monmouth and anti-York riots on Gunpowder Treason Day 1682 were described by one hostile newsletter
writer as 'hundreds of Butchers men and other mean fellowes'.[38]
Another author, writing in defence of the Tory apprentices of
London, referred to those who sided with the Whigs as the 'giddy
Multitude', and claimed that those who signed a petition for the
sitting of Parliament were 'Porters and Broom-men'.[39] The Tory
apprentices, by contrast, were 'the greatest, and best bred part of
London Apprentices'.[40] Nathaniel Thompson, discussing a loyal
apprentice address presented to the king in June 1681, insisted 'that
not only those that carried [it] were of the most eminent Rank (viz.)
4 Merchants, 2 Mercers, 2 Drapers, and a Goldsmith' but also that
'the subscribers in general (who were above 20,000)' were 'those of
the greatest hopes both for Fortunes and Ingenuity in the City'.[41]
Pedigree was also important to the Whigs, however, who repeatedly
insisted that those youths who sided with the Tories were 'made up
of the Scum and Refuse of the Places where they live', such as
porters and chimneysweeps.[42] Thus Richard Janeway maintained in
his *Impartial Protestant Mercury* that those apprentices who signed Tory
addresses were 'Ruffians and Beggerly Vermine, drawn in by Pots of
Ale, and not Prentices'. 'The Real Apprentices of London, who
Remember they have Substantial Parents in the Countrey, and
Trades to expect', supported the Whigs.[43] The Whig apprentices, he
later wrote, were 'ingenious well bred Youth[s]'.[44]

It was never simply a question of breeding, however, even for the
Tories. Thus L'Estrange acknowledged that his long-running periodical, *The Observator*, was intended for the common people and written
in a vulgar idiom in order to win over their allegiance and keep them
loyal to the Crown. Honesty was more important than class. Those
members of the upper classes who stirred up the masses against the

[38] Library of Congress, MS 18,124, VIII, fo. 257.
[39] *Vox Juvenilis: Or, the Loyal Apprentices Vindication of the Design and Promoters of their Late Humble Address to his Majesty* (1681), pp. 1, 3.
[40] *A Letter of Advice to the Petitioning Apprentices* (1681), p. 1.
[41] *Loyal Protestant Intelligence*, no. 35, 5 July 1681.
[42] Library of Congress, MS 18,124, VIII, fos. 83, 98; *An Impartial Account of the Nature and Tendency of the Late Addresses* (1681), p. 12; L'Estrange, *The Observator*, I, no. 30, 6 July 1681.
[43] *Impartial Protestant Mercury*, no. 15, 10–14 Aug. 1681.
[44] *Ibid.*, no. 34, 16–19 June 1681.

government were just as bad as the mobile themselves. Man is judged not by his pedigree or wealth, L'Estrange wrote, but by his 'Life', 'Manners', and 'Intrinsick Value', 'according to the Received Estimate, of Good and Evil'. When he spoke of the mobile, he understood it to be 'made up, out of the Rubbish of both Great, and Small; with Veneration to the Honesty even of a Tinker, as well as of a Cavalier'.[45]

If honesty was crucial, then it followed that people had to be acting of their own free will. Whigs repeatedly complained that Tory crowds were orchestrated from above. Richard Janeway, describing the crowds that cheered the duke of York as he made a public progress through London on his way to dine with the Artillery Company on 20 April 1681, reported how the guards frequently had 'to put the Boys and Mobile in mind of their Duty, to shout and Hallow', though even then 'the Noise was not extraordinary'.[46] Writing of the pro-York bonfire celebration that took place in Ludgate that evening, Janeway recalled how 'a parcel of Blades', planted in the balcony of the local tavern, 'threw out money to the Rabble bidding them cry out "a York!" which they did only as long as they got Liquor'.[47] With regard to the signing of Tory addresses, Whig publicists insisted that apprentices were often forced to sign by their masters, or else were bribed into signing. Because Charles II sponsored a lavish feast to reward his loyal apprentices, Whigs alleged that the Tory youths acted more from a love of venison than loyalty. One Whig pamphlet, which is structured as a dialogue between a Whig and a Tory apprentice, has the Whig apprentice allege not only that the Tories forged signatures to their loyal apprentice address but also that they bumped up the number of signatories by getting 'Journeymen, Carmen, Porters, Tapsters' to sign, 'with many others of a far more inferior degree'. His Tory counterpart confesses that they did indeed do this, 'as very well knowing that all persons of such an inferior rank and profession, would easily be bribed to set their hands to that which their judgements approved of not'.[48] The Tories, predictably, denied such

---

[45] L'Estrange, *The Observator*, III, no. 206, 4 Sept. 1686.
[46] *Impartial Protestant Mercury*, no. 104, 18–21 April 1681.
[47] *Ibid.*, no. 105, 21–25 April 1681.
[48] *A Friendly Dialogue between Two London Apprentices, the One a Whig, and the Other a Tory* (1681), pp. 2–3; *War Horns Make Room for the Bucks with Green Bowes* (1682); Library of Congress, MS 18,124, VIII, fo. 64.

allegations and threw them back at the Whigs.[49] Both sides claimed
that their own supporters acted of their own free will, and did not
need to be coerced.[50]

It was also important to represent one's own supporters as acting
in an orderly and respectable way. The Tory journalist Nathaniel
Thompson talking about the bonfires staged in London on 8 April
1682 to celebrate the return of the duke of York to the capital after a
lengthy spell in Scotland, reported how several householders in the
liberty of the Savoy sought permission for their street party in
advance from the Captain of the Guard for that night.[51] A pro-York
bonfire celebration in Covent Garden that night, Thompson further
pointed out, 'was carried on without the least Violence, Affront or
Incivility whatsoever'. Although there was trouble in some parts of
London that evening, that was caused, Thompson alleged, by the
Whigs. Thus at Ludgate, 'some persons being enraged at the great
Joy and general satisfaction expressed there . . . endeavoured to
hinder it, by managing a great number of the Rascality, and giving
them Drink, which caused them to offer some violence'. They could
not do much, because they were outnumbered by the loyalists (a
Tory journalist was bound to claim that his own party's supporters
enjoyed a numerical superiority), so they withdrew to Paternoster
Row, 'where between 20 and 30 of these Animals fell upon 6 or 7
[loyal] Youths . . . and abused them'.[52] The language Thompson
uses is in itself highly revealing. For another example, let us consider
the way he chose to describe the scuffles that developed between
rival Whig and Tory crowds on Gunpowder Treason day 1682. He
refers to the multitudes at the Whig bonfires as 'the Mobile' and 'the
Rable', and claims that they 'behaved themselves very insolently to
several Gentlemen', reporting how they 'barbarously pull'd' one
Captain Bloomer 'out of his Coach, and knock'd [him] down several
times'. Not only did the mobile not respect social rank, but they
engaged in dishonest tactics. Thus 'about 40 or 50 of the Rable got
together' and went to a bonfire where they cried out 'a York, a York',
in order to see who else would do the same. When the loyalists
revealed themselves, they would 'knock them down . . . in a base

---

[49] *Vox Juvenilis*, pp. 2–3; *Loyal Protestant Intelligence*, no. 23, 24 May 1681; L'Estrange, *The Observator*, III, no. 203, 25 Aug. 1686.

[50] *Impartial Protestant Mercury*, no. 33, 12–16 Aug. 1681; *Vox Juvenilis*.

[51] *Loyal Protestant Intelligence*, no. 141, 13 April 1682.

[52] *Ibid.*, no. 140, 11 April 1682.

fanatical cowardly manner'. The man they set up as their leader, moreover, Thompson tells us, was 'a Porter'.[53]

Again, however, Whig publicists were keen to represent their own followers as peaceful, law-abiding people. Thus Langley Curtis, writing of the great pope-burning of 17 November 1681, proudly observed that despite all the people, there were no riots or disturbances.[54] He also reported that although 'the Bells rang and Bonefires were made in divers Streets' when the Earl of Shaftesbury was released from prison on 24 November 1681, 'we hear not of any Tumult or Damage done to any Person, but that everyone retired peaceably home'. (Curtis was being economical with the truth; there was considerable trouble that night.)[55] Those who supported the Tories, on the other hand, were drunken thugs. Thus in early July 1681 Richard Janeway carried an account of how 'Four young men' stopped 'a Person of Eminency and worth of this City Travaling Homewards . . . in a Coach' and 'without any Provocation began to Swear, Rail and Curse at one of the Company in the Coach, calling him and the Earl of Shaftesbury, Rogues, Dogs and Traitors', and demanding money for alcohol. When a constable was later sent out to execute an arrest warrant against 'one of these Young Tories', he found him at a tavern in the company of 'Forty or Fifty. . . that went under the Denomination Apprentices', who threatened to beat him up if he tried to make the arrest.[56] In September of that year Janeway carried a report of how 'four Debauchees passing the Streets, would force many people to say God bless the Duke of York, and those who refused, they either knocked them down, or otherwise abused them'.[57]

So far we have been documenting simple inversion, with both sides tapping into similar positive and negative stereotypes. What, if any, were the differences in Whig and Tory representations of the crowd? To oversimplify, the Whigs tended to emphasize their supporters' attachment to liberty and to parliament, whereas the Tories put a greater emphasis on duty (especially the duty to be loyal to the sovereign). We need to unpack this assertion, however. Loyalty, in and of itself, was not a Tory preserve. The Whigs, as one

---

[53] *Ibid.*, no. 231, 9 Nov. 1682.
[54] *True Protestant Mercury*, no. 91, 16–19 Nov. 1681.
[55] *Ibid.*, no. 93, 23–26 Nov. 1681. For the disturbances, see Harris, *London Crowds*, pp. 180–2.
[56] *Impartial Protestant Mercury*, no. 21, 1–5 July 1681.
[57] *Ibid.*, no. 44, 20–23 Sept. 1681.

might expect, were insistent that their supporters were loyal. Indeed, they were quick to allege that the activities of the Tory crowds were coordinated and encouraged by the political and religious enemies of the state. Thus, when news broke of an alleged plan by the Tory apprentices of London to hold a Rump-burning procession on 29 May 1680, in protest against the Whig pope-burning of the previous November, the Whig journalist Benjamin Harris alleged that 'the principal Ringleaders' were 'Papists' and 'that a considerable number of the Popish Party were in the Conspiracy'.[58] Significantly, 29 May was both the anniversary of the Restoration and Charles II's birthday, and when it started to become the focus for Tory demonstrations in the early 1680s, the Whig press could scarcely come out and condemn those who chose to commemorate the day. Thus describing the events of 29 May 1682, Langley Curtis reported how the day had been 'kept very solemnly by all true Lovers of their King'. He nevertheless alleged that many of those who had lit bonfires two days earlier, on the 27th, to commemorate the duke of York's return to Whitehall (after a brief trip to Scotland), 'made none' on the 29th (thereby implying that York's supporters were not truly loyal to the Crown). Curtis further recounted how on the 29th 'several Tories, or Papists, or such as endeavour to create Englands Troubles, being very zealous to express what they desired, burnt several Protestants in Effigy', and recalled that when Tory youths had burnt an effigy of Jack Presbyter in Westminster the previous 5 November, 'an honest Gentleman' had written 'from France' to report 'that the Papists there seemed to rejoyce at the News, saying, that they hoped ere long to burn the Karkasses of all the Hereticks in England'.[59] Richard Janeway, reporting on the bonfire celebration for the Queen's birthday in Cheapside on 15 November, which had been paid for by the Queen's laceman, observed how 'the Boys and Rabble' happily toasted the healths of the king and queen, but when 'one of the promoters of the Bone-fire' started 'an Health to the Pope', they immediately 'began to kick out the fire, and fling the lighted brands at the Head of this Roman Health-drinker'.[60]

Whig activists were themselves quick to protest that they were loyal to the king, and they were somewhat defensive about the fact that they found it necessary to take a public political stance. Thus

[58] *Protestant (Domestick) Intelligence*, no. 76, 26 March 1680, and no. 77, 30 March 1680.
[59] *True Protestant Mercury*, no. 146, 27–31 May 1681.
[60] *Impartial Protestant Mercury*, no. 60, 15–18 Nov. 1681.

when the City Whig apprentices began to promote an address in the summer of 1681, dissociating themselves from a recent Tory apprentice address delivered to the king, they decided, 'out of an awful deference to Majesty', 'not to Importune their Sovereign', but instead to petition the lord mayor of London.[61] When they delivered it at the beginning of September, the apprentice who made the presentation 'Humbly Acknowledg[ed] . . . that the Presumption we may seem Guilty of in this Matter (Considering our present Stations,) requires a far greater Apology, than we are able to make', but insisted that they acted from a desire to demonstrate their 'Loyalty to His Sacred Majesty' as well as their 'Zeal for the Protestant Religion'.[62] An address to the king which the Whig apprentices drafted in June 1682 (though never actually presented) opened by protesting that the petitioners were 'your Majesties most Loyale and Obedient Subjects' who had 'been abused and scandalized as being phanatically affected and given to tumults, by the enemyes of your Royall person and Government and the public peace of the Kingdome, only for showeing ourselves true Loyalists and Zealous Protestants', and went on to acknowledge 'the Blissings we have and doeth enjoy in our Religion and Liberties under your Princely and most Gracious Reigne over us'.[63]

The Whigs' loyalty to the monarchy and zeal for the Protestant religion, however, were related to a championship of parliament, even though the king himself had condemned the actions of the exclusionist parliaments following his dissolution of the Oxford Parliament in March 1681.[64] Hence the Whig apprentices sought to distance themselves from the Tory addresses: they did not want the world to take them 'for Tories, or Enemies to Parliaments, but for Sober, and most Loyal Apprentices'.[65] As Janeway insisted in his *Mercury*, 'the Reall Apprentices of London', though 'ready to Serve His Majesty to the Utmost', were resolved 'never to be Papists, or Slaves', but had 'a just Veneration for Parliaments, and the Liberties of English Men, without which their Civil Moderated and necessary Apprenticeships, will at the Expiration of their Indentures, but turn

---

[61] *Ibid.*, no. 33, 12–16 Aug. 1681.
[62] *Ibid.*, no. 39, 2–6 Sept. 1681.
[63] Library of Congress, MS 18,124, VIII, fo. 64.
[64] Charles II, *His Majesties Declaration To All His Loving Subjects, Touching the Causes and Reasons that Moved Him to Dissolve the Two Last Parliaments* (London, 1681).
[65] *Impartial Protestant Mercury*, no. 18, 21–24 June 1681.

them over to an Absolute and Life-lasting servitude'.[66] The apprentice petition of September 1681 was to ask the lord mayor to bring
pressure on the king to call a parliament, the petitioners protesting
'the Veneration and Esteem we have, and ought to have for
Parliaments'.[67] Mr Stillingfleet, the apprentice responsible for coordinating some of the Whig apprentice demonstrations, told his
associates in a speech delivered in May 1682 that it was important
for them to take a stance against popery and tyranny; it was no good
looking to the king, for 'His Majestie being too Credulous entertained and harkened to the faneing words of Papists and tymserving
Rogues'. 'Let us endevvor', he therefore implored, 'to defend our
Rights and Libertyes and Religion, for when it is gon, our Lives goes
Likewise . . . Let us rather dye Like men then be butchred and
Brunt by Papists.'[68]

For the Tories, the Whigs were not loyal subjects but rebels.
Whereas the Whigs 'heartily' rejoiced at the release of Shaftesbury in
November 1681, after the Whig leader had been saved from a treason
charge by an *ignoramus* jury, they staged no such bonfire celebrations
– the authors of the Tory periodical, *Heraclitus Ridens*, claimed – for
the return of the king from Newmarket on 8 April 1682. (The paper
omitted to remind its readers that Charles was bringing his brother
back to London after a period of exile in Scotland.)[69] L'Estrange was
consistent in his belief that the activities of the Whig crowds and
petitioners were illegitimate: 'What are all your Popular Remon-
strances, and Addresses . . . but so many Attempts of the Mobile, to
Confound, and Subvert the Order of the Publique, by Intermeddling
in Matters which they have Nothing to do withall? . . . The Subject's
Part is Resignation, and Obedience.'[70] By contrast, the Tories'
supporters out-of-doors were not intermeddling in matters that had
nothing to do with them; they were demonstrating that they were
loyal and obedient. L'Estrange himself insisted that the aim of his
long-running periodical, *The Observator*, was the 'Instilling of Dutyfull
and Honest Principles into the Common People'.[71] A tract pur-
porting to be a self-vindication by the Tory apprentices for their loyal
address of the spring of 1681 stated that the Tory youths wanted to

[66] *Ibid.*, no. 15, 10–14 June 1681.   [67] *Ibid.*, no. 39, 2–6 Sept. 1681.
[68] Library of Congress, MS 18,124, VIII, fo. 57.
[69] *Heraclitus Ridens*, no. 64, 18 April 1682.
[70] L'Estrange, *The Observator*, III, no. 26, 6 April 1685.
[71] *Ibid.*, II, 'To the Reader'.

show that they could not be imposed upon by rebels who sought to effect their own designs (as had been the case back in the 1640s), and that they would 'never again be decoy'd out of our Duty to our Sovereign'. Although they were willing to take direct action, it was not to defend their own rights or liberties, but to protect the king against traitors: their 'hearty Affections to his Person and Government, and their Loyal Union among themselves', they declared, 'would make them not afraid', when commanded by the king, 'to Confront the Most Resolute and Formidable Rebel' and provide a 'Guard to his Royal Person'.[72]

Both sides played the numbers game, in the sense that they tried to argue that their own supporters outnumbered those of their opponents.[73] They did so, however, to different ends. For the Whigs, numbers added legitimacy to their position; they wanted to show that their cause represented the voice of the people. The Tories were interested in documenting loyalty, and showing that the Whigs did not have everyone on their side, thereby hoping to deflate any potential for rebellion, because the evidence of loyalist crowds revealed that people would rally behind the Crown in time of crisis. Yet numbers by themselves did not add any extra legitimacy to their position. As L'Estrange asked in his *Observator*: 'what's the Majority, or the Minority of the People . . . to the Merits of the Cause?' 'I am no Friend to Appeals, from Westminster-Hall, to Billingsgate, or from a Council of State, to a Bear-Garden . . . I am ready to be Try'd by the Proper Judges of the Controversy: As a Convocation, in Matters of Religion; The King's Privy-Councel, in Matters of State; by the Law, in a Question of *Meum* & *Tuum*.'[74]

This chapter has sought to explain the schizophrenic attitude of contemporaries to the London crowd in the seventeenth century, and to suggest that it is related to the struggle over how to represent the crowd in what was a fiercely polarized political culture. I have focused in particular on the years of the Exclusion Crisis towards the end of Charles II's reign, when the Whigs were in opposition and the Tories staunch defenders of the royal administration. Let us address briefly, by way of conclusion, the question of change over time, and

[72] *Vox Juvenilis*, p. 4.
[73] Library of Congress, MS 18,124, VIII, fos. 83, 95, 97; *True Protestant Mercury*, no. 49, 22–25 Jun. 1681; *Impartial Protestant Mercury*, no. 33, 12–16 Aug. 81; *Vox Juvenilis*, p. 2.
[74] L'Estrange, *The Observator*, III, no. 217, 13 Oct. 86.

consider what happened when the roles became reversed after the Glorious Revolution, and ministerial Whigs found themselves opposed by an alliance of Tories in parliament and discontented elements in the streets. How did Whig and Tory polemicists respond to the disturbances that occurred at the time of the trial of Dr Henry Sacheverell in March 1710, when high-church mobs went on the rampage through the metropolis tearing down non-conformist meeting places to express their support for this inflammatory Tory divine?[75] The remarks offered here are preliminary, intended to raise questions rather than present definitive conclusions, but hopefully they will serve as a stimulus to future research.

Before we became familiar with the existence of loyalist crowds under Charles II, the very visible nature of the Tory crowds under Queen Anne, and the forthright condemnations of such activity by leading Whig polemicists, seemed to present a puzzle: why were Tories now for the crowd and Whigs against it? The interpretation offered here, however, reveals that there is no puzzle. The Whigs, at the time of the Sacheverell riots, were doing exactly what they had done during the Exclusion Crisis, namely condemning the activities of Tory crowds. And they were doing so largely for the same reasons and on the same grounds – that is, that they were rented mobs who were not fighting for the true interests of British Protestants. Thus William Bisset described the Sacheverell crowd of 1710 as 'a French-fiy'd Mob'. 'It can never enter into my Head, that the late were true British Mobbs: There are all the Signs that can be of an Artificial hired Mobb.'[76] John Dunton said that Sacheverell knew that 'London was never a Friend to his detested Cause, but always appear'd for Liberty, Property and Religion', and accused the doctor of having 'Brethren of Rome' and the Pretender for 'his Master'.[77] The Whig-dominated House of Commons proposed that the Queen should issue a proclamation against the rioters, as being 'set on foot by papists, nonjurors, and other enemies to her majesty's government'.[78]

Sacheverell's crime had been that he had delivered a sermon on the previous 5 November attacking dissenters, occasional confor-

---

[75] For the riots, see Geoffrey Holmes, 'The Sacheverell riots: the crowd and the Church in early eighteenth-century London', in Paul Slack (ed.), *Rebellion, Popular Protest and the Social Order in Early Modern England* (Cambridge, 1984), pp. 232–62.

[76] William Bisset, *The Modern Fanatick* (1710), preface.

[77] John Dunton, *The Bull-Baiting* (1709), p. 5.

[78] Narcissus Luttrell, *A Brief Historical Relation of the State of Affairs from September, 1678, to April, 1714* (6 vols., Oxford, 1857), VI, p. 551.

mists, and low churchmen alike, and vindicating the principles of non-resistance and passive obedience, which to the Whig government of the day seemed tantamount to a malicious and seditious attack on the Revolution settlement in church and state. Whig polemicists predictably had fun ridiculing the idea of rioting in support of the notion of non-resistance. Nevertheless, they were still prepared to defend mob activity, so long as the crowd was engaged in the right sort of cause. Daniel Defoe, in a tract written in the form of a letter from the supposed 'captain' of earlier Whig crowds to the Sacheverellite mob, labelled those Londoners who rioted in support of Sacheverell 'Degenerate Boobys': if they believed Sacheverell's teachings on passive obedience and non-resistance, why did they rise and resist their lawful governors? But these doctrines were not worth defending, he told the Sacheverellites, since by them they gave up

your Wives, and your Children, your Goods and Fortunes, all to the Pleasure of a Tyrannical Prince; and if he comes to take your Lives, ravish your Wives and Daughters, and make Ducks and Drakes of all your Mony, you are only to cry, 'Welcome, Sir, here's my neck at your service: Will you please lie with my Wife or my Daughter? And please to accept of all I have in the World?'

This was no 'Cause for freeborn Subjects to engage in', Defoe's captain insists, adding that he is 'asham'd and griev'd that such slavish Souls should dishonour the Name and Title of Mobb'.

You are the first, and I hope will be the last Mobb, that ever stood up against Liberty and Property, and the Freedom of the Subject. You a Mobb! You are the Scum and Dregs, the Tools and Vassals of the Romish Brood, and sent from their dark hellish Cabals, once more (if you could) to blow up the Queen and Parliament.

Yet the truth was that few of the members of the Sacheverellite crowd stirred 'for this Cause alone'; rather, their main intent was 'to plunder, and rob, and pilfer Houses', and 'force Mony from them, who dare not deny you'. In short, they were nothing more than 'Thieves', an 'everlasting Blot and Disgrace to the Honour of the Mobility!' 'When I and my Friends rose', the captain recalled, 'it was for Justice, and Liberty, and the Government, and the Protestant Religion; and any of mine that should take the value of a Penny to enrich himself, I would have hang'd him'.[79]

---

[79] Daniel Defoe, *A Letter from Captain Tom to the Mobb, Now Rais'd for Dr Sacheverel* (1710), quotes on pp. 2, 3, 6.

The Tories found it difficult to boast about the Sacheverell crowds because of the violence in which the crowds engaged. They tended, therefore, to distance themselves from the crowd, claiming that they were in no way responsible for what the mob chose to do.[80] Some even went so far as to blame the disturbances on those people whom they traditionally regarded as enemies of church and state. Thus one correspondent appears to have genuinely believed that 'the body of the transgressors' responsible for 'the gutting of Burgess's meeting house . . . was a compound of dissenters headed by an Anabaptist'.[81] One pamphleteer openly accused the Whigs of raising the mob, since it was the Whigs and their predecessors who had taught people the doctrine of resistance, 'that they were the original of government, that kings and queens were creatures of their making'. Even though 'this Mob was against you . . . they learnt of you to rise'. The same pamphleteer further suggested 'that the Dissenters pulled down some of their Meeting-houses, and charged the High-church with it', to win over the Queen's favour, 'and set the High party at a greater distance from her good esteem'.[82] Yet Sacheverell also had plenty of respectable supporters – as evidenced by the reception he received in many places as he made his journey from London to Shropshire following his sentencing – who needed to be distinguished from the riff-raff who engaged in rowdy behaviour. 'If People would come Crouding to stare at him', one pamphleteer asked, 'if they would Hoop and Hollow, make Bonfires, ring Bells, etc. could He help it?' 'The Bulk of the Nobility and Gentry of a County, and the Magistracy of Cities and Corporations', the same author continued, 'are no Mob, I hope, tho' some have had the manners to make no distinction between Them, and those that Hollow'd and Huzza'd about them'.[83] We may wonder what had changed. Indeed, it sounds not unlike Mr McGivan's plea to distinguish between our 'real fans' and 'the minority of hooligans who crudely attach themselves to our game'.[84]

---

[80] *An Ordinary Journey no Progress; Or, A Man doing his own Business No Mover of Sedition. Being a Vindication of Dr Sacheverell* (1710), p. 4.

[81] *HMC, 10th Report*, Appendix, part VI, p. 186.

[82] William King, *A Vindication of the Reverend Dr Henry Sacheverell* (1711), in *The Original Works of William King* (3 vols., 1776), II, pp. 192–5.

[83] *Ordinary Journey*, pp. 5–6.

[84] McGivan, 'How we will bring football home'.

CHAPTER 10

'Making fire': conflagration and religious controversy in seventeenth-century London

Nigel Smith

[Fire is] internal or external; the external fire is mechanical, corrupting and destroying, the internal is spermatic, generative, ripening.

> Nicholas de Locques, *Les Rudiments de la Philosophie naturelle touchant le système du corps mixte* (Paris, 1665), pp. 36, 47, quoted in Gaston Bachelard, *The Psychoanalysis of Fire*, trans. Alan C. M. Ross (1987), p. 73.

PHILOSOPHER: By what Law then was he burned?
LAWYER: By the Common-Law.
PHILOSOPHER: What's that? . . . if you will say he was burn't by the Law of Reason, you must tell me how there can be Proportion between Doctrine and Burning.

> Thomas Hobbes, *A Dialogue between a Philosopher and an Student of the Common Laws of England*, ed. J. Cropsey (Chicago, 1971), pp. 130–1.

I HERESY AND HOLLYWOOD

Few have noticed the fact that Arnold Schwarzenegger's film *Terminator 2* appears to be an account of the theological divisions between English Civil War radical religious factions. Remember that the film is based in Los Angeles, and chronologically strung between the 1990s and a future thirty years hence. A nuclear holocaust was started in 1997 by a computer called Skynet; this begins a war between the survivors of the human race and the machines. The latter send back from the 2030s a robot called a Terminator whose job it is to eliminate the future leader of the humans, John Connor.

I am grateful for the helpful comments of audiences and seminars at Harvard University, the University of North Carolina, Chapel Hill, and the University of Pennsylvania, and, in particular, Eric Wilson, Marjorie Garber, Leah Marcus, Megan Matchinske, Peter Stallybrass, Rita Copeland, Margreta de Grazia, David Wallace, and Genelle Gertz-Robinson.

In turn, Connor sends back his own Terminator (Schwarzenegger) in order to protect his adolescent self.

Both Terminators are heretical bodies. The humans' Terminator has a fleshly, organic carapace, but a metal and electronic skeleton. He is flesh and machine: Hobbesian man writ to perfectibility, yet constructed in dualistic terms. The machines' Terminator is an updated model, being made, so we are told, of 'liquid metal'. He is in fact mortalist man: the flesh and the spirit are inseparable liquid particles. However they are buffeted, blown apart, frozen, and shattered, they reconstitute themselves into the awesome silver Terminator (looking like a version of Van Helmont's soul, a crystal man), who can change his appearance at will. The only way to destroy both Terminators is to melt them in a blast furnace, an unmistakeable image of eternal punishment in Hell, a Dantean boiling-pot that burns away the flesh of the Schwarzenegger Terminator and removes the metal identity of each. The mortalist Terminator suddenly gains human dimensions, a face screaming in a molten surface, as he is melted to annihilation. To a late twentieth-century seventeenth-century scholar, it is as if the scriptwriter was Richard Overton, with the screenplay by Christopher Marlowe.

The film is framed by shots of the city, and the scenic leitmotif is a view of downtown Los Angeles, seen from a children's play park. A nuclear bomb is detonated over the city and the firestorm sweeps across the landscape, ultimately consuming the flesh of the film's heroine, who is revealed to have a bone rather than a metal skeleton. It is apocalypse now.

II APOCALYPSE AND THE FIRE-ENGINE

We should not be surprised by this modern version of apocalyptic destruction associated with the city. The city is the site of the violent happenings of the Book of Revelation, where Babylon is burned away and the human race (or its elect) refined by a fire in order to prepare them for the Holy City. In Rev. 8: 5–9, after the seventh seal is opened, consuming fire visits the earth, burning a third of the trees, all of the grass, turning the sea to blood and destroying all marine life. Fire is mentioned at least once in eight of the following fourteen chapters that complete the book. The Book of Revelation repeats figures of fiery consumption in the prophetic books of the Old Testament: 'For behold the Lord will come with fire, and with his chariots like a whirlwind, to render his anger with fury, and his rebuke with flames of fire' (Isa. 66: 15). Even the gospels contain the same image of burning punishment. Matt. 13: 42 is a prophecy where angels sent from the Son of Man gather up the iniquitous and cast them into a fiery furnace.

These texts were known intensely within English Protestant culture, and especially within early nonconformity.[1] Fire had an imagined presence inside London radical Puritanism since the later sixteenth century. For these people and communities, fire was close to the centre of religious inspiration because it was a figure for divine inspiration, as well as a manifestation of divine wrath. The 'cloven tongues like as of fire' (Acts 2: 3) that sat on the heads of the Apostles when they were filled with the Holy Spirit is the most famous biblical image that sanctions preaching. On the one hand, fire is the ultimate means of destruction, a wholly uncontrollable force. On the other hand, it signifies the power of holy inspiration. Its occurrence in the Bible as a means of punishment is part of what modern anthropologists would identify as its power of purification. Fire cleanses the elect, burning away the tainted dross in the world.[2] In some imaginations, the two senses of fire come together. The divine fire that is the preaching of God's Word must bring down a purification of the faithful.

The anticipation of cataclysmic fire was not, of course, the special property of the non-conformists. In a society without a regulated system of insurance against loss, fire, along with burglary and rape, was seen as a major cause of absolute deprivation of property.[3] To survive a fiery death was worse than suffering one, for what followed could be naked, wretched destitution. These fears are readily understandable in the context of London's demographic realities. Cities, and certainly the early modern metropolis, have a population density and dwelling proximity far, far greater than that of either provincial towns or rural places. In the city, life is lived with a claustrophobia induced by the breaking down of boundaries between one body and the next. There is little or no suppression or

---

[1] For a literary consideration of the impact of these texts in this period, see Madeleine Forey, 'Language and revelation: English apocalyptic literature, 1500–1660', DPhil thesis, University of Oxford (1993).

[2] See Hazel Rossotti, *Fire* (Oxford, 1993), p. 243.

[3] See e.g. Edmund Scott, *An Exact Discourse of the Subtleties . . . of the East Indies* (1604), p. 112; see also the discussion in Heather Dubrow, *Shakespeare and Domestic Loss: Forms of Deprivation, Mourning and Recuperation* (Cambridge, 1999).

hiding of the human presences (i.e. waste) that we know today.[4]
Urban life is neurotically, nauseatingly close, exaggeratedly so in the
concertina-ed dwellings that artisans (non-conformists among them)
inhabited. No wonder it felt on the edge of time: just about ripe for a
Second Coming. The habit of casting even domestic or artisanal
London fires in terms of ultimate destinies is not uncommon in the
period. Thomas Dekker likened the perpetual fires of the glass-
blowing furnaces at Blackfriars to hell; John Webster, blown glass to
a pregnant woman burning in hell.[5] The latter reference is preceded
by a madman's threat to realize a fiery doomsday with a magnifying
glass – another product of an urban, artisanal workshop.[6]

   Nor indeed were fires new in the City of London in the seventeenth century. In the city's early history, when even more of the
buildings were made of wood than was the case by 1600, large parts
of the city were regularly consumed. A large fire destroyed the
second St Paul's Cathedral in 961, and another devastating fire
followed only twenty-one years later. After the Norman Conquest,
there were four fires between 1071 and 1136, so that the city was
rebuilt four times in sixty years.[7] Smaller fires were frequent and
numerous: one wonders quite how many failed to feature in the
records. There were substantial fires in 1630, destroying fifty houses,
and in 1633, destroying one-third of the houses on London Bridge,
and eighty in the parish of St Magnus Martyr. Smaller fires in 1650
and 1654 were caused by exploding munitions, and carried in
consequence a disproportionately heavy death toll.[8] The Great Fire
of 1666 was the last in a long tradition of near-complete annihila-
tions of the capital by fiery consumption. In its aftermath came not
only the famous rebuilding of the city, but also the first modern
attempts at fire control and safety (although the 'fire-engine', a
mobile device that pumped water through a spout, had already been
brought to England from Germany in the late 1620s). Only with the

---

[4] Piero Camporesi, *The Incorruptible Flesh: Bodily Mutilation and Mortification in Religion and Folklore*,
   trans. Tania Croft-Murray (Cambridge, 1988), ch. 2. See also Mark Jenner's forthcoming
   monograph on filth and its management in early modern London.
[5] Thomas Dekker, *A Knight's Conjuring* (1607), sig. C4v; John Webster, *The Duchess of Malfi* (first
   performed 1613–14), 2.2.6–12; 4.2.77–9; John Webster, *The White Devil* (first performed 1612),
   1.2.136–9.
[6] Webster, *The Duchess of Malfi*, 4.2.73–5: 'Doomsday not come yet? I'll draw it nearer by a
   perspective, or make a glass that shall set all the world on fire upon an instant.'
[7] See Roy Porter, *London: A Social History* (1994), pp. 20, 22.
[8] Stephen Porter, *The Great Fire of London* (Stroud, 1996), pp. 3–5.

aerial raids of the Second World War would London be ablaze to this extent again.

III FROM HISTORY TO PROPHECY: WRITING FIRE

In the early modern histories of London, fires constitute the breaks in the narrative. They are the destructive counterparts in the text to the celebratory bonfires that punctuated the calendar of early modern England.[9] Firebreaks are made by removing flammable foliage in a forest, in order to stop a fire's progress. The break caused by fire in John Stow's history of places and buildings is equally abrupt:

> In place of this church [the house of Crouched Friars], is now a carpenters yeard, a Tennis court, and such like. The Fryers hall was made a glasse house, or house wherein was made glasse of diuers sortes to drink in; which house in the yeare 1575. on the 4. of September, brast out into a terrible fire, where being practised all meanes possible to quench, notwithstanding as ye same house in a smal time before, had consumed a great quantite of wood by making of glasses, now it selfe hauing within it about 40000. Billets of woode was all consumed to the stone wals, which neuerthelesse greatly hindered the fire from spreading any further.[10]

Fire and churches go hand in hand, partly because of the centrality of ecclesiastical buildings in Stow's urban memory, partly because of the proximity of churches to the sites of fires, and of course, the steeples of churches attracted lightning: in their architectural praise of the almighty, churches became sacrifices of divine or natural wrath.[11] They even became figured as bodies: the published account of the fire of 1561 records molten lead from St Paul's Cathedral flowing like blood in the streets at the 'martyrdom' of the church.[12] On this occasion both St Paul's Cathedral and St Martin's were hit by lightning, and the fire subsequently descended from the top of the buildings. The fires were thus readily seen as judgements of Providence in the published literature of the time, which, in this instance, was just three years after the Elizabethan Settlement.[13] Most of the

---

[9] See David Cressy, *Bonfires and Bells: National Memory and the Protestant Calendar in Elizabethan and Stuart England* (1989), ch. 5.

[10] Stow, *Survey*, I.148.   [11] E.g. *ibid.*, I.299, 347.

[12] The feature of molten lead was repeated in the accounts of the Great Fire of 1666 (most famously in John Evelyn's Diary), after which only 43 out of 130 churches remained.

[13] For a discussion of the theological content of this dispute, see Norman Jones, *The Birth of Elizabethan England* (Oxford, 1993), p. 44.

fires that Stow records are sixteenth century, and if not connected
with churches, they are associated with loss of precious objects, such
as the fire of 1541, in which many of the King's jewels were burned
or otherwise lost. Beyond mere record, the fire becomes a symbolic
record of royal and church history within the walls of the city.

The real and the symbolic come together most strongly in the
Reformation history of John Foxe, where the fiery martyrings of
several early Protestants soon became parts of the most remembered
sections of the *Acts and Monuments*. London's sixteenth-century history
was in fact saturated with burnings, usually in Smithfield. In the reign
of Queen Mary, the most intense period of such persecution, forty-six
burnings are recorded between 4 February 1555 and 27 June 1558.[14]
In Henry Machyn's diary, lists of funerals vie for space with lists of
burnings.[15] Purifying fire cleanses the taint of heresy, and then
punishes the heretic with a painful death.[16] But the instances of
martyrdom by burning (most memorably in London that of John
Rogers, vicar of St Sepulchre's) turn the symbolism of punishment
into one of commemoration: the martyrs test their faith by placing
their hands in the flames, and in the accompanying woodcuts as well
as the text, they appear as statues preserved in flame.

The anticipation of a fire in the City of London was common in
the seventeenth century. Lady Eleanor Davies, for instance, prophesied the burning of the city before Easter Day, 1639. Her prophecy
proved false, but she managed to raise popular fear because there
had been several local but nonetheless damaging fires just before
that time.[17] People lived with the permanent sense that fire was
immanent. In 1665, Sir Roger L'Estrange, the government's censor
of the press, suppressed almanacs prophesying great fires of London
for fear that they would cause popular disorder. And when the Great
Fire came in September 1666 – 'destroying four-fifths of the
historical, commercial, topographic, and imaginative center of
London within four days'[18] – the poets, among many others, saw it
as a fiery apocalypse, even when they were literally describing the
domestic surety of a hearth:

---

[14] Susan Brigden, *London and the Reformation* (Oxford, 1989), pp. 608–12.
[15] J. G. Nichols (ed.), *The Diary of Henry Machyn, Citizen and Merchant Taylor of London, 1550–1563*, Camden Society, 42 (1848).
[16] A related feature is the torturing of arson suspects with hot irons in order to obtain a confession: see Scott, *An Exact Discourse*, pp. 119–22.
[17] *CSPD (1638–9)*, p. 620 (27 March 1639).
[18] Cynthia Wall, *The Literary and Cultural Spaces of Restoration London* (Cambridge, 1998), p. 5.

God's bellows blow the Coals, and ev'rywhere
Toss wanton Fire-balls dancing in the Air.
The liquid pitch in flaming clouds doth rowle,
(The draught of Heaven shrivell'd to a scrowle)
And clammy Lightnings in strange Figure, falls,
Like sparks, from beaten Links at Funerall.
To watch the downfall of the hovering blaze:
Till, where least fear'd, it lights; and fatal showres
Through Chimney-tops into their dwellings powres.[19]

With hyperbole like this, we should not be surprised that the rhetoric of many sermons suggested that the Apocalypse had all but arrived with the fire.[20] The same is true of more private kinds of writing, such as diaries: 'The whole world had not seene the like since the foundation of it, nor to be outdone, 'til the universal conflagration of it, all the skie were of a fiery aspect, like the top of a burning oven burning.' . . . 'I left [London] this afternoone burning, a resemblance of Sodome, or the last day.'[21]

IV RETRIBUTION, DIVISION AND THE GREAT FIRE OF 1655

Elsewhere, the charge that the fire was linked to the threat of foreign invasion was associated equally with harmful internal division: 'Sin was the Common Cause, no faction freed; / Here all *dissenting* Parties were agreed.'[22] These sins were commonly identified by men of all parties with the moral shortcomings of Charles II's court. For instance, the official religious response – in a series of sermons that treat the Plague and Fire as divine-induced punishments for national sins – is no less concerned with interior matters than are the radicals of the previous decade:

dream no longer of *Granadoes* or *Fire-Balls*, or the rest of those witty Mischiefs; search no more for *Bontefieus* or *Incendiaries, Dutch* or *French*: The Dutch Intemperance, and the French Pride and Vanity, and the rest of their

[19] Simon Ford, *The Conflagration of London* (1667), in Robert Arnold Aubin (ed.), *London in Flames, London in Glory. Poems on the Fire and Rebuilding of London 1666–1709* (New Brunswick, 1944).

[20] See Thomas Brooks, *Londons Lamentation: Or, A Serious Discourse concerning that Late Fiery Dispensation that Turned our (once renowned) City into a Ruinous Heap* (1670); Wall, *Literary and Cultural Spaces*, pp. 17–18.

[21] John Evelyn, *Diary*, 2–3 Sept, 1666.

[22] John Crouch, *Londinenses Lachrymae* (1666), pp. 55–6. The Parliamentary committee investigating the fire heard testimony that foreigners (in this case, Portuguese people) threw fireballs, which they had been able to conceal in their pockets, into houses. For a further association of the Portuguese with fireballs, see Scott, *An Exact Discourse*, p. 116.

Sins, we are fond off, are infinitely more dangerous to us, than the Enmity of either Nation; for these make God our Enemy too. Or if you'l needs finde out the Incendiary, look not abroad . . . Turn your Eyes inward into your own Bosoms; there lurks the great Make-bate, and grand *Boutefieu* between Heaven and us.[23]

But there was also an identification of civil or religious division with fire: 'The Quakers say [the Fire has occurred as a punishment] for their Persecution. The Fanaticks say tis for banishing & silencing their Ministers. Others say tis for the Murther of the King & Rebellion of the City. The Clergy lay the blame on Schism & Licentiousness, while the sectaries lay it on Imposition and their Pride.'[24] Too much factious preaching under the inspiration of the Spirit's holy flame might bring about a real conflagration as punishment for one side or the other in the religious politics of the English Revolution. The destruction of London by fire had already been so prophesied by the Quaker Humphrey Smith in 1660.[25]

When religious division caused political turbulence, as it did when the Fifth Monarchists challenged the rule of the Protectorate in 1654, the description of nonconformity as a destructive fire became irresistible. William Spurstowe wrote that resistance to the Protectorate was 'a fire of sedition, that is ready to brake forth into a flame.'[26] He was repeating a trope that was more readily found not so much in the sermons and tracts of puritan divines as in the writings of their opponents. But this mode was extremely attractive to puritan journalists like Henry Walker, who was prepared to print in his newsbook verse that one might more readily find in the Royalist *Mercurius Democritus*. Thus, *Perfect Occurrences* printed *An Epitaph upon the Itinerants of these Times*: 'Here *Propagation* lies that did aspire / Like *Phaeton* to set the world on fire.'[27] Just as many Fifth Monarchists looked back to the revolution of 1648–9, when the chance for truly godly rule had in their view begun, so the Protectorate apologists were repeating and modifying a conservative fear that was voiced in the late 1640s, a fear that was not merely

---

[23] William Sancroft, *Lex Ignea: Or the School of Righteousness* (1666), pp. 21–2.
[24] 'Letters concerning the Great Fire in London Sept. 1666'; Bodl., MS Gough London 14, fo. 38r.
[25] Humphrey Smith, *The Vision of Humphrey Smith, Which He Saw Concerning London, in the Fifth Month, in the Year 1660* (1660).
[26] William Spurstowe, *The Magistrates Dignity and Duty* (1653), p. 11.
[27] *Perfect Occurrences*, 1 (39 [i.e. 30] Jan.–6 Feb., 1654), 140. Nelson and Seccombe, 519.1; Thomason Tracts E717 (18).

urban but essentially to do with London: 'When the whole kingdom shall rise in a flame, what will be your lot but smoke in our eyes, and at last a consuming fire in your bowels: when you only should be left to maintain this domineering Army with your blood?'[28] Rising out of the fire of religious division in London was, in the view of this author, a terrible Phoenix, in fact, a terrible, consuming disease: a tyrannous and ravenous New Model Army that would be a terrifying and costly burden on the citizens. For the poet John Dryden, the 'banishment' of monarchy, wit, and true religion during the Commonwealth was as if the nation, imagined as a city, burned: 'when Troy was wrapt in fire and smoak'.[29]

Imagined apocalypses and millenniums in seventeenth-century London were as much to do with metals as they were to do with glass. Those who worked in the metal trades – goldsmiths and silversmiths for example – lived with an imaginative continuity of apocalyptic texts, the value of precious metals, and the possibility that the raw material of their livelihood might become (through the secrets of alchemy) the means by which a kind of Paradisal city might be created. Furthermore, satire of Dissenters from the Restoration makes the association between metalworkers and nonconformists explicit: *A Comical New Dialogue between Mr. G–ff, A Pious Dissenting Parson, and a Female Quaker (A Goldsmith's Wife) near Cheapside* (n.d.). Ben Jonson seems to have seen all this in his play *The Alchemist* (1610), where London becomes the site for the supposed millennium of Sir Epicure Mammon's money industry and the Anabaptist cash-flow welfare nirvana of Ananias and Tribulation: the market and separatist faith go hand in hand. In Jonson's world, the anticipated millennium dissolves in the farce of exploding flasks and the victorious deceit of a mischievous butler. However, many godly sectaries worked in the precious metals trade, and the voice of religious radicalism provided the strongest critique of London's parasitical luxury a few decades later. Gerrard Winstanley claimed that the old world would disappear like parchment burning in a flame, and Abiezer Coppe asserted that money would burn in the pockets of selfish, rich people.[30] Others still took what Jonson regarded as an illusion quite seriously.

---

[28] Anon., *A Seasonable Caution to the Citie of London* ([2 June], 1648), p. 7.
[29] John Dryden, 'To my Lord Chancellor, Presented on New-years-Day' (1662), p. 19.
[30] Abiezer Coppe, *A Second Fiery Flying Roule* (1649) in Nigel Smith (ed.), *A Collection of Ranter Writings from the Seventeenth Century* (1983), p. 101.

Retributive fire was the solution recommended by William Finch
in 1655 for persistent selfishness: fire started by people but coming,
so to speak, from God. Finch was a follower of the silversmith
prophet Thomas Tany, and like Tany fused Leveller, Digger, and
Ranter injunctions to share wealth.[31] Property has to be consumed
by fire if the birthright of every man is not honoured, and, taking the
Lord's work into his own hands, Finch appears to have attempted
several great fires of London:

This saith the Lord God, the searcher of all hearts, You have prophesied a
Lye in your own Consciences; and I will make your prophesie true on your
Persons and Estates: There's a Fire kindled in your houses shall consume all
your Goods; and when you have nothing, you shall cry unto me, and I will
say to you, I have nothing for you, Prov. 1. and so shall all you lying
Hypocrites perish. Remember my Fire kindled in Fleet-street, and secondly
renewed in Thred-needle-street, in the bowels of that proud City, who in
their contemning Pride say to my Poor, *We have nothing for you;* so you shall
not for your selves, saith the Lord God: so Now I have bid a Fire-price
once, and given a Fire-Earnest-peny in good Earnest for all your estates:
But now I am coming to take full and final posession by Fire and Sword on
all flesh, Isa. 66 for by fire and sword doth the Lord plead with all flesh.[32]

Finch was doing nothing more than literalizing a simile employed by
the Leveller William Bray: 'God hath appointed a day wherein he
will judge the world in righteousnesse at which time wicked deeds
shall have no glory in power and rules, God will destroy *Machavell*
more and more even by a Law which is like unto fire which shall
enter into the inmost parts.'[33] That Finch's third fire is actually a
pamphlet raises an incidental but important theme in this chapter. It
is not merely, or in some cases, at all, that we are dealing with urban
perceptions mimetically represented in a text. Rather, the text is
instrumental in the social activity that makes up city life, or, in this
case, apocalyptic life. Francis Hacket and Abiezer Coppe deal in
prophetic gestures that can be embodied on the page; Finch lights a
fire in your head; nothing is stopping you from making a spill of his
pages.[34]

---

31 I am deeply indebted to Ariel Hessayon, '"Gold tried in the fire": the prophet
   TheaurauJohn Tany and the puritan revolution', PhD thesis, University of Cambridge
   (1997).
32 [William] [Finch], *A Third Great and Terrible Fire, Fire, Fire* (1 June, 1655), p. 4 (Thomason
   Tracts E841(5)).
33 William Bray, *A Letter to his Excellencie Sir Thomas Fairfax* ([3 June,] 1647), pp. 3–4.
34 See Alexandra Walsham, '"Frantick Hacket": prophecy, sorcery, insanity and the

The figural play in Finch's writing should not detract from the fact that he and his group seem to have had some success in both raising fires and in sowing monitory fears in the heads of their fellow citizens and the government. Nehemiah Wallington noticed fires in Fleet Street and other places between February and May 1655, cataloguing them as 'Notices of God's Judgements'.[35] On 10 April 1655, the Common Council of London appointed a day of fasting and prayer after the 'great fires in London'.[36] They hoped that religious observance would assuage the divine wrath to come, and this was widely felt. The astrologer William Lilly wrote in 1656 that 'God hath in this last year 1655 sent his fearfull Messengers of Fire so frequently into several parts of this City as an Alarm of some further judgement he intends to go on with, if there be not a general, timely and serious repentance in the Inhabitants thereof, or an aversion from sin and iniquity.'[37] The prophets Reeve and Muggleton were more starkly colourful in what they imagined: 'What is this ground think you of so many dreadful fires this year in this City, and other parts, above the memory of man? . . . These fires came not merely by natural causes, but by a divine power as a fore runner of the eternal burning [of] this world.'[38]

The conflagration that Finch seems to have attempted to realize is prefigured and repeated in the literature of enthusiasm from the late 1640s onwards, and particularly in the group of texts associated with the Ranters. George Foster's remarkable visions of millenarian justice contain repeated imagery of burning. God is a 'consuming fire' who will annihilate all property, so that the godly must *be willing when he appeareth* to forsake all, *and to count that what for the present is* their God, *as gold and silver, as nothing* that they may cloath and feed the hungry, *and so scape the day* that shall burne as an Oven'.[39] Foster's sense of context is every bit as urban as Finch's: he was moved to come to London to have his visions printed, and for all that he is told by a divine voice that the flaming city in his vision is spiritual 'Sodom and Egypt', the frantic attempts at extinguishing flames remind the reader of the capital. Indeed, if the narrative was not in other ways

Elizabethan puritan movement', *Historical Journal* 41 (1998), 27–66; Nigel Smith, *Perfection Proclaimed: Language and Literature in English Radical Religion, 1640–1660* (Oxford, 1989).
[35] BL, MS Sloane 1457, fos. 96r–99r.
[36] CLRO, Jour. 41, fo. 116v. See also Porter, *Great Fire*, p. 5.
[37] William Lilly, *Merlini Anglici Ephemeris* (1656), sig. A3v.
[38] John Reeve and Lodowick Muggleton, *A Divine-Looking Glass* (1661), p. 198 (written in 1655).
[39] George Foster, *The Sounding of the Last Trumpet* (1650).

so symbolic, we could be reading an account from the first night of
the Great Fire itself: 'and the people which their surest running to
quench it, as Kings, and Lords, and great men, and of all sorts of
men, with buckets of water, and hookes, to pull down some of it, that
was on fire, but they could not quench it, as then didst see . . . the
tenth part of it was consumed'.[40] And as we have seen, some
narrative accounts of the Great Fire were in fact structured as
apocalypses: survivors were shown to have experienced a levelling
effect in the instant abolition of the familiar social, psychological,
and physical boundaries.

Foster's vision leaves bodies intact however – or at least the bodies
of the elect. In another vision, a woman wearing a white garment
covered with black spots (the symbolism is not subtle) is set on fire.
She survives naked and is reclothed in pure white: purification is
achieved.[41] And when Foster represents in his other tract the
working of the Lord of Hosts as an act not of consumption but of
rapine, the emphasis on the imminent destruction of earthly institutions is clear.[42]

V GOODNESS GRACIOUS, GREAT BALLS OF FIRE

That some modern arsonists have reported a connection between
fire and sexual arousal suggests a link between Ranter sexual
theology and fire, but it is hard to find a literal instance of this
perception in the surviving evidence. Yet the unsigned publication of
January 1657, *Divine Fire-works*, often attributed to Abiezer Coppe
himself, contains a woodcut in which a Crowned lion holding a
flaming sword stands against a landscape that is plainly on fire. He is
apparently emptying coins from a chest, which are being consumed
too. A lamb sucks from his breast while he is depicted with an erect
penis.[43] Whatever this aspect of the picture means, the conflagration
is presented as a purging of Londoners.

The tract itself articulates a burning purgation caused by the

---

[40] *Ibid.*, pp. 22–3.   [41] *Ibid.*, p. 35.
[42] George Foster, *The Pouring Forth of the Seventh and Last Viall* (1650), p. 16. In the vision, a man
with a knife disembowels his victims. This is interpreted as a representation of the Lord's
discernment of people's souls.
[43] Another interpretation would be that the genitals of the lion represent the masculinity of
God, femininity by the suckled lamb. But in the lines underneath the woodcut, the lion is
'rouzed'. Do the genitals suggest the iconography of devils and demons? The lamb in the
woodcut bears no relation to the sacrificed lamb in Rev. 5.

arrival of 'BLVI', Coppe's way of writing the Latin letters of the year 1656 (of course, it should be MDCLVI). 'BLVI' also spells 'blue', a stone with a power greater than the alchemists' 'philosopher's stone', that facilitates the transformation of base metals into gold by a fiery refinement. What follows is hot stuff: 'The Spirit of Burning . . . took such real possession of me, That it not only waxed hot within me; But also (on a sudden) set my body on such a flame; that (at a distance) it would warm the stander by, as if they were warming their hands at a burning fire, &c. Then was I raised to sit up in my bed (in my shirt) smoaking like a furnace.'[44] Then we learn that the 'BLVI' is God's appearance in the colour of truth, and Coppe hears the sound of whiplash, coupled with the crack of burning. Is the sound of whipping a reference to Christ scourging the merchants and money-changers in the temple (John 2: 13–17), or an aural echo of early modern punishment? The fire searches inside everyone, as well as consuming everything, so that the 'IN-side' is turned 'out-wards'. Finally, the fire consumes the 'Daughter of Sodom', an allegorical figuration for urban luxury, and also a quintessentially Ranter configuration of feminine pride. Startlingly, we realize that the literal smell of burning flesh is elicited by God's flaming arrival: 'And the roaring ramping Lyon, with the sharp two-edged Sword, wil run her through and through. And with unquenchable fire / Will burn up the bravery of their tinkling Ornaments. / The bracelets, &c. The changeable Suits of apparel, &c. The Glasses, and fine Linnen. The Hoods and the Vails, &c. And instead of sweet smelling there shall be a stink; and BURNING instead of Beauty.[45] Earthly sexual prowess, as presented in a courtly mistress, is replaced by the flaming energy of the lion – erect godly power. One of the woodcut's meanings is thus revealed; and we may conjecture that Coppe's abjection in the face of courtly luxury – his own sexual disempower-ment – is answered by a flaming holy hard-on.[46]

Where the terms of Coppe's reference are unclear, for Thomas

[44] ?Abiezer Coppe, *Divine Fire-Works* (1657) in Coppe, *Selected Writings*, ed. Andrew Hopton (1987), p. 100.

[45] *Ibid.*, pp. 103–4.

[46] For abjection, see Coppe, *A Second Fiery Flying Roull* in Smith, *Collection of Ranter Writings*, p. 105; Coppe's sexuality is discussed in Clement Hawes, *Mania and Literary Style: The Rhetoric of Enthusiasm from the Ranters to Smart* (Cambridge, 1996), pp. 50–76. Cf. Freud's discussion of the legend of Servius Tullius, whose mother, a slave in the household of King Tarquin, was inseminated by a phallic flame that leapt out of a domestic fire: Sigmund Freud, 'The acquisition and control of fire' in *Complete Psychological Works*, ed. James Strachey (24 vols., 1953–74), XXII, pp. 187–93.

Tany, the purification of the body would literally be a consumption of the dross in each individual, a refinement down to the purity that the fleshly body imprisons in this life in a living hell. This was the most extreme and most individualistic view of the uses of fire in the period. Yet if Tany's views, and those of his followers, seem extraordinary and part of a heretical and lunatic fringe, related concepts and perceptions occur in the writings of the more orthodox. In Simon Ford's poem of the Great Fire, for instance, the soul is certainly not refined by calcination, but the poet's vision (under the influence of the 'sacred Flame' of inspiration) can reveal the *inside-Flames*: the effect of the fire on the interior mental life of those who witnessed it.[47]

VI URBAN FIRE INTERPRETED

The poet John Dryden, who was a pupil at Westminster School in the 1640s, and who worked for the Protectoral government in London during the 1650s, thought the Great Fire was a punishment for the sins of regicide and the puritan commonwealth. In his vision of the Fire in *Annus Mirabilis*, the ghosts of the regicides (whose heads had been left on spikes rising above London Bridge), and other puritans, are not purged by holy fire, but simulate their future life in Hell in a Satanic ritual: 'The Ghosts of Traitors, from the Bridge descend, / With bold Fanatick Spectres to rejoyce: / About the fire into a Dance they bend, / And sing their Sabbath notes with feeble voice.'[48]

For Dryden, the Great Fire was a way of bringing back into the present the punishment of the regicides that he had formerly imagined would be postponed until the Last Days. Just so, for the former royalist journalist John Crouch, the fire brought back memories of when 'fiery Cromwell domineer'd'.[49] Elsewhere in the poetry on the Great Fire, the alleged desecration of St Paul's Cathedral during the Commonwealth is followed by its martyrdom in the Fire. A hoped-for resurrection will, we are promised, be in accordance with the ancient, episcopal British church, and looked over by the king: a national cure from nonconformity is finally

---

[47] Aubin, *London in Flames*, p. 17.
[48] John Dryden, *Annus Mirabilis* (1666), 889–92.
[49] John Crouch, *Londinenses Lachrymae* (1666), pp. 73–4.

achieved in the post-conflagrational rebuilding of the cathedral, the city, and its culture.[50]

Within that non-conformity itself, the gathered churches and prophetic conventicles of Civil War and Interregnum London, apocalyptic biblical texts became a means by which the city could be appropriated for a millennial narrative. The Fifth Monarchist prophet Anna Trapnel's visions place London inside the chronological simultaneities afforded by apocalyptic narrative. The visions that she delivered in Whitehall in January 1654 (during the interrogation of the Fifth Monarchist Vavasor Powell) involve an initial extended vision (like a repeated dream) that she seems to have had first in 1647, before August, when the New Model entered London via Southwark. The vision involves a military muster on Blackheath, overlooking the east end of the city (she came from Poplar):

after this there was a day of thanksgiving that I kept with the Church of *Allhallows* in *Limestreet*, for the Army that was then drawing up towards the City, in which I had a little discovery of the presence of the Lord with them, in which day I had a glorious Vision of the New Jerusalem . . . repairing to my Chamber [which was in the Minories] again, I looked out at the window, where I saw a flag at the end of the street; this word I had presently upon it, thou seest that flag, the flag of defiance is with the Army, the King of *Salem* is on their side, he marcheth before them, he is the Captain of the Salvation; At the other end of the street, I looking, saw a hill (it was *Black-heath*) it was said to me, thou seest that hill, not one but many hills rising up against *Hermon-hill*, They shall fall down and become Vallies before it. It was then said unto me, Go into the City, and see what is done there: where I saw various things from the Lord in Order to his appearance with the Army; as I was going, hearing of a Trumpeter say to a Citizen these words, we have many Consultations about our coming up, but nothing yet goes on, presently it was said to me, the Councels of men shall fall, but the Councel of the Lord stands sure, and his works shall prosper: So repairing home, I had many Visions, that the Lord was doing great things for this Nation.

And having fasted nine days, nothing coming within my lips, I had upon the ninth day the Vision of horns; first I saw in the Vision the Army coming in *Southwark*-way, marching through the City with a great deal of silence and quietness, and that there should be little or no bloud spilt; this was some weeks before their coming in.[51]

Her authority as a prophet rests upon the continuing presence of that magnificent entry, that she supposes will bring on the millen-

[50] John Tabor, *Seasonable Thoughts in Sad Times* (1667), pp. 365–97.
[51] Anna Trapnel, *The Cry of a Stone* (1654), pp. 4–5.

nium. The interruption of that process is the dissolution of Bare-
bone's Parliament (although she held no particular faith in it) and
the beginning of the Protectorate. The result is an urban nightmare
where the initial vision revisits without its original expectations, and
where a triumphant army is replaced by an inverse carnival of
dangerous, charging beasts, and, in some of the songs that accompany the accounts of the visions, the Lord Mayor, Aldermen, and
Sheriffs are blamed for sating Cromwell with rich food and wine,
committing him to backsliding lusts.[52]

The vision of a coming conflagration is as real to her as anything
in her own exterior world. London becomes an apocalyptic landscape as Whitehall and the white tower (which she links to the
tower of strength in Prov. 18: 10) are juxtaposed. The vision is a
kind of refigured gunpowder plot: the council rooms in Whitehall
are strewn with gunpowder. The Saints wait in the white tower
'with their eyes fixed toward Heaven, their countenances shining as
the Sun'. Round about the tower are 'a great many of the Colonels
and Chief of the Army, with their Pistols cock'd, and lighted Match
in their hands, beating the fire toward the white Tower, but they
could not, for the fire would not take'.[53] The gunpowder represents, we are told, the 'Wisdom, Power and policy' of the comman-
ders: if it does not blow up the saints, the inference is that it will
certainly destroy these enemies. Was she living with this scripture,
uncited in her text: 'And they went up on the breadth of the earth,
and compassed the camp of the saints about, and the beloved city:
and fire came down from God out of heaven, and devoured them'
(Rev. 20: 9)?

The greatest literary monument to the capital in this and in
several other respects is Andrew Marvell's *The First Anniversary upon
the Government of the Lord Protector*, a poem written by a probable
republican against Fifth Monarchist agitation but in defence of a
religious radical, Oliver Cromwell, and his Protectoral rule.[54] The
poem appears to present the Protectorate as a functional republic,
made so by the presence of the Protector, the 'protecting weight' of
the roof of the senate. This is a reference to the gathering of the first

---

[52] Untitled folio volume, Bodleian Library, S.Th.i.S, p. 55.
[53] Trapnel, *The Cry of a Stone*, p. 12.
[54] Feake and Simpson are the two prominent Fifth Monarchists mentioned by Marvell at line
305: surprisingly, there is no mention of Trapnel. For the poem's broader context, see
Andrew Marvell, *Complete Poems*, ed. Nigel Smith (forthcoming).

Protectorate Parliament in September 1654, around which crystallized a good deal of millenarian expectation, and which was intended by some to wrest back a measure of power from the Protector himself. It is remarkable how the poem's envisioning of the perfected state is in the image of the city of London, fused again with Jerusalem (as well as ancient Thebes): 'ere he ceased, his sacred lute creates / Th'harmonious city of the seven gates' (lines 65–6). The image of the constitution as a building made strong through the operation of mutually opposing forces derives directly from Milton's London-influenced defence of literary freedom, *Areopagitica* (1644). At the same time, Marvell's Cromwell functions as the first London fire brigade, dousing apocalyptic fires with apocalyptic showers, an image that three years later embarrasses Richard Cromwell in Marvell's elegy on Oliver, since Richard will only produce a little rain: 'Cease now our griefs, calm peace succeeds a war, / Rainbows to storms, Richard to Oliver. / Tempt not his clemency to try his power, / He threats no deluge, yet foretells a shower' (lines 321–4). No less than Trapnel or Finch, the poem is making capital of the possibility of apocalypse within the city: Cromwell is presented as the deliverer of an urban millennium, but he does it by damping fires.

Like Finch and Trapnel, Marvell's vision is implicitly urban, and represents the extent to which the urban and biblical (apocalyptic) narratives had been fused within the London gathered churches by the mid-1650s. And yet, we often remember Dissent as a rural or a provincial thing. Think of the classics in the non-conformist tradition: Bunyan's *The Pilgrim's Progress* down to George Eliot's *Felix Holt*. Bunyan's *Mr Badman* (1680) has unlicensed conventicles meeting in fields rather than surreptitious huddlings of people in citizens' houses. *The Holy War* figures not London but the Bedford corporation, as James II attempted to interfere with local government. The Marprelate or Richard Overton of the Restoration was Ralph Wallis, who hawked his tracts on the streets not of London but of Gloucester. In the classic printed statements of Dissent after 1660, the specificity of London's geography begins to disappear from the text. Dissenters found it easier to present the world where it had its earlier, relatively undisturbed, origins: the provincial town (especially market places) and the country. The quest for respectability among all non-conformist groups after 1660 meant that printed pastoral literature tended to present itself as belonging to nowhere, yet deeply cultural: witness, for instance, the 1660s sermons of William Spur-stowe.[55]

The reason for this is not difficult to discern. It was not possible to be quite so public in London while the penalties against Dissenting worship during the Restoration stood. Of course, many (especially the Quakers) were persecuted in the provinces, but they were able to function in a way that was continuous with their original missionary ideals. The Quakers even looked here for an equality of communication that would make 'Country people' less prone to exploitation by the city.[56] It is no surprise that fires away from the metropolis could be more readily appropriated for pious purposes: loss of property and shelter can turn the mind to heavenly things that really matter.[57]

But London had its 'public sphere', its crossable boundaries, and its hiding places. It was full of points of contact across the divisions that the Act of Uniformity (of 1662) enforced. Hence George Fox's visits to Richard Marche, one of Charles II's grooms of the bed-chamber, an avenue both to Charles II and the Jesuits. By the early 1670s, Dissenters offended by the attacks of Anglican bishops like Samuel Parker were joining Andrew Marvell in the kind of stylistic bravado of *The Rehearsal Transpos'd*, where the trappings of Restoration comedy were taken inside the universe of the pamphlet and the lexis of non-conformity for the purposes of satirical attack. At the end of the same decade, Samuel Jeake, the influential Independent lawyer of Rye, found it safer to avoid arrest by hiding in London. It was this sphere that the early Friends subjected to criticism, even to the extent of burning newsbooks publicly, while also making astute use of the press.[58]

This is why it is so apt that Marvell's greatest depiction of burning punctuates a depressed commentary on the plight of the English in their capital city during the Restoration. In a passage in *The Last Instructions to a Painter* (1667) that is considered one of the finest in his verse, after the description of the Great Fire of London – the beginning of a year of national calamity in the poet's opinion –

[55] See e.g., Spurstowe, *The Spiritual Chemist* (1664); N. H. Keeble, *The Literary Culture of Nonconformity in the Later Seventeenth Century* (Leicester, 1987), chs. 1–3.

[56] *To the Parliament of the Comon-wealth of England* (1659).

[57] See e.g. Anne Bradstreet, 'Upon the burning of our House, July 10th 1666'.

[58] The most well-known Quaker newsbook burner in the Restoration was John Pennyman: see *DNB* and Quaker Biography Dictionary files, Friends House Library, London.

Captain Archibald Douglas is described dying on a burning ship during the Dutch raid on the Medway (July 1667), which included the burning of Chatham. Douglas becomes a burnt offering for the sins of the helpless English nation, preserved as a monument within the flame as bees are preserved in amber, and rather like the martyrs depicted in Foxe's *Acts and Monuments*. That Douglas was in all probability a Roman Catholic suggests that the poet hopes the fiery sacrifice will overcome the religious division that has torn the nation: the division that is the cause of so much fire in the land.

The poem may have been related to another confessional explanation of the Great Fire. *Pyrotechnica Loyolana, Ignatian Fire-works* (1667), supposedly written by a loyal Catholic, blames the fire on the Jesuits.[59] The body of the work is a historically informed attack on the Society of Jesus, but the occasion is the Great Fire of 1666. Even in the name Ignatius is the nature of the man: ignition. A woodcut depicts a Pope charging a flaming London with bellows, while Captain-General Loyola orders foxes (who represent Jesuit agents; in Judges 15: 4 Samson set the tails of the foxes ablaze in order to destroy the crops of the Philistines) on to the attack: 'what ayles / These *Foxes* to wear *Fire-brands* in their tayles? / What, did *you* teach these Cubs the World to *burn*, / Or to *Embottle* London in its Urne?'

VII FIRESPEAK

In all of the writing on fire examined here (that is to say, the expectation of urban apocalypse for one reason or another in the 1650s, or reportage of and reflection upon the Great Fire of 1666), it is notable that there is little speculation on the nature of fire itelf. Perhaps with the exception of Tany, there is no register of the questioning of the age-old view that fire was one of the four elements.[60] No doubt it was assumed that God would pour fire upon the earth from its location in the outermost of the four spheres. Jacob Boehme had already claimed that fire did not purify, and Robert Boyle challenged the view that fire was an indivisible element in print from the early 1660s. No-one seemed to doubt that, on the basis of evidence, it consumed.

To the commentators of the 1640s and 1650s, fire explained the

---

[59] I am grateful to my colleague, Eileen Reeves, for drawing my attention to this work.
[60] See the discussion of the consequences of ancient fire theory in Gaston Bachelard, *The Psychoanalysis of Fire* (1938), trans. Alan C. M. Ross (Boston, 1964).

events of those decades: not merely civil war, the national church put into abeyance, and the execution of a monarch, but also, and perhaps more importantly, the new forms of writing and activity that came into existence in the early 1640s. That is to say, journalism, pamphleteering, and popular movements like the Levellers, Quakers, and Fifth Monarchists, orchestrated by the printed word. That these events seemed to fit with the approaching Apocalypse helped these perceptions to cohere. From fire would come more fire. To the orthodox and the conservative puritans, this was the apogee of the 'fire' of dissent. In short, fire represents a consumption of a solid, certain world in which information did not travel, and dissent or protest did not exist. The popular politics of the 1640s was an energetic proliferation of speech, print, and martial activity: the nation was on fire. Those who could imagine the fusion of outward fire and inward fire believed that they were being seared into a new future of material, spiritual, and sexual equality.

That seventeenth-century people seemed to move so effortlessly from the literal to the figurative and back again in their talk about fire suggests that they made little distinction between the two categories.[61] There seems no end to these mutual nourishings of one area by the other: they are an anxiety machine. Fire is not tied down to any one explanation or phenomenon: hence it can appear anywhere as a means of articulating a threat to the reliable and the safe. Since the city was the site of the most intense change, be it social, political, or religious, fire becomes the leitmotif of both civilization and the fear that civilization will end in annihilation.[62] To put the ashes of the city into an urn, as the poet of the prefatory verse in *Pyrotechnica Loyolana* imagined, is to end the energy of the city, much as Marvell punningly pictures Captain Douglas going to rest in bed in the sheets of the flames engulfing him. Fire is heightened activity bringing to a rapid conclusion the activity that is life. Its presence in the early modern urban mind is always to connect the literal and the figural, and in doing so to make the quotidian or the contingent part of the narrative of the last days. Fire remains with us in this way today, especially in the images

---

[61] Much like the dream discussed by Freud, where a father is visited in the dream by his newly dead child to warn him that she is burning: he wakes to find that the watchman guarding her corpse has fallen asleep, while the candles surrounding her body have ignited it: Sigmund Freud, *The Interpretation of Dreams*, trans. and ed. James Strachey (1965), pp. 547–8.

[62] See also the discussion in Johan Goudsblom, *Fire and Civilization* (1992), p. 11.

provided by popular culture, even though what combustion is – high-temperature oxidation – has been known for two hundred years, tied down to a fixed meaning. In early modern London, fire is always a possibility, indeed, in some of its meanings, it is always there; and as the Book of Revelation prophesies, in the end, we will all burn in the city.

There were new fire theories in the later seventeenth century and early eighteenth centuries, in which it was accepted that combustion depended upon an extra substance in the air: either John Mayow's particles of 'nitroairial spirit' of the 1660s, or Stahl's 1702 hypothesis of 'phlogiston', an 'essence of fire' released during combustion and reabsorbed by the air. Both of these would have been entirely suited to articulating that which the previous generation meant by fire: speaking in public, in many often contrary voices. Somewhere in *Leviathan* there should have been a description derived from Boyle's experiment of a flame being extinguished as air was pumped out of a chamber. It might well have helped Hobbes to conceptualize the relationship between obedience and belief. But Hobbes was writing fifteen years too soon, and in any case, he did not accept that a pure vacuum could be created. For him, and his generation, fire was always a possibility.

Index

Act of Settlement (1662), 12, 140, 181
Acton (Middlesex), 150, 160
Adams, Thomas, 9, 110, 24, 245–6
Addison, Joseph, 144, 199, 207
administrative jurisdictions, 135, 137, 140
adultery, 227, 239, 243, 244, 245
advice literature, 163–4
air, 18, 35, 196–9, 203–5, 210, 211; *see also* pollution
alchemy, 281, 285
alleys, 6, 121, 125, 127, 131, 186, 199
Allington, Richard, 43
almshouses, 32, 33, 79, 93
Anabaptists, 45, 272
Anglo-Saxons, 39
anonymity, 11, 12, 13, 14
anti-Catholicism, 39, 40, 44–5, 62, 69–70, 108, 253, 255, 268, 270
    of Munday, 54
    of Strype, 77–8
antiquarianism, 28, 37–51, 69
apocalypse, 21–2, 274, 278–9, 281, 288, 291, 292
apprentices, 251, 252, 253, 255–6, 258, 259, 261, 266
Archer, Ian, 4–5, 37
archery, 30, 33, 36, 37, 198
architecture, 3, 71, 72, 73
Arden of Faversham, 236–7, 244
aristocracy, 71, 128, 150, 163, 200, 201, 230, 231, 234, 241, 247, 262
arson, 282, 283, 284
art, 72; *see also* portraits
Artillery Company, 62, 263
artisans, 161, 239, 242, 243, 276
Aston, Margaret, 33
Aylmer, Bishop John, 79

Baldwin, William, 44
Bale, John, 39, 40
ballads, 227

sellers, 167, 171, 174, 177
singers, 176–7, 179
Barking, 76, 79
Barlow, Thomas, 88
Barnardiston, Sir Samuel, 258–9
Battersea, 159
Beaumont, Francis: *The Knight of the Burning Pestle*, 112–13
Becket, St Thomas, 40, 77
Bedloe, William, 69
Beer, Barrett, 41–2
beggars, 13–14, 166
    female, 173–4, 176–7
    itinerant domestic, 168, 174–5, 182
    language of, 172–3
    policing, 171–2
    prosecutions, 171, 178
    the public poor, 177–8off.
    'self-employed', 13, 168, 174, 175–7
    social policy, 178–84
    stationary, 14, 168–74, 182–3
Bellot, Thomas, 110
benefactors, 32, 89–90, 91, 93, 94, 95–6, 97–8, 99, 100–13
    attitudes to, 110–13
    Munday and, 56–8, 59, 60
    power inequalities, 112
    women, 89, 90, 146
    see also charity; donations
Bernard, Francis, 22
Bethlehem Hospital, 35, 80, 198, 210
Bible, 58, 274–5, 285
Bills of Mortality, 134–5
Bisset, William, 270
Blackheath, 140
Blome, Richard, 73, 87
Bloomer, Captain, 264
Bloomsbury (Middlesex), 156, 190, 202, 235
Bodley, Thomas, 111
body, 22, 194–5, 196, 210

Boleyn, Anne, 45
Bolton, Edmund, 67
bonfires, 263, 264, 266
Book of Revelation, 22, 274–5, 288, 293
Bossy, John, 224, 225
Boswell, James, 12
Boulton, Jeremy, 11, 12, 35, 181
boundaries, 10, 56, 87, 135, 137–8, 140
bowling alleys, 34, 35, 36
Boyle, Robert, 196, 291, 293
Braun and Hogenberg: *Civitates Orbis
    Terrarum*, 118, 119, 187; *see also* maps
Briggens, Peter, 153
Bromley, 66
brothels, 230, 235, 236, 239, 241, 248, 251,
    252, 257, 258
Brown, Thomas, 144, 147, 148, 169
Bruster, Douglas, 243
Buckingham, duke of, 255
buildings, 6, 12, 29, 33, 36, 63, 87, 122, 123,
    124, 125, 127, 128, 130
    public, 71
Bunyan, John, 289
Burnet, Gilbert, 253
burnings, 278, 285
Buxton, Henry, 170–1
Byrd, Max, 23

Calverley, Mr, 227–8, 229
Cambridge University, 57, 58, 59, 76
Camden, William, 37–8, 39, 44, 50, 51, 68
Carew, Bampfylde, 175
Carew, Richard: *Survey of Cornwall*, 28, 47–51
carmen, 19, 71, 259, 263
Catholicism, 4, 42–3, 45, 53, 60, 62, 68, 69,
    70, 76, 78, 80, 253, 256, 268, 291
    and antiquarianism, 37–8
    and commemoration, 91, 93
    see also anti-Catholicism
censorship, 85
chantries, 93, 94
Chapman, Edmund, 60
charity, 4, 29, 32, 37, 56–60, 63, 66, 75, 78,
    79, 180
    and commemoration, 89, 90, 91–3, 95–6,
        101–11
    critics of, 110–12
    distributions, 106–7
    power inequalities, 112
    and ritual, 101–2, 105–7
Charles I, King, 65, 81, 82, 260, 261
Charles II, King, 82, 190, 201, 207, 260, 261,
    263, 266, 268, 279, 290
Chelsea (Middlesex), 66, 153, 157, 158, 159
Cheyne, George, 193–4, 195

children, 104–5, 106, 168, 173, 176, 178, 226,
    227, 239
Christ's Hospital, 104–5, 106, 112
church courts, 3
Church of England, 46, 54, 69, 138
churches, 4, 32–4, 36, 41, 55, 56, 57, 58, 70,
    71, 84–5, 89
    attendance at, 145
    and begging, 175
    building, 46–7, 59–61, 66, 69, 86
    destruction of, 68, 69
    fires, 277, 278
    and memorialization, 90, 100–5
    organization, 138
    repair, 47, 59–61, 78, 86, 102, 138
    windows, 60, 62, 63, 100, 102, 103
'C.I.', 65, 66
circulation, 194–5, 196, 204, 210
city ditch, 125
City gates, 169, 176
city walls, 125, 135
civic regalia, 90
Civil War, 2, 5, 81–2, 287, 292
Clark, Stuart, 217
classical imagery, 6, 14, 15, 20, 66, 221, 238,
    239
clergy, 51, 80, 84, 106, 280; *see also* preachers
Clerkenwell (Middlesex), 156, 235
    St James, 84
clubs, 154
coats of arms, 64, 96, 97, 99, 100, 102, 113
coffee houses, 141, 149, 150, 153, 154
Cole, William, 44
Collinson, Patrick, 4
commemoration *see* memorialization
    common fields, 187; *see also* green space
communion cups, 102
community, 11, 12, 13, 32, 37, 91, 127, 139, 145
    imagined, 51
    and the public poor, 177, 178, 180
Compton, Bishop Henry, 76, 78, 84, 85
consistory court depositions, 145, 148, 153,
    154, 156, 159
consumption, 2, 152, 219, 223, 226, 233
continuity, 3, 4, 5, 6, 23, 63–4, 107
Coppe, Abiezer, 281, 282, 284–5
Cornish, Sheriff, 257
Corporations of the Poor, 180, 183
Corpus Christi, feast of, 31
corruption, 17, 36, 218, 232, 235, 236, 238,
    241–3, 245–9
Cosgrave, Denis, 211
Counter-Reformation, 42
craftsmen, 155–6
Cressy, David, 90

crime, 16, 130, 225–39, 240, 244ff., 250
Cromwell, Oliver, 288, 289
Cromwell, Richard, 289
Cromwell, Thomas, 29, 36, 188
crowd/mob, 20–1, 178, 250–72
  ambivalence towards, 252, 253–4, 256–7,
    259–61, 269
  and authorities, 256–8, 259–60
  composition of, 258–9
  denunciation of, 251, 253, 254
  legitimacy of, 260–2
  and politics, 251, 252, 254, 258, 259ff.
  praise of, 251–2, 254
  and public opinion, 260–1, 262
  violence, 251, 252, 253, 258, 260, 261, 272
  see also demonstrations; riots
Crowley, Robert, 44
Crown, the, 20–1, 98, 130, 189–90, 260–1,
  262ff.
  and City, 81–2, 85
Cunningham, Robert, 80
Curtis, Langley, 265, 266
Cust, Richard, 37
customs, 28, 29–32

Dabhoiwala, Faramerz, 243, 244
Dalton, James, 21
De Laune, Thomas: *The Present State of London*,
  69–70, 71
death rates, 133–4, 192–3
Defoe, Daniel, 36, 123, 135, 137, 193, 271
Dekker, Thomas, 16–17, 21, 220–1, 222, 223,
  228, 238, 242, 249, 276
  Britannia's Honour, 220–21
  The Honest Whore, 228, 242, 246
  If You Know Not Me You Know Nobody, 89
  News from Gravesend, 221
  The Seven Deadly Sinnes of London, 16
demonstrations, 251, 255, 258, 261, 262,
  264–5, 267, 268
desecration, 4
  see also iconoclasm
diaries, 3, 43, 148, 153, 279
Dickens, Charles, 13–14
directories, 7, 8, 10, 140
disease, 15, 23, 193, 194, 203, 204, 207, 210,
  248; *see also* plague
disorder, 15, 44, 137, 144, 167, 171, 194, 210,
  252, 254, 255, 261, 278
  and order, 217–19, 224–5, 226, 235–9,
    244–5
  and parks, 20
  toleration of, 257–8
Dissenters, 70, 76, 77, 138, 145, 270, 272, 275,
  276, 278, 280, 281, 287, 289, 290, 292

divine judgement, 19, 21, 22, 277, 279–84
Dixie, Sir Wolstan (d.1593), 57
documents *see* records
donations, 56–9, 85, 89–90, 93, 94, 99–100,
  101, 102–5, 112; *see also* benefactors;
  charity
Douglas, Captain Archibald, 291, 292
Dow, Richard, 105–6
drama *see* plays
drunkenness, 29, 219, 222, 230
Dryden, John, 281, 286
Duffy, Eamon, 30, 37
Dunton, John, 270
Dyson, Humphrey, 64, 65, 87

Earle, Peter, 153, 154
East End, 35, 122, 131, 134, 156, 160, 165
  development, 128
  parishes, 139
  social structure, 146
Eastward Ho!, 242
Echard, Lawrence, 253
economy, 11, 15, 17, 31, 75, 78, 224, 243, 244,
  246, 247, 249
Elborough, Robert, 19
elites, 137, 167, 168, 172, 177, 252
  corruption of, 16, 232
  and gender, 147–8
  and London mob, 256–8
  memorialization of, 90, 97, 110–11, 112, 113
  perceptions, 14, 17, 146, 147, 161–5
  and the public poor, 180–4
Elizabeth I, Queen, 95, 100, 108
  church monuments, 61–2, 69, 86
Elkin, Alice, 59
Ely House, 187
Emmanuel College, Cambridge, 58, 59
enclosures, 36, 187
encroachments, 29, 34, 35, 130, 185, 186, 187
engravings, 73, 118, 119, 210
epitaphs, 55–6, 58, 63, 69, 72, 92, 100, 101,
  110, 111, 112
Erdeswicke, Sampson, 37
Evelyn, John, 18, 19, 188, 196, 197–8, 204
Exclusion Crisis, 254, 255, 261, 269

Fairchild, Thomas, 189
Faithorne, William, 142; *see also* maps
families, 133, 183; *see also* households
feast days, 31–2
Fielding, Henry, 166, 184
Fifth Monarchists, 280, 287, 288, 292
Finch, William, 22, 282, 283
fire, 22–3, 29, 65, 75, 193
  apocalyptic, 274, 278–9, 281–4, 291

fear of, 278
language of, 291–2
religious meaning, 274, 275–7ff., 292
scientific understanding of, 291, 293
sexual connotations, 284–6, 292
urban, 23, 276, 286–91
see also Great Fire (1666)
Fitzstephen, William, 4, 28–30, 31, 35, 40, 45
foreigners, 36, 58, 77, 250, 253, 257
Foreigners' Guide, The, 191, 198
Foster, Agnes, 89
Foster, George, 283–4
Foxe, John, 45, 58
    Acts and Monuments, 43, 45, 69, 278, 291
Freeman, Thomas, 123, 137
French immigrants, 36, 58, 77
Fulham (Middlesex), 66
funerary sculpture, 95, 100–2

gaming houses, 34, 35, 36, 230, 235, 237, 239,
    241, 242
gardening, 188–9
gardens, 13, 34, 124, 125, 128
    ambiguity of, 212
    Inns of Court, 190–1
    and physical exercise, 194–6
    private, 187–9, 192, 203
    public, 191–2, 212
    and retirement, 206, 207, 211
    see also green space
Gay, John, 169, 170, 176
gender, 10, 146–65, 168
    east and west ends, 162
    perceptions, 146–9, 161–5
    and social mobility, 149–62, 163
    see also men; women
genealogy, 37, 48, 101
gentry, 128, 149–51, 161, 162, 200, 201, 203,
    226, 237, 242, 247, 262
Gibson, Avis, 90
glass, 276, 281
Glorious Revolution, 5, 70, 76, 82, 252–3
good works, 91, 92, 93, 109–11, 113; *see also*
    charity
Goodcole, Henry, 21, 234, 235, 238, 239
    London's Cry, 238
Gowing, Laura, 11, 243–4
Graunt, John, 123
Great Fire (1666), 2, 5, 6, 7, 19, 71, 86, 127,
    276
    apocalyptic accounts of, 284, 286, 291
    blamed on Catholics, 69–70
    churches and, 138
    and divine judgement, 22, 278–9
    see also monuments

green space, 18, 23, 35, 128
    access to, 187, 201, 203, 211, 212
    formal, 186, 192, 197–8, 202–3, 209
    and health, 192–9, 203–4
    and morality, 19–20, 164
    public and private aspects, 202, 212–13
    and retirement, 206–9, 211
    and social exclusivity, 18–19, 199–206, 211,
        212–13
    see also gardens; parks
Greenwich Hospital, 210
Gresham, Sir Thomas, 89, 98, 113
Griffiths, Paul, 257
Grindal, Bishop Edmund, 42, 79, 96
guidebooks, 7, 8–9, 17, 72
guilds, 31, 137, 145

Hackney (Middlesex), 36, 76, 198
Hall, Joseph, 78, 105, 110
Hampstead, 149, 190, 198, 199, 204
Harding, Vanessa, 7, 10, 11, 12, 153
harmony, 209, 210, 211
Harrington, Sir John, 109
Harris, Benjamin, 266
Harris, Tim, 20, 21
Hatton, Edward: *A New View of London*, 71–2,
    74
health, 11, 18, 23, 131, 133–4, 192–5ff.,
    203–4
Hearth Tax returns, 131–2
Hell Upon Earth, 164
Henry VIII, King, 18, 30, 33, 187, 188
heraldry, 37, 96–7
Heywood, Thomas, 89
Highgate (Middlesex), 123, 190, 198, 199, 204
Hitchcock, Tim, 13, 14, 162
Hobbes, Thomas, 293
Hogarth, William, 174–5, 176, 179
holidays, 257
Hollar, Wenceslaus, 128, 129; *see also* maps
Horne, Thomas, 74
horticulture, 187, 188–9, 196–7
hospitals, 33, 80, 104, 105, 106, 166, 179, 180,
    183, 184, 198, 210
Houndsditch, 32, 122, 125
House of Commons, 69, 270
households, 11, 127, 131, 132, 152, 158, 183–4,
    244
houses, 6, 33, 34, 36, 71, 124, 125, 127, 128,
    130, 131, 132, 182, 187–8, 189
Howell, James: *Londinopolis*, 67–9, 70–1, 83
Howes, Edmund, 64
Hoxton (Middlesex), 36, 189, 210
Hunt, Margaret, 152
Hutton, Ronald, 30

iconoclasm, 40–1, 60, 61, 63, 68, 69, 83, 89, 95, 99
identity, 3, 5, 7, 11, 12, 90, 95, 96, 113, 139, 140, 161, 162
immorality, 5, 15, 16, 17, 79, 192, 230, 233, 279
  and green space, 19–20, 193–4, 198, 204–5, 206, 211, 212
  inversions of, 217, 218, 219, 221ff., 247
  see also sin
Independent churches, 138
individuals, 3, 9, 11, 12, 14, 19, 23, 140, 178;
  see also Londoners
infanticide, 226, 227, 228, 237, 246
information, 7, 9, 10, 71
Inns of Court, 141, 190–1, 230, 234
inscriptions *see* epitaphs
insurance, 71, 75
Interregnum, 67, 287
inversion, 16, 217–20, 226, 235–9, 244–5, 249, 265
Islington (Middlesex), 66, 123
'I.W.', 84

Jaggard, William, 91
James II, King, 76, 82, 253, 255, 256, 260
James, Mervyn, 31
Janeway, Richard, 262, 263, 265, 266, 267
Jefferay, Richard, 222–3
Jefferey, William, 43
Jesuits, 290, 291
Jewel, Bishop John, 47
Johnson, John, 76
Johnson, Richard, 91
Jones, Emrys, 11
Jones, Norman, 248
Jonson, Ben, 16, 249
  The Alchemist, 249, 281
  Bartholomew Fair, 249

Kalm, Pehr, 189
Katherine of Aragon, 45
Kebyll, Henry, 95, 96
Kensington (Middlesex), 149, 153, 159, 198
Kent, 38–9, 51, 118
Killigrew, William, 111
King, Bishop John, 59–60, 78
Kingsford, C. L., 32, 41, 52, 53
Kirk, Robert, 9
Klein, Lawrence, 150
Knepp, Elizabeth, 153

labourers, 156, 158
Lake, Peter, 16, 20, 21
Lambarde, William: *Perambulation of Kent*, 28, 38–40, 41, 51

Lambe, William, 58–9, 108, 111
Lambeth, 150, 157, 191, 197
Lambeth Palace, 255
landlords, 123, 127, 130
language, 10–11, 17, 50, 146, 172–3, 217, 220, 224, 234, 247, 264, 291–2
Laslett, Peter, 27
law courts, 141, 145, 148
leases, 123, 125, 153
leisure, 10, 28, 29–32, 36, 49, 189, 191, 198, 202; *see also* sports and pastimes
L'Estrange, Roger, 251, 260, 262–3, 268, 269, 278
Levellers, 282, 292
Lightfoot, John, 76
literature, 16, 17, 18, 19, 20, 27, 54, 74, 90, 91, 111, 112–13, 146, 177, 179, 296, 207–9, 219
  celebration, 220–1, 224
  crime, 225–49
  denunciation, 221–5
  fire, 278–9ff., 281ff., 286, 288ff.
  gender, 147, 163–4
  religious, 21–2, 42–3
  social contagion, 204–5
  urban growth, 122–3
livery companies, 3, 64, 75, 86, 188
  halls, 4, 90, 96–9
  memorialization, 93, 94, 107
  power inequalities, 112
  wardens, 106
Lockman, John, 207
Lodge, Sir Thomas, 44
Lodge, Thomas: *An Alarum against Usurers*, 241–2, 246–8
London
  criticism of, 17, 21, 217, 221–5, 238
  growth, 1–2, 3, 8, 9, 15, 34–5, 66, 117–31, 135, 144, 185, 186–7
  moral reform, 80, 223, 241
  physical size, 8–9, 121–3
  positive/negative images, 217–19ff.
  praise of, 13, 14–15, 29, 220–1, 224, 238
  pre-Reformation city, 2, 4, 37, 40, 56, 57, 91, 107
  Protestant character, 62–3
  rebuilding of, 5–6
  rural environs, 34–5
  social reform, 166, 167, 168, 180–4
  social structures, 131–5
  see also London, City of; East End; Southwark; suburbs; West End; Westminster
London, City of, 31, 61, 144, 146, 150, 151, 188
  Corporation, 125

and Crown, 21, 81–2, 85
government of, 85, 135
legal records, 64–5, 85
population, 1–2, 124, 125
see also livery companies; lord mayors
London, companies:
  Armourers, 97
  Clothworkers, 97, 99, 107–8, 113
  Goldsmiths, 99, 101, 107, 113
  Grocers, 99
  Haberdashers, 98
  Ironmongers, 98, 99
  Mercers, 98
  Merchant Taylors, 91, 94, 96, 99, 106
  Skinners, 57
  Vintners, 98, 99
London, parishes:
  All Hallows the Great, 57
  All Hallows in the Wall, 56
  St Andrew Undershaft, 41, 63, 79, 100
  St Antholin, 235
  St Bartholomew Exchange, 96, 108
  St Benet Gracechurch Street, 57
  St Botolph Aldgate, 56, 60, 84, 103, 105, 106,107, 127
  St Botolph Billingsgate, 33, 46
  St Botolph Bishopsgate, 36, 66
  St Christopher le Stocks, 159
  St Edmund Lombard Street, 58
  St Dunstan in the East, 107, 108
  St Giles Cripplegate, 44, 134
  St James Garlickhithe, 60
  St Katherine Coleman Street, 56
  St Katherine Cree, 63
  St Katherine by the Tower, 121, 122, 123
  St Lawrence Jewry, 102
  St Lawrence Pountney, 58
  St Leonard Eastcheap, 140
  St Magnus, 33, 44
  St Margaret Lothbury, 111
  St Margaret New Fish Street, 44
  St Martin Outwich, 99
  St Martin in the Vintry, 46
  St Mary Aldermary, 96
  St Mary at Hill, 94
  St Mary Woolnoth, 101
  St Michael Basinghall, 57
  St Michael Cornhill, 33, 57, 99
  St Michael le Querne, 86
  St Mildred Bread Street, 62, 100, 103
  St Olave Hart Street, 56
  St Pancras Soper Lane, 108
  St Stephen Walbrook, 102
London, places:
  Aldgate, 35, 36, 121, 124, 132, 133, 256

Austin Friars, 33, 61
Bishopsgate, 33, 36, 79, 121
Charterhouse, 210
Cheapside, 124, 134, 137, 235, 255, 266
Cheapside cross, 40–1, 68, 83
Coldharbour, 130
Fetter Lane, 43
Golden Square, 190, 202
Gray's Inn, 190–1, 210, 235
Gresham College, 150
Grey Friars (later Christ Church), 33–4, 95
Guildhall, 256
Hog Lane, 121
Holborn, 118, 128, 132, 155, 188
Holy Trinity Priory, Aldgate, 32–3
Holy Trinity (St James), Duke Place, 102
Houndsditch, 122, 125
Inner and Middle Temples, 190, 191, 198
Lincoln's Inn Fields, 130, 169, 170, 176, 190, 191, 198, 200, 208
London Bridge, 44, 65, 169, 176, 276
Ludgate, 40, 263, 264
Minories, 125, 156
Moorfields, 33, 91, 191, 192, 198, 257
Newgate, 235
Northumberland House, 35
Old Jewry, 141, 142
Paternoster Row, 264
Petty France, 36
Royal Exchange, 89, 96, 113, 151, 169
St Bartholomew's Hospital, 179
St Martin le Grand, 130
St Mary Spital, 104
St Paul's Cathedral, 83, 95, 182, 276, 277
St Paul's Cross, 41, 44, 57, 110, 221
St Thomas's Hospital, 170
Smithfield, 169, 235
Temple Bar, 36, 169, 170, 176
Tower Hill, 130, 169
Tower of London, 65, 69, 130
Londoners, 58–9
  charity of, 32, 56–9, 75, 89–90, 93, 100–13
  experience of, 10, 15, 117
  mental maps, 7, 10, 11, 140–1, 145, 161
  social structure, 145–6, 149–60
  visual perceptions, 121
lord mayors, 30, 44, 57, 64, 65, 70, 93, 256
  pageants, 54, 63, 112, 220–1
lower classes, 20, 165, 204, 234, 237, 258, 260
  female, 157, 158, 159–60, 163, 164
  male, 155, 158
Lucar, Elizabeth, 58
lunatics, 80
Lute, John, 108

luxury, 193, 194, 206, 219, 223, 225, 233, 242, 245, 285, 288

Machyn, Henry, 278
Mack, Maynard, 206
Macky, John, 188, 202
magistrates, 137, 238, 239, 241, 256, 257, 259
Mandeville, Bernard, 18
Manley, Lawrence, 122
Manning, Roger, 255
Manningham, John, 34
maps, 7–8, 67, 73, 87, 117–21, 125, 126, 140, 142, 187, 188
    'Agas', 187
    Braun and Hogenberg, 118, 119, 187
    Faithorne, 142
    Hollar, 128, 129
    Ogilby and Morgan, 7–8, 125, 126, 135, 136, 188
    Oliver, 118, 120
Marston, John: *The Dutch Courtesan*, 228–9
Martin, Betty, 150, 153
martyrs, 278, 291
Marvell, Andrew, 288–9, 290–1, 292
Marylebone, 198
Mary I, Queen, 46, 278
Mayday, 30, 35, 41, 63
medical metaphors, 18, 22, 23, 194–5, 203–4
medicine, 193, 194–5
memorialization, 4–6, 278
    attitudes to, 112–13
    collective, 90–1, 104, 113
    company halls, 96–9
    contestation of, 110–12
    motives of, 108–11
    new forms of, 90, 91
    oral, 90, 99, 105, 107
    parochial, 99–108
    power inequalities, 112
    sermons, 107–8
    and sociability, 113
memory, 4, 5, 90–1, 93
men, 145–6, 147–8, 149–60, 179, 243, 244, 258
merchants, 97, 110, 141, 242, 243, 246
    social mobility, 151–3, 161
Merritt, Julia, 92, 102
'Merry England' theme, 27, 30
metals, 281, 285
middle classes, 152–5, 162, 163, 168, 189, 237, 242
    and London crowd, 259–61
Middleton, Thomas, 16
migration, 13, 35, 179–80
Mile End 'New Town', 122

military musters, 28, 30
Miseries of Enforced Marriage, The, 227, 228–9
Misson, 'Monsieur', 166, 174
mobility, 10, 11, 140–1, 145, 148
    and gender, 148, 149–62, 163
    and social class, 149–62
    see also social mobility
modernity, 123, 163, 177, 178
money, 15, 101, 181, 243, 245–7, 249
monuments, 4, 37, 55, 58, 60, 62, 72, 89,
    funerary, 33–4, 37, 46, 54, 58, 60, 65–6, 72, 84, 92, 95, 100–2, 110
    Great Fire, 70, 78
    Queen Elizabeth, 61–2, 69, 86
morality, 3, 14, 15, 16, 79–81, 110–12, 137, 209, 210, 221–5, 240–1ff.
    and cleansing, 18
    miasmatic theories, 203–5
    and parks, 19–20, 213
    reform, 223, 241
    see also corruption
More, John, 43
More, Sir Thomas, 208
Morgan, William, 7–8, 125, 126, 135, 136, 188; *see also* maps
Munday, Anthony, 5, 7, 9, 53, 54–67, 70, 77, 78, 86, 87, 88, 91, 122
    and charitable donations, 56–9
    civic triumphalism, 63, 64, 65
    perambulations, 55–6
    and Protestantism, 56–65
    'Remaines, The', 65–6, 74
    1618 edition of the *Survey of London*, 54, 56, 59, 60, 64, 91
    1633 edition of the *Survey of London*, 54, 59, 62, 64, 65–6, 74, 91–2, 101
    and Stow, 55, 56, 63, 66–7
murder, 16, 225–6, 227, 231, 232, 234, 239, 240, 244, 245

Nalson, John, 261
nature, 18, 19, 186, 194–9, 207, 209, 210; *see also* gardens; green space; parks
neighbourhoods, 10, 11, 12, 127, 145, 146, 154, 160, 161, 162
New Model Army, 281, 287, 288
Newcastle, earl of, 252
newsbooks, 280, 290
newspapers, 9
nobility *see* aristocracy
non-conformists *see* Dissenters
Norton, Sir Edward, 259
nostalgia, 4, 5, 27–8ff., 34–5, 37, 53, 68, 69, 87
Nowell, Alexander, 58

occupations, 10, 161
Ogborn, Miles, 20
Ogilby, John, 7–8, 125, 126, 135, 136, 188; *see also* maps
Oliver, John, 118, 120; *see also* maps
open spaces, 128, 130, 187, 195; *see also* green space
oral commemoration, 99
order, 133, 202, 205, 211, 212, 221, 250, 255, 261
    and disorder, 217–19, 226, 235ff., 244, 245
overcrowding, 35, 192, 193
Oxford University, 57, 59

pageants *see* lord mayors
pamphlets, 3, 15, 17, 78, 152, 251, 258, 263, 280, 282, 290, 292
    advice, 163–4
    crime, 225–34, 235, 238, 239–42, 244, 246–8
    plague, 16, 221, 222
Paris, 72, 123, 128
parishes, 10, 12, 55–6, 59, 60, 61, 86, 87, 145, 180
    government of, 83–4
    lectureships, 92
    local charities, 92
    memorialization, 93–4, 99–108
    perceptions of, 138–40
    plague mortality, 134
    poor law, 139–40, 181, 182
    population growth, 139
    suburban, 66
    see also under London; Southwark; Westminster
Park, Robert, 12
Parker, Archbishop Matthew, 47, 79
parks, 18, 192
    access to, 19, 187, 201, 203, 212
    and immorality, 19–20, 164, 193–4, 198, 204–5, 206, 211, 212
    and physical exercise, 194–6
    royal, 189–90
    and rural retreat, 207–9
    and social contagion, 204–6
Parliament, 69, 162, 260, 265, 267–8, 270, 288, 289
Pepys, Elizabeth, 141, 149–50, 158, 165
Pepys, Samuel, 105, 112, 141, 148, 149, 150, 151, 153, 158, 160, 161, 162, 165
perambulations, 2, 55–6, 67, 71, 85, 86, 87, 89
petitions, 251, 258, 261–3, 268
Petty, William, 123
philanthropy, 89, 111; *see also* charity

physical exercise, 18, 194–5, 204, 210
Pilkington, Sir Thomas, 70
Pipkin, John, 161
plague, 22, 100, 193, 223, 225
    mortality, 133–4
    pamphlets, 16, 221, 222
Plaistow, 159
plants, 196–7, 202, 203, 205; *see also* gardens
plate, 94, 98–9, 102
plays, 9, 16, 17, 31, 54, 69, 81
    and charities, 89–90, 112–13
    crime, 225–6, 227, 228–30, 232–3, 236–8, 239, 242–3ff., 249
    miracle, 49–50
poetry, 35, 111, 232, 286, 288–9, 290–1, 292
pollution, 194, 204, 205
    air, 2, 18, 193, 197, 203
poor, the, 29, 32, 33, 37, 57, 61, 75, 80, 101, 105, 106, 107, 108, 139, 193
    active role of, 167–8
    deserving, 182
    mobility, 159
    'public', 13, 14, 177–8off.
    see also beggars
poor relief, 12, 14, 89, 95, 139, 175, 181, 182, 183; *see also* charity
Pope, Alexander, 207, 208
Popish Plot, 70
population, 71, 123, 139
    City, 124, 125
    density, 123, 124, 193, 275
    growth, 1–2, 3, 117, 124, 144, 185, 186, 187, 254–5
portraits, 90, 91, 97–8, 100
poverty, 2, 15, 49, 131, 132, 167, 182, 183, 184, 227
    see also beggars; poor, the; poor relief
power inequalities, 5, 90, 112
Power, Michael, 146
preachers, 19, 41, 44, 51, 57, 59, 104, 105, 107, 109, 110, 221, 225
Presbyterianism, 76, 138
Price, Daniel, 109
Price, Joseph, 168
Price, Sampson, 221
prophecies, 22, 278, 280, 282, 283, 287
prostitution, 17, 148, 159, 160, 161, 163, 164, 165, 176, 226, 230, 232, 234, 235
Protectorate, 280, 288, 289
Protestantism, 4, 5, 38, 40, 41, 43, 46, 53, 56ff., 68–9, 70, 77, 78, 79, 80, 262, 267, 271
    and commemoration, 90–1, 92–3, 95–6, 109–11
    and fire, 275

providence, 22, 62, 68, 90, 108, 240, 277
public spaces, 14, 172, 176, 182, 183; *see also*
    gardens; green space; open spaces; parks
punishment, 239, 240, 275, 278, 280, 286
purification, 18, 22, 23, 275, 278, 284, 286
puritanism, 44, 45, 58, 62, 275, 280, 286ff.,
    292

Quakers, 280, 290, 292

radicalism, 21, 22
Ranters, 282, 283, 285
Ratcliff (Middlesex), 122
readers, 52, 240, 241
records, 3, 64–5, 84, 85
Red Lyon Square, 190, 203
Reformation, 1, 4, 56, 60, 68, 79, 81, 89
    antipathy to, 37, 38, 69
    and collective memory, 90–1
    and memorialization, 93–5
    see also iconoclasm; Protestantism
religion, 6, 21–2, 40–7, 51, 68–9, 75, 76,
    77–80, 83, 86, 138, 240, 266, 292
    feast days, 32
    and fire, 28off.
    and memorialization, 90, 91
    and nostalgia, 5, 28, 37ff., 53, 69
rents, 124, 125, 127, 131
republicanism, 20, 288, 289
Restoration, 2, 82, 155, 266, 281, 290
retirement/retreat, 206–9, 211
retribution, 22, 278–9ff., 286
Richardson, Charles, 110
Richmond, 159
Ridge, Thomas, 57
riots, 251–2, 253, 254–5, 261, 270, 271
    toleration of, 256–8
ritual, 4, 5, 18, 90, 100, 101–2, 105–7, 218
Robertson, James, 135
Robinson, Richard, 91
Rome, 66, 221, 238, 239, 241
Romford, 140
Rous, John, 226–7, 229
royal accessions, 90
royal parks, 189–90
rural life, 15, 17, 19, 35, 189, 194, 205, 206,
    208, 209, 289–90
Ryder, Dudley, 150, 154, 160, 161, 164

Sacheverell, Dr Henry, 77, 270–1
Sackville, Sir Edward, 238
St Giles in the Fields (Middlesex), 151, 155,
    170, 173, 235
St James Park, 195
St Pancras (Middlesex), 235

satire, 16, 17, 54, 112, 205, 290
Saussure, Caesar de, 152, 202
Saxby, Mary, 176
Seleski, Patty, 157, 158
Sennett, Richard, 194, 202
sermons, 16, 41, 44, 57, 80, 90, 154, 221, 222,
    279, 290
    funeral, 103–5, 107–8, 110
servants, 29, 133, 157–9, 161, 163, 227, 239
settlement, 12, 13, 140, 148, 157, 178–9, 180,
    181, 182
sexual behaviour, 159–60, 212, 224, 226, 229,
    230ff., 240, 243–4ff.
    and fire, 284–6
    women, 148, 160, 161, 163, 164–5
Shadwell (Middlesex), 122, 130, 132
Shaftesbury, earl of, 259, 265, 268
Shakespeare, William, 20, 31
Sharpe, Kevin, 217
Shirley, Sir Thomas, 37, 38
Shoemaker, Robert, 10, 11
Shoreditch (Middlesex), 122, 132
    church, 34
silversmiths, 281, 282
sin, 16, 17, 22, 193, 211, 217, 218, 221ff., 235,
    237, 244–8, 279, 285, 286, 288
Skinner, Quentin, 218
Slack, Paul, 7, 17, 134, 181
Smith, Nigel, 21
Smithfield, 169, 176, 235, 278
Smyth, Richard (d.1675), 141, 142, 153
social classes, 10, 11, 18, 128, 131–2, 145–6,
    149–62, 163, 164, 236, 242–3
    and London crowd, 259–63
social mobility *see* mobility
social status, 10, 18–19, 145
    and green space, 199–206, 210, 212–13
    see also social classes
social unrest *see* disorder
Southwark, 11, 118, 191
Southwark, parishes:
    St Olave, 61
    St Saviour, 61
Southwark, places:
    Boroughside, 11, 12
spatial meaning, 6, 135–40, 149–62, 165
Speed, John, 122
Spitalfields, 122, 191
sports and pastimes, 28, 31, 33, 36, 49, 80–1
squares, 13, 19, 130, 182, 190, 202–3, 212
Stansell, Christine, 147
Steele, Sir Richard, 169, 178
Stepney (Middlesex), 118, 122, 134, 139,
    156
Stevenson, Laura, 248

Stow, John, 7, 55, 105
    Annales, 64
    and Becket, 40
    library, 42–3, 47
    'life' of, 79, 88
    nostalgia, 4, 5, 27–8ff., 32, 34–5, 37, 53
    old age, 34
    perception of London, 140, 143
    and religion, 37, 40–7, 53, 58, 60, 92
    self-censorship, 46
    Summarie of Englyshe Chronicles, 30, 44, 45–6, 47
    visual perception, 121
    see also Stow's *Survey of London*
Stow, Thomas, 42
Stow, William, 2, 8, 10
Stow's *Survey of London*, 1, 9, 15, 21, 125
    contrasted with Strype, 117, 122, 143
    editions, 5, 52–4ff., 67, 74–5, 86, 87
    green space, 185–6, 187, 188, 189, 192, 198
    lord mayors, 64
    omissions, 31, 46, 58, 60, 92
    on physical size, 121–2
    purposes, 7, 89
    readers of, 52
    reputation of, 88
    scope of, 144
    wards, 12, 137
    see also Munday, Anthony; Stow, John;
      Strype's edition of the Survey of London
      (1720)
Strafford, earl of, 255
Stratford, 198
streets, 6, 13, 18, 29, 72, 87, 121, 122, 125, 127, 135, 164
    and begging, 166, 169, 170, 172, 182
    cleaning, 133
    lighting, 71
    maps, 6, 7, 8, 87, 118, 140
    vendors, 176, 177
Strype, Hester van, 76
Strype, John
    as author/editor, 73–4
    moral views, 79–81
    political views, 76–7
    religious views, 76, 77–80, 83
    and Stow, 74–5, 79, 88, 122, 143
    and stranger community, 77
    see also Strype's edition of the *Survey of London* (1720)
Strype's edition of the *Survey of London* (1720), 1, 5, 7, 9, 21, 53, 72–88, 168, 251
    and City authorities, 85
    and Civil War, 81–2
    contrasted with Stow, 117, 122, 143

Crown–City relations, 81–2, 85
    difficulties of, 143
    economic data, 75, 78
    editorial voice, 87
    format of, 72–3, 75, 86, 87
    green space, 186, 188–9, 191, 198, 199, 210
    'life' of Stow, 79, 88
    marginal annotations, 75, 87
    omissions, 83, 84, 86, 87
    on physical size, 122
    popularity of, 87–8
    religious history, 75, 78–9, 83, 86
    research methods, 84–6
    scope of, 144
    social and health aspects, 199, 200, 203
    sports and pastimes, 80–1
    and Survey tradition, 86–7
    time constraints, 85–6
    wards, 12, 137
    see also Munday, Anthony; Munday's
      editions of the *Survey of London*; Stow's
      Survey of London; Strype, John
suburbs, 12, 35, 36, 66, 118, 122, 123, 125, 127, 128, 131, 135, 137, 144
    health, 133–4
    households, 132, 133
    parishes, 139
    plague, 134
    population growth, 1, 15, 185, 186–7
    problems of, 15
    social differences, 146
    sureties, 148, 151, 153, 156
Swift, Jonathan, 180
Swinnerton, Sir John, 93

Tany, Thomas, 282, 285–6, 291
Tatler, The, 150, 207
taverns, 152, 153, 154, 230, 234, 235, 237, 239, 241, 242
taxation, 12, 132, 137
Thames, river, 62, 65
theft, 231, 232, 234, 244, 245
Thomas, Sir Keith, 27
Thompson, Nathaniel, 262, 263
tithe survey (1638), 127
Tittler, Robert, 90
Topcliffe, Richard, 54
topography, 10, 11, 66, 121, 123, 235
    social, 131–5
Tories, 76, 254, 259, 262ff.
'Town', 11, 146
Townshend, John, 155
trade, 10, 14, 15, 75, 77, 239
    social mobility, 151–3
    women and, 152–3, 156–7

transport, 2, 20
Trapnel, Anna, 21, 287–8
Trevor-Roper, Hugh, 41
Trip Through London, A, 152, 163–4
Trip Through Town, A, 164, 168–9, 172–3
triumphalism, 5, 63, 64, 65, 70
Troy, 220, 221, 222, 223, 238, 249
Trusty, John, 80

urban life, 2, 194, 289
  denunciation of, 16, 17, 217ff., 238, 241ff.
  fear of, 15, 16
  praise of, 14–15, 17, 20, 29
  and rural values, 205, 206, 208, 209–10
  and social contagion, 203–4
urbanization, 5, 186–7, 209, 210
  impact of, 3, 14–24, 52, 53
usury, 43, 224, 241, 242, 243, 246–7, 249

Vagrancy Acts, 166, 174, 179, 182
Varey, Simon, 202
Vauxhall Gardens, 20, 191–2, 208
vestiarian disturbances (1566), 44–5
vestments, 94
vestries, 83–4
vice *see* immorality
violence, 218, 237, 238, 240, 251, 252, 253, 255, 258, 260, 261, 272
visual media, 90, 91, 97–8, 100, 117, 118ff.

walks, 192, 195, 206
Wall, Cynthia, 6
Waller, Edmund, 207
Wallington, Nehemiah, 140–1, 283
Wapping (Middlesex), 118, 121, 122, 123, 156
  chapel, 122
Ward, Edward, 72
Ward, Joseph, 137, 144–5
Ward, Ned, 177–8, 209
Ward, Sir Patience, 70
wards, 12, 31, 137
  maps, 8
Warning for Fair Woman, A, 232–3, 244, 245
water supply, 133
wealth, 10, 15, 75, 93, 131, 139, 145, 161, 193, 194, 205, 219, 224, 247, 249, 282
Weever, John, 110
West End, 2, 11, 131, 141, 160, 162, 182
  development, 128, 189, 202
  green space, 186–7, 188, 189–90
  social structure, 146, 150, 151
Westminster, 10, 11, 36, 118, 120, 128, 131, 141, 144, 146, 186, 188, 200, 266
  Abbey, 68
  and gender, 152

households, 132
infirmary, 184
social mobility, 149, 150, 153, 159, 162
Westminster, parishes:
  St Margaret, 10, 111
  St Martin in the Fields, 10, 139, 151, 181, 188
Westminster, places:
  Berkeley House, 200
  Buckingham House, 188, 200
  Burlington House, 200
  Charing Cross, 160, 169, 170, 176, 188
  Covent Garden, 128, 129, 130, 169, 170, 171, 264
  Drury Lane, 129, 149, 160, 165
  Grosvenor Square, 190, 199
  Hanover Square, 123, 157
  Haymarket, 150, 169
  Hyde Park, 18, 19, 189, 190, 204
  Leicester Square, 190, 202
  Long Acre, 132, 150
  Mayfair, 189
  New Exchange, 153
  New Palace Yard, 130–1, 132
  Picadilly, 118, 188
  St James's Park, 19, 150, 189, 190, 192, 195, 197, 200–2, 204, 205, 208, 209
  St James Square, 130
  Salisbury House, 187
  Soho, 77, 188
  Somerset House, 188, 210
  Spring Gardens, 19, 188, 191, 196, 197
  Strand, the, 36, 169, 170, 188
  Tothill Fields, 123
  Westminster Hall, 87, 150, 153, 169
  Whitehall Palace, 18
Whetstone, George: *A Mirror for Magistrates of Cities*, 230, 238, 239, 241–2
Whigs, 84, 254, 259, 260, 262ff.
Whitechapel (Middlesex), 34, 132, 160, 186
Whittington, Sir Richard, 89, 98, 113
whores, 17, 148, 164, 165, 228, 229, 230, 234, 235, 237, 243–4ff.; *see also* prostitution
widows, 133, 151, 156
Willet, Andrew, 92–3, 112
William III, King, 82, 253
Williams, Laura, 19
Williams, Raymond, 206
wills, 95–6, 97, 101, 103, 107, 108, 111
women, 44–5, 226, 227, 243, 244–5, 285
  attitudes to, 164–5
  beggars, 167, 173–4, 176–7
  benefactors, 89–90
  gentry, 149–51
  lower class, 159–60, 163, 164

marital status, 148
middle-class, 152–5, 163
mobility, 10, 141, 150
perceptions of, 146–9
prostitution, 148, 160, 161, 163, 164, 165
servants, 157–9
sexual behaviour, 148
and trade, 152–3, 156–7
upper-class, 163
vagrants, 178, 179

Woodward, John, 23
workhouses, 75, 79, 80, 166, 180, 183
Worthington, John, 74n.

Yarrington, Robert: *Two Lamentable Tragedies*, 225–6
York, James, duke of, 70, 263, 264, 265, 266; *see also* James II, King
Yorkshire Tragedy, A, 227, 228